# PRAIS[E FOR]

# *Our Vision for Liberation*

"At a time when the world desperately needs hope and guidance toward habitable futures, these moving visions of a decolonized, democratic and free Palestine will resonate wherever collective yearnings for freedom have survived. Palestinian intellectuals, activists, and artists are a beacon both for the future of Palestine and the destiny of our globe."

—ANGELA DAVIS, American activist, author and professor known internationally for her ongoing work to combat all forms of oppression in the US and abroad

"This landmark book will destroy any doubt that Palestine can be freed. Its multiple truths and dimensions will strike fear into those who conspire to destroy the possibility of a resurgent Palestine from the river to the sea. The Palestinian voice and vision articulated in this masterpiece of lived experiences and intellectual memory possesses the strength, culture, intellect, organizational creativity and dynamism that foreshadows a vision of liberation that will triumph—because it is rooted in the indestructibility of a people's just cause. Read this book and you will be strengthened and inspired. It's a death knell to the Zionist fantasy and imperialist domination. Every page breathes the scent of freedom—sooner than is thought. This is an ode to joy, freeing us all from colonialist horror, and an uplifting glimpse into the possible future."

—RONNIE KASRILS, South African author, politician and anti-apartheid icon

"This book deserves a warm welcome. It celebrates the achievements of Palestinians and the rich diversity of their culture. Clearly, their spirit of resistance is alive and well. The book's implicit challenge is to all who care for justice and the rule of law—free the Palestinians from their cruel oppression by Israel."

—KEN LOACH, renowned British filmmaker (his works include *Kes* and *I, Daniel Blake*)

"There is eloquent, optimistic logic to this outstanding anthology edited by Ilan Pappé and Ramzy Baroud. It is that Palestine will be free when, like a seed beneath the snow, the power of a universal movement emerges from below: truly a people's liberation matched by our solidarity."

—JOHN PILGER, acclaimed Australian journalist, writer, scholar and documentary filmmaker

"It is so important to pay attention to the brave and smart voices of Palestinians, those particularly who are active every day to bring decency and justice into a world getting uglier by the day. This book carries these voices, Palestinian voices, but also voices that echo inside our heads, voices that urge us on, tell us to go out there onto the streets to make the world by marching."

—VIJAY PRASHAD, Indian historian, editor, journalist and director of Tricontinental: Institute for Social Research

"The first-hand testimonies in this collection of essays send a clear message to the racist apartheid occupiers of Palestine: your attempts to obliterate us have failed. Here we stand. Here is the evidence of the culture, the archeology, the history and the land that you have tried to persuade yourselves and the world that didn't exist, here we stand as living proof of the presence you could not erase even after more than a century of trying.

These essays underscore the continuing strength of resistance to the totalitarian nature of the Zionist enterprise. It was not just the people who had to be removed, the villages destroyed, the land taken and shorn of its native growth but Palestine in its totality, so the day would come when future generations would not even know it ever existed.

Yet even after a century, this goal has not been reached and now, with more Palestinians between the river and the sea than their oppressors, clearly, it never will be.

These essays take the reader deep into personal Palestinian experiences. An archeologist, imprisoned women, weavers of tapestries, college professors, an agriculturalist, journalists, poets, musicians, cineastes and exiles living far from their homeland are united in the twin messages sent to their oppressor: defiance and the unshakeable certainty that one Palestine will again be free."

—PROFESSOR JEREMY SALT, author of *The Unmaking of the Middle East: A History of Western Disorder in Arab Lands*

"This is a fascinating, great book."

—ROGER WATERS, world-famous English songwriter, musician, bassist and singer, founding member of progressive rock band Pink Floyd and lifelong anti-apartheid, human rights, and pro-Palestine activist

*In the reading of this great book*
*I came across Mahmoud Darwish's ID Card poem from 1964*
*I have a message for my dead master*
*And my dead mother, and my dead father*
*And the land they fought for.*

*So, so you think you can tell*
*Heaven from hell*
*Blue skies from pain*
*And can you tell a green field*
*From a cold steel rail*
*A smile from a veil*
*Do you think you can tell*
*And did they get you to trade*
*Your heroes for ghosts*
*Hot ashes for trees*
*Hot air for a cool breeze*
*Cold comfort for change*
*And did you exchange*
*A walk on part in the war*
*For a lead role in a cage*

*No, you didn't Mahmoud*
*And neither did my mother and father*
*And neither will I*
*We will all be here*
*Living and dead*
*Shoulder to shoulder*
*Side by side*
*Until Palestine is Liberated.*

Roger Waters*
December 22, 2021

---

*Roger Waters' father, Eric Fletcher, was killed in the battle of Anzio in the Second World War, fighting against Fascism and Nazism; it is this memory that he brings to the fore, when thinking of those who fought, and are fighting, for the liberation of Palestine.

# OUR VISION FOR LIBERATION

## Engaged Palestinian Leaders and Intellectuals Speak Out

EDITED BY

RAMZY BAROUD & ILAN PAPPÉ

Clarity Press, Inc.

ECPS
The European Centre
for Palestine Studies

ISBN: 978-1-949762-44-0
EBOOK ISBN: 978-1-949762-45-7

Production team: Romana Rubeo, Sylvia Fernandes, Samah Sabawi
In-house editor: Diana G. Collier
Cover design: Zarefah Baroud
Cover model: Iman Baroud
Book design: Becky Luening



Library of Congress Control Number: 2021952182

Clarity Press, Inc.
2625 Piedmont Rd. NE, Ste. 56
Atlanta, GA 30324 USA
https://www.claritypress.com

The European Centre for Palestine Studies
Institute of Arab and Islamic Studies
University of Exeter
Streatham Campus
Exeter EX4 4ND, United Kingdom

To Suha Jarrar.

*The trees die standing.*

# TABLE OF CONTENTS

## SECTION II
## THE MANY FACES OF RESISTANCE



## SECTION III
## ON LIBERATION, CULTURE & EDUCATION

## SECTION IV
## ON LIBERATION, POLITICS, EMPOWERMENT & SOLIDARITY

# ACKNOWLEDGMENTS

IT WOULD TAKE more than a page or two to thank all the people who have helped us in the process of creating this volume, from the time when it was just a mere idea to having it published. The inspiring authors, whose writings have graced this book, are but a small representation of the many more who engaged with us in terms of research, discussion and various contributions, including translation, editing and proof-reading.

Thank you to Diana G. Collier of Clarity Press for her enthusiasm and support of the idea from its inception. Her feedback and constant encouragement made this intricate, time-consuming and urgent project possible.

Romana Rubeo, Italian journalist, editor and translator, has played an integral part in the production of this book. She has played several essential roles, from administering the project, to translating part of the content, to proof-reading. Thank you, Romana, your help and support were indispensable.

Sylvia Fernandes has served more than the role of the copyeditor of this book. Her feedback, ideas and attention to detail have allowed us to streamline the work of many intellectuals into one volume. She took on a massive project and fulfilled her role with patience and grace. To her, we are indebted.

Samah Sabawi was a critical part of this work. Her essay "Writing in the Blank Spaces" is an essential read, as it fulfills an important part of the Palestinian narrative, one that is often neglected. However, she has been much more than that. Her brilliant translations of several essays, from Arabic to English, have allowed us to create a more inclusive space enabling Palestinian intellectuals to have their voices heard.

Our gratitude also goes to the University of Exeter and The European Centre for Palestine Studies for agreeing to be part of this important project, one that we hope will advance more pro-active thinking on Palestine, while espousing the kind of discourse that is centered on Palestinian intellectuals.

The real stars of this project are the engaged intellectuals whose legacies, thoughts—and also patience—made this book what it is today: the genesis of an urgent conversation that concerns all Palestinians and supporters of justice and human rights in Palestine and everywhere. Thanks so very much to all of you. Your sacrifices and indefatigable efforts for a free Palestine will be appreciated for generations to come.

Thank you to all of our brilliant translators who were involved in the production of this book, who, aside from Sabah Sabawi and Romana Rubeo, include Ahmed Almassri and Nahed Elrayes.

A special note of appreciation goes to Palestinian author and journalist, Ali Abunimah, for all of his help and support.

Thank you also to Yousef Aljamal, Iain Chalmers, Marisa Consolata Kemper, Yafa Jarrar, Sheryl Bedas, Ahmed Yousef, Rabab Abdulhadi, John Harvey, Salman Abu Sitta, Maren Mantovani, Louis Brehony, Noha Khalaf, Islah Jad, Triestino Mariniello, Aida and the late Carl Bradley, Tamara De Melo, Richard Falk, Omar Aziz, Mark Seddon, Erica Aloang Aquino, Issam Adwan, Vincenzo Rubeo and Anna Cacace.

We would also like to acknowledge the contributions and support of the Palestinian Centre for Human Rights (PCHR), Center for Islamic and Global Affairs (CIGA) and Palestine Deep Dive.

Thank you to our families for their patience, support and encouragement every step of the way. A special thank you goes to our cover page model, Iman Baroud, our creative designer Zarefah Baroud, and our sports consultant, Sammy Baroud. They are the rising stars of Palestine.

# PREFACE

*"Los libertadores no existen. Son los pueblos quienes se liberan a sí mismos." – "Liberators do not exist. It is the peoples who liberate themselves."*

—ERNESTO CHE GUEVARA

THIS FAMOUS QUOTE, attributed to the Argentinian revolutionary, is as true in the case of Palestine as it is of South America.

In Palestine, however, we have been quite unfortunate in having too many liberators or, more accurately, self-designated liberators. From self-serving Palestinian leaders, to corrupt Arab rulers, and even to confused western ideologues, many have claimed, with much fanfare though little action, that the "liberation of Palestine" is central to their political agendas.

I grew up in a refugee camp in the Gaza Strip. My father's intellectual circle consisted mostly of like-minded socialists, ex-political prisoners and true revolutionaries—that is, engaged organic intellectuals in the full Gramscian sense. Like my father, they were all justifiably cynical, making constant reference to the "treason of the Arabs," the hopelessness of the international order and the stranglehold Zionists have over America. Yet, though they would have been utterly offended by the following suggestion, they were also—to a degree—politically innocent, if not outright naive. Despite their constant tirades against their "Arab brethren," they still hoped that some liberating Arab army would, miraculously, come to Palestine's rescue.

During the First Intifada, the popular uprising of 1987, rumors abounded: that the Egyptian military was crossing the Sinai desert to confront the Israeli occupation army in Gaza; that Saddam Hussein had ordered the Iraqi army to march to Palestine through Jordan; and that even the Algerians whom, we were told, were particularly fond of Palestinians, were fed up with the silence of Palestine's Arab neighbors before the Israeli atrocities, and had thus decided to dispatch their navy through the Mediterranean. Though my father and his friends would always claim that they had known, all along, that these were silly rumors, I remember hearing the giddiness in their voices and seeing the excitement in their eyes whenever a new rumor would surface, hoping, perhaps, that this time around, the stories of approaching Arab liberators were true.

The liberating Arab and, by extension, the liberating Muslim, have occupied much space in the Palestinian popular discourse. The Imam of our local mosque would always end his Friday sermon with the supplication, "May Allah awaken the sleeping Arab and Muslim Ummah so that they would liberate Palestine and Al-Aqsa Mosque." We, the faithful, including my father and his allegedly communist friends, would repeat in unison, "Ameen." By the end of the Intifada, it was clear that no one was coming to liberate us, not then, not now, and, most likely, not any time soon.

Since then, I have lived and traveled in many countries and interacted with numerous intellectual spaces in which solidarity with Palestine is central, or at least relevant, to various political or ideological movements. The true love and genuine concern that ordinary people across the globe have for Palestine is more than touching; it is invigorating. A Native American woman in Colorado told me that her biggest regret, knowing that she was dying with cancer, was that she would not see the day in which Palestine is free—her dying wish was to visit Palestine and her community actually made it happen. A newly-wed South African couple told me that the happiest day in their life was the day they prayed at Al-Aqsa Mosque in occupied Palestinian East Jerusalem. A former Irish fighter and prisoner assured me that he is as committed to the freedom of Palestine as he is to the true freedom of his people…

Judging by the rise of global solidarity with Palestine and the tremendous success of the Palestinian Boycott, Divestment and Sanctions (BDS) movement—coupled with the greater awareness of the interconnectivity/intersectionality among the struggles of all people against injustices in all of its forms—one can rest assured that solidarity with Palestine is not a fleeting phenomenon. However, since a centralized Palestinian political strategy, one that emanates from a representative Palestinian leadership, remains missing, many often take the initiative to speak for, and on behalf of, the Palestinian people.

A few years ago, while visiting the United Kingdom on a speaking tour, I repeatedly asserted that Palestinians own political discourse, their cultural, their national aspirations, history and so on—should serve as the guiding principle of any true solidarity with Palestine. To my surprise, a British activist protested: "Our solidarity should not hinge on a deep understanding of the people in need of solidarity," he argued. He said that it was "his generation" that "liberated Vietnam from American imperialism" and, yet, he, to this day, still knew nothing about Vietnamese culture. I was dumbfounded at this clear misrepresentation of that heroic struggle. That interaction has afforded me the most jarring insight into the extent of the disconnect between those who seek to appropriate the role of liberators, and the people who, as per Che Guevara's words, are the only ones capable of truly liberating themselves.

For many years, the Palestinian people have been caught in a seemingly impossible political dichotomy. On the one hand, they have proven capable of shouldering immense sacrifices and sustaining a national struggle for justice and freedom over the course of a century while, on the other hand, in the words of the late Palestinian Professor, Edward Said, they have also been "woefully cursed by bad leadership."

Clearly, it is not by a curse but by political design that the Palestinian people have been afflicted with such a "bad leadership," despite the fact that Palestine is endowed with some of the most accomplished, capable, educated and well-informed women and men in every field of leadership. This book is but a microcosm of what Palestine has to offer. The problem, however, is that such potential leadership is often marginalized, silenced, imprisoned and even assassinated. With the true engaged Palestinian leaders and intellectuals sidelined or eliminated altogether, the political space is deliberately opened for fraudulent leaderships, political wheelers and dealers and money-hungry charlatans.

*Our Vision for Liberation* is our attempt to offer a new way of looking at Palestinian liberation. For the kind of liberation championed in this book to succeed, the Palestinian people must be placed at its core, and truly engaged Palestinians must take center stage, not only to convey the victimization of their people but also to mobilize and empower them as well. Such engaged Palestinians are also critical to the international solidarity movement. Solidarity that is not guided by authentic Palestinian voices is simply futile; it cannot reflect the true desires of the Palestinian people, and therefore cannot effectively mobilize what is most essential: their support.

As an admirer of the great historian, Ilan Pappé, I felt truly privileged to be his Ph.D. student at the University of Exeter's European Center for Palestine Studies. My focus at that time was on finding an alternative, non-elitist way of conveying the history of the Palestinian people. I wanted to imagine a different way of telling the history of Palestine that does not go through the traditional routes of powerful clans, wealthy leaders and political factions, but through the narrow and impoverished alleyways of Gaza, the dusty roads of Ein el-Hilweh refugee camp in Lebanon, and the heaps of rubble to which the refugee camp of Jenin, in the Occupied West Bank, was reduced following the Israeli invasion of 2002. I wanted to tell a different kind of narrative, stories about ordinary Palestinian men and women who defined Palestine, its tragedies, its triumphs and its aspirations. Though I earned my degree in 2015, I remain a forever student of this inspiring teacher.

In an article, published in 2018, Pappé wrote,

> ... Thus, 70 years on, one has to resort to a term that might seem outdated in order to describe what can genuinely bring peace and reconciliation to Israel and Palestine: decolonization. How exactly this will occur is yet to be seen. It would require, first of all, a more precise and united Palestinian position on the political endgame or the updated vision of the project of liberation.

Palestine is in need of a radical form of decolonization, as the forces that conspire to deny Palestinians any form of liberation, let alone justice and freedom, are too powerful to be left to crumble under the weight of their own contradictions. Indeed, caught between a decided Israeli colonial project, irrelevant Palestinian "leadership," and the self-aggrandizing authoritarian Arab regimes, Palestinians have no alternative but to be their own liberators.

Our Vision is not an intellectual exercise aimed at dissecting or dwelling on the past, but a serious attempt at looking forward, at envisioning that "unified Palestinian position" urged by Pappé, by allowing the engaged Palestinian intellectuals, each in his/her respected field of work, study and struggle, to articulate that coveted road map of liberation.

I am honored to have co-edited this book with my mentor and friend, Professor Ilan Pappé. I am also honored and humbled to have worked with many inspiring Palestinian leaders and engaged intellectuals, who have much to teach us all, not just Palestinian readers, but justice warriors the world over.

*—Ramzy Baroud, November 2021*

# INTRODUCTION

THE PALESTINIAN STRUGGLE for liberation takes many forms and is based on diverse modes of resistance. This struggle is usually—and understandably—described as the collective effort of a nation that was colonized in the late 19th century and is still under occupation and colonization today. Since the struggle continues, it is useless to make any reasonable judgment on its success or failure. What is reasonable and most important to do at this point in time, in our mind, is to record and recognize the individual struggles that form this collective effort. They are sometimes forgotten or overlooked, but they are crucial for understanding why those who are part of the liberation struggle and those who support it have not given up hope for its eventual success in the future.

When we decided to record these individual stories of struggle for freedom and liberation, we first hoped to have a full picture of the personal contribution and experience of each contributor. However, we were fortunate enough to receive much more than this. Each individual account has a biographical section that opens a window into a recent or more distant Palestinian past, whether in the homeland or in exile. This is very much about what was lost as a result of the ongoing *Nakba,* as well as what was regained by sheer resilience, steadfastness and commitment.

Take for instance our opening chapter by Hamdan Taha that assesses the role of Palestinian archaeologists and archaeology in the struggle for liberation. It begins with a glimpse into the life of a 12-year-old village boy on the day of the Israeli occupation of the West Bank in 1967. In a moving passage in the chapter, Hamdan tells us how this boy, and later teenager, became one of Palestine's leading archaeologists; it was his first encounter with the new, oppressive reality imposed by the occupation. It set him off on an incredible career as one of Palestine's leading archaeologists. Even today, Hamdan has to struggle daily against an archaeological narrative of denial and erasure. This sinister campaign is not only done through distorting ancient historiography but also by the production of a misleading discourse and the invention of a deceptive vocabulary.

Just how distortion of language can misrepresent past and present realities in Palestine is an essential part of Ibrahim G. Aoudé's life story, whose professional commitment brings to the fore the role of discourse and language in the liberation struggle. His professional life has been devoted to countering a Zionist vocabulary that has promoted and sustained the fraudulent denial of the Palestinian existence from the very start. His particular mode of cultural resistance is performed day in and day out and finally, in this century as he tells us, has produced tangible and encouraging results.

The public domain is influenced by this discourse and it is mainly the media that disseminates it, hence the crucial role the media plays in the struggle for liberation. Our contributors who work in the media domain tell a life story that will encourage young Palestinians to follow suit and become influential journalists and media persons in the future.

While a strong educational background provided at home and at school is a typical route to media success, in the Palestinian case, one often has to be self-taught and learn through sheer personal determination, as Qassem Ali Kafarneh's life story illustrates. Qassem shares with us how he started out on the road to become one of Palestine's leading journalists:

> The next part of my journey turned out to be a formative and fundamental ingredient to my engaging meaningfully with journalism as a powerful tool in the struggle for liberation. It was a journey digging to the roots of my people; collecting their experiences of life; debating on political visions; disagreeing on ideology, religion, cultural constructs.

It was both formal and informal education that prepared him for his role as a leading journalist in the future. One such informal site was the Israeli prison:

> The crucible blending and catalyzing our nationalism, uniting us as a people, erasing gender, socio-economic, religious and ideological barriers, and all of this provided on a silver platter by our Israeli oppressor: PRISON.

Samaa Abu Sharar also played a crucial role in the media struggle, and ponders the choices Palestinians make in the course of their struggle for liberation:

> We are often told that "our life choices are those of our making"; in the case of most Palestinians, I believe it is a luxury that we often dare not indulge in.

And yet, as Samaa's chapter shows, such a destined role, not chosen but accepted, can lead to pioneering work in building media outlets and bastions of professional journalism which generate people's recognition of the Palestinian plight and, in particular, shed constant light on Palestinian refugees' right of return. This is a significant achievement given the attempts to deny access to Palestinian realities by a huge Israeli propaganda machine oiled with Western help and support.

Palestinians' sense of belonging and recognizing their identity as such, displaced due to historical circumstances, is occurring everywhere around the globe. Anuar Majluf Issa tells the story of the *Club Deportivo Palestino*, one of the best football clubs on the continent, where young people who "have it all" now have still not forgotten their roots, identity and nation through its most difficult times. Their support will make sure that abnormal realties of occupation and colonization would not deny the joy and crucial importance of sport in Palestinian life and future.

Indeed, being a Palestinian out of Palestine for most of one's life does not diminish a bit one's commitment and contribution to the liberation struggle. Ghada Karmi recalls an incident when she was invited to tell her life story at a special event where people were asked to do so, but was then censored by the organizers who feared a Palestinian life story might be "provocative" or "offensive." This occurred in London, not under a callous dictatorial regime. Ghada devoted, and still devotes, her life to ensure Britain does not forget Palestine and its own role in its catastrophic history. At times it was a lonely struggle, later it was carried out in tandem with others and all of it part of the struggle of the PLO since its inception and until the 1980s, and then within other networks of support to the liberation effort on the ground in the homeland.

Randa Abdel-Fattah demonstrates that this struggle abroad is a daily, at times consuming, part of one's life and identity by shedding light on Palestinian resistance in Sydney, Australia. Generation after generation of people experience a reality that alternates between being tied to Palestine while being elsewhere. As Randa beautifully puts it:

> On the one hand, a claim by a Palestinian here to bear witness to what is happening in Palestine there. On the other, a claim by a Palestinian child here to control the here, to keep what is happening in Palestine there.

Samah Sabawi too begins a poetic journey into history and identity from the Redlands Coast of Queensland, Australia, while visiting her aging father. This is where the history of the Australian settler colonialism and its genocide of the indigenous population meets the story of the Zionist settler colonialism and its ethnic cleansing of the Palestinians. The geographical and historical background are all the time consciously present in the life of a Palestinian woman who writes about, and experiences daily, the nexus between exile and trauma and in the middle ponders on post-memory. This self-reflection helps Samah challenge the erasure and denial and pass that determination to the next generation:

> We cannot move on while our loved ones are under falling bombs, under siege and under occupation. So we do not. And we pass this on to our children.

Palestinians draw courage, inspiration and orientation from different sources. One of the most important one is religion, whether they are Christians or Muslims. The theology of liberation is both Christian and Islamic. The life story of Father Manuel Musallam is a powerful antidote to any colonialist and apartheid regime's colonialist attempt at "divide and rule" tactics by driving a wedge between Muslims and Christians in Palestine. Father Musallam writes:

> I will resist from a religious standpoint, stemming from the theology of my church, and my strong conviction in this theology.

Sami Al-Arian discusses Islam within a wider context of exploring the different parameters in which the liberation struggle can move forward, without flinching in the face of difficult realities and current imbalances of power. The role of political Islam in the liberation struggle has been recognized by many. This chapter situates the struggle within the story of the lifelong commitment of an intellectual, who has paid highly for his devotion by suffering a long term in American prisons, including in solitary confinement. His intellectual reach is extraordinary, from a deep knowledge of Western philosophy to a profound knowledge of the Islamic visions and perceptions. Sami is not only looking at the past, he is viewing the future and believes in grand visions, without which there is no hope for a proper liberation—a vision that is situated in Islam as much as it is in general human values of freedom and justice.

Religion also inspired Hanadi Halawani's personal struggle to protect Jerusalem in general and the Al-Aqsa Mosque that is its striking centerpiece. This young Jerusalemite Palestinian woman has been the moving spirit and inspiration behind the Palestinian determination to defend Jerusalem and the Al-Aqsa Mosque. She recounts the amazing and courageous efforts of Palestinian women in particular to defend this site sacred to Islam and highlights how children and young Palestinians are enrolled in such a struggle at a place where the massive Israeli presence should have prevented any form of resistance, and yet it exists. Hanadi's struggle takes place in the classroom, on the streets of Al-Quds and wherever she is, now that she is banished from her beloved Al-Aqsa.

Faith in one's religion or nation, alongside incredible human courage, is what keeps the Palestinian political prisoners resilient and determined not to cave in when faced with callous incarceration and denial of justice. Khalida Jarar, still in prison when this book was being prepared, was denied the right of participating in the funeral of her beloved daughter—may she rest in peace—to whom we dedicate this entire collection.

Jarrar's description of her trials and tribulations shed light on the power of conviction that keeps Palestine's political prisoners steadfast in their commitment to the liberation struggle. Such a route inevitably demands sacrifices and can end in martyrdom, imprisonment or loss of one's home and career. The courage and resilience of those who have experienced the most brutal aspects of oppression is illuminated in this extraordinary piece that was conceived within the four walls of an Israeli prison, amidst torture and endless brutality. Here we find no self-pity, no hate, just an incredible display of commitment, resilience and hope. Jarrar writes:

> While it is important that you must comprehend the suffering endured by prisoners, such as the numerous acts of physical torture, psychological torment and prolonged isolation, you must also realize the power of the human will, when men and women decide to fight back, to reclaim their natural rights and to embrace their humanity.

Popular resistance demands not only commitment and courage but also organization. Jamal Jumaa explains the essential role of networking, to which he contributes to this day, providing us with an overview of the popular struggle from a level above it. Institutions, organizations, and networking were at the heart of the more successful years of the PLO's struggle. They were deemed lost for a while as a result of the events of 1982 and the Oslo Accord but, as Jamal demonstrates, are still there and have the potential to reignite and regenerate more coordinated and organized successful uprisings in the future.

Organized or individual struggle on the ground in Occupied Palestine leads, as we have seen, to prison. It takes someone who has been in prison to devote his life to defending other prisoners as their lawyer. This is the life story of Gaza's most famous human right advocate, Raji Sourani. His work is done both in Israeli and international courts. The former is almost an impossible arena in which to turn for justice and the other, as Raji tells us, in recent years has been politicized and become a more difficult venue for prosecuting the crimes against Palestinians. But he insists that these difficulties would not deter him from continuing his work, in particular in the international area, pointing out the special attribute of international law:

> So international law is a way of demonstrating that we are equal. All we are asking for is the equal application of the law that we are treated the same as everyone else, that we enjoy the same rights as everyone else. That we are held accountable just like everyone else.

To be treated as equal is also a constant challenge for those who have devoted their life to education as a means of struggling for liberation. This became a particular mode of cultural struggle in the refugee camps, as can be learned from the next chapter written by Ghada Ageel. Life in refugee camps quite often resembled life in prison and refugees, as much as political prisoners, can tell us stories not just of their suffering but mainly of their struggle against the oppression. In the refugee camps, education was a key element in maintaining one's humanity and ability to continue the resistance. Ghada is of the third generation of refugees from the Gaza Strip and her journey into choosing education as a mode of resistance helped others to see what the West refuses to recognize—the deeply racist nature of the Zionist project and its implication for the Palestinians. Against this racism, Ghada used the field of education as a springboard to make her unique contribution for the liberation struggle.

There is more than one way of educating people about the Palestinians history and heritage, and one such way is the unique Palestinian History Tapestry Project. Jehan Alfarra and Jan Chalmers show how this incredible project keeps alive an old artisanry while reflecting through its beautiful embroidery historical scenes of the Palestinian oppression and the struggle against it. This project is mobile and displayed both in exhibitions and on the internet. These fine products are prepared by devoted artisans in the Gaza Strip, and Palestinians from across the occupied territories, and in refugee camps in Lebanon and Jordan, bringing together women who share a perception of their work as an act of liberation.

Next, Terry Boullata gives us an overview of the role of heritage in the liberation struggle in its cultural mode. Defending that heritage, as Terry shows us, is not always a conscious act of liberation, it occurs because:

> I would argue that, for the greater majority of Palestinians outside the homeland, myself included, being Palestinian is not so much a decision but rather a reflection of who we are.

The way Terry chose to struggle against the cultural erasure in the West and the Zionist campaign of cultural suppression adds another layer to the liberation struggle and its record of individual victories, which might be small in the big scheme of things, but will prove, one day, to be an accumulative transformative and powerful factor in the liberation of Palestine.

In this respect, singers, and their songs, like poets and their poetry, play a crucial role. Reem Talhami. Reem is a '48 Arab and a renowned singer, who recounts the long, impressive history and reservoir of Palestinian liberation songs (which hopefully one day will be archived and accessible to all). These songs have helped to articulate, in the most beautiful and passionate way, one of the major predicaments of the '48 Arabs: their alienation in their own homeland. The songs Reem chooses and performs paint in stark colors this alienation. As Reem puts it, "with songs, we wage wars without shedding a single drop of blood".

The cinema and the movies are a relatively modern form of art connected to the individual and collective struggles for liberation. Here, Farah Nabulsi assesses the role of cinema in oppressing and resisting the liberation struggle, while her work exemplifies how it can be used for liberation as well. Born in London, her personal and professional engagement with the world of cinema was never divorced from her Palestinian identity and did not diminish her outrage at the injustice done to the Palestinian people. While realizing that "art alone, of course, cannot free Palestine," she nonetheless emphasizes that "I believe that without it, Palestine will never be free!"

Sometimes art or any other interest or profession is not enough to help one survive in such a struggle. Being a victim of Israeli brutality and being immersed in the long experience of the struggle takes a mental toll. Samah Jabr's contribution, which comes next, helps unveil these hardships and how to confront them. As is fitting for a psychiatrist, her account starts from the very moment she was born and continues through her rise to become one of Palestine's leading psychiatrists. Aware that collective and individual trauma has only more recently been recognized as a mental health area of concern, Samah has assigned for herself as her future contribution to the struggle the twin missions of raising the recognition of the importance of mental health treatment in the overall liberation struggle on the one hand, and the need to critically examine Western notions such as PTSD and their relevance to both to oppression and the struggle against it in the Palestinian context, on the other.

Just as Samah's path was a mixture of commitment that did not compromise her professionalism, the role of science in the liberation struggle emerges very strongly in Mazin Qumsiyeh's chapter. Science is a human capital that is not always accumulated via the classroom or the laboratory for those who are occupied or colonized. Zionism attempts to destroy this ecological wisdom, as after all its project has led to an ecological disaster. Mazin's path in life and contribution to the liberation struggle is exercised in multiple contributions for popular resistance; here, he highlights the role of human knowledge of nature and science played in this popular resistance. This is a very timely contribution for our times for, as Mazin writes, in Palestine: "a harmony between humans and nature persisted for millennia" and now we struggle to maintain it due to the disharmony sowed by Zionism since its arrival in Palestine.

In the last section of this book, we meet personal stories of liberation struggle that are pursued vis-à-vis the international community, through diplomacy, engagement with the global civil society and with the state of Israel and its Jewish society.

It begins with the moving account of Hasan Abu Nimah, a Palestinian who became a senior Jordanian diplomat while being fully aware, at every juncture of his life, of his Palestinian identity and commitment to the struggle. His life story reflects that of the Palestinian people from the day he was born and through his rich life, until today. He reminds us not to focus just on the Palestinian moments of nadir but recall also the crumbling of Israeli sinister plans and projects, providing a hopeful reappraisal of the past with a view to the future where liberation is a doable and successful possibility. He writes:

> I am convinced that the violent partition of Palestine that I witnessed as a child will end, and the country will be made whole again, with people free to live and move wherever they wish. There is no room for an apartheid regime in Palestine.

In the following chapter, Johnny Mansour follows the development of Israeli studies on the Palestinian side, explaining how the liberation struggle needed to avoid stereotyping and superficiality as it sought to understand the destructive nature of Zionism and the nature of the Israeli Jewish society. A project that was begun by the late Issam Sirtawi has now reached a high professional level with the establishment of an institute for Israeli Studies in Ramallah, *Madar*. Johnny followed the early stages of the development of this institution and his deep knowledge of both the Israeli and Palestinian history and societies, and he continues to serve faithfully the ongoing project of *Madar* and similar projects in his and my hometown Haifa, such as *Mada al-Karmil.*

Haneen Zoabi; a founding member of the *Tajamoa* party and representative of this party in the Israeli parliament, describes a different struggle. Haneen's political career evolved around the attempt of the '48 Arabs to transit from politics of recognition to politics of liberation. Her involvement in the Freedom Flotilla in 2010 exposed for her the hypocrisy of the Liberal Zionist Left and forced her somber recognition of the limitations of being active for liberation under an apartheid state that has wide support among its Jewish society. Haneen's contribution is important for anyone who still has illusions of changing the Israeli society from within:

> In conclusion, Israeli citizenship was not granted to Palestinians as a means of introducing them into Israeli society; rather, it was the manifestation and exercise of Israel's victory over us. Palestinians engaging in Israeli politics must preserve the clarity of the inherent contradiction between justice and colonial citizenship.

Nonetheless, the '48 Arabs do not lose hope in building a new decolonized space with at least some of the settler Jewish community, as happened in post-Apartheid South Africa. When progressive anti-Zionist Jews who currently live in Israel are involved in such an act of genuine solidarity, inevitably they are concerned also with the vision of a liberated Palestine and their place in it. Awad Abdelfattah, in his chapter, tells the struggle for a democratic state over all of historical Palestine that would emerge once the ill-fated two states solution is buried deep down in the dustbin of history. Such a vision of liberation is based on both the very sacred principles of the Palestinian liberation movement from its outset, and on a mode of decolonization that entails a joint democratic vision, not only for the Palestinians but also for the Jews who are willing to live in a liberated Palestine.

Solidarity cannot remain a soundbite. It has to be translated into action in the face of the abnormal realities of settler colonial

Israel and the occupied Palestine. Both Laila Al-Marayati and Nora Lester Murad make the point, in separate chapters, that an effective liberation will have to have a clear view of how to recruit financial resources for the struggle and how to employ them in the best way possible. Each one of these two activists founded an organization that catered to the special circumstances in which such work is being done. Laila woke up to the need to do it differently when she became aware that:

> Barriers were created, seemingly overnight, to anyone around the world who wanted to provide humanitarian support to Palestine, from Europe to the Gulf.

As a result, she established with friends KinderUSA (Kids in Need of Development, Education and Relief). She advises that charity work for Palestinians in the US is never straightforward, as the pro-Israeli lobby keeps demonizing it as in support of terrorism. No matter: it nonetheless connects people, and whatever they can give, directly with places such as the besieged Gaza, the occupied West Bank and the refugee camps, eschewing possibly questionable intermediaries.

Nora Lester Murad also founded her own organization, the Dalia Organization, through which she deals daily with questions of how to institutionalize and professionalize aid to the struggle, without forgetting the crucial role by grassroots individuals and organizations in it. This is an inspiring template that will be referred to in years to come.

My own article tries to tap into this solidarity and expand it by chronicling the rise and actions of the international solidary movement. The potency of this movement lies in its ability to empower speaking the truth, so that even people who were nurtured as Zionists, in Israel or abroad, were able to cross the Rubicon and join the movement in solidarity with the liberation struggle. This is a growing phenomenon, and it will play a crucial role in the future in bringing freedom to Palestine.

Armed struggle, different modes of cultural struggles, of knowledge production, recruitment of resources and support of mental and physical ailments caused by occupation, imprisonment, and colonization—all form the struggle for liberation. The various individual stories in this volume do not cover all the aspects of this struggle, nor can they represent all the groups, locations and generations that kept the liberation struggle alive. But even as a sample it is a testimony to the human capital that Palestine was blessed with before the *Nakba* and has managed, despite the ongoing catastrophe, to regenerate and expand. One day, this human treasure will be employed for the benefit of everyone who lives between the River Jordan and the Mediterranean, and for all those who were expelled from there over the years.

*—Ilan Pappé, November 2021*

# SECTION I

# ORIGINS AND MEMORIES OF LIBERATION

HAMDAN TAHA *is an independent researcher and former Deputy Minister for Heritage in the Palestinian Ministry of Tourism and Antiquities. He served as Director General of the newly established Department of Antiquities and Cultural Heritage from 1994–2012. He has directed a series of research and salvage excavations in Palestine. He acted as National Coordinator of the World Heritage File in Palestine from 2002–2014, and is currently Coordinator of the Palestine History and Heritage Project, for which he has recently co-authored an introductory volume,* New Critical Approach to the History of Palestine. *He is the author of many books, field reports and scholarly articles.*

# EXCAVATING EARTH AND MEMORY
# The Role of Archaeology in Our Liberation[1]

*Hamdan Taha*

I WAS BORN at dawn on the fifth of November 1954, to Mohammed and Fatima, in our family summer cabin in Wadi Abu Safar, east of our home town of Shiyukh. The Shrine of Sheikh Ahmed, which was next to an oak tree by the same name, was regarded as God's eyes that oversee the place. As children, we were tasked with carrying the vows and prayers of the visitors, little matchboxes and candles that they left behind to the Hedmi mosque in the village. I recall memories from my early childhood in the family yard, the scent of the seasons in the earth, the games I played with my friends, running through the narrow alleys of our tranquil village.

## The War I Forgot to Mention

I was twelve years old in 1967. My family was working on our farm east of the village during the summer planting season, when we saw planes in the sky. I was asked to fetch some things from home and on the way, I heard people say, "The war has started." When I went back to the farm, I forgot to tell them that the war had started.

The next day, young people from the town gathered volunteers to fight in the war. They went to the Hebron Governor's headquarters asking to be armed but came back empty-handed. People wondered what was happening. They listened to radio broadcasts about the

---

1 This essay was originally written in Arabic and was translated by Samah Sabawi.

heroic battle in Jerusalem and heard sporadic rumors about the arrival of the Iraqi army, but then they saw with their own eyes Israeli air raids on a withdrawing Jordanian army convoy in the neighboring town of Sa'ir, turning most of the convoy tanks into smoldering hulks.

Some people took refuge in the caves around the village. The children set about playing and smoke soon rose from stoves in the caves. It was as if they were having a family holiday.

The town became a crossroads for fleeing soldiers and civilians heading east towards the Jordan River. It was not long before the Israeli military patrols stormed our village; soldiers wearing netted helmets came in their dusty sand-colored military jeeps and posted flyers on the doors of the shops. We heard that some people were severely beaten. A curfew was imposed on the town so that the Israeli army could conduct a population census.

On November 6, 1967, we experienced the first real meaning of Occupation, when military forces stormed the town in the afternoon and imposed a curfew. Military helicopters hovered east of the town and paratroopers landed in the Al-Bayyada area. Rumors spread about a battle taking place with the *fedayeen* in the caves of Umm Qarmoul, which lasted about four hours. Martyrs buried at night were turned into legends, and the beautiful image of one of them, Youssef, was etched in our minds.

Next morning, loudspeakers called for all men over the age of sixteen to gather in the vacant lot not far from our house. We did not hear the announcement from our house, and then we did not want to go when we saw, from our windows, the brutal beating of those who arrived late.

## Antiquities Fever

After the Occupation, work stopped, and crowds of young unemployed men searched for archaeological material in the nearby ruins. Eyes sparkled when an artifact was found! Things were to such a degree of ease that middlemen traders came to the excavation sites to reap the bargains. This was an indicator of the end of the antiquities protection system. I found a bronze coin, most likely from the Roman period.

The antiquities fever spread stories of treasures and gold. My grandfather told my mother a story about when he was a young man during the British Mandate period and how he found gold pieces in a small basin. He took the pieces to an antiquities shop in Jerusalem to sell them, but the dealer at the shop asked if he had more, and when he said that he did, the dealer asked him to wait, and went to the adjacent room to make a phone call. My grandfather realized that he was calling the police, so he ran away! As he ran, he took off his green headscarf that identified him, and tossed the gold coins left and right into the open fields. I think no archaeologist would guess that these coins had been contaminated and removed from their original archaeological context.

## School Days

I attended the town's preparatory and primary schools and the Secondary School of Halhul.

During this period, I became enamored with reading novellas by Arab and foreign writers, including novels from the school's library. I lived the events of these novels in my dreams. I came across the story of Anne Frank and was deeply affected by it, but did not link it to Israel and Zionism. I also obtained a copy of the Palestinian National Charter with its Hebrew translation at a secondhand bookstand in Halhul. That was the first time I saw literature written by the Palestine Liberation Organization. However, over time, I came to understand that the village with its people, who preserve the wisdom handed down to them, was the most important school in my life.

## Birzeit: My First University

In 1973, I began attending Birzeit University. I first moved into the student dorms but found that the accommodation there was governed by strict laws, so I decided to move in with a group of colleagues into a house located at the entrance of the town. The house became known as the "Commune." We later learned that it used to be a base for meetings of revolutionaries before 1948.

That period witnessed the emergence of a new generation as the university became a stronghold for our national movement; the curriculum was arabized and the first student council was established. This was also the period in which municipal elections took place and we saw the emergence of a unified national Palestinian leadership.

I have always been influenced by the ideas of the Peasants' Revolution and inspired by Frantz Fanon, so my friend, Yasser Ibrahim, and I purchased and collected book donations. We established the first public library in our village, which he ran from a small room in his house.

On one of my visits home, a curfew was imposed, and men were summoned and herded together at a school which I had attended as a child. A crowd of us huddled under the trees, while the army ran their interrogation in the classrooms. When my turn came, I was ordered into the classroom and saw the army interrogator sitting on what used to be my teacher's chair. He asked about my name, family, work, and when he found out that I was studying at Birzeit, his attention peaked. The interrogator wanted to know who my friends were, and he was not impressed with my vague response. That was when I received a slap in the face from another interrogator who suddenly appeared beside me. I was told to go to the Al-Amara military government building in Hebron the following Wednesday.

At the Al-Amara, the scene was different. The interrogator was sitting at his desk with a pile of files in front of him. After the introductory questions, he said, "Listen, we know everything about you. It's all in this file in front of me. I advise you to confess." He said this in a confident tone. I told him that while I was at his office, I was missing out on lectures at the university so, to save both my time and his, he should just read the file. He got angry and told me to leave, warning me that he would be watching me.

In my third year of sociology, I enrolled by chance in "Introduction to Archaeology," a course taught by Dr. A. Glock, which was offered as part of a minor. I was completely captivated by the new world that it opened up to me. It was as if I had wandered into a cave filled with treasure, the cave of Ali Baba.

This is how an elective minor became central to the course of my future. Immediately after graduation, I took up a job as an academic assistant in the Department of Archaeology, while also completing the university requirements for a double major in archaeology. I participated in training excavations at Tell Jenin and Tell Ta'annek, developed my field work skills and learned more about cultural artifacts, especially pottery which, as Flinders Petrie says, constitutes the alphabet of archaeology. The Jenin excavation camp experience was unique; it led to the emergence of the first locally trained team, and it made us feel that we had the responsibility to dig into our history with our own hands.

## Studying at the University of Jordan

I was accepted into a part-time Master's program at the University of Jordan in 1980 and during my studies, in order to cover the expenses of my stay, I worked as a day laborer for the Jordanian Department of Antiquities in a number of salvage excavations. I also participated in a survey of the Ajloun area together with Robert Jordan. It was during this survey that we received news of the Sabra and Shatila massacre in Beirut. We were shocked by this ruthless Occupation that terrorized and expelled Palestinians and then chased them as they fled to seek asylum in other countries, only to continue killing them there.

For my Master's thesis, I chose to research the origin and civilization of the Philistines (Taha 1983). My thesis was based on a clear distinction between Philistines and Palestinians, as two distinct terms denoting two divergent historical contexts, despite the linguistic link and despite the fact that the Philistines clearly gave their name to the country. I concluded that the ethnic origin of the Philistines, which was a subject of great controversy among biblical researchers, is not important, and that the real importance rather lies in the cultural continuity of a people.

On my return journey home, I was interrogated at the border crossing. The Israeli interrogator, agitated to see me, barked, "Why have you come back?" I was told to check in at Al-Amara in Hebron for a second round of questioning the following day, which I did. On the third day, our house was shot at, with two bullets going through the window but, fortunately, no one was hurt. During that time, our village was being terrorized by militias affiliated with the Occupation. I returned to lecture at Birzeit University in 1984 and spent a semester at the university until I traveled abroad to study in Germany.

## My Studies in Berlin

I was awarded a German Academic Exchange Mission Scholarship and completed a Ph.D. in Archaeology at the Institute of West Asian Archaeology at the Free University of Berlin. I studied German at the Goethe-Institute in Göttingen.

I married Samar Jarrar, whom I met during my studies in Jordan. She joined me in Germany and we had three children there—Dalia and the twins, Suhail and Lubna. My youngest daughter, Noura, was born in Jerusalem after we returned to Palestine. In Germany, I lived in Dahlem Dorf, and often cycled to the university. One day, while browsing through a magazine at the university, I was taken aback to read about the martyrdom of my brother, Abdul Karim. He was 24 years old and had been martyred on Land Day, during the First Intifada.

The topic of my thesis was "Mortuary differentiations in Palestine (Taha 1990) from the Mousterian period until the beginning of urbanization." It was a new experiment in applying the methodology of mortuary analysis to archaeological artifacts that had been unearthed by hundreds of archaeological excavations in Palestine, including a sample of Middle Bronze Age burials from Tell Ta'annek in what is known as the children's cemetery, which was found under the floors of houses in the Middle Bronze Age. The whole mortuary theory is based on the assumption developed by Saxe (1970), Binford (1972) and others that social differentiation, whether by age, sex, social position etc., is reflected by the mortuary differentiation of the dead.

## Coming Home

Again, on my way back home, I was asked at the bridge to go to Al-Amara to be interrogated. I was returning as an adjunct professor at Birzeit University. I was eager to participate in the setting up of the Archaeology program but had to negotiate stifling procedural obstacles. The director of the institute had reservations regarding my ability to teach, believing that I was only fit for research. The case was referred to the university councils and the staff union. An agreement was reached in the office of the late university president, G. Baramki, that I would return to teaching. I was assigned two courses in archaeology. A few days later, I heard the tragic news of the murder of Dr. A. Glock, from whom I had learned a lot, and had worked with, for many years.

## Participation in the Negotiations

I was working at the university when Palestinian preparations for the 1992 Madrid Conference began, and I was selected to coordinate an advisory Antiquities Team, one of many technical teams tasked to prepare for the negotiations (Taha 1994d).

I participated in the technical negotiations in Taba where I noticed our plan was not clearly articulated. I prepared an amended paper and informed the head of the Palestinian delegation, Dr. N. Shaath, about this. Later that morning, we met with the Israeli side, and I submitted my amended paper, but the Israeli side insisted on working from the first version which, in my opinion, did not constitute a basis for negotiation. The session was quickly adjourned. In the evening, Dr. N. Kassis whispered to me that the Israelis had accused me of sabotaging the negotiations.

The next session was with Dr. M. Sadiq in Eilat. The discussion stalled during a procedural session over a disagreement about a requirement, listed as point No. 9, which stipulated that the Palestinian Authority needed to obtain Israeli approval to work in a number of archaeological sites. I asked for this provision point to be deleted, but all attempts to reach an agreement on that point failed. On the third day, the Israeli negotiator lost his temper and warned that I would not be allowed to return for future sessions. I registered a complaint and asked for him to be removed, which he was, but the deadlock was not broken, and I was not called to participate at the next session in Cairo, where the agreement was actually signed.

## Reclaiming History

The establishment of the Palestinian Department of Antiquities in 1994 was a momentous event. It was viewed as inaugurating the revival of the Department of Antiquities established in 1920, which had been dissolved on account of the *Nakba*, and marked an official reclaiming of history.

Following the Palestinian-Israeli agreement signed in Oslo in 1993, and the subsequent agreement in 1994, the Palestinian side was given control of several administrative domains, including archaeology in areas designated A and B under the Oslo Accords. There was an understanding that responsibilities in Area C would be transferred gradually to Palestinians, on the understanding that the peace process was to be concluded by May 1999. However, this mutually agreed timetable was never honored by Israel. In the absence of a final peace agreement, Israel, therefore, remains a military occupier in the Palestinian Territories, with responsibilities set out in international law (Taha 1914: 29).

I was appointed Director of the Department of Antiquities on August 10, 1994 and led the process of managing the handover of antiquities offices and employees that had, until then, been part of the Israeli Civil Administration. There was only a small staff working in a handful of offices. Their main responsibility had been to follow up on licensing issues and to serve as an operational base for the Israeli antiquities officer.

Palestinians had inherited, from this period, a negative view of archaeological work, perceiving it to be part of the Occupation, because antiquities were being used as a pretext to confiscate land for settlement purposes, and many settlements had been established on the back of archaeological excavation campaigns, such as Khirbet Siloun, Mount Gerizim, Tell Rumeida, etc.

The new era of archaeology in Palestine began with the work of a small but dedicated and enthusiastic team, who worked out of a field office by the ruins of the ancient Hisham's Palace in Jericho. This team included Muhammed Ghayada, Youssef Abu Ta'a, Iman Saca, Jihad Yassin, Juliana Neiruz and Iyad Hamdan, among others. We started from scratch, with no qualified personnel, no logistical capacity and no archival or archaeological materials in our custody. The department that we built considered itself a natural extension of the Mandate Department of Antiquities that had ceased to exist in 1948.

The department began work to promote a modern understanding of cultural heritage in Palestine (Taha a-c1994). The new situation after Oslo allowed Palestinians to write the history of Palestine on the basis of its primary sources, a privilege reserved, until recently, for foreign and Israeli archaeologists (Curtis 1994, 1914: 29). The first fieldwork activities began at a small site in Jericho known as Jiser Abu Ghabush (Taha 1994), under the blazing August sun. The team felt empowered, as they were now in charge of their own archaeological sites and writing their own past.

The new Department of Antiquities shouldered a number of responsibilities, including formulating new legislations, training staff in salvage excavation, combating looting of archaeological sites and the illicit trade in antiquities, and building a museum sector (Taha 2014: 31). The department's founding vision emphasized the role of archaeology as a scientific enterprise, tasked itself to safeguard the integrity of different aspects and layers of cultural heritage and recognized antiquities as a source for sustainable development and an integral part of Palestine's national cultural identity (Taha 2003).

## Writing History Using Primary Sources

The newborn department was involved in archaeological excavations, and it became possible to start the first ambitious project: excavating the Great Water Tunnel at Khirbet Balama (Taha and van der Kooij 2007) alongside a large cluster of tombs from different periods. One of the most notable of these discoveries is the Qabatiya silver coinage collection (Taha and van der Kooij 2006). We gave priority to cleaning up a hundred archaeological sites (Taha 1998) and developing sites that were excavated and abandoned by previous archaeological missions, which had transferred archaeological materials and excavation archives to various European and American museums.

## The Formula for Post-colonial Cooperation

I received the first letter of international cooperation from Prof. Paolo Matthiae of the University of Rome La Sapienza, proposing to begin joint cooperation at Tell es-Sultan in Jericho. This venture paved the way for establishing the first model of post-colonial cooperation (Nigro 2006:96). Although Palestine is still under Occupation, excavation permits were replaced by memoranda of understanding based on equality and mutual respect. The colonial principle of appropriating archaeological materials was abolished. The cooperative model was extended to other sites. Most notably, these included joint excavations in Khirbet Balama and Tell Balata with Leiden University in the Netherlands, Palestinian-French excavations in Tell al-Blakhiya, Tell al-Nuseirat and Tell es-Sakan in Gaza, Palestinian-Norwegian excavations at Tell al-Mafjar, Palestinian-American excavations at Hisham's Palace, and Palestinian-Russian excavations at the Sycamore Tree site in Jericho (Taha 2014).

Dr. D. Baramki had stopped the excavations at Hisham Palace due to the turbulent events in Palestine preceding the *Nakba* of 1948. My heart pounded when I read in his thesis the following line:

> It is hoped that at some future date some enthusiastic person may supply the funds necessary for the resumption and conclusion of the work.
>
> (Baramki 1953: 95)

I began the excavations in 2006 and completed "the work" between 2012–2015, together with Don Whitcomb, working in the area adjacent to the Umayyad Bath and the northern area to expose the Abbasid aspects of the palace (Taha and Whitcomb 2014).

## Museums and Galleries

On the understanding that museums play an important role in preserving cultural memory, the new department began the establishment of archaeological and ethnographic museums in Hebron, Bethlehem, Jericho, Tulkarm and Gaza. At the same time, a series of international archaeological exhibitions were organized, including "Mediterranean Gaza," in Paris in 2000, "Gaza at the Crossroads of Civilizations" in Geneva in 2007 and "Gaza the Gateway to the Sea," in Oldenburg in 2009 and Stockholm in 2010 (Taha 2014: 38–39). These initiatives were an important component of our efforts to part ways with the model of colonial control over Palestinian cultural institutions (Taha 2021) represented by the pre-1948 Mandate era Palestinian Department of Antiquities and the Archaeological Museum in Jerusalem.

## Intentional Destruction of Cultural Heritage

We documented the deliberate destruction of cultural heritage, especially in Jerusalem, Hebron and Nablus, since the Occupation in 1967, which constituted an extension of the displacement and destruction in 1948 of more than 500 Palestinian villages, together with all their heritage (Taha 2019: 26–28). We also documented the damage inflicted on archaeological sites and historical buildings during successive Israeli assaults on Gaza.

A major challenge that we confronted, as a department, was the threat posed by Israeli settlements constructed in the Palestinian territories since 1967, which control more than 50% of cultural resources in the West Bank and Gaza. The other significant problem was the threat posed to archaeological heritage by Israel's Separation Wall, including those parts of it built in and around Jerusalem. The Wall separates people from their land and history and has a devastating impact on archaeological sites and cultural landscape (Taha 2014: 37–38).

## Archaeology and the Occupation: An Ongoing Debate

Archaeology in Palestine must be viewed as archaeology under Occupation (Taha 2016). It is an arena of struggle between two competing narratives, an indigenous Palestinian narrative, and the settler colonial narrative of Zionism. The Israeli narrative tends to give overwhelming priority to Jewish heritage in Palestine, and to scantily mention Palestine's non-Jewish and Arab history. At the first International Conference on the Archaeology of the Near East, which was held in 1998 in Rome, the relationship between archaeology and the Occupation was raised, and the conference affirmed its commitment to the stipulation of the UNESCO Charter pertaining to excavations in occupied territories.

One problem that we face as Palestinians is that Israelis fabricate our narratives, sometimes even well-meaning Israelis. As for instance, in an essay criticizing Israeli archaeology, architect Eyal Weizman quoted me as saying something that I had never said, in connection with Israeli excavations at Khirbet Seiloun, controlled by Shiloh settlement. But then, this story was later repeated by an Israeli journalist, now in an incendiary article written after Palestine gained membership in UNESCO, which accused the Palestinian Authority of re-writing Jewish history (Giulio 2011) and constituting a scandal worse than Holocaust denial in the view of the right-wing Israeli archaeologist, G. Barkay. Muddling facts as well as names, the article confused me with the Palestinian poet Mutawakel Taha, who wrote a treatise on the Wailing Wall.

## Building an International Network

After Oslo, Palestine became a member of a series of international and regional organizations, including UNESCO, ALECSO and ICESCO. International engagement in Palestine took the form of crises management, rather than offering substantive solutions to the problem of the Occupation.

While attending the International Conference on the Archaeology of the Near East in Rome in 2008, I said, in my closing speech, that the land might be divided for political reasons, but history is indivisible, and this means that Palestine will remain the physical and moral homeland for the Palestinians.

In 2005, Palestine prepared (Taha 2005/2009) a tentative list for World Heritage Sites in Palestine. The list includes twenty sites of cultural and natural heritage. In 2009, the Department of Antiquities began preparing the Bethlehem file (Taha 2012a, 2012b), although Palestine was not yet a regular member in UNESCO. At the 2010 World Heritage Conference in Brazil, the Palestinian delegation refused to be seated until their place was marked with a plaque bearing the name of Palestine, as is the case for other country delegations.

UNESCO's recognition of Palestine in 2011 culminated a long struggle (Taha 2011, TWIP 2011b). The sites of Bethlehem in 2012, the cultural landscape of Battir in 2014 and the old city of Hebron in 2017, were inscribed on the World Heritage List. UNESCO's recognition of Palestine represented the first official international cultural recognition, which marked the beginning of rectifying part of the historical injustice that has befallen the Palestinian people.

## Reconstructing the Past to Build the Future

After my official appointment with the Department of Antiquities ended on November 5, 2014, I turned to the world of research and scholarship. I took on some advisory and teaching work, before I devoted myself to the completion of a publication on the findings of previous excavations (Taha, H. and van der Kooij: 2016) and coordinating "The Palestine History Project," which involved a group of local and international researchers. This culminated in the publication of a book entitled *New Critical Approaches to the History of Palestine* (2019).

In my view, the role of archaeology is to reconstruct the past in order to build the future (TWIP 2011a). Palestinians are now contributing, in writing, an inclusive narrative of their history, drawing on primary sources that incorporate the voices of all peoples, groups, cultures and religions that have lived on the land of Palestine, in stark contrast to the exclusivist fantasy advanced by Zionism's settler colonial narrative. I remain inspired by D. Baramki's admonition (Baramki 1969: 239) that all archaeological and historical evidence shows that Palestine was inhabited by many peoples, from the early times of Homo sapiens until the twenty-first century and that, over this history which was marked by many wars, invasions and conversions—religious and political—the indigenous population was never completely eliminated. We Palestinians, the indigenous people of this land, have always endured, and this gives us hope in our struggle for liberation from Israel's settler Occupation and the regime of apartheid that it has established in the land of Palestine.[2]

2 My role would not have been possible without the support of my family, my friends, and the help and efforts of those I worked with on this journey, in particular, my colleagues in the Department of Antiquities and all its partner institutions. Although I am not able to acknowledge all by name, I owe them my thanks and gratitude. A full list of references is in my publications and is available on my website, https://independent.academia.edu/HamdanTaha.

IBRAHIM G. AOUDÉ *is Professor of Ethnic Studies at the University of Hawai'i—Mānoa. He is the Editor of* Arab Studies Quarterly *and holds a Ph.D. in political science. His publications include articles, book chapters and edited volumes in political economy, globalization and inter-ethnic relations about Palestine, Lebanon, Iraq, Turkey, Egypt and Hawai'i. He is the author (pen name: B. J. Odeh) of* Lebanon: Dynamics of Conflict *(Zed Books, 1985). Since 2001, he has been the producer and host of the TV show "Island Connections" on the Educational Channel, sponsored by the Department of Ethnic Studies.*

# THE STRUGGLE TO CONTROL THE NARRATIVE

## When Pursuing Liberation, Watch Your Language

*Ibrahim G. Aoudé*

THE MAY 2021 EVENTS in Palestine reignited passions and heightened hopes that, this time around, the Palestinians would accomplish a leap forward in their struggle for liberation. The 2021 Ramadan Al-Aqsa uprising turned into a torrent of resistance, with masses of Palestinians from the 1948 occupied Palestinian territories participating in the defense of Palestinian Jerusalemites facing ethnic cleansing (not "evictions," as Zionist propaganda would have us believe) from Sheikh Jarrah, Silwan and other Palestinian neighborhoods.

As I watched live coverage of events on Al-Mayadeen TV, I was transported into a different era. The scene was Beirut, seventeen years after the *Nakba*. The event was the first armed operation against the Zionist entity, established in Palestine on May 15, 1948. The operation itself was not significant militarily, but it dominated the news in the Arab world. I read in a Lebanese newspaper the first communiqué from the Palestinian National Liberation Movement, known also in Arabic as "*Al-Fatah*," the inverse acronym of its Arabic name. I was captivated. You see, I was born in Jaffa and was three years old when the family fled Nazareth and took refuge in the southern Lebanese town of Marjayoun. Two understandings were instilled in me from a young age: First, I am a Palestinian Arab. Second, Palestine must be liberated. About 750,000 Palestinians had been ethnically cleansed.[3] Those who survived Zionist massacres had become refugees in neighboring countries. My refugee status left an indelible mark, like a compass pointed towards Palestine, and a vision of the return of all Palestinians to the homeland.

Galloping events in Lebanon and the region reinforced that vision. Those events included the July 23, 1952, military coup that toppled the Egyptian monarchy, the 1954 Algerian Revolution, the Baghdad Pact of 1955,[4] the 1956 tripartite invasion of Egypt by Britain, France and the Zionist entity, the unification in 1958 of Syria and Egypt in the United Arab Republic, the 1958 civil war in Lebanon, the 1958 landing of US Marines in Lebanon and the July 14, 1958, military coup in Iraq that toppled a Hashemite monarchy. As I was growing up in Beirut, I read books about Arab history and listened to many views among friends and relatives about recent events. I arrived at the conclusion that Western imperialism, led by the US ruling class, was the enemy of the peoples of the world and that the Zionist entity in Palestine was its main tool in the Arab world.

A few weeks after reading about the armed operation, a friend mentioned that perhaps I should meet with his co-worker at the office. Within days, I was having coffee with my friend and that mysterious individual, who handed me the communiqué on an *Al-Fatah* letterhead. I was elated. The language of liberation was nothing new to me, but there I was reading a group's communiqué whose goal was Liberation.

I remember my teenage years in London, when my main concern was getting involved in Arab student politics and reading Marx. Shortly after the Palestine Liberation Organization (PLO) was established by the Arab League on May 28, 1964, a colleague in the Marxist study group asked me to write a short essay about the event for the group's Arab language newsletter. In the essay, I pointed out that the PLO was created to contain Palestinian liberation aspirations.

---

3 Ilan Pappé, *The Ethnic Cleansing of Palestine* (Oxford: Oneworld, 2006).

4 Charles D. Smith, *Palestine and the Arab-Israeli Conflict* (Boston, MA: Bedford/St. Martins, 2010), 235–37, 239, 260.

However, I still thought that the PLO would be a useful vehicle to contact and organize Palestinians for liberation.

Back in Beirut at the end of 1964, I immediately started working with Palestinian youth and joined a Lebanese Marxist study group as a carry-over from my London activities. My focus was the liberation of Palestine in the struggle against imperialism. In early 1965, I worked with Palestinian youth while maintaining contact with the study group. My work with Palestinian youth lasted till October of 1967, i.e., after the *Naksa,* the debacle resulting from the 1967 war. Given the sum total of my political activities, I had no choice but to leave Lebanon for Canada. Fifteen months later, I moved to the US. I often reflected on an interesting matter years later: I had been a transnational individual even before transnationalism as an academic discipline had been seriously theorized or came into vogue. I also wondered if there had been many others in my situation. The most the academy had been concerned with, until fairly recently, were diasporas. A second matter that I had reflected while in the "diaspora" was what I had sensed as an Arab compromise and the beginning of a Palestinian compromise, officially revolving around UN Security Resolution 242 of 1967.[5] In hindsight, I attributed the compromise to the fact that the Palestinian revolutionary movement had been led by the Palestinian bourgeoisie. It was clear to me, when I was still active with the Palestinian youth, that the lack of democracy on the one hand, and the absence of any organizational discipline on the other, could become fatal for the popular movement, but not necessarily for its bourgeois leaders. Be that as it may, the dialectics of revolution are expressed in its ebb and flow.

In opposition to the winds of compromise, were "The Three No's" of the Arab Summit Meeting in Khartoum, Sudan on August

---

5 On June 12, 1974, the Palestinian National Council (PNC) replaced the PLO's goal of a "secular democratic state" with an "independent Palestinian state." The diplomatic dynamics surrounding the adopted change in language shows the coordination between the PLO and the Arab states at both the Algiers 1973 and Rabat 1974 Arab Summit Meetings. See Samih K. Farsoun and Naseer H. Aruri, *Palestine and the Palestinians: A Social and Political History* (Boulder, Colo.: Westview Press, 2006), 189, 214.

27, 1967. "No Peace, No Recognition, No Negotiations" appeared to be the dam that would stop all compromise with the Zionist enemy.[6] However, knowing the nature of most of the Arab regimes, it was hard for me to believe that Saudi Arabia's position on total liberation had its roots in the firm belief in my people and the Arab masses across the Arab world. That belief was based on what I had witnessed while working with Palestinian youth and during the 1967 war, being at the scene when droves of young men were crossing the border from Lebanon to Syria to join in the fight in the ranks of *Al-Fatah.*

A third matter I reflected on was that compromise by Arab states was not surprising, since many of them had been created either by the Sykes-Picot Accord or the British, in the case of the Arabian Peninsula. But to have the Palestinian leadership compromising at that point was devastating.

These reflections took me back to Beirut in early 1967 when I was having a discussion with a member of a Palestinian organization that was not engaged in the armed struggle. I could not believe my ears—this organization was promoting a "two-state solution!" That logic did not make sense at all. It was couched by nonsense such as "we shall establish a state on any liberated part of Palestine." One did not need to be a radical political scientist to see the illogic in that thesis, given the upheaval that was going on in Palestine and the Arab world at that time.

I spent my time in Montreal trying to understand the French-English divide and steeped myself in Marxism. I saw, first-hand, the repression of the State against the Quebecois nationalists, as I had been caught twice in the midst of huge demonstrations and running battles between the demonstrators and the police. Those were the heady days of 1968 and 1969. I also kept in touch with developments in the US. The Civil Rights movement was still going on, as was the war in Southeast Asia.

---

6 The cautioning against any Arab state reaching a separate peace with the Zionist entity was considered a "Fourth No." See, for instance, Ghada Hashem Talhami, *American Presidents and Jerusalem* (Lanham: Lexington Books, 2017), 103.

After arriving in the State of Hawai'i, the headquarters of what is now known as USINDOPACOM (United States Indo-Pacific Command), I continued to follow the news of the antiwar movement and began to pay more attention to "American politics." The antiwar movement had been strong here, given that the entire State is dotted with bases and installations that had fed the war machine in Southeast Asia. This fact belies the stereotype of Hawai'i as the backwater of the empire.

My extracurricular activities had been limited to part-time work, reading Marxist classics and books on Palestine, and attending antiwar rallies and panels. Concurrently, news from the Arab world was not encouraging. The Cairo Accord of November 2, 1969, gave the Palestinian Resistance Movement the right to operate from Lebanese territory against the Zionist entity. However, the Jordanian army's defeat of the Palestinian Resistance between September 1970 and July 1971 represented a major setback for the liberation struggle. Initially, the October 6, 1973, war was a pleasant surprise. Egypt and Syria undertook a coordinated attack, presumably to liberate their respective territories lost in the 1967 war. Anwar Sadat's decision to halt the advance of Egyptian troops and leave Syria's Hafiz al-Asad on his own in the fight against the Zionist enemy, constituted not only a military, but also a diplomatic strategic setback. "The Three No's" of Khartoum completely vanished, as the world witnessed Sadat's descent into the abyss of treason and ignominy. The road to November 19, 1977, the day Sadat visited the Zionist entity and gave a speech at the Knesset in Jerusalem, was paved with the blood of Egyptian and Syrian soldiers. Negotiations that had subsequently ensued with the settler-colonialists initially included discussions about presumably securing "autonomy" for the Palestinians.[7] However, those had been pro forma negotiations, not meant to arrive at any agreement between the Zionists and Egyptians. At any rate, "autonomy" was a far cry from liberation. The Peace Treaty between Egypt and the Zionist entity was signed on March 26, 1979. Concurrent with Egyptian

7 Harvey Sicherman, *Palestinian Autonomy, Self-Government, and Peace* (New York: Routledge, 2019). See also Farsoun and Aruri, 198.

developments, the Lebanese scene, beginning with the Zionist entity's 1968 raid on Beirut International Airport, had deteriorated into "civil war" by April 13, 1975. The PLO, with *al-FATAH* leader, Yasser Arafat as its chairman, beginning February 4, 1969, fought on the side of the Lebanese National Movement in the civil war against the right-wing Phalangist Party.[8]

Those events were watersheds in the ebb and flow of the revolutionary movement for liberation. They provide a base for a language of politics governing specific events. A lexicon for a particular situation is created through the ability to promote that terminology and have it disseminated by media outlets in the service of the event and its desired goal. A war of words, ideologies and doctrines ensues. The objective is to socialize the target public to accept the narrative woven around or against an event. Zionist narratives dominated the media scene in the West. In contrast, Palestinian narratives consonant with social reality were weak or totally absent. Hence, for instance, the Zionist false mantra of "a land without a people, for a people without land" was able to gain traction, despite the fact that the *Nakba*, it should be underscored, was in actuality reliant on superior firepower and international diplomatic support bolstering a process to which the far more accurate designation, "ethnic cleansing," was never applied.

The beginning of the Palestinian armed resistance movement necessitated a language to support the event that was contrary to the main Zionist narrative. It emphasized achieving national liberation through armed struggle. Several factors, however, militated against the continued success of the armed struggle narrative and, by implication, the continuation and development of that struggle until liberation. The Arab-state system, by and large, had been pro-western and worked to abort the armed liberation struggle. Furthermore, Arab states, such as Egypt and Algeria, were weak compared to the Zionist entity and its Western creators. In the West, the Zionist-Western narrative triumphed by branding the Palestinian movement as "terrorist" and

---

8 B. J. Odeh, *Lebanon: Dynamics of Conflict* (London: Zed Books, 1985), 131–134.

Arafat (nom de guerre, Abu Ammar) as "Abu Haddam." "*Ammar*," in Arabic means "Builder" and "*Haddam*," means "Destroyer." In fact, while still in Lebanon, I heard the "*haddam*" description of Arafat, from a relative, prominent in Lebanese society.

Western propaganda had not been able, on its own, to overcome the Palestinian resistance. It took two wars to seriously weaken it. The first was the 1970–71 war in Jordan and the other was the 1975 war in Lebanon. These two events point out that, while control of the media narrative is a necessary condition for success, propaganda on its own is not sufficient to arrive at victory. To enhance the chances of success, one must have fire power. When the Zionist entity's military reached Beirut in the summer of 1982, the Palestinian Resistance was defeated and had to depart from Lebanon on August 30 of that year. This resounding strategic defeat made it easier for the bourgeois leadership of the PLO to move away from the language of liberation. The new language needed new events to bolster it and secure its dominance.

In less than a year after the Palestinian Intifada of December 8, 1987, the PLO met in Algiers on November 15, 1988, where Arafat declared a virtual independent State on the West Bank and Gaza, with East Jerusalem as its capital. It was a Machiavellian move, in that the PLO used the Intifada as a veil to hide its selling out of the revolution. Given the nature of the two-state modality of the Algiers declaration, it was clear that Arafat had aligned the Algiers declaration with the Fahd Plan declared (but scuttled) at the Fez, Morocco Arab Summit Meeting of August 7, 1981, which called for an independent Palestinian State in the West Bank and Gaza with East Jerusalem as its capital.[9] Furthermore, the first US Gulf War of 1991 had transported the Arab leadership to the Madrid Peace Conference on October 30, 1991.

Arafat, the PLO, the Arab states and the US began to develop a language of "peace." Perhaps the presence of several Palestinians in Madrid, albeit as part of the Jordanian delegation, was viewed

---

9 The April 2002 Arab Summit Meeting in Beirut adopted a similar version of the Fahd Plan. See Farsoun and Aruri, 292.

by some in the PLO as a significant success. However, the entire Madrid spectacle had been repulsive to those of us who thought that compromising on principles could be deadly for the cause of liberation.

Revolting as that spectacle had been, it paled in comparison to the Oslo Accords of September 13, 1993. I remember a few days after the signing of Oslo, a friend of mine from Egypt and I did a show on Public Access TV in Honolulu, in which we both condemned the Accords as treasonous acts that sold the Palestinian cause down the river. The Oslo language was a variant of the "two-state solution." Its dictionary had terms such as "Gaza-Jericho First," "Final Status Negotiations," and "Confidence Building Measures." In a major way, Oslo consecrated the recognition of the Zionist entity and gave up on liberating 78 percent of Palestine. It relegated, among other things, the matter of (East) Jerusalem, UN Resolution 194 governing the Right of Return, Zionist settlements and water for Palestine to the "Final Status Negotiations." On the TV show, we pointed out the intentions of the Zionist entity and the compromised PLO leadership position and emphasized the existential nature of the struggle between Zionism and US imperialism, on one hand and the Palestinian and Arab peoples, on the other. Giving up on liberation was treachery.

On August 1, 1994, I was in Cairo meeting with the Secretary-General of one of the Egyptian opposition parties who asked, jokingly, why I was not in Gaza on that day to witness the Gaza-Jericho First celebrations. He knew where I stood on the Oslo Accords, but said that, under the circumstances, it was the most that could have been achieved to advance the Palestinian cause. That was the language of politics that fit the occasion. Incidentally, he was a friend of Arafat. It seems this new language of politics had permeated all levels of Arab officialdom, including the Palestinian leadership that fancied itself as part of that officialdom. Hearing PLO officials describing how state building, including the economy, could be achieved so that, for instance, Gaza would become the "Singapore of the Middle East" was very disturbing. In fact, it was despicable hearing wealthy PLO officials uttering such nonsense.

Since the Oslo debacle, the defeatist language of negotiations through all of its iterations became the official language of the Palestinian National Authority (PNA). Simply by accepting the language of the "two-state solution," the PNA, by definition, accepted the division of Palestine. In each phase of negotiations there would be talk about "confidence-building measures" between the Zionist entity and the PNA. This meant that the PNA was succumbing to the US-Zionist agenda that sought to have the PNA agree to the legitimacy of the Zionist entity in 1948 Occupied Palestine. It also meant, insofar as the PNA was concerned, that the Palestinians living in the 1948 areas need only struggle within the settler-colonial entity against "racism" for "equality" with the settler-colonialists. Their struggle would be limited to "dismantling" the "apartheid state" and bringing "equality" between occupier and occupied. Quickly forgotten by the PNA was that a settler-colonial entity that has been adamant about creating a "Jewish state" would never allow "equality" between a Jew and a Palestinian. The *raison d'être* of Zionism is expansionism through expulsion and genocide, even beyond Palestine and the Palestinians. This fact, proven time and again by daily events of land theft and ethnic cleansing in all of Palestine, belies the notion of a peaceful existence between occupier and occupied or between a Palestinian State and a Zionist entity. While Zionists continued their crimes against the Palestinian people, Zionist propaganda adopted the language of "peace" and "victim." They claimed that the Palestinians did not want peace or that there was no Palestinian "partner for peace" or that the Palestinians "refuse to live with us" (in the West Bank) and that is why they opposed the construction of settlements. This was the manipulative trajectory of the Zionist discourse.

Once the PLO agreed to a "two-state solution," it automatically agreed with the Zionists to divide not just the Palestinian land, but the Palestinian people. A bourgeois leadership intent on having a land base, however restricted, would opt for negotiations, knowing full well that such a track would be against the interests of the dispossessed Palestinian population. This sort of leadership that sees no other avenue before it but that of "negotiations," is a leadership that engages in "security coordination" with the enemy, a euphemism for collaboration, that serves the needs of the settler-colonial entity and the Palestinian bourgeoisie.

Zionist crimes against the Palestinians raise questions primarily regarding the PNA and the matter of the Zionist practices in dividing the occupied Palestinians: (1) Why acquiesce to the Zionist strategy of splitting the main force that Palestinians will have to rely on to achieve liberation? (2) Why rely on a "peace process" that has pushed Palestinians farther and farther away from even reaching autonomy on isolated spots of territory cut out by Zionist-settler roads and settlements? (3) What sort of leadership would agree to such provisions?

Those competing discourses and narratives transformed over time. They were driven by events on the ground, initiated either by the Palestinian movement for liberation or the imperialist-Zionist axis. The PLO leadership surreptitiously moved to a compromising position camouflaged by a declaration of an independent state, as previously noted. The dominant language since, became the language of Western narratives. In the Donald Trump era (2017–2021), it was relatively facile for Gulf Arab states to engage in open relations with the Zionist entity through the "Abraham Accord." It appeared that the Palestinians, including the PNA leadership, were going to have their cause erased from history. It was a surreal moment watching PNA personalities condemn the Gulf Arab states for moving forward with open relations with the Zionist entity while leaving the Palestinian bourgeoisie behind facing an existential crisis.

The Ramadan Al-Aqsa uprising, however, radically changed the equation. Again, events on the ground became the basis for a renewal of political language, emphasizing the pillars of the Palestinian struggle for liberation (total liberation and the return of the Palestinians to the homeland). The May 2021 Intifada unified the Palestinian people. This unity contradicted the "two-state solution" that the Palestinian bourgeoisie has been clinging to for decades. Gaza's support of the "Unity Intifada" underscored the centrality of the armed struggle for liberation. Unity meant that the struggle of the Palestinians in 1948 Occupied Palestine was not for "equal rights" between the settlers and the indigenous Palestinians. It was an existential struggle between a Zionist entity seeking to displace them, and the Palestinian people. Zionist attacks on Al-Aqsa showed the steadfastness of the people in defending the holy site. A PNA in crisis appealed to the UN to oppose these Zionist attacks even as it maintained security coordination with the Zionist enemy. Protests erupted in Nablus, Hebron and other areas despite the PNA's attempts to contain them.

The ceasefire revealed several attempts to roll back the gains of this Unity Intifada in all its dimensions, including the emergent language of liberation that it asserted with blood. The Zionist entity and the EU, led by the US, quickly began to create new events to defeat the Unity Intifada's asserted language. They refloated the "two-state solution" and propagated the "conflict" as between Hamas and the Zionist entity. It completely sidestepped the existential struggle between the Zionist entity and the Palestinian people. The US is supporting Gaza's reconstruction, provided that it goes through the PNA with a long-term truce as a central part of the deal. It also mentioned that the PNA should be reformed without stating what it meant by "reformed."

The PNA's continued position of security coordination with the enemy is equally damaging. Mahmoud Abbas has not budged one iota from his compromised position of seeking crumbs for a Palestinian "State." On a June 6, 2021 "al-Massa'iyyah" program on al-Mayadeen TV, Khalil Qarajah al-Rifaa'i, a Ramallah writer and political analyst closely linked to the PNA, openly said that Oslo had paved the grounds for the Palestinian struggle to establish the Palestinian State "agreed upon" by "all" Palestinian factions. His reference was clearly to Arafat's declaration of the establishment of a Palestinian state in 1988. However, it behooves us to note that, at that time, several fighting Palestinian organizations (Hamas, Islamic Jihad and others) did not exist and the terrain of the Palestinian struggle has since changed. The PNA's language of politics completely disregards the nature of the Zionist entity, which has no intention of agreeing to a Palestinian state, as amply demonstrated by the expansion of the settlements and the flood of settlers already established on the West Bank.

In conclusion, the 1948 ethnic cleansing produced two contradictory discourses. One Zionist, the other Palestinian. The first supported the ethnic cleansing events, while the second focused on returning to a liberated Palestine. Over time, Palestinian liberation discourse lapsed into what became the dominant discourse of compromise. The PNA language overlapped considerably with the US and Zionist discourse of "peace," which acted as a cover for the Zionist establishment and expansion of settlements after June 1967. But the socialization of the Palestinians around the discourse uttered through PNA officialdom nonetheless ultimately failed to rein in the liberation discourse that had been suppressed.

By contrast, the recent Unity Intifada engendered events that in turn revived the language of liberation. It is absolutely critical at this stage to not allow the enemies of the Palestinian people to create events on the ground that support their discourses at the expense of the language of liberation. The PNA often claimed that it engaged in armed struggle against the Zionist enemy when it was necessary. They evoke the September 2000 Al-Aqsa Intifada as an example. The point, however, is to ask a critical question: Is the armed struggle adopted as a main method for liberation, or to pressure the enemy to acquiesce to a "two-state solution?" Parenthetically, it should be remembered that while Sadat attacked the Zionist entity on October 6, 1973, his goal was not liberation, but "peace" with the settler-colonialists in Palestine. It is incumbent upon Palestinians everywhere to create new events that build on the accomplishments of resistance to enable us to bolster our discourse against that of our enemies. The torture and killing of Palestinian activist Nizar Banat in June 2021 while in PNA custody shows the desperation of the PNA to return events toward the language of compromise. However, judging from the uprising all over Palestine in response to Banat's murder, it appears that his martyrdom has backfired against the PNA and the Zionist entity. The language of liberation seems to have asserted itself, so far.

The dialectical relationship between language and events cannot be overemphasized. It begins by recognizing that, on the road to liberation, it is absolutely essential to watch your language.

QASSEM IZZAT ALI *is a media specialist, a founder and innovator in the television news industry. Ali's journalism career has evolved over the past three decades, from covering the First Palestinian Intifada to leading the only Arabic television news agency to international renown. As a pioneer in the news industry, he established Ramattan News Agency, a Palestinian news agency based on solid, strategic, grassroots news gathering within Palestinian communities. In this way, Ali has shaped the international media focus on key historical events, including the Israeli reaction to the outbreak of the First Palestinian Intifada in the camps of Gaza, the response of Iraq to the first Gulf War and the 2008–2009 War on Gaza. Politically active as a student in Birzeit, New York and Oxford Universities, Ali broke new ground in the early '90s with his research on the evolution of* walait il faquih *(Islamist political thought) and its diverse interpretations and relationship to political resistance movements from North Africa and the Middle East to Pakistan and India. This focus evolved to shape the social and political underpinnings of the Arab Spring movements and the ongoing international geopolitical dynamics that continue to impact contemporary Middle East.*

# REFLECTIONS ON THE MEDIA
# A Powerful Tool for Palestinian Liberation

*Qassem Izzat Ali*

MEDIA. JOURNALISM. These were meaningless words to me, whether in Arabic or in English, until my early thirties. I was consumed with fighting to protect my family, my land, and my people from being removed and erased. With time, I found that the best way for me to resist was to keep us in the world's eye by being the first to report on what was happening in Gaza and the rest of Palestine. Through journalism, I was able to communicate directly to the world—and not through the flawed and ineffective political structures set up by Oslo to dictate the Palestinian story.

My life started in Beit Hanoun, a village that is a symbol of Palestine: dispossession, migration, generosity, resilience, frontier. And, after all my travel, displacement, deportation, escape and denial, my life will likely end there, too.

My life—and my identity—is intricately interwoven with the struggle. To be born in Gaza is to be born a liberation fighter. There is no other destiny. It is only the means that differ. Shopkeeper, nurse, business owner, farmer—our very existence is a symbol of resistance on this land, having witnessed the injustice of the past 70 years.

Alongside the struggle, a defining feature of my life has been the powerful influence of women. At the center of my life is my mother, Khadra Zweidi, forced out of her home at 10 years old. In the 1948 *Nakba*, Israeli forces cleared her village (Dimra) of its houses, mosques, markets and crops and forced the exodus of its residents. Most of the villagers ended up in Beit Hanoun, whose larger tribes followed Arab tradition by "adopting" the families fleeing the *Nakba*. In this way, my mother—our *yumma*—became part of the Kafarneh clan, a brawny and stubborn tribe of over 10,000 members. She went on to marry one of its grandest figures, Izzat Qassem Ali: prominent businessman, elegant dresser, deeply respected and (all importantly) eldest brother.

My grandmother (her mother-in-law), *sitti* Hissen, also had a strong hand in shaping me. Daughter of the *mukhtar*, or tribal chief, *sitti* Hissen was a true *fellaha*, a country woman in whose veins coursed the rich soil of Mother Palestine. Her home was in the *bayarat*, the orchard of oranges, lemons and pomelo that embraced our village, where she worked the land endlessly: loving each tree by day, boiling tea and sleeping serenely beneath them by night. The greater part of my youth was spent with her, learning. I admired her stamina, her attachment to the land, her physical strength and the knowledge stored in her mind, all gained from our most valuable asset—the land on which we lived. My mother, Khadra, rarely saw me but knew that I was spoiled in the lap of true luxury—the love of a grandmother and the embrace of the land.

*Sitti* Hissen's husband was Qassem, my grandfather and namesake. As a prominent man in the village, Qassem decided to take a second wife. His new wife, *hajjé* Sarah, was the daughter of a prestigious martyr from our clan, hanged by the British police for bearing arms. As life would have it, *hajjé* Sarah was unable to bear children, this defining measure of a woman at the time. Destiny had other plans for *hajjé* Sarah, who became the leader from the shadows; the force in our tribe of strategic mind and extraordinary tact. Unlike *sitti* Hissen, *hajjé* Sarah was an intellectual force, comprehending social, clan, human and tribal power dynamics with such perspicacity that her counsel was mandatory on key decisions, from approvals of marriage to conflict mediation and tactical calculations with village tribes. Although she lost her husband at the age of 28, she chose not to return to her family but stayed with us, continuing in her role as businesswoman, clan leader and the voice of authority in our village.

As luck would have it, the fourth woman to grace and shape my young life was an outsider to our family, my first-grade teacher, Miss

Salwa Yaffawiyyeh, Miss Salwa was educated, tall, sophisticated, impeccably dressed and absolutely beautiful. At the age of six, I felt the butterflies of love in my stomach. Miss Salwa inspired me to learn through focus and discipline, to love knowledge and understand the power of education. Inadvertently, she also provoked in me the resistance fighter that I would remain for life. One day, as a reward for excellent academic performance, she gave me a "white card"—the equivalent of food stamps from the United Nations to get special provisions and food from the agency. I hated the notion of a handout and felt ashamed to be carrying it but loved Miss Salwa. Once out of her sight, I ripped the card into a million pieces and ran home to tell *hajjé* Sarah. Sarah was pleased. "*Ya* Qassem, *ya habibi*, we are proud people, and proud people do not accept to eat from the hand of the United Nations." From that day, I wondered why the UN was giving us food. What did they want from us? Were they trying to buy us? Influence us? Foster a dependency? We did not need handouts; we were proud people of lengthy lineage living on incredibly fertile lands! My young mind was already simmering …

Growing up in a life of palpable power and influence, buttressed by my father, *hajjé* Sarah and our clan, life took a dramatic turn at the age of nine, when the 1967 war ushered in the Israeli Occupation. The timing of the invasion corresponded with one of my father's many business trips to Cairo and, with the new Israeli control over all Egyptian territory east of the Suez Canal, an impenetrable frontier now separated him from his wife, seven children, tribe and homeland. Ten years would pass before we saw my father again. There was to be no facilitation of his return, given his prominence in the PLO leadership. Circumstance gave Israel this golden opportunity to trap him outside.

The next chapter of our lives was marked with the trauma of not knowing my father's fate, and a dramatic collapse in our economic status in his absence. It revealed a depth of grit and determination in *yumma* Khadra and *hajjé* Sarah that shaped my siblings and me for life. These two women, with no formal education or literacy, began a business of selling fabric from the only village shop. It became a success, and—one by one—these two women sent all seven of us to university, starting with my eldest sister, Fairuz, to Cairo, Marwan to Baghdad, Azza, Nihad, Nasser and me to Birzeit and Marwa to Bethlehem. Among us, today, there are holders of Ph.D., Master and Bachelor's degrees.

In that land without electricity, let alone media, we grew up vividly aware of the dramatic injustice that had befallen our country, our people, our families, our lands. For me, it meant figuring out how to become a man at the age of nine; how to maintain the family status with no market for our citrus, no income from my father's business; how to help my mother and my family. In addition to other side gigs in the village (including becoming a skilled and successful poker player and gambler), this meant excelling in my studies, achieving top grades in *tawjihi,* and getting a full scholarship to study engineering in Cairo.

At that time, to study in Cairo was the greatest achievement: it was also the most meaningful gift of gratitude that I could give *yumma* and *hajjé* Sarah. But it was not to last. In Cairo, I was far from the struggle and unable to meaningfully engage, confront and mobilize against the entity attempting to snuff out my people. I knew I had to find my place in Palestinian political life, at its beating heart—Birzeit University. Devastating for my family—I went from working towards a career in engineering to studying political science, known as a fast-track to prison rather than a career. Since my namesake, grandfather Qassem, died in the 1956 war at the hands of the British and the French when they invaded in opposition to Jamal Abdel Nasser having nationalized the Suez Canal; and my family doppelganger, my maternal uncle Hassan, kidnapped by Israelis in 1948 and never heard of again, I would say, in hindsight, that my destiny was set. Activism and political leadership would see me spending the next 10 years of my life in and out of Israeli political prison.

By this point, you may be wondering where the media comes in. The next part of my journey turned out to be a formative and fundamental ingredient to my engaging meaningfully with journalism as a powerful tool in the struggle for liberation. It was a journey digging to the roots of my people; collecting their experiences of life; debating on political visions; disagreeing on ideology, religion, cultural constructs. It was a collection of exchanges as minute as sharing a cigarette, as profound as enduring torture rather than reveal a name. It was the most formative and (ironically) meaningful period in my life, building my understanding of my people, my oppressor and myself. The crucible blending and catalyzing our nationalism, uniting us as a people, erasing gender, socio-economic, religious and ideological barriers, and all of this provided on a silver platter by our Israeli oppressor: PRISON.

Without any of the material tools of journalism—no camera, no paper, no microphone or feed equipment—my memory became my vault. Listening, recording, processing, analyzing conversations, experiences, ideas, strategies … it was all accumulating in my head and perfectly safe from Israeli confiscation. It would serve me well.

My exit from prison and from politics corresponded with my graduation from Birzeit University with a B.A. in Middle East Studies, minor in Political Science, fundamentally useless under the Occupation. Armed with my useless diploma, deeply disgruntled with Palestinian political factions, and as a Palestinian from the "inside" (as opposed to those trapped outside the country following the 1948 and 1967 wars), I would not direct my fiery passion to support the PLO, the supposed "sole legitimate representative of the Palestinian people" because I, like so many others, had lost faith in that dilapidated and exclusive institution. With tomes of personal stories, opinions, ideological positions, debates, arguments and contradictions bouncing around in my head like free radicals, I knew that I had to find an alternative to politics. Some way to speak to our occupier and to the world about our stories, challenge colonial narratives and shape perceptions to a deeper realization of who "we" are—the people whom Israel claimed did not exist.

Nothing seemed evident. I worked in Israel as a laborer and then started a farm with a friend. It took some time, but the realization came to me that Gaza needed me more than Birzeit, Ramallah or the West Bank. To Gaza I returned.

Gaza was always the lesser-known entity, and a place where Israel had a different strategy of engagement—a level of complete impunity with brutal repression of any space for democratic expression. In Gaza, community groups, associations and clubs were not permitted to emerge. The Israelis exerted tight control over a population that seethed with militancy and armed struggle. It was in this environment of absolute penetration and coercion, where jobs were linked either to the Israeli Occupation authority or the United Nations Relief and Works Agency, that I had to figure out how to earn a living while channeling my fury and indignation at the grotesque level of injustice that had befallen my community and my people. As a revolutionary spirit, former prisoner and political junkie, trusted comrade, and effective organizer, I still could not see a course of action for myself.

Then in 1987, the Intifada exploded and a path for my future finally emerged. My friend, Ali Ka'adan, asked me to work as a producer with WTN in Gaza. I had no idea what that meant. Producer of what? We did not have televisions readily available and could not conceptualize news through that medium. A camera for me was used in cinema, for producing Egyptian soap operas, Jordanian television programs. These networks were not about news but about extolling kings, presidents and other popular personalities. WTN provided me with two hours' training on a VHS video camera at Erez checkpoint, and I began my television media career.

In one of my first pieces of footage, I filmed children and women throwing stones at helicopters in the Rafah refugee camp on the border with Egypt. Jumping between the corrugated metal rooftops, I collected raw footage that would become one minute of explosive video aired internationally against the Israeli narrative. Accustomed to perceiving the news "embedded" in the Israeli army (i.e., "aggressive" Palestinian youth throwing stones), with news collected, filmed, produced, narrated and dubbed by Israeli journalists and technicians, the big networks were now able to access material with the visual counternarrative, and they were all over it. My camera gave quite a different story: I was filming from amongst women in traditional dress and children with school backpacks throwing stones, while in the aperture, Apache helicopters launched missiles and Israeli jeeps fired from grenade launchers and mounted guns. To get the tapes out of (pre-internet and pre-digital) Gaza, I had to rely on my community networks—the mothers and fathers who trusted me and their sons and daughters to whom I had grown close in prison. That trust made everything possible and smuggle the tapes we did—much to the chagrin of the Israeli army commanders, who—recognizing that the international public was becoming increasingly sympathetic to the Palestinian cause—went ballistic when they realized that they had lost control of the imagery.

Little did I know that my evolution into a journalist was to leap forward, in large part thanks to a small hotel—and its dynamic manager. Marna House: a tiny place in the beachside Rimal neighborhood, adorned with lovingly tended plants and flowers, with aromas of lavender, jasmine and citrus. Every foreigner coming to Gaza wanted to stay at Marna House and would wait for weeks to get a room. It was run by a woman of sharp intellect, incisive instinct and stalwart principle. A woman who was to become my mentor, my friend, my confidante, my third mother: Alia Shawwa.

An excellent listener and infrequent talker, Alia was my teacher, my enabler and my conscience in shaping my understanding of the media. She was educated, objective and principled, trusted by the top personalities in the industry at the time—Robert Fisk (writer), Gloria Emerson (*NYT*), Sarah Roy (Harvard researcher), Peter Jennings (ABC), Larry Register (CNN), Paul Taylor (*Time Magazine*), Bob Simon (CBS), Joe Sacco (Maltese graphic author). Alia did not give a spit about class, wealth or VIP status. Everyone was afraid of her—"fearfully reverent" would be one way to put it. She loved Marna House, this long-established "institution," serving intellectuals, diplomats and international organizations. She made of it the best Ministry of Information, with herself the Minister, deeply aware and insightful regarding the significance of the media industry and the needs of the personalities who made it work.

Marna House was the secure venue for sharing valuable information amongst Palestinians and with trusted journalists, fostering an atmosphere of nationalism and intellect that—along with the American Colony in Jerusalem—has seen no rival in Palestine. Alia had the network and the sources to guarantee the identity of every single person staying at the hotel, specifically ensuring they were not Shin Bet officers, frequently placed into Gaza undercover as journalists to collect information, arrest and kill activists. This cover, well played, was able to provide them access to camps, villages, and the many centers of the national resistance movement. The physical protection of this precious venue was in the hands of my village clan.

Alia reshaped the focus of journalists to write about the core issues of the conflict, not about Palestinians as a humanitarian issue. At Marna House, a new narrative was shaped. It became one of the most significant Palestinian institutions for refining, sharing and amplifying the media messaging that would influence the course of one of the most spectacular popular uprisings in contemporary history.

Every day, I would travel with my VW Bug from Rafah in the south to Beit Hanoun in the north, gathering news and bringing it back to Alia, updating her with events, sitting with her, Dr. Haidar Abdel Shafi and *sit* Yusra al Barbari to ensure they had the freshest, most accurate grassroots information on what was happening on the ground and what people were thinking.

The Oslo Accords marked a tectonic shift in our vision for liberation and the popular nature of our struggle. A cheap deal struck with no representative support, the Palestinian "gains" from Oslo were similar in style and substance to negotiations that took place in jail. Seeking small improvements in the comfort of our compatriots and ourselves, we would negotiate a phone call, a cigarette, an extra ladle of *mulokhia*. Our Oslo "political leadership" was negotiating in such a way—to get a "better" Occupation, not to free our people.

What we did not anticipate at the time was how we as a people were to change in its wake. Not only did the liberation agenda become politicized and transacted like vegetables at the market, but it also became a tool for individual promotion and conceit. We converted our collective belief in popular activism to worshiping a golden calf; believing that liberation could be achieved by "political leaders," "government," "negotiations." We lost our dedication, our willingness to talk through our differences, to put our unity as a people over individual or party agendas. No good was to come from this short-sighted compromise.

As the years moved along, so did my involvement with the media. I started a company that covered the return of Yasser Arafat and his entourage of PLO people to Gaza in 1994, all of whom had been living in exile for decades. Once fulsomely distressed with the evolution of the new Palestinian Authority, I left for New York and then Oxford to study. Upon my return in 1999, I worked with several journalists from different political backgrounds with whom strong bonds had been created in prison to found Ramattan News Agency as an independent platform for free expression. An incredibly successful undertaking, Ramattan served as a different form of resistance, mobilizing and training hundreds of young Palestinian women and men as technicians and journalists, obtaining and disseminating through mainstream international media both incredible imagery and incisive analysis of the continuum of tragedy that has been brought on by the failed Oslo formula.

Trust. Integrity. Unity. Activism, organization, mobilization. A collective and individual willingness to take risks. Our people will, through the generations that succeed us, forge a path forward through this stalemated atmosphere of petty political bickering and increasing international indifference. Faithful to our plight, we will continue, generation on generation. This is the foundation enabling us to speak of media as a tool of liberation.

Looking back 30 years, to the '70s and '80s era of collective struggle and sacrifice, I am convinced that—should social media have existed at the time, dovetailing with the intense spirit of nationalism and grass-roots activism—our country would have been liberated long ago. What incredible risks we took in those days to organize a strike or a protest, to print leaflets letter by letter, distributing them door to door under the noses of the Israeli army, when getting caught meant, at best, six months in prison and at worst, getting shot. It is tragic that such instantaneous tools were not to intersect with our most glorious time of belief in ourselves, in one another and in our collective ability to take on the might of Israel and the Western colonial agenda.

Now, beholding our young generation in Gaza, the West Bank, historical Palestine and in the diaspora, I see another opportunity for media to become a tool of liberation. Over the past months, young Palestinians have turned to social media to mobilize against the ethnic cleansing of East Jerusalem, document the devastating bombardment of besieged Gaza and talk about what the future of the Palestinian leadership could be, in the wake of the killing of human rights activist, Nizar Banat. The swift and untrammeled reactions of social media have meant that people around the world are finally hearing the Palestinian story directly—uncensored, raw and human. Thirty years on from the time that I picked up the camera to show the world what was happening in Gaza, Palestinians now have a new tool that will drive, shape, change the way our story is heard—and acted upon.

SAMAA ABU SHARAR *is an independent journalist and researcher based in Beirut, Lebanon. She has covered issues pertaining to the Middle East for several Arab and international media outlets and conducted research work for many local and international organizations, including the United Nations and the European Union, regarding Palestinian refugees in Lebanon. She has published numerous articles and research papers in Arabic, English and French.*

*Abu Sharar also heads the Majed Abu Sharar Media Foundation (MASMF), a non-governmental organization that works to empower youth in Palestinian refugee camps and gatherings in Lebanon in the field of media in order to convey their messages away from the misrepresentation and stereotypes of mainstream media. She also oversees* Shababeek, *a training website for Palestinian youth in camps and gatherings in Lebanon.*

# TO LIBERATE PALESTINE, EMPOWER ITS REFUGEES

*Samaa Abu Sharar*

DURING A VIRTUAL CONVERSATION with a South African friend at the beginning of the month of June, Nurah made a striking contrast between what is happening in Palestine and the apartheid system that had existed in her home country. Watching the ethnic cleansing taking place in the Sheikh Jarrah and Silwan neighborhoods in Occupied East Jerusalem brought back memories of horrific stories Nurah had heard from her parents during apartheid in South Africa.

Nurah and several other foreign friends felt the resemblance more than ever during the Palestinian *Habah*, the rise of Palestinians everywhere during the uprising of May 2021. "Something seems different this time," they all agreed. Something actually does seem different, even for us, Palestinians. The world's championing of our cause for the first time ever, along with the rise of promising new, young activists, eloquent and capable of reaching out to millions of audiences on social media, while live-streaming unfolding events in Palestine and, ultimately, spurring the relative change in the terminology used to describe the long-term Israeli colonization of Palestine—all are notable changes.

My generation has inherited the defeats of our parents and grandparents before them and I thought, until very recently, that I would pass on these defeats to my daughter, Meena. Nothing on the horizon seemed to give me a glimmer of hope that this would not be the case, until the Palestinian *Habah* heralded a new reality which, if not sabotaged by the Palestinian "leadership," could be the first step on the long road to dignity, liberation and return to our homeland.

We are often told that "our life choices are those of our making." In the case of most Palestinians, I believe choice is a luxury that we often dare not indulge in, as we have inherited a heavy load—a lingering political cause, from even before we were born. I was born to Palestinian parents from Hebron: my father, Majed Abu Sharar, originated from the village of Dura while my mother, Fatima Al Azzeh, originated from the village of Beit Jibrin. Their marriage and, later, their life choices have certainly framed my journey, despite their early and abrupt departure from my life.

My life was a rollercoaster of events, thanks to my parents and more so to my father, who chose to include us in the life he was leading and not exclude us as other Palestinian Liberation Organization (PLO) leaders did with their children.[10] This meant that we would follow the PLO to wherever it took as a base.

My parents brought me to life in Khoubar, Saudi Arabia, where my father worked at the time as a Chief Editor of *Al Ayam* newspaper before joining and heading the "Fatah" movement in the Gulf country. Jordan was his next obvious stop, where we lived for a few years, until the PLO's departure following the events of Black September in 1970. My only vague recollection of that period, as a kid, is that of my brother Salam and I hiding under the dining table, believing what our mother would repeatedly tell us—that this would protect us from the shelling outside.[11]

Lebanon was our next stop, as it was for many of the PLO cadres and families. Lebanon, the closest to what I would ever call home, became the country where my life took some shape. The land of cedars is where I witnessed, and continue to witness, all forms of wars, conflicts, injustices, discrimination and suffering. This tiny country would become the place where I would become reconciled with the many losses I endured on both the public and personal level, would discover the pride of being a Palestinian and translate it into activism, despite all odds.

---

10 A number of PLO leaders chose, for security reasons, to distance their families from where the PLO was based and, accordingly, many lived in countries such as Syria, Jordan, Kuwait, Egypt, etc.

11 Clashes were taking place in the streets of Amman and elsewhere in Jordan between the Jordanian Army and Palestinian Fedayeen, which came to be known later as the "Black September."

I lost my birth mother to cancer at the age of eight and, along with her, my safe haven in life. My brother, Salam, and I spent the next few years moving from one boarding school to another. My father, overwhelmed by the loss of a wife and the heavy responsibility of two children, probably thought it was best to enroll us in a boarding school. He thought wrong because, despite his busy schedule, the little time we spent with him on some weekends was the closest we ever felt to the warmth of a home after my mother's death.

Between boarding schools, occasional stays with my father and sleep-ins at his friends' houses, Salam and I managed to survive and cope with the huge void left by our mother. We celebrated our father's decision to get married after resenting it initially, since our compensation was to leave boarding school and live at home with him and his new wife, Inam, and her daughter, Azza, from a previous marriage.[12] The unusual setting, although bumpy at the beginning, turned out to be the home which I had longed for, for years. All of a sudden, Salam and I were under the same roof with our father, and I had gained a sister and a second Mom. Our father Majed and Inam decided to have my sister, Dalia, to crown us as a real family, not only bonded by their marriage but also by blood.

My father embraced Lebanon in all its aspects but remained loyal to his identity and convictions and made sure he passed this on to us. "You can choose to speak the Lebanese dialect with your friends outside the house but at home we speak the Palestinian dialect," he would often tell us, explaining that we are mere guests in the country.

Majed was a master at passing on subtle messages without enforcing his opinion. Nonetheless, at times, he pushed us to our limits by expecting us to abide by his decision for a benefit that we might not realize instantly. Introducing us to new things, ideas and people was probably Majed's subtle way to trigger our curiosity to ask questions and instill pride in our Palestinian and Arab culture and identity.

---

12 Inam Abdel Hadi was first married to PLO leader Hani el Hassan, with whom she had her daughter, Azza.

I did not realize Majed's worth in his lifetime; I actually only discovered who he was, on the political and national front, following his assassination. I only learned, years after his death, of the numerous death threats he had received. At the time, Edward Said shared his concerns with us. Said sent, with a mutual friend, a cutting from an American newspaper on which it was written "Majed Abu Sharar: the rising star of the PLO," with a note warning him that this was a bad sign and an indication that he was being watched. Despite that, he was never cautious about his security.

Majed's abrupt departure devastated our lives. October 9, 1981 will be engraved in my heart and soul as the day my world collapsed, the day when I lost my rock in life. My initial feelings of anger and resentment towards my father for choosing Palestine over us and my feelings of jealousy and outrage at Palestine for stealing my only remaining parent, stayed with me for years. For my sanity, I buried my problematic relationship with my father and Palestine in the back of my mind, in order to move forward. Little did I know that, a few years later, both my Dad and Palestine would become the very compass of my existence!

The Israeli invasion of Lebanon in 1982 came a few months after my father's assassination and I swallowed my personal pain temporarily in the face of the collective devastation. My encounter with the war had, until then, been relatively sheltered, despite the fact that we were living in war-torn Lebanon. The Israeli invasion of Lebanon was like nothing I had previously experienced until then, as I witnessed, first-hand, the displacement and suffering of people and the devastation of the war.

I volunteered at a Talmudic center, hastily turned hospital in Hamra, lending a helping hand to the injured.[13] Many horrifying images of the atrocities of the war still linger in my mind, one of which is the unforgettable image of a young man bleeding all

13 Hamra was a safe haven in comparison to other areas in West Beirut, and was spared from the Israeli bombardment thanks to the presence of foreign journalists and diplomats.

over while rushing into the center, holding his ear in his hand and screaming, “Save my ear, save my ear.”

The suffering of people went hand in hand with numerous daily challenges. Long humiliating queues of people waiting for their turn to fill a bottle or a gallon of water became a regular scene, as did spending hours by candle light due to severe power cuts, as well as struggling to find basic commodities because Israel and its collaborators prevented international and humanitarian aid from entering West Beirut. Sadly, Lebanon of 1982 resembles, in many aspects, Lebanon in 2021.

All of us cheered for the Palestinian and Lebanese Resistance in the South, while following the news, believing that our fighters had a chance against one of the strongest and most cruel war machines in the world. As it became apparent that Israel was planning to enter Beirut, many of our acquaintances and friends started to leave the country through East Beirut, the only point of exit available at the time.

Taking the trip was a risk many people undertook in order to flee the hell of a war that was taking place in parts of the tiny country. When the decision was taken for us to leave for Jordan, upon the advice of some of my father’s friends, I dreaded the trip. I am not sure which I dreaded more, the idea of leaving Beirut or the trip through the forbidden part of the capital. Up until then, we were strictly prohibited from even thinking of visiting East Beirut, which was controlled by the Phalange’s forces, known for their hostility towards Palestinians. All the stories that we had heard about the atrocities taking place at checkpoints in East Beirut came rushing into my mind and I imagined the worst. For me, facing the war was easier than taking this trip.

The trip was surreal from start to end. Leaving Beirut felt like a betrayal of every person I left behind and of every corner of the city that had embraced me for many years. The feeling of betrayal grew as we were approaching safety, thanks to the fake Jordanian passports that we carried, which secured our journey to Syria.[14] Images of Israeli soldiers amicably chitchatting with members of the Phalange's forces, or those of young Lebanese women wearing T-shirts that read "We love Israel," or the strange contrast between East Beirut, beaming with life and people, and war-torn and dilapidated West Beirut, still linger in my mind.

As I returned to Lebanon in 2001 and lived through the 2006 Israeli war, countless conflicts in the country and, most recently, the horrifying massive explosion at the Beirut port and the unprecedented economic collapse we are experiencing at present, I came to understand that the Lebanese people would never share one common friend or one common enemy. Thus, an entity like Israel will remain a friend for some and an enemy for others, as long as the interest of the sectarian leaders or the sects comes before that of Lebanon.

The undeclared war we are living through today is proof of this. The complex sectarian mosaic of the country, along with the corrupt sectarian leaders, each with an outside agenda that serves their pockets more than anything, makes of this country a fertile soil ready to embrace all kinds of conflicts and wars. Sadly, even in the most dire of times, such as the one we are living through at present, the Lebanese still fail to unite against these corrupt sectarian leaders for their own good and that of their country.

As a Palestinian married to a Lebanese, I have been privileged to enjoy the rights denied to my people in Lebanon. My return to Lebanon in 2001 came after years of living abroad for the purpose of study and work. Palestine was never absent from anything I did. In the US and France during my university studies, I was a fierce defender of our cause and gained, along the way, many friends and a number of enemies.

Upon my return to Jordan, I landed a job as an editor and a contributing writer at *The Star* English weekly newspaper, an affiliate with *Ad Doustour* daily Arabic newspaper. Issues pertaining to

14 Many people who left through East Beirut during the Israeli invasion carried fake passports and we were no exception, since it was dangerous for us to leave with our father's name on the real passports.

Palestine always took center stage in my writings for *The Star* and other media outlets outside the country for which I was freelancing.

It was in Jordan that I became more familiar with Palestinian refugee camps through my numerous visits while accompanying foreign journalists. It was also in Jordan that I got to meet, as a journalist, Palestinian icons and PLO figures that I had only heard of previously, like Leila Khaled, Mohammed Oudeh (Abu Daoud) or Abdel Rahim Malouh and others.

It was not, however, until I moved to Lebanon that I truly understood the meaning of being a Palestinian refugee. A Palestinian refugee in Lebanon is like no other Palestinian refugee elsewhere in his/her place of displacement. The successive generations of Palestinian refugees in Lebanon have been deprived, ever since they took refuge in this country, of their basic human rights such as the right to work in tens of professions and the right of ownership, to name a few. I cannot even count the number of times I heard Palestinian refugees speak of the scams they experienced because they were forced to register their life savings for an apartment, a piece of land or a shop in the name of a Lebanese relative or friend.

The Palestinian camps are bastions of poverty, high unemployment and numerous social and security problems. The unprecedented economic crisis in Lebanon today has hit everyone in the country, but particularly Palestinian refugees, who already suffer from extremely harsh living conditions and are left to face their fate on their own.

Most live in dwellings that resemble caves rather than houses, that do not see the sunlight and lack any kind of ventilation, from which the unpleasant smell of humidity emanates, allowing all kinds of illnesses to affect the residents. People spend their days and nights in the narrow streets of the camp to escape the unbearable summer heat of their homes due to permanent power outage and the absence of diesel fuel to operate generators. Most survive on a day-to-day basis as the purchasing power of refugees has decreased significantly, since the prices of basic commodities have skyrocketed due to the severe devaluation of the Lebanese lira against the US dollar. Apart from random humanitarian aid—food, baby milk, diapers and medication—from different non-governmental organizations and volunteer groups, refugees are literally on their own. Today, like they did previously, they hold the United Nations Refugee Agency (UNRWA), the Palestinian factions, the PLO and the Palestinian National Authority (PNA) responsible for failing them again and again, especially at such times of crisis.

Despite my strong feelings against the injustice, discrimination and racism to which Palestinian refugees have been subjected by the consecutive Lebanese governments, I also believe that the PLO has failed them on more than one level. Failure to set up sustainable projects in the camps that could have created hundreds of job opportunities for refugees and allowed them to sustain themselves rather than to continue to rely on relief for their livelihood, as well as failure to improve the poor infrastructure in the camps and gatherings—these are major shortcomings, given the political and financial power that the PLO has enjoyed in Lebanon for years. Given the high concentration of refugees in Lebanon, albeit significantly diminished since then, the PLO officials were either short-sighted or the issue of refugees was never their priority.

My knowledge of the camps and the living conditions of Palestinian refugees in Lebanon was, upon my return to Lebanon, superficial and limited to the one- to three-minute reports I made for "Future TV," for which I worked for a few years. It was not until I started working as an independent researcher that my knowledge developed, thanks to the countless readings on the issue and the numerous long focus groups I had with Palestinian refugees of all ages and genders in camps and gatherings across Lebanon.

In 2014, a dream came true. With the help of my siblings and some loyal friends, The Majed Abu Sharar Media Foundation (MASMF) came to fruition. On the one hand, the mission of the organization is to carry on the legacy of Majed and continue his unfinished work in the field of media and, on the other, fill an existing gap in the refugee camps in that domain. Majed was a firm believer in the power of media to reach out to the world and gain Arab and international supporters for our cause.

MASMF was set up to engage, empower and train Palestinian youth in refugee camps to produce various types of media in a professional manner, away from the stereotypes of the mainstream media. This stemmed from our firm belief that no one is more capable of conveying the stories of refugees than the refugees themselves, since no one knows better the living conditions and problems facing Palestinian camps and gatherings than they do. In a country like Lebanon, where countless misconceptions and stereotypes exist about Palestinian refugees, this kind of work is extremely crucial.

The Lebanese people are either strong supporters of Palestinians, aggressively hostile or simply indifferent. During a conversation with a renowned Lebanese journalist when I first moved back to Lebanon, he pinpointed the problematic relation of the Lebanese people with the "other," Palestinians included, by saying: "The Lebanese don't like each other, how on earth can you want them to like Palestinians or anyone else for that matter!"

Although a small organization with limited human and financial resources, MASMF was able to operate in partnership with local and international organizations and institutions, offering training in all forms of media under the guidance of renowned journalists free of charge. This training attracted hundreds of aspiring young journalists in the camps and gatherings around Lebanon.

The work produced by the youth at the end of these trainings touched on issues highlighting different aspects of life in the camps, existing problems and potential solutions and success stories. Selected work was published in different media outlets such as *Al-Hal* newspaper of the Birzeit University Media Development Center, *The Palestine Chronicle,* and MASMF's website and Facebook page, amongst others.

The need to find an outlet to continue the learning process following our training, or in its absence, urged us to establish *Shababeek.* The four-year-old *Shababeek* provides young journalists with continuous supervision to empower them in the field of media, along with the space to publish their work. We do aspire, with time, to have *Shababeek* develop into a vibrant web magazine that reflects the voice of refugees by refugees themselves and to become their window into the outside world.

Our work falls short, though, in the face of the huge challenges that non-governmental organizations (NGOs) like ours, civil society organizations (CSOs) and even volunteer groups encounter in the field in the camps and gatherings across Lebanon. The enormous problems facing Palestinians in their places of residence not only puts the priority of refugees elsewhere but also makes the work being done a drop in the ocean! I say this from first-hand experience of observing our work, and that of other organizations, during the last few years.

When we first launched *Shababeek* with two consecutive funds from two renowned Palestinian organizations, the enthusiasm of the trainees was contagious. *Shababeek* was set up as a training website, not one for employment, that primarily aims to sustain the learning journey in the field of media, and symbolic remuneration would be given to the young journalists for their efforts only when funding is available. With this understanding, tens of journalists joined *Shababeek.* However, with the challenge of sustaining the funding came the challenge of holding on to these young journalists, as the challenges of life in the camps were bigger than both of us. "I have always dreamt of becoming a journalist and I found myself in a place like *Shababeek* in which I was able to train and write at the same time, and gain a bit of money, but I had to find a job that pays me to live," said one of our best trainees, whom we lost along the way.

I genuinely believe that the Palestinian cause deserves a better media apparatus and more eloquent spokespersons than those existing at the official level. Unfortunately, we have spent the last 73 years mainly talking to ourselves rather than addressing the Other to present a credible narrative and mobilize supporters for our cause. Our failure to have a sound and unified media discourse in the face of a very sophisticated Israeli propaganda machine has brought our just cause nothing short of disasters. Through our work with the youth in the camps, we hope to start the long process of empowering refugees in the field of media in order for them to become spokespersons of their people and cause in the Diaspora.

This does not mean that the work MASMF and others are doing is in vain, but it does mean that our work will always remain secondary to the real work that needs to be done to ensure refugees are granted the basics to live a dignified life, until the internationally-enshrined Right of Return—a right all refugees consider sacred—is reached, and they are able to return to their homeland.

Those in charge of the Palestinian refugees, like the United Nations Relief and Works Agency (UNRWA), the Palestinian factions and the popular committees, in addition to the PLO, Palestinian Authority and various host countries, should each assume the responsibility of transforming the lives of refugees in the camps. UNRWA should resume the services it reduced, or cut altogether, under the pretext of lack of funding. The Palestinian factions and the popular committees should put their factional differences aside and work together towards improving the lives of refugees while embracing initiatives that come from outside their frameworks, especially those by youth, in order to pump in new blood. The PLO, quasi-inexistent at present, should regain its role as the representative of the Palestinian people and start acting as such for the benefit of its people.

As long as these continue to fall short in assuming their mandate and fail to do the job for which they were created, the enormous lack of trust will continue to exist between them and the Palestinian refugees. As long as the refugees feel they only have God to resort to and have to create WhatsApp groups to solicit and exchange medicine and collect food items to distribute to those in need, we will continue to lose people on many levels. As long as the disastrous current policies adopted by the Palestinian leaders and all parties involved in relation to refugees and the Palestinian cause, in general, persist, we will continue to see our people and our cause slip further away from us.

Majed's dream was to retire, after the liberation of Palestine, in a small village called Fkekise, next to Dura, where he could spend his time writing and gazing at the Mediterranean Sea in Gaza. Majed was not naive to envision the liberation of Palestine during his lifetime; he was convinced that Palestine will be liberated principally because of the unbeatable will of its people and the indisputable justice of its cause. I do, too. I firmly believe that Palestine might not be attainable in the near future, but with our most powerful weapon, the Palestinian people, their invincible will and contagious zest, Palestine will be liberated.

My bet was, and remains, on martyrs like Bajes Abu Attwan, Basel al-Aaraj, Naji el-Ali, Ghassan Kanafani, Kamal Naser, Kamal Adwan, Majed Abu Sharar and so many others to keep inspiring us with their teachings. My bet was, and remains, on the young generation of Palestinians, inside and outside of Palestine, to keep inspiring us with their confidence, vision and innovative ideas to challenge the Israeli occupier on more than one level. My bet is, and will remain, on every Palestinian refugee to keep the flame of the Right of Return burning until we all return to our villages and towns in Palestine. The Palestinian cause was never solely the issue of a stolen land but also that of a stubborn, steadfast people who, despite the cruelty of their colonizers, continue to hold on to the dream of a free Palestine and their return to what is rightfully theirs.

ANUAR MAJLUF ISSA *is a Chilean lawyer of Palestinian origin. He studied Law at the* Adolfo Ibáñez University, *where he also received a minor in Political Science. Majluf studied Arabic language at the University of Jordan (2010), with a scholarship from the Palestine International Institute (PII) and has Diplomas in "Arab and Islamic Culture" from the Center for Arab Studies of the Faculty of Philosophy and Humanities (2012) and "Current Problems of Civil Responsibility" by the Faculty of Law (2020), both from the University of Chile. Between 2008 and 2009, he was president of the General Union of Palestinian Students (UGEP-Chile), where he raised awareness of the situation of Palestine in many universities.*

*He worked as executive director of the Palestinian Community of Chile until June 2021. In this capacity, he worked in Chile and Latin America, and planned advocacy work with Chilean authorities. As he has become more involved, thus a recognizable personality in the struggle for Palestinian rights, the Israeli government has, in 2017, prohibited him from entering Palestine.*

# NO FUTURE WITHOUT MEMORY
# Deportivo Palestino and the Story of Palestinians in Chile[15]

*Anuar Majluf Issa*

THE FIRST Palestinian immigrants to Chile arrived in the country at the beginning of the last century, when Palestine was still under Turkish Ottoman rule. As of today, there are an estimated 500,000 Chileans of Palestinian descent.

When the Ottoman Empire collapsed, European powers took over and in 1920, Palestine fell under the so-called "British Mandate." Almost immediately, the British began to facilitate Jewish emigration, mostly from Europe, to the newly-conquered Palestinian homeland, leading to much hardship among the native inhabitants of Palestine. This, in turn, resulted in a new migratory wave from Palestine towards many places, including Chile.

Predictably, British and Zionist colonialism in Palestine led to communal strife and, ultimately, violence. Britain turned to the United Nations, which had neither the power nor the mandate to determine the fate of Palestine, especially as the Palestinian people themselves were hardly considered or consulted on decisions pertaining to their very future. Ultimately, the UN General Assembly resolved in 1947 that Palestine should be partitioned into two separate entities, Jewish and Arab. Thus, the State of Israel was created on May 15, 1948, and 70% of the Palestinian population was expelled. No Palestinian Arab state was ever established.

---

15 This essay was originally written in Spanish and was translated by Romana Rubeo.

The mass expulsion of the Palestinians and the complete destruction of hundreds of Palestinian towns and villages set the stage for a prolonged exile, or *shatat*. Hundreds of thousands of Palestinian refugees sought shelter in neighboring countries. Others crossed continents, settling in Europe, the United States and Latin America. The Palestinian Community of Chile is part and parcel of this Palestinian diaspora, which is still ongoing.

Our community here is fully integrated into Chilean society at all levels, including the economy, sports and politics. Such communal triumph, however, was a result of countless hardships and struggles that deserve to be documented for the sake of future generations.

Every migratory process is grounded in its own historical contexts and thus has its own unintended consequences. Bearing that in mind, Palestinians in Chile represent a success story of integration and preservation of identity. My family stands at the heart of this inspiring collective experience.

If I were a member of any other group of people, maybe my contribution here would be of less significance. But, like all Palestinians, we are forced to relentlessly affirm and reaffirm our existence as a people and culture. The mantra created to justify Zionist colonialism of Palestine, that Palestine "was a land without people for a people without a land," was deliberately designed to cancel our own existence as Palestinians, thus depriving us of our legitimate rights. This led Palestinian writer Rashad Abu-Shawir, to conclude that "the Palestinian question is not merely a problem of borders, (but) an existential problem."

Since existence is not a passive act, it has to be fueled through an active memory. "There is a single element that Palestinians, regardless of where they are, can indeed control: their collective memory, which remains the main motivator of their legendary steadfastness," Ramzy Baroud wrote on the 72nd anniversary of the *Nakba*.[16] "Israel is afraid of Palestinian memory, since it is the only facet of its war against the Palestinian people that it cannot fully control; the more Israel labors

16 Ramzy Baroud, "Why Israel fears the Nakba: How memory became Palestine's greatest weapon," *The Jordan Times*, October 17, 2021.

to erase the collective memory of the Palestinian people, the more Palestinians hold tighter to the keys of their homes and to the title deed of their land back in their lost homeland."[17]

Using my family history as one microcosm of the collective Palestinian experience, I will attempt to tell a collective story, which is the story of most, if not all, Palestinians in Chile, a country that has welcomed us with open arms.

## My Story

In 2007, I was in my second year in law school, and people knew me for my commitment to Palestine. For years, I had been involved in organizing talks and debates concerning Palestine. Our events had attracted many Palestinian students and auditoriums were always filled whenever we hosted such events. Zionist students were interested in our gatherings, too. Their presence and the students' debates that preceded and followed our events made the atmosphere always heated and tense.

I do not recall the precise moment when I became an activist. But I perfectly remember all the activities at the *Colegio* Árabe from which I graduated, including *Dabke* dancing, Arabic music and much more. Thanks to these cultural interactions, I became even more attached to my Palestinian identity, which my family was always keen on preserving. True, we did not speak Arabic at home, but our Palestinian spirit was present in every aspect of our life, from family gatherings to the food we ate, to the music we listened to.

Every year, scholars from all over the world came to learn more about the Palestinian community in Chile, because they found it difficult to understand how such a large, well-integrated and active Palestinian community could exist so far away from Palestine. The oft-repeated question is, "Do you feel more Chilean or Palestinian?", as if the two identities necessarily opposed one another. My answer remains unchanged: "I am both Chilean and Palestinian."

But it is not always so easy or straightforward. At times, I do question myself, especially if the inquirer is a Palestinian: do I truly

---

17 Ramzy Baroud, Ibid.

feel Palestinian? Am I Chilean of Palestinian origins, or a Palestinian who was born in Chile? There are no easy answers. But what I know is this: I am indeed a Chilean of Palestinian origin. But when I am in a Palestinian context, I truly feel a Palestinian who was born in Chile.

Possibly, the reason behind the seeming inconsistencies is the fact that Palestinian exile remains an open wound. Our *shatat* is still unresolved. When I speak of exile, I am not only speaking of the *Nakba* of 1948, but the harrowing journeys that preceded the *Nakba* as well.

The Majluf family arrived in Chile in 1906. I am the great-grandson of Palestinian immigrants on my father's side and the grandson of Palestinian immigrants on my mother's side. According to my grandfather, Gabriel, they decided to migrate from Palestine "to seek a better future and to escape Turkish domination."

My grandfather remembers the day his family left Palestine—possibly from the Haifa or Yaffa port. Their first stop in their sea journey was Marseille, in southern France, and from there, to Buenos Aires. From the Argentinian capital, they took the train to Mendoza and then crossed the Andes Mountains to Santiago. That leg of their very long journey was accomplished in the course of three months. Crossing the mountain range was particularly tough, requiring a whole week of constant travel on the back of a mule.

It is not easy for me to even imagine the hardship my family had to endure. There are no photos left, and only stories continue to shape our memories of that harrowing history. The main source of these stories came from my grandfather on my father's side. Gabriel was the youngest of ten siblings. He lost his father when he was only eighteen years of age.

According to my grandfather, his poor family only possessed enough money to cover some basic expenses of the long journey. When they traveled by sea, they could only afford third-class tickets. They traveled along with other families, for safety and protection. According to old documents that remained in the family, most of the travelers were men, who left their wives and children behind, not knowing whether they would ever see them again.

Every aspect of that journey spoke of untold hardship, from the rat-infested accommodation on the boat to the violent and often deadly storms of the Andes Mountains. All of this to end up in a country with a completely different culture, language and way of life.

My great-grandfather, Nicolás—Gabriel's father—did not talk much about the reasons that drove him to leave Palestine. The common understanding is that heavy taxations, imposed by the Ottomans, and intense pressures on Palestinians to be drafted into the army were some of the motives that forced young Palestinian males to migrate. Considering that many of these young men had left with the "clothes on their backs"—per Nicolás' own words—the success of Palestinians in Chile becomes even more remarkable.

Both branches of my family come from the city of Beit Jala, which fell under Israeli Occupation following the 1967 war. In the first waves of migration, only adult males left. Their intention was to make enough money to eventually return to Palestine to start a better life. But after spending four years in Chile, Nicolás and his brother, Musallam, agreed to have their families in Palestine join them in Chile instead, as the situation in Palestine was moving from bad to worse.

Beit Jala is a small village, located east of the city of Bethlehem, about 15 kilometers from the city Al Quds, Jerusalem. Most of Beit Jala's residents are Christians, namely Orthodox Christians. This beautiful village is known for its olives, grapes and also for the Church of Saint Nicholas. My great-grandfather was probably named after Saint Nicholas, as were thousands of fellow villagers, all fervent believers in the Saint's miracles.

Endogamy, or in-marriage, was quite common in the Arab world at the time, for such a practice allowed a family or a clan to maintain its cohesion, thus guaranteeing a certain degree of respect for the existing hierarchy. Back then, Beit Jala consisted of four main neighborhoods and 25 clans, or "Hamaiel." My family belonged to the Hamule of the Nawawiyeh.

When his economic situation in Santiago worsened, Nicolás decided to settle in the city of Victoria, in the southern Chilean region of Araucanía, since many families who lived there belonged to his Hamule—the likes of Abu Abbarah, Elias, Barham and Eluti.

My great-grandfather, Nicolás, married Luzbeth, the daughter of his first cousin, Selim, while all of my grandfather Gabriel's siblings married immigrants from Beit Jala, and most of them married people from the same Hamule.

On my mother's side, Ode Majluf arrived in Chile with his wife, Sara Cassis. They settled in Los Andes, where a sizable Palestinian community lived at the time. They had five children, including María, my maternal grandmother, who lived in our house until she passed away in 2015. She was a woman of strong character, very rooted in the Palestinian Arab traditions, but also very kind-hearted and loving. She was the one who passed on Palestinian traditions to our family, including food recipes and many Arabic words.

Alas, the next generations did not hold on to the Arabic language. Nowadays, hardly anyone in the Palestinian community speaks Arabic, though every family preserves elements of Palestinian traditions, especially food. When Palestinians from other parts of the world come to Chile they are impressed by our Palestinian cuisine. They often say that it was as if time had stood still. Indeed, certain elements of the Palestinian identity from the early twentieth century were passed from generation to generation, as if they were frozen in time.[18]

## Life in Chile

In 1911, my great-grandfather Nicolás bought a weaving machine and started a small business. His wife Rosa looked after the children, as per tradition of those days.

Nicolás' wool came from Germany and for a while, business was good. But when World War I started, obtaining raw material from

---

18 Early Palestinian immigrants to Chile were mostly peasants, whose unique Arabic accent was characterized by unique sounds such as the mispronunciation of the Arabic letter that stands for "k" with the sound "ch." Therefore, their descendants now say "Chif" instead of "kif" (meaning "how") and "Chnafe" and not "knafeh."

Germany was no longer possible. Sadly, in 1917, Nicolás' promising business was shut down. Along with his whole family, my great-grandfather moved to Victoria, in the South. There he opened a store and called it "El Martillo." Essentially, it was a grocery store, but also a warehouse, and eventually, a parcel shop as well. My grandfather Gabriel was born in Victoria in 1926.

Nearly a decade later, the family decided to move back to Santiago to reopen the old factory in Calle Loreto, located in the heart of Barrio Patronato, in the municipality of Recoleta, where the majority of Palestinians in Chile had settled. Barrio Patronato became the Palestinian community's "Little Bethlehem," as it was mostly populated by immigrants from the Palestinian towns of Bethlehem, Beit Jala and Beit Sahur.

Given the concentration of the Palestinian community there, the early migrants managed to emulate Palestine's own's social system, patriarchal with a strong social network that is predicated on extended families. This system proved critical to the survival of the Palestinian community, especially as they were the victims of discrimination, which was common in Chile at the time. The Palestinians were referred to as "The Turks." Speaking Arabic, along with any other language—with the exception of German—was frowned upon in the Spanish-speaking country.[19]

The Palestinians of Chile quickly fortified their presence by establishing various community organizations and institutions, starting with the first Orthodox Christian Church, "San Jorge," in the town of Recoleta.[20]

Other institutions followed: the Club Palestino, in the municipality of Las Condes; Arab clubs, scattered throughout almost

---

19 The nickname "The Turks" was a cause of distress, as one of the main reasons why many Palestinians left their country in the first place was because of the Turks' attempt to draft them into the military of the Ottoman Empire. But since early Palestinian immigrants carried passports issued by the Ottoman Empire itself, they were erroneously perceived to be "Turks."

20 A Roman soldier with a Palestinian mother, Saint George is revered by Palestinian Christians for his fierce opposition to the persecution of Christians in the Holy Land.

all cities of Chile, as well as the pride and joy of the Palestinian community in Chile until this day, Club Deportivo Palestino. The football club, wearing jerseys with Palestinian colors and symbols, currently plays in Chile's top Primera División.

Patronato, or Batronato,[21] became a residential neighborhood but also a meeting place for the community. Over the years, Patronato gradually became a commercial area, where large Palestinian-owned factories, mostly specializing in the textile industry, were established.

Concurrently, in other regions of Chile, Palestinian immigrants became traveling salesmen, who eventually settled in city centers, opening their own stores.

## Deportivo Palestino

Over a century later, the Palestinians of Chile have maintained their unique identity. True, we do not speak Arabic, but our diet relies mostly on Arabic food; nearly half of our marriages are inter-Palestinian; we have established more than 50 Arab and Palestinian institutions throughout the country. Although many of these institutions have gradually lost part of their identity as a result of cultural assimilation, some are being revitalized by the youth, who are seeking to reclaim their identity, especially as their rapport with their brethren in Palestine is being constantly strengthened.

One of the greatest displays of Palestinian identity in Chile is linked to the Club Deportivo Palestino, founded in 1920, the most iconic representation of institutionalized Palestinian presence in Chile. Every weekend, thousands of football fans gather at the Palestino's stadium, the Estadio Municipal La Cisterna, a popular district of Santiago. The club is not only popular among Palestinians, as many people, especially those belonging to the poorer sectors of Chilean society, are also die-hard fans. The reason for that is that the club dedicates much energy and resources in helping the community

---

21 In the Arabic language there is no letter corresponding to the sound "P," which is why Arab immigrants mispronounced the name of the neighborhood where they settled.

at large, including support for children and youth, thus reducing risk factors for drug abuse and other destructive habits.

Indeed, many of the Club's Chilean fans do not have Palestinian or Arab origins. They simply support the club because of its social work, and also as a way of expressing their solidarity towards the Palestinian people.

In fact, Deportivo Palestino is more than a football club. It has already proven its ability to transcend national borders. It brings joy to its supporters and to its fans in Occupied Palestine and in the diaspora. Its victories are celebrated from Santiago to Jerusalem. Its achievements represent a rallying cry against injustice and an opportunity for the oppressed to claim a moment of happiness.

Quite often, Deportivo Palestino is viewed as the second Palestinian national team. The club does not hide its Palestinian identity. On the contrary, it displays it proudly. A hundred years later, we can say with much confidence that this football club has helped unite the Palestinian community in Chile and has been a major platform in integrating Palestinians to the larger Chilean society, without ever losing sight of its Palestinian identity.

The so-called "Turks" have eventually managed to write their own history, using sports as a medium. True, the success story of Deportivo Palestino is not only about sports, but that should not take away from the fact that this team has won Chilean Primera División (First Division) title in 1955 and 1978, in addition to the Segunda División (Second Division) in 1952, 1972 and also "Copa Chile" in 1975, 1977 and 2018. The latest title was particularly special for my generation as we had never witnessed that great achievement in our lifetime.

The strong connection between the club and Palestine was one of the main reasons behind its establishment, as envisioned by its founders a hundred years ago. The founders wanted Palestino—name, symbols, chants and mission—to keep the Palestinian identity alive in Chile. The *Nakba*, the catastrophic destruction of the Palestinian homeland in 1948, was the reason why the leaders of the Palestinian community in Chile decided to turn the club into a professional football team, which continues to be the case to this day.

The achievement of the club throughout history was not measured by goals and trophies but also by the many exchanges between Palestinians in Chile and Palestinians at home through the many matches played between the Palestinian National Team and Deportivo Palestino. These games have taken place in both Palestine and Chile, and each game was joined with a massive celebration of culture and reaffirmation of identity.

One of the club's most memorable milestones was the decision to replace the number one on the team's jerseys with the map of historic Palestine. This decision triggered a harsh reaction by Zionists in Chile, who lodged an official complaint with the Asociación Nacional de Fútbol Profesional (ANFP). The Zionists wanted the club to remove the map from the jerseys. But their campaign backfired, as the subject garnered significant media attention and generated a wave of solidarity from the fans of other Chilean teams which, in turn, resulted in a large spike in shirt sales, both in Chile and abroad.

It is telling that Club Deportivo Palestino was founded in 1920, that is, 28 years before the very creation of the State of Israel on the ruins of historic Palestine. When Zionists arrived in Palestine to establish their colonial regime, they claimed Palestine as "a land without a people for a people without a land." Of course, that claim was entirely fabricated as there was even a thriving Palestinian community in Chile at the turn of the 20th century, a community known as such, that enjoyed its own institutions, houses of worship and even football clubs.

This is why Deportivo Palestino is not an ordinary football team. It is a witness to history and to the durability of Palestinian culture and to the Palestinian people as a whole. Deportivo Palestino represents a cause that has generated much solidarity, even among rival teams. Deportivo Palestino is the tangible proof that Palestine is alive in us, wherever in the world we may be. It also represents a model of how sports can be a platform for resistance and a generator of solidarity. While Palestinians at home are often prevented from, if not punished for raising Palestinian flags, in Chile we raise it every Sunday, during our games. Whenever we cheer, following every goal that the team scores, we scream the name of Palestine and constantly remind ourselves of who we are and where we come from.

But there is more: the club has played a supportive role for the Palestinian football league in Palestine and has "exported" several Palestinian Chilean talents back to the homeland. Several of our Chilean players of Palestinian origins now play in the Palestine National Football team, including Jonathan Cantillana, Yashir Pinto and Matías Jadue. Even when political unity eludes at times, sports can always unite us.

Deportivo Palestino players are always aware of the events transpiring at home, as they are also aware of what their club represents for Palestinians everywhere. They do their best at each game, not only to win but also to send a message and to bring joy and pride to Palestine.

## Our Mission

Being the largest Palestinian community outside the Middle East, and certainly the largest in South America, we have a critical mission that we must continue to fulfill. Our work in Chile focuses on two major fronts: first, keeping the Palestinian identity alive in our new generations and then, continuing our advocacy for the Palestinian cause.

Regarding identity, we have launched several projects, such as the "I am a Palestinian" program, which teaches young Palestinians about the history of their homeland and the traditions of their people. Towards that end, we constantly organize educational travel programs to Palestine; we teach our children traditional Palestinian dance *Dabke*; we screen movies on Palestine, among other activities, which mainly take place in "Club Palestino."

As for advocacy, we are committed to teaching ordinary Chileans about the Palestinian cause. This is implemented at three different levels: first, through lobbying the executive and legislative authorities; second, advocating for Palestinian rights with civil society organizations and educational institutions, from elementary schools to universities; and, finally, by harnessing the energies of the Palestinian community itself. In the final analysis, we do more than disseminating information, educating and raising awareness; we also mobilize and push our supporters to carry out specific and concrete actions.

The Chilean "Congreso"—the country's equivalent to a parliament—is particularly sympathetic to the Palestinian cause. Unsurprisingly, the most supportive group of our cause in the Chamber of Deputies is the Chilean-Palestinian Inter-Parliamentary Group, which consists of more than 90 members, some of whom are of Palestinian origin. Interestingly, this influential group comprises left and right-wing members and at times, they seem to be only united by their support for Palestine.

The lobbying with the government often results in tangible outcomes, not mere political platitudes. One of many examples is that, in July 2020, the Chilean Senate approved a draft resolution, which called for President Sebastián Piñera to introduce a draft law that prohibits the import of Israeli goods produced in illegal Jewish settlements in the occupied Palestinian territory.

Later, on June 2, 2021, the Chilean Chamber of Deputies introduced a Bill that served the same purpose. The Bill, which was met with intense Israeli lobbying pressure in Congress, has already been under discussion by the Legislation, Justice and Constitution Committee. Although the legislation is not binding, it is nonetheless an important first step towards holding Israel accountable for its crimes. Indeed, the Israeli Occupation has to come with a cost.

These kinds of actions are motivated by our belief that it is time for us to move from solidarity into measurable actions. The situation in Palestine is dire, and statements of goodwill alone will not end the illegal Israeli Occupation.

It must be said that the role of the Palestinian community in Chile goes far beyond the numerous activities surrounding the Club Deportivo Palestino. Indeed, the football club is merely one of many Palestinian social, cultural, charitable and political institutions that were created in Chile over the years. Our aim is to constantly attempt to balance out the natural cultural assimilation of Palestinians in Chilean society, by maintaining strong ties with the Palestinian homeland. This particular objective is more urgent now than ever, as Israel relentlessly attempts to erase Palestinian history, culture and identity. For us here in Chile, this mission is not carried out at random, but it is part of a centralized, strategic plan.

One pillar of this strategy is the constant dialogue between the leaders of our community and other Palestinian communities in South America. A few years ago, we organized a regional conference entitled, "*Taqalid*"—meaning Tradition. The conference was hosted by Club Palestino in Santiago, with the decided purpose of uniting the Palestinian communities in Latin America around the values of Palestinian culture and identity. The 2017 conference was attended by more than 5,000 people, who traveled from every part of Latin America. In 2019, the conference was hosted in Lima, Peru, where a comparable number of Palestinians attended. These are perfect examples of how such action can mobilize and revitalize our communities, which become stronger when they meet, converse and organize together. The Palestinian community in the diaspora can, indeed, do much more than "spreading the word." It can strategize towards influencing the very political processes and decision-making of governments.

The achievements of the Palestinian community of Chile have been earned through hard work and dedication. As an active member and organizer with the Palestinian Chilean community, I can summarize the key points of our success as follows:

• *Embedding Palestine's historical memory:* Defending the Palestinian homeland requires more than passion and enthusiasm but knowledge, training and deep understanding of history.

• *Truth-telling:* Teaching the truth about Palestine is not a haphazard process. It requires a strong foundation or proper tools—inspiring talks, documents, videos, testimonials, and such.

• *Pursuing political power:* Obtaining knowledge and teaching the truth must eventually be translated into actual political leverage, which can only happen when the members of the community themselves become engaged in the political process, whether in government, in political movements or civil society organizations.

• *Empowering others:* The power obtained throughout the community as a direct outcome of its own mobilization must translate into generating our own leaders, representatives and spokespersons which could—in fact, should—include non-Palestinian or Arab political actors. It is critical that our cause is presented as a universal one, because, indeed, it is. Therefore, we must reach out to all people from all backgrounds who are united by the values of justice, equality, freedom and human rights.

• *Networking:* Communal energies and political achievements are often weakened by the lack of reliable networks. The fragmentation of Palestinians in the diaspora between various political parties, religions and ideologies, is a major pitfall that we, here in Chile, do our best to avoid. To move forward, we must harmonize all of our actions and network, at every level, to achieve the desired outcomes.

• *Planning ahead:* Generally, Palestinians tend to react rather than plan ahead. We react to specific Israeli actions such as their repeated aggressions and wars on Gaza or the expansion of illegal Jewish settlements, etc. But, quite often, we do not organize around a pro-active strategy. Palestinians must not allow Israeli provocations and aggressions to be the catalyst for their mobilization and activism. We must remain proactive, guided by a clear and permanent strategy and agenda. Palestinian action must be permanent, as long as the Israeli Occupation is also permanent.

• *Remaining inspired:* Frustration and demoralization are not an option. It is understandable that people who are truly committed to the Palestinian cause can grow frustrated at times as the result of the ineffectiveness of our leadership or the lack of progress on the ground, or the absence of a political horizon and so on. But we must not allow ourselves to be demoralized, because this is precisely what Israel hopes to achieve. Demoralization leads to apathy, and apathy to inaction. We must remain strong and active under every circumstance.

Over seven decades have passed since the Palestinian people were expelled from their homeland following the brutal ethnic cleansing of Palestine, a genocidal campaign that continues to this day. The daily Israeli aggressions and the perpetual Occupation are constant reminders that the *Nakba* has never truly ceased.

Our people here in Chile, though grateful for the hospitality and the opportunities offered to them, are fully aware of Palestine's painful reality and are fully committed to defending the Palestinian cause and the Palestinian people, until freedom is finally attained.

Though many thousands of miles away, here in Chile we believe that Palestinians are one, whether in Jerusalem, Nazareth, Gaza, Beit Jala, Lebanon, Syria, Jordan or Santiago. Those of us who are based outside Palestine are entrusted with the compounded responsibility to serve as ambassadors for the Palestinian cause, wherever we are in the world. Like Palestinians at home, we, too, believe in the significance of the unity of our people.

We are eager to see the reactivation of the central role of the Palestine Liberation Organization (PLO) that offers Palestinian communities in the diaspora, like ours, a direct political platform, so that we may play a role in shaping the Palestinian discourse and be part of a larger strategic plan that aims at ending the Israeli Occupation, ensuring the Right of Return for Palestinian refugees, and achieving full equal rights of citizenship to Palestinians, whether in the Occupied Territories or in Palestine 1948.

GHADA KARMI *is a Palestinian physician, academic and writer. She is a former research fellow at the Institute of Arab and Islamic Studies at the University of Exeter, where she lectured on the Palestinian-Israeli conflict. Her major work has been in this area, on which she has published widely. Her books include an acclaimed memoir,* In Search of Fatima, a Palestinian story *(Verso Press, 2002);* Married to Another Man: Israel's Dilemma in Palestine, *which deals with the one-state solution (Pluto Press, 2007); and a second memoir,* Return, *(Verso, 2015).*

# AN EQUAL RIGHTS CAMPAIGN
## Key to the End of Zionism

*Ghada Karmi*

IN EARLY 2020, when London went into lockdown because of the coronavirus pandemic, I enrolled, like many others, in an online course that I could study at home. The subject, "Concepts in Psychoanalysis," was something that had always interested me. The lecturer was a Jewish South African and, whether by coincidence or not, many of my fellow course students were Jewish, too.

During a session on memory, the lecturer asked for volunteers to put forward their own significant memories for analysis by the class. It so happened that I had earlier given her a copy of my memoir, "In Search of Fatima," which relates the story of my family's forced departure from Jerusalem in 1948 and our subsequent life in exile. Presumably because of this, she asked me to contribute a personal memory to the class. I decided to choose the moment in April 1948 when we left Jerusalem for the last time. I was a child, and my memory was of clinging to the garden gate, trying to soothe the much-loved family dog we would have to leave behind as he clambered frantically to be let out. I could have been any child in similar circumstances, and I thought it would come across as poignant and touching.

The lecturer agreed to my choice but, on the day of the class, she phoned me, clearly very agitated, to say that she had been thinking it over and feared my revelations would provoke a political argument in the class. Her course, she insisted, was academic not political, and things might get out of control. At that time, May 2021, dramatic Palestinian uprisings were taking place in Israel and the Occupied Territories, and she was afraid passions would already be inflamed amongst her Jewish audience. None of my efforts to point out that she was the one in control of the class and could stop a discussion that got out of hand succeeded in pacifying her. Her anxiety was that the Jewish members would be upset by my memories because they related to the events of Israel's creation. A Jewish friend, also on the course, explained to me afterwards that describing my pain and loss could assign the blame to Jews. That, in turn, could suggest that Israel should not have come into existence. What a terrible calamity that would have been, she lamented, depriving Holocaust victims of their only refuge at the time.

Apparently, when the lecturer agreed earlier to my speaking at the session, she had not realized the implications of her decision, and had now panicked. It appeared that the upset that my story might cause a Jewish audience outweighed my own in losing my home and country. She would not change her mind, and I felt that I had no choice but to withdraw my contribution altogether—whereupon she was enormously apologetic and begged me to understand, which left me wondering what exactly it was I had to understand. That Jewish feelings were more important than Palestinian ones?

This small anecdote encapsulates, for me, the essence of the Palestinian predicament with Zionism: how it insists on the primacy of Jewish suffering over that of its victims; how it assumes that Jews have a right to settle in another people's homeland because they have suffered; and how it promotes the non sequitur of linking Jewish suffering in the Holocaust with Palestine, whose people had in no way been responsible for it. Such arrogant, self-centered notions might have made sense in a context of revenge exacted on an antisemitic Europe, but they made none when exercised against an innocent people who had never harmed Jews as a collective. In order to disguise this flawed logic, it has been necessary to silence the Palestinian version of events from the start, just as, in her own way, our Zionist lecturer saw no alternative but to silence me.

That, essentially, has been the story of my life in exile in England. I grew up suffocated by the assumption of everyone around me that Jews were entitled to Palestine. This view was entrenched in the Britain of the 1950s and, despite a later awareness of Palestinian suffering, it never changed. That a whole population of Palestinians had been ejected from their homeland to make Israel happen, was largely unknown and of no concern to anyone at the time. Our flight from Jerusalem, amidst the violence and disruption of the Jewish takeover of our part of the city in 1948, had been part of a much larger and immensely tragic Palestinian exodus. Yet, in the 1950s and most of the '60s, Palestinian history formed no part of Israel's story, and no alternative narrative was given a platform. Our silence was the condition enabling Israel's credibility.

My understanding of Palestine's modern history was shaped by this experience. Israel's legitimacy as a member of the community of nations was so firmly implanted into Western consciousness it was impossible to dislodge, even from those who knew the truth. We stuck to the conviction of our undying right to our homeland—one day, we said, our country would be free, and it would be returned to us. In those early days we did not think of this natural right in the context of "liberation": the foreign settlers who had taken over our country were seen as more like thieves and outlaws, to be evicted to wherever they had come from as soon as possible. Our ire was focused on Britain as the treacherous colonizing power that had given Palestine to these people. However, this view could not hold out against a changing reality. The outlaws of earlier times morphed into a State admired and cherished by the West. The late 1960s saw Israel celebrated as a heroic victor over three Arab states which, together, could not defeat this "plucky little State." The Arab-Israeli war of 1967 which brought about this Arab defeat also led to the loss of the rest of Palestine. Israel expanded its colonial rule to East Jerusalem, the West Bank and Gaza, where its hold was rapidly consolidated by building Jewish settler colonies in these territories.

It was in this environment that the Palestine Liberation Organization (PLO) became established and was coming into its own. Created in 1964 to liberate the homeland, as its name clarified, its effect on us was profound. It changed the language of struggle against Israel, making it one of anti-colonial liberation and part of the other national liberation struggles. The PLO came to support all progressive and revolutionary movements, such as those in Cuba, Nicaragua, Namibia and South Africa. This dimension influenced our understanding of the national struggle and gave those of us in exile an aim and a role in it. After all, the PLO had sprung up out of exile, its leaders and fighters were in exile, and it held out the promise of regaining the homeland and ending that exile. In those years, the PLO's existence was a marvel for us, a symbolic homeland to which we could belong while waiting for the true liberation. It is hard to overestimate its importance as a foundation of our renaissance, and a beacon of hope for the prospects of regaining Palestine. Its ambitious bid to represent the whole of the Palestinian community through its 740-member "parliament-in-exile," the Palestine National Council, was a balm to the soul of a battered and fragmented people.

My political activism and that of many others were nurtured by the PLO's existence, the breadth of meaning it gave to our ubiquitous struggle and how it must be fought in every arena. Despite this euphoria, I was not blind to the PLO's shortcomings and the limitations of its ability to achieve its ambitions. The chances of success for any liberation movement were poor under the conditions the Palestinians had to operate in, fighting against Israel from outside Palestine, and forced to contend with a range of unreliable Arab states which might betray them. At the same time, though, I felt released from the impotence of having to watch my compatriots fighting and dying in Palestine, while unable to help them from afar. The PLO showed me the way to join the struggle.

Though Fatah's first military operation against Israel in 1965 reaffirmed the Palestinian right to resistance through armed struggle, it was never the only or the most successful path to liberation. This took many forms: political, diplomatic and cultural. In the late 1960s and '70s, the PLO developed a governing structure and established an array of civil society institutions and professional unions. It reflected at once the aspiration to create a State, even though in exile, and a wished-for return to some semblance of Palestinian life as it had been before 1948.

Given the power imbalance with Israel and the global consensus to maintain it, these were wild aspirations at that time. Nonetheless, the PLO, as an idea just as much as a concrete reality, succeeded in inspiring the majority of Palestinians. It was a call to arms that they could not resist, and it galvanized them and the growing number of their supporters into action. I remember the dizzying excitement of feeling that I was sharing in a great enterprise, as if our efforts really would achieve Palestine's liberation, and I saw myself as a warrior in this endeavor. But what did liberating Palestine mean when I did not live there or even in its vicinity?

This became the spur to the realization that literature and storytelling, poetry and art, films and plays and the media, could become weapons equal—or even superior—to any on the field of battle. In the pro-Israel environment of the England I grew up in, I saw my work of liberation as a battle using these means to change hearts and minds and bend them towards our cause. The early 1970s saw a ferment of Palestine activism, commencing with Free Palestine, a small organization, which briefly wrote and spoke about the Palestine cause. In 1972, a number of us founded Palestine Medical Aid, the first medical charity of its kind in Britain later to become Medical Aid for Palestinians (MAP). In the company of a few colleagues, I started Palestine Action, (not to be confused with the group of the same name currently active in Britain) a year later. It was the first political organization for Palestine dedicated to lobbying the British government and British public opinion. We used the conventional methods of letter-writing to influential people, demonstrations, media appearances and newspaper advertising. We met the Foreign Secretary at the time, Alex Douglas-Home, along with other junior members of government, and wrote to the Queen, gratified to receive some positive responses.

Our aim in all this was to put the Palestine issue on the political map in Britain and counter the Zionist narrative that had taken hold of the British public. In 1974, the first PLO representative to the UK, Said Hammami, was appointed as part of a Palestinian diplomatic effort to solidify the Palestine cause internationally. This development boosted our work and, ultimately, superseded it. Palestine Action went on being active until the end of the 1970s, when it finally petered out. Not long afterwards, the Palestine Solidarity Campaign was established, to be followed by other British solidarity groups, and the trend towards organized Palestinian support in Britain was established. Together with others, I became active in writing opinion pieces for the press and publishing books and research studies. Edward Said's highly influential *The Question of Palestine* was released in 1979, and his writings continued to promote the case effectively until his death in 2003, and beyond.

Two important literary genres that came later, and should have appeared far earlier, were the memoir and the novel. Nothing is more calculated to open the eyes and reach the hearts of people than a personal account and an imaginative tale that conveys the Palestinian experience. Such books had long been published in the Arab world, but unless translated, they were inaccessible to the Western reader. In the context of liberation, personal histories and stories were best written in European languages and, in view of the role they played in the Israeli-Palestinian conflict, the English language of Britain and the US was particularly important. In these literary and artistic endeavors, we sought to synchronize our efforts with the political and military actions on the ground to make the struggle more effective.

These days the Palestinian experience, conveyed in literature, theater and film, has become increasingly familiar in the West. However, the liberation we strove for, and the point of the exercise, is no closer, perhaps even further away. The reality today is that Israel is in colonial control of the whole of historic Palestine. In this space, the Palestinians are either second-class Israeli citizens, or non-citizens without rights in the post-1967 territories. The latter are doubly controlled by the Palestinian Authority, which is subservient to the colonial power and is ordered to police Palestinian lives and oppose any resistance against their oppression. How can liberation happen under such conditions, and what does it mean? The two-state solution, touted for decades as the best way forward for Israel and the Palestinians, would not constitute liberation, even if it ever were to happen. The 22 percent of Palestine that would make up the Palestinian state, as offered by this solution, is no substitute for the freedom of the whole country. Partly because of this, though mostly by conviction, many have turned to the one-state solution as the route to liberation: the creation of a democratic, equal society for Palestinians and Jews.

The aim of replacing the colonialist, apartheid State of Israel with a democracy with equal rights for all is not new and was first proposed by the PLO in 1969. In a remarkably forward-looking vision, given the circumstances at the time, Fatah had put forward its idea of "the Palestine of tomorrow," a progressive, democratic, non-sectarian state where all would have equal rights. It acknowledged, for the first time, the physical presence in Palestine of a Jewish community that included not just native Palestinian Jews, but also settlers who had to be accommodated in the new state with justice and equality. The proposal rejected the idea of a Palestinian mini-state, for example in Gaza and the West Bank, which would merely amount to a Bantustan; and equally rejected a binational state that could replicate Lebanon's failed confessional arrangement. In the non-sectarian state, the PLO envisioned that the Palestinian Right of Return would be fulfilled, with other migrations to come later, and instituted according to an agreed state policy.

The democratic state proposal was not welcomed by most Palestinians. For many, it meant an acceptance of the Zionist invader in Palestine, and an intolerable concession to the enemy. Others feared exploitation and domination in a single state by the more technologically advanced Jews; still others feared the new state would form a legitimized bridgehead for Jewish economic penetration into the Arab world and, most importantly, the proposal threatened to weaken the Palestinian fighting spirit and quash resistance. Similar fears are still present today and used to oppose the proponents of the one-state solution. Nevertheless, the idea has caught on amongst many Palestinians and in public opinion at large, where it is no longer seen as a utopian dream of a few oddballs and idealists. Many groups and individuals have adopted the unitary, democratic state idea and have been striving to make it happen. Their progress is slow, but unforeseen events could accelerate it, especially given the current wave of unprecedented popular support for Palestine in Europe, the US and among American Jews.

Despite this growing popular acceptance, however, there is currently no formal support for the one-state solution in any country. No state or political institution has adopted it and, even though it has gained increasing recognition in the last two decades, it has attained nowhere near the international consensus reached over the two-state solution. Meanwhile, Israel will not remain idle in expanding its colonizing project, stealing more Palestinian land and expelling more Palestinians. Parallel to this, it will be working overtime to reverse its negative image in the world, using every ruse and straining every muscle to counter the push from the other side. The fight between the parties was always unequal, and the odds are still tipped in Israel's favor.

So, what is to be done? If we agree that full liberation can only come about with the creation of an equitable, inclusive democracy in place of the current Zionist, apartheid state that is Israel, then the only question to be answered is, "How can it be brought about?" Israel today is de facto one state from the Jordan River to the Mediterranean Sea. It has a population of 6.6 million Israeli Jews with citizenship and full rights, 1.8 million Israeli Palestinians with citizenship and partial rights, and 4.7 million Palestinians with no citizenship and no rights. So far, Israel has managed to maintain this inequitable arrangement, even to normalize it, for more than 50 years, evading international conventions and violating human rights norms. No world power or international body has been able, or willing, to end this blatant inequity—or looks likely to. In the absence of such intervention, it is the victims themselves who must find a way to end it.

Imagine, therefore, if the disenfranchised Palestinians of Jerusalem, the West Bank and Gaza were now to pose this challenge to Israel: we reject your rule over us while giving us no rights. Either you withdraw from our territory, or you give us citizenship equal with the others over whom you rule. Imagine further that, when Israel refuses to withdraw and ignores the challenge, as it will, these Palestinians do not back down but demand Israeli citizenship. At the same time, they mount a huge campaign of civil disobedience to accompany their demand if Israel refuses, and publicize their case to the world, exposing to public gaze the reality of their situation and Israel's ugly conduct towards them. Then the Palestinian Diaspora, and all who support Palestine, come out in solidarity with their compatriots' demands, creating a two-pronged campaign, coordinated between the inside and the outside, much as the anti-apartheid movement campaigned to assist the internal South African struggle. The ubiquitous, disparate activities promoting Palestine, with each individual and group starting up their own initiatives and dispersing their energies, then begin to unite towards this one end.

Staying with this project, let us now imagine that Palestinians can be persuaded to adopt the equal rights strategy, recognizing that no other has helped them so far, and put their shoulders to the wheel. Suppose, as a result, the strategy is finally implemented and they acquire Israeli citizenship. Their gains would be considerable: they would stay on their own land by right, to live in dignity and security; the whole of historic Palestine would become available to them once more; and their displaced compatriots could look forward to returning home, once a representative parliament is enabled to pass laws permitting it. Above all, their call for equal rights will get to the heart of Zionist ideology predicated on Jewish majority rule and Jewish exclusivity. If all Palestinians become citizens, Israel's demography will irrevocably alter towards pluralism, and so bring Zionism to an end.

Had this been a chess game, the strategy I have outlined above would mean checkmate for Israel. In the real world, however, it is most unlikely to happen. The task is too hard, with a Palestinian population still hoping for their own state, in spite of all the evidence, and a Palestinian intelligentsia persuaded to go along with the favored international position on two states they believe it will deliver. They will not unite behind a different strategy while this illusion lasts. Nurturing the hope of independence for Palestinians, while doing nothing to abort Israeli colonization of Palestinian land, is another crime in the list of the many committed against the Palestinian people.

An equal rights campaign, putting forward a simple, straightforward message the whole world can understand, would cut through the prevarication and obfuscation shrouding the Palestinian struggle today. It does not negate but, on the contrary, may potentiate, the current unitary state initiatives, and is potentially the fastest and most direct route to attaining what Palestinians passionately wish for: the end of Zionism and the liberation of their country.

RANDA ABDEL-FATTAH *is a Palestinian Egyptian Australian Muslim writer, academic, activist and former lawyer. She is a postdoctoral research fellow in the Department of Sociology at Macquarie University. Abdel-Fattah's books include* Islamophobia and Everyday Multiculturalism *(2018), the co-edited anthology* Arab, Australian, Other: Stories on Race and Identity and Coming of Age in the War on Terror *(2021). Abdel-Fattah is also the multi-award-winning author of 11 novels published in over 20 countries, including her best-selling debut novel* "Does My Head Look Big in This?" *Abdel-Fattah has been nominated for Sweden's 2019 and 2018 Astrid Lindgren Award, the world's biggest children's and young adult literature award.*

# ETHICS OF LIBERATION
## Palestine as a Mode of Existence

*Randa Abdel-Fattah*

OUR PALESTINIAN FAMILY of thirty, nineteen of them grandchildren, spill out of a Sydney suburban house onto the front lawn. A Palestinian flag and an *Eid Mubarak* banner are draped over the front porch. The smokers huddle on the driveway, sucking on their first morning cigarette since Ramadan. A few of the girls, dressed up for Eid, balance their phones on a windowsill and record a Tik Tok video. My mother-in-law sits on a rattan outdoor chair that is too big for her, gripping a cup of Arabic coffee. The younger children play soccer, using my father-in-law's lemon trees as goalposts, ignoring the cries of the aunties to watch out for the branches. The rhythm of this 2021 Eid morning hums along to the invisible cadence of "We teach life, sir."

We constantly encounter our life in exile through a lenticular lens. Viewed from one angle: joy, love, privilege. Viewed from the slightest tilt of an angle: injustice, oppression. We dismiss the self-indulgent temptation to feel despair in the safety of diaspora, and cajole the children to pose in family photos. The angle tilts. We scroll through social media, watch videos of Israeli mobs chanting "Death to Arabs," hear Mona Al-Kurd's anguished cry, "You are stealing my house"; recoil at attacks on worshippers in Al-Aqsa. The lens tilts again: we send Eid gifs in WhatsApp groups.

My mother-in-law's phone rings. "They're a few minutes away," she cries, and tips her coffee onto the grass.

My phone rings. A journalist from the Australian Broadcasting Corporation (ABC) who had no time for us yesterday, suddenly wants a story on a Palestinian family about "how Eid celebrations have been affected given the situation."

The situation is this. Gaza is being bombed. And my husband and father-in-law are on the way back from the hospital with his cancer test results.

Israel pounds Gaza with airstrikes for eleven days. Within 26 days, my father-in-law is dead.

* * *

About a week after my father-in-law's diagnosis, less than two weeks before his death, I sit beside him at his home, computer propped on my lap. I am in multi-tasking activist daughter-in-law mode. "How do you feel, *Amo*?" I ask, as I email colleagues about an open letter, Academics for Palestine.

"*Alhamdulilah*," he replies with stoic calmness.

Al-Jazeera news is on the television, reporting on Gaza. I can hear Disney's Aladdin from my seven-year-old son Adam's I-pad, with him beside me singing along, uninhibited, out of tune, mutilating the lyrics. I raise the volume on the television. Adam raises the volume on the I-pad, letting out a frustrated cry, "I can't hear the song!"

"We're watching the news," I say.

*Amo* shoots me a look of disapproval and turns off the television.

Here, two competing claims to the family space offer an insight into how our Elders teach us life in the quotidian spaces of a Palestinian diasporic family. On the one hand, a claim by a Palestinian here to bear witness to what is happening in Palestine there. On the other, a claim by a Palestinian child here to control the here, to keep what is happening in Palestine there.

I think about my father-in-law's gesture of solidarity with his grandson to allow him the space to be a child, to play and sing while I watch Palestinian children being murdered and terrorized in Gaza by the Israeli State. I think about when the right time for a child is to understand the connection between here and there. Not just in the migration sense proposed by Ambalavaner Sivanandan, but to understand, as Palestinians outside of Palestine, that we are not mere spectators to a geographical place. To understand Palestine as a mode of existence.

"Are you in pain?" I ask *Amo*. He smiles. "How can I complain? Look what's happening in Gaza. *Alhamdulilah*." I apologize for being on the laptop. For the past few days, I had neither called nor visited, consumed by what is happening. "No," he says, cutting me off. "Keep doing it." He takes out his phone and shows me WhatsApp videos from Palestine, shared with him by family and friends.

Crouched beside *Amo's* grave days later, I remember this scene and sob. I sob for the missed moments in *Amo's* last days, but not out of guilt. *Amo*, himself a tireless advocate for justice, understood that Palestine is a way of life, not just a cause.

I cry because I am haunted by the constant questioning of what commitment to a liberation struggle yield in families—in how we teach our children in the Diaspora that *sumud* is an embodied way of life. I say "in the Diaspora" because, first, that is where I write from and second, because the children in Palestine are the ones who teach me the meaning of *sumud*, not the other way around.

Working with children and young people as an author and academic, I am constantly exploring what political life means: how we make sense of our purpose and identities, how we relate to each other, what children learn about the world through their families and themselves, how we find balance, how we know when to resist by facing Israel and when to turn away. A life defined solely in resistance risks "becoming an end in itself and for itself," as Ghassan Hage argues. Cultivating a "space or a dimension of life that is free from both Occupation and the resistance to Occupation" is to cultivate a space of "heroic normality."

One, out of all the images that haunt and invigorate me, is that of a little Palestinian boy and girl standing in the most recent crime scene that is Gaza, smiling as they hold their pet fish amidst the rubble and debris.

To be clear, I am not fetishizing resilience. We must reject the pontificating of those who expect the occupied, bombed and traumatized to exercise "restraint" and demonstrate resilience.

The image affected me deeply for another reason. Here was what scholar Nadera Shalhoub-Kevorkian describes as Israeli "kill-ability" facing off with Palestinians' livability. Here were two children momentarily claiming a space of "heroic normality," reminding us that in our struggle for liberation we must sometimes pause long enough to consider who we will be, what we will do, what we will mean, when Palestine is free.

When our intrinsic, non-negotiable rights and dignity as a people are honored, what will it mean to live fully human? If we suspend the human, postpone joy, creativity, play, stillness, laughter, frivolity until we are liberated, what will be left of us when liberation comes. These two children with their fish reminded me of this.

There is much to lose in the fight to achieve freedom and justice if, in thinking about what we are fighting against, we neglect to think about what we are fighting for. Children, precisely because they do not mean to, remind us of this. When Adam called out "I can't hear the song!" he was reminding me that we are fighting not simply for the right for Palestinian children not to be killed, but for their right to live, and it is for this reason that my father-in-law, wiser than me in that moment, turned off the television to let Adam hear his song, and to let us hear Adam sing.

* * *

In our efforts to resist the political and media establishment's denial of Palestinians' "permission to narrate," as aptly described by Edward Said, Palestinians have, by necessity, spent years demanding space, and labor mobilizing voices to speak against denial in its entirety: *Nakba, Naksa*, two-state/one-state, apartheid, blockade, borders, green line, ethnic cleansing and so on. Counter-narration has been central to our collective resistance, especially among diasporic, exilic populations in the West. At the rightful center of the Palestinian narrative of struggle and liberation are young people, not as supporting characters but as leading narrators whose occupied lives, blockaded dreams, checkpoint births and grievable deaths must remain the central story.

With 51% of Gaza's population under the age of 15, a war on Gaza is a war on children. With 45% of the West Bank population under the age of 15, Israel's military Occupation is waged against babies, toddlers and teenagers. With over 30% of the total Palestinian population aged between 15–29, young adults live in oppressive conditions, brutalized by Israel's settler colonial apartheid regime.

Children and young people are fundamentally at the core of the Palestinian liberation movement. Israeli political elites know this.

We see this in how Israel has normalized the dehumanization of Palestinian children—what Nadera Shalhoub-Kevorkian calls "unchilding."

During the 2018 Great March of Return, Israel's then Defense Minister, Moldovan-born settler and ultra-right nationalist Avigdor Lieberman, declared "there are no innocent people in Gaza." The IDF's official Twitter feed posted a graphic listing, "Molotov cocktails," "rocks," "wire cutters," "arson kites," "children," "disabled civilians" and "rope tied to fence" as "Hamas' Tools for Infiltrating Israel." In other words, Palestinian children are fair game, legitimate targets.

We see this when Israel purposely excludes eight-month-old baby Leila Ghandoor[22] and all the other babies and children killed or permanently maimed from the political category of "innocent"—and Western politicians and journalists endorse this exclusion by asserting Israel's "right to defend itself," whilst meekly requesting that Israel use "proportionate violence." Apportioning life and death is only possible in a world where Palestinian children count as a ratio of human: non-human, sub-human, less-human. With Israel as representative/embodiment of the West, there is no more powerful

---

22 *Al Jazeera* English, "Laila Anwar al-Ghandour becomes the face of Gaza carnage," May 15, 2018, https://www.aljazeera.com/news/2018/5/15/laila-anwar-al-ghandour-becomes-the-face-of-gaza-carnage last accessed November 5, 2021

and mobilizing signifier for the non-human than the "terrorist." A signifier moored in the global cartography of racialized power hierarchies in which Israel, as local defender of "Western" interests and settler colonial values, finds its legitimacy in the racist trope of fighting the "violent," "extremist," the "radical" East. In this representational prison, Leila Ghandoor can never be innocent. Her murder is justified by terms such as "Hamas human shield," or blamed on Hamas' supposed "dead baby strategy," as a Zionist defender once put it to me during my appearance in May 2018 on Australia's national Q&A television program.

Israel's most recent bombardment of Gaza killed 256 Palestinians, including 66 children. According to the Israeli Meir Amit Intelligence and Terrorism Information Centre, at least 48% of Palestinians killed were "associated with terrorist groups" with "many" of the children characterized as "family members of terrorists"—in other words, justifiably exterminable.

Ahed Tamimi, the Palestinian teenager who slapped a soldier a few hours after an Israeli soldier shot her 15-year-old cousin in the head at close range was, according to Israel's then Culture Minister, Miri Regev, "not a little girl," but "a terrorist."

There is no end to Israeli's instrumental invocation of the language of the so-called "war on terror" to legitimize its criminalization of Palestinian children's existence and resistance. Israel has invested heavily in a sustained discursive regime which seeks to normalize the meaning of "Palestinian resistance" as "terrorism" and transform "Palestinian child" to "terrorist." In the last twenty years, in particular, the narrative of Palestinian youth as terrorists, as "national security threats," has been calculated to plug neatly into the fundamental, organizing grammar and imperial logics of the "war on terror." Israeli strategists know only too well how the imperative of messaging the Palestinian child as culpable terrorist serves the purpose not only of fighting the war on terror as an agent of the West, but also of escaping international scrutiny. After all, the spectacle of dead innocent children puts a lucrative multi-billion-dollar military, surveillance technology and armaments industry at risk, with Gaza being the ideal "weapon-testing laboratory." Framing

Israeli military campaigns as counterterrorism serves a political economy in which Western governments are heavily invested. The racial scripts, securitized imagination and pre-emptive logics of the war on terror have always operated against young Muslim, black and brown people who have been constructed as a central category of the terrorist figure.

How, then, does all this bode for Palestinian youths' imaginings of liberatory futures?

National liberation must start with self-liberation and self-liberation first demands self-knowledge of one's positionality.

In my most recent project, I have been interrogating the violence exercised against young Muslims by the State, and so-called neutral policies and political practices in a war on terror context and how this leaves its traces on youth born into a post 9/11 world. I have sought to mine deep into how this violence is experienced and resisted by young people in the micro-context of their lives, in particular their schools, and how years of "countering violent extremism" policies and political and media rhetoric have normalized a hyper-sensitivity to and policing of Muslim/Arab (because they are treated as synonymous) youths' bodies, speech and the spaces they move in. Living in what academic Sunaina Marr Maira describes as "the everyday of surveillance," young people shared with me how they engage in both adaptive and maladaptive coping strategies in response to attempts to contain and manage their political expression and dissent: from a young Palestinian girl who was forbidden to wear a "Free Palestine" t-shirt at school because it was "political," to a young Muslim boy who was interviewed by ASIO for writing an essay on terrorism and Western interference in Muslim countries, to students who confessed to pursuing strategies of self-censorship in order to demonstrate their "safeness," or pushing back and claiming the right to speak on their own terms. I also encountered students who pursued assimilation, sought to perform as "good"/"moderate"/"apolitical" Muslim/Arabs. They were, to borrow from Bhabha, miming whiteness and, in the process, reduced to ambivalence, finding themselves always "almost the same, but not quite." On the other hand, there were Palestinian students who, faced with their dehumanization in the syllabus taught to them in school—which almost always insisted on "two-sides"/ Israel has a right to self-defense/BDS is anti-Semitic/Hamas this and Hamas that"—refused to "prove" their humanity.

One of the ways to mute young people's voices is to devalue their emotions, dismiss their political passion and anger as subjective and irrational. There are the explicit attempts to censor young people who support Palestine—cases such as that of Rahmaan Mohammadi who wore a "Free Palestine" badge to school and was referred to the police by his teachers under the UK's counter-radicalization Prevent program. There is also the epistemic racism that young people face, which denies them their anger, emotion, resistance and political voice in the name of the myth of "neutrality."

Ramon Grosfugel argues that Western hegemonic identity politics and epistemic privilege is sustained by certain myths, one of which is what Colombian philosopher, Santiago Castro-Gomez, called the "point zero" perspective. Grosfugel explains: "The 'point zero' perspective is the Western myth of a point of view that assumes itself to be beyond a point of view."

The hubris of "point zero" is what epistemologically animates the narrative of "both sides," "balance," "neutrality," "conflict," "negotiations." Students told me about teachers telling them not to "bring politics into the classroom," or cautioning them to be "factual, less angry." One student's essay was marked down for being "too personal and emotional" and not "academic enough." Students spoke to me about learning to "tone down" their anger because, as one student said, "I get told to sort of not be too, how should I say it, angry in my voice…anything I say sort of comes out as, not aggressive, but almost I guess being seen as an attack. I can't tone down my emotions. They don't want to hear my anger."

The Orientalist trope of the angry, irrational Muslim/Arab is pernicious. The resistance to self-censoring and the pressure to do so in classroom contexts is a common theme among many students I encounter. Anticipating how one's tone, words, emotional register will be interpreted through racial and Islamophobic tropes bears down on students' self-presentation and contribution to classroom discussions because of how effectively a deep-rooted collective image of the "angry Arab" works to curtail political speech.

One university student told me: "I always feel like I have emotion and others don't care. Then it hits me at the end of class, oh shit, I'm embarrassed. You're the only one so passionate about it. It's annoying because I think: why don't they care? Like when it came to Palestine, the Middle East and brown and black lives, Syria, drones, Yemen and stuff, why don't they get passionate? I'm sitting there and saying this is so wrong and they say I shouldn't be so emotional, shouldn't bring what's happening overseas here, that I should leave it at home."

To not care, not be affected, is emblematic of privilege—distinguishing what counts as "publicly grievable lives," on the one hand, from "unremarkable" lives on the other, as Judith Butler theorizes. This enforced privatization of grief over "what's happening overseas" is also about neutralizing school and university spaces, creating a binary between the "rational," "apolitical" classroom space and the "emotional," "irrational" private space.

The "point zero" epistemic racism that drives narratives of "balance," "dispassion" and "neutrality" obscures the fact that Palestine is engaged in a liberation struggle where, to claim to be "beyond a point of view," is in and of itself a point of view. The claim that one is not taking sides is taking sides. A posture of actual neutrality is not just impossible but indefensible when the fact of Israeli hegemony, belligerence and defiance of international laws is so clear.

In my work with young people, both Palestinian and non-Palestinian, I am unequivocal: Palestine is a site of knowledge which teaches us to repudiate the Western myth of a neutral, apolitical, ahistorical subject and rather to proudly announce ourselves as people who self-reflexively claim a political, social and emotional orientation and intellectual posture rooted in seeking justice and thereby, necessarily "taking sides."

It is only conceivable to imagine future possibilities if this posture is nurtured from the moment children can understand the concept of justice and accountability, pursuing what Paula Abood describes as "models of selfhood that don't privilege the cult of the individual, but rather are multifaceted and relationally kinetic." To be Palestinian must be about embodying an ethics of practice, a way of navigating the world, constantly assessing the balance of privileges and denials, the weight of our words, the impact of our actions on others. We can only reject the epistemological and ontological presumptions and conceits of the so-called "point zero" perspective if children understand that there is no such thing as a point zero perspective and that we are all located on an axis of power relations based on historical forces.

To come to identity as a young Palestinian is about adopting an ongoing ethical, intellectual and political praxis of locating oneself beyond the local: searching for self-knowledge, reckoning and understanding in the silenced, erased, redacted spaces of histories taught. Unlearning and then relearning what it means to be Palestinian. I share with students my own genealogy of self-knowledge. To engage in "decolonial thinking" is to trace what Mignolo characterizes as the "imperial wound" of identity: the British imperial project that supported and enabled the creation of the State of Israel and dispossessed my father from his homeland, brought my father to another British imperial project—Australia. A settler colony that can, therefore, never claim a "point zero" perspective of "neutrality." Understanding my positionality as the daughter of a dispossessed Palestinian born and living in Australia on stolen land, empowers me to embrace alternative epistemologies of identity, agitate for epistemic disobedience against the structures, laws, discourses and forces that seek our obedience, conformity, silence, erasure, dehumanization and containment.

To keep politics "out of classrooms," treat "what's happening overseas" as irrelevant, is to also elude the fact that Palestine is an international struggle. One of the most effective ways to promote despair is to make Palestinians feel isolated, to treat their cause as "just another Middle Eastern conflict," "complicated," "obscure," "intractable." This masks the intersections of state-sanctioned violence. The racial violence against indigenous, Black, racialized minorities and Palestinians is enacted through ongoing structures of race and settler colonialism which are based on a historical matrix of power. As we enter the twentieth anniversary of the war on terror, young Palestinians need the intellectual tools to grasp the imperial logic of the war on terror and connect the dots between what is happening in Gaza, or Sheikh Jarrah or the censored social media accounts of Palestinians in Israel, with their own experiences in Western contexts, such as in their classrooms. They need to understand the wider context of attempts to contain their dissent and deny them their resistance; understand what and who is served by the weaponization of the war on terror's language of "radical," "extreme," "national security," "terrorist" against particular social justice movements (Black-Palestinian solidarity activists, BDS activists, Black Lives Matters protestors, anti-racism activists, decolonial environmental advocates, youth campaigners). When young people insist on these connections, they herald ongoing and historic affinities and convergences between different movements against systemic and institutionalized state violence, systemic oppression and brutality.

Ultimately, to be Palestinian is about creating an ethics of liberation that is rooted in fighting for justice, not as a transactional gesture, a kind of "I scratch your decolonization back so you can scratch mine," but because Palestinian liberation embodies what it means to be unapologetically committed to justice, truth-telling, dignity and freedom, no matter which part of the world you are in. This is liberating. This is empowering. Which is why shared global struggles are a threat, not only to white supremacy and Zionism, but also to neo-liberal multiculturalism which limits anti-racism to diversity politics or interpersonal nondiscrimination, never decolonization, never dismantling global power structures.

* * *

My father-in-law was born in Jaffa and is buried in the unceded sovereign land of the Gadigal people. In June 1967, he walked from Palestine to Jordan. He lay down beside corpses and "played dead" to avoid capture. Uprooted from Palestine, he ended up in Australia, where he spent his life devoted to helping refugees, migrants and marginalized communities. He also spent his life laughing and making people laugh. Nadera Shalhoub-Kevorkian and Sarah Ihmoud write: "The significance of the past and its ruins starts from our responsibility to build a home for our humanity, our psyches and our communities." *Amo* embodied this responsibility. As Israel bombed Gaza and his cancer spread, we spoke more about Palestine than we did about his health. He carried Palestine in him to the very end.

In *I Saw Ramallah,* Mourid Barghouti writes: "The Palestinian has his joys, too. He has his pleasures alongside his sorrows. He has the amazing contradictions of life, because he is a living creature before being the son of the eight o'clock news."

What kind of "living creature" are we fighting for? Our political imagination and political labor are only as good as our insistence that to be Palestinian is to fight, even as we make music and dream without reference to Israel. Basma Ghalayani, in her introduction to "Palestine + 100: Stories from a Century After the Nakba," contemplates the relevance of science/speculative fiction to Palestinians: "The cruel present (and the traumatic past) has too firm a grip on Palestinian writers' imaginations for fanciful ventures into possible futures." Yet, these fanciful ventures are critical. They allow us to "practice" our "humanity," as Palestinian writer, Adania Shibli, puts it when she speaks of why words offer her a "rescue," a way to "create parallel possibilities where dehumanization thrives." There is a time for practices of aesthetic and embodied resistance and resilience—such as baking Eid cakes during war or setting up a barber"s mirror and chair in the rubble. However, there is also, crucially, a need for there to be a parallel, autonomous space to experience joy, not simply carve it out. To stop, as poet Sara Saleh writes, "writing about borders and bloodshed and war and death and home…" To dream without borders, walls, checkpoints or cages; laugh because it feels good, not because it is a defense mechanism; sing loudly to the lyrics of Aladdin with Al-Jazeera in the background. Affirm our humanity not as a reply, but because to be Palestinian is a life worthy of being celebrated and a death worthy of being grieved.

*Allah yerhamak, Amo.* We will instill in our children that their right to resist is just as important as their right to play.

SAMAH SABAWI *is a writer and scholar. She is a recipient of multiple awards including the prestigious 2020 Green Room Award for Best Writing. Her critically acclaimed theater credits include* Tales of a City by the Sea *and* THEM. *Sabawi co-edited* Double Exposure: Plays of the Jewish and Palestinian Diasporas, *winner of Patrick O'Neill Award and co-authored* I Remember My Name: Poetry by Samah Sabawi, Ramzy Baroud and Jehan Bseiso, *edited by Vacy Vlazna, winner of the Palestine Book Award. Sabawi received a Ph.D. from Victoria University for her thesis "Inheriting Exile, transgenerational trauma and the Palestinian Australian Identity."*

# WRITING IN THE BLANK SPACES

*Samah Sabawi*

I WRITE THIS on the land of the Quandamooka people, in the Redlands Coast of Queensland, Australia. I spend a lot of time here, visiting with my aging father, Abdul Karim Sabawi, a perpetual refugee who whispers poetry like sacred prayers, even as his droopy eyelids give way, and his body slumps into a restful sleep. I watch him recite revolutionary verses as he drifts into his dreams and I smile, "Free Palestine!"

I have a theory: a poet is only truly alive for as long as his poetry lives. In the same way, a cause is only truly alive for as long as there are people who believe in it. And, here, at the end of the world, I believe in Palestine and because of it, also seek the truth of the land that I actually live upon.

How did we end up in this place? Uprooted and exiled from our colonized land—now settlers and colonizers of another people's land. The irony does not escape me. We are beneficiaries of the white settler colonialist invasion and, from where I sit to write this, my eyes shamelessly consume the stretch of tropical green plantations that spread across the fields and into the arms of the tall palm trees that line up along the emerald coast. In the distance, the deep blue sea collides against a pale blue horizon that holds up the magnificent sky. How abundant and rich is this land! My heart aches at the impossible beauty that surrounds me, and at the knowledge of the historic pain of its indigenous inhabitants, magnified by their deliberate absence from view. This was once part of a thriving Aboriginal culture and way of life, but I do not think I've seen any indigenous person during any of my visits here, neither have I seen any reference to the history of these First Nations people. In this part of Queensland, I have only seen a carefree whiteness, occasionally dotted with freckles and adorned with eyes that mirror the greens and blues of this landscape.

I do my own research and I learn that the Quandamooka people lived here, that they farmed and fished for tens of thousands of years in villages around these coastal areas, islands and campsites. This ended when the Europeans came in the early 1800s and began decades of ethnic cleansing and genocide that almost erased all presence of these native nations. Will this happen to us in Palestine? Will we be erased, too?

The answer lies in the persistent need to confront erasure with the demonstrated presence of culture and memory. For Aboriginal and Torres Strait Island people here, as well as for Palestinians in the homeland, it is impossible to imagine moving forward without acknowledgement of the traumatic events of the past and removal of the shackles of oppression from the present, in order to begin the journey of reconciliation into a just and peaceful co-existence.

For this reason, I must do my part. I acknowledge that I, the victim of settler colonialism and erasure in my home country, an exiled spirit severed from the earth that I belong to, that I live on stolen colonized land, and I pledge my solidarity and pay my respect to the elders past, present and emerging of the Quandamooka people and all Aboriginal and Torres Strait Islanders, all survivors, all freedom fighters, and I thank them for the privilege of being on their land, the land from where I write this.

## Trauma and Exile

I am Generation *Naksa*, born in Gaza in 1967, wrapped in a shawl and whisked away in a baby basket from our home in Tuffah, all the way into exile. I am the age of exile.

I uttered my first words and took my first steps in a refugee camp in Jordan before we moved to Saudi Arabia and from there, to Australia. If not for a twist of fate, I could still be one of the two million Palestinians trapped today in the refugee camps in Jordan, or one of the two million Palestinians trapped in Gaze and surviving its siege and periodic Israeli bombardment campaigns. This feeling of having the privilege of having survived that my cousins and loved ones do not enjoy, has lurked like a shadow, following me throughout my life's triumphs and tribulations. A source of shame and guilt, it inhabits my thoughts and actions, manifesting itself in my advocacy, poetry and theatrical productions. This shadow, my lifelong companion, sometimes inspires me; at other times, especially during the bombardments of Gaza, it leaves me traumatized and utterly devastated.

The first time I became aware of the presence of this shadow, I was 14 years old, standing in Melbourne's City Square in 1982, protesting the massacres of the Sabra and Shatila refugee camps in Lebanon. I had been to Lebanon when I was seven. I knew people there. I played with children *from* there. My uncle, Abdel Muti, who was later martyred in Gaza, *was there*. He told me once, as he scooped me up into his strong loving arms, that he was "fighting for freedom." *He* was there. *They* were there. And *there* was a massacre.

On the day of the protest, I saw photos of Palestinian families for the first time on the front page of *The Age* newspaper. At any other time, I might have been excited to see this. Not this time. Not like this. The families were not sitting in a circle around a tray of rice and meat. They were not standing facing the camera in their Eid clothes. They were not dancing at a wedding. The families on the front page of *The Age* newspaper were piled on top of each other, lifeless, limbs drooping, blood dripping, mouths open, bellies bloated … and, worst of all … worthless. They were worthless in the eyes of the world that I had just become a part of. Damn it! This was my new world, my new Australia, the country that gave me citizenship, dignity and worth: how could it care so little about the life of Palestinian refugees and align itself with the butchers? For a teenager, desperately trying to belong, that realization was detrimental. I knew, at that moment, I would never belong.

The most recent time this shadow appeared to taunt me is right now—as I write these words, the bombs are falling on Gaza, yet again. I'm riddled with fear at what might happen to my cousins and my in-laws and all those beautiful children whom I know. How is it that, in the eyes of the Western world, I, as a citizen of a settler colonial nation, have more human worth than they do, my relatives and loved ones, who are besieged refugees? Guilt drapes its shadow over me, my chest tightens, my heart races and my tears fall. Here we go again. Trauma. Do I have a right to claim trauma in the luxury of exile?

## The Absence of the *Nakba* from the "Trauma Genre"

When I did my doctoral research,[23] the question of trauma in exile was foremost on my mind. How is it that we, as Palestinians in exile, some of us never having lived in Palestine, inherit this agonizing sense of collective trauma? And how much does this trauma contribute to our understanding of our Palestinian identity and to the urgency of our advocacy?

It only took a few months at the start of my doctoral research to come to an astonishing, yet not surprising, discovery. The Palestinian experience of dispossession and trauma in 1948, the *Nakba,* which literally means "catastrophe," the most significant traumatic event in Palestinian history, is absent from the "trauma genre." In fact, research by Rosemary Sayigh[24] confirms that the most highly cited literature on war and collective trauma excludes any mention of the *Nakba* or the larger ongoing Palestinian experience of trauma. According to Sayigh, the theoretical conceptualization of the "trauma genre" peaked in the early 1990s, with studies by theorists such as Caruth,[25] Felman,[26] and Felman and Laub.[27] She argues that these studies focused, at first, on the Holocaust, then expanded to addressing the suffering of peoples from around the world—except for the suffering of Palestinians. Sayigh offers a critique of these studies, challenging

---

23 Samah Sabawi, *Inheriting Exile: Transgenerational Trauma and Palestinian-Australian Identity,* Ph.D. thesis, Victoria University, 2020.

24 Rosemary Sayigh, "On the exclusion of the Palestinian Nakba from the 'Trauma Genre.'" *Journal of Palestine Studies* (2013) 43(1), 51–60.

25 Cathy Caruth, *Unclaimed Experience: Trauma and the possibility of history* (Baltimore, John Hopkins University Press, 1991).

26 Shoshana Felman, "In an era of testimony: Claude Lanzmann's Shoah," Yale French Studies 79 (1991), 39–81.

27 Shoshana Felman and Dori Laub, *Testimony: Crises of Witnessing in Literature, Psychoanalysis and History* (New York/London: Routledge, 1992).

their claim of "universality and inclusiveness" on the basis of their exclusion of Palestinian suffering, and raises the question of whether the "trauma genre" sets up "cultural frames of reference" to what is suffering and what is not and, by extension, to who is suffering and who is not. She notes that the "glaring absence" of the *Nakba* within the "trauma genre" in Western academic research is a phenomenon that both reflects and reinforces "the marginalization of Palestinian claims to justice," highlighting the notion that the exclusion of Palestinian suffering from the "trauma genre" is part of the political and cultural myopia which we see in relation to many aspects that concern Palestine and the Palestinian people. This myopia is substantially constructed or enabled by the Orientalist and colonialist representations of Palestinians and Arabs.

In fact, Western power structures, and especially Western academia, have played a major role in the violence perpetrated against the Palestinian people. This was clear in the works of the late Palestinian icon, Edward Said.[28] In his 1978 book, *Orientalism*, a foundational text for postcolonial studies, Edward Said argued that early scholarly writing from America and Europe was misleading due to its presentation of stereotypical and inaccurate depictions of the East, which hinders the true understanding of its cultures and also enables the exploitation of its resources. Said made the point that such stereotypes were deliberate and vital for the West, serving not only as a rationalization of colonial rule, but also as a means to justify it in advance by painting a picture of an Eastern world that needed to be rescued, civilised and accultured.

Said's writing on the theory of Orientalism was sparked by the Western media coverage of the Arab Israeli war, as well as his own personal life and experiences as a Palestinian-American. In a 1998 video interview,[29] he spoke of the great disparity between the representations of Arabs and Palestinians in most scholarly works and his own lived experience as a Palestinian and an Arab. These

---

28 Edward W. Said, *Orientalism* (New York: Pantheon Books, 1978).

29 Edward W. Said, "Edward Said on Orientalism," interview by Sut Jhally, University of Massachusetts–Amherst, 1998.

representations created fixed images of a stagnant un-developing region, an Arab world that is frozen in time and "falls outside of history." It was a world which he, as an Arab who grew up in that region, did not recognize, but projected a vision of one that was necessary for the creation of an oppositional "Other" for Europe.

Said defines Orientalism as both research and writings about the Orient from a particular Western-focused perspective that presents itself as objective knowledge, but which is driven largely by the impetus to support and maintain a discourse of racial superiority in furtherance of colonial/imperial interests. For example, American Orientalism, according to Said, is ideologically driven and highly politicized in order to support America's interests in the oil resources of the Middle East as well as to prop up its ally, Israel.

Seeing the Palestinians through an Orientalist lens makes it impossible to understand the context of the Palestinian/Israeli conflict yet, for decades, this was the only perspective on offer for Western scholars. Unfortunately, this perspective still persists, allowing the disappearance of an event as significant as the *Nakba* from the "trauma genre" of Western academia.

## Growing up outside the "Moral Communities"

Sayigh proposes two theoretical frameworks to consider when trying to understand how this disappearance, this erasure, is possible: The first, she suggests, is that Palestinian suffering falls outside what literary scholar David Morris calls "moral communities." Morris[30] builds on the late philosopher Tom Regan's term "moral communities"[31] in order to illustrate the ways in which writers often work within exclusive social parameters determined by culture and history. These parameters often do not include stories of suffering of others, who are deemed to fall outside of their defined "moral

---

30 David B. Morris, "About Suffering: Voice, Genre, and Moral Community," *Daedalus* 125, no. 1 (1996): 25–45. Accessed July 7, 2021 at http://www.jstor.org/stable/20027352.

31 Tom Regan, *The Three Generation: Reflections on the coming revolution (*Philadelphia: Temple University Press, 1991).

community." Israel's lobby groups have, for decades, acted as the gatekeepers of the Western world's "moral community." In order to justify Israel's past and ongoing crimes, the Palestinians needed to be seen to fall outside of the world's "moral community."

I have experienced this first-hand whenever I have tried to present stories of the Palestinians to the wider public. The attack was most severe in 2016 when the Israeli lobby group, B'nai B'rith, launched a campaign led by Dvir Abramovich to remove my play, *Tales of a City by the Sea* from the Victorian Certificate of Education (VCE) drama playlist. Their heavy-handed approach led to an interruption of the Budget Hearings of the Victorian State Parliament, as the Opposition confronted the government with their demands. It was surreal; the Victorian Opposition actually "used a budget hearing to attack the Government" over the inclusion of what they claimed was an "anti-Israel" play[32] on the VCE curriculum. This made my modest piece of independent theater, a Palestinian love story set in Gaza, to be amongst the few, if any, independent theater productions to be debated in the Victorian State Parliament.

For days, while the controversy raged, I was talked about but never talked to by the mainstream media, who readily gave a platform to the Zionist lobby but never thought to invite me to speak. This event could have been another story of great anguish and injustice, but in fact, it turned into a positive story, a sign that the times are changing. For the first time, this Palestinian writer did not have to fight her battles alone. Australian theater-makers, artists, writers and friends spoke up in defense of my work, and my right to tell a story about my people, without running the story through the Israeli filters for approval. "Censorship" was the word many used in describing the pressure the Zionist lobby was creating. The play remained on the VCE curriculum and won two Victoria Drama Awards. The magnificent and brave La Mama Theatre was unfazed by the

---

32 Stephanie Anderson, "'Anti-Israel' play in VCE curriculum prompts attack on Government," *ABCNews,* May 10, 2016, https://www.abc.net.au/news/2016-05-10/anti-israel-play-in-vce-curriculum-government-questioned/7402176

"controversy" and their support was overwhelming. *Tales of a City by the Sea* sold out its entire season, with nightly standing ovations, before going on a national and international tour. As of the time of writing this, the play has had more than 100 performances around the world and has been studied by thousands of students worldwide.

When I finally responded to the false accusations leveled at me in an opinion piece published in *The Age*, I wrote: "The problem with this play is not that it may dehumanize Israelis—it does not. The problem is it humanizes the Palestinians. Apparently, for some, this is too much to handle."[33]

## Palestinians as "Ungrievable" Populations

The second framework to explain the erasure and absence of the *Nakba* from the "trauma genre," according to Sayigh, can be found in Judith Butler's idea that "forms of racism [which are] instituted and active at the level of perception, tend to produce iconic versions of populations who are eminently grievable, and others whose loss is no loss, and who remain ungrievable."[34]

We see this all the time: Palestinian children who are pulled from under the rubble of Israel's wars are nameless, their stories seldom told, while Israeli deaths are given the dignity of a name and a story. Palestinians are seen through the eyes of Western media and scholars as "ungrievable" populations who fall outside of their "moral community."

I look back at the 14-year-old teenage me. She is standing with her "Free Palestine" placard, protesting the massacres of Sabra and Shatila in 1982 in Melbourne City Square. She did not need to do a doctoral research to discover that Palestinians are deemed "ungrievable." She could see it on the front page of *The Age*

---

33 Samah Sabawi, "Vision of everyday life in Palestine too bleak for some," *The Sydney Morning Herald,* June 2, 2016, https://www.smh.com.au/opinion/vision-of-everyday-life-in-palestine-too-bleak-for-some-20160602-gp9tmc.html

34 Judith P. Butler, *Frames of War: When is life grievable?* (New York: Verso, 2009).

newspaper, in the nameless Palestinian dead and the bloated corpses that had no stories. She could read it in the editorials that mentioned something about Palestinian "Terrorists" and Israel's right to defend itself. She could hear it in the voices of the news anchors who invited Israeli "experts" to explain the "conflict." She knew it. It was her life. I wish I could go back in time and put my arms around her and tell her that this will change. She just needs to be patient.

## The "Guardianship" of Palestine in the "Exile Milieu"

Simone Weil wrote that being rooted is "the most important and least recognized need of the human soul."[35] Weil explains that we establish roots by belonging to a place, a community, a culture and a history that "preserves in living shape certain particular treasures of the past and certain particular expectations for the future." This process of preservation is often the first casualty when a people are dispossessed and uprooted. Reviving it becomes both a necessity for the survival of those dispossessed, and an obstacle to the process of planting new roots. The hearts of exiles, Weil contended, are so "irresistibly turned towards the homeland in distress that few emotional resources are left for friendship for the land they happen to be living in."

Edward Said wrote about the formation and nourishment of the Palestinian national identity in the "exile milieu."[36] He described exile as "a jealous state," a condition of "estrangement" and "alienation" that guards its existence in order to establish "an exaggerated sense of group solidarity" and "a passionate hostility to outsiders" (2001, p. 141). I learned, growing up, that embracing my Palestinian identity was a duty, a conscious political decision, a familial obligation and a minimum gesture of solidarity with loved ones who are still trapped in Israel's Occupation.

---

35 S. Weil, *The Need for Roots: Prelude to a Declaration of Duties towards Mankind* (A.Wills, Trans.) (New York and London: Routledge, 1952).

36 Edward W. Said, *Reflections on Exile: And Other Literary and Cultural Essays* (London: Granta Books, 2001).

However, while identifying as a Palestinian might be a "conscious decision" and a "political" choice, I would argue that for the greater majority of Palestinians outside the homeland, myself included, being Palestinian is not so much a decision but rather simply a reflection of who we actually are. Palestinian mothers laboring over the perfect *Maqluba* while recounting stories of growing up in Palestine are not consciously keeping the cause alive. They are sharing a part of themselves, revealing their past and passing on the treasure trove of knowledge they inherited from past generations. When my sisters got married, my mother did not insist on having a Palestinian wedding to spite the Zionists, or to sing songs as old as the sycamore tree in her home in Palestine in order to wipe Israel from the map. She insisted on celebrating in the manner that she knew. This is her reality. Her world. Her memories. And she is Palestinian. When I joined the *Dabke* dance group at the Palestinian Arabic Club in Broadmeadows in my early teens in Australia, it was not because I had read Edward Said's theories on exile and decided to nourish my national identity in the "exile milieu" through dance moves. I did it to socialize with others who shared my interests and who understood what it felt like to grow up in families like mine. This is to say that Palestinian families outside the homeland do not see their Palestinian identity as a political choice but rather as an inescapable part of who we are. What, I believe, *politicizes* the Palestinian identity is the negation of our right to identify as Palestinian.

Zionists have often made the argument that the Palestinian identity is a fiction that is constructed or created only to destroy Zionism. Israel's fourth Prime Minister, Golda Meir, infamously said, "It was not as if there was a Palestinian people in Palestine and we came and threw them out and took their country away from them. They did not exist."[37] More recently, Ted Lapkin,[38] the director

---

37 Judd Yadid, "Israel's Iron Lady Unfiltered: 17 Golda Meir quotes on her 117th birthday: the wise, the whimsical an the downright polemical," *Haaretz,* May 3, 2015, https://www.haaretz.com/.premium-17-golda-meir-quotes-on-her-117th-birthday-1.5356683

38 Ted Lapkin, "Palestinian national identity and the roadblock to peace," Opinion, *Australian Broadcasting Corporation,* September 3, 2015, https://

of Public Affairs for the Zionist Federation of Australia, wrote this response to an article I had published in the ABC about being Palestinian: "The construction of a Palestinian something-from-nothing constitutes the most remarkable triumph of fable over fact in living diplomatic memory."

This is the discourse and the environment in which I grew up concerning my hyphenated identity. There was no Palestine on any of the maps in my high school. There was no Palestinian food on any of the menus in restaurants. There were no Palestinian voices or characters in any of the shows or movies on television. There was no mention of Palestinians—only now and then, Arab terrorists bent on destroying Israel. The only place where Palestine existed was in our homes, at our dinner tables and within our community.

## Writing Palestine into the Blank Spaces of Erasure

It is, indeed, remarkable how we Palestinians have filled up the blank spaces of erasure with a proud sense of identity and fierce resistance. Unlike families whose homes were filled with memory objects that tell their stories: a grandmother's sewing machine, a grandfather's old record player, family heirlooms and libraries filled with books and historic archives, I belong to a generation that had all of these—everything—taken away. I belong to the Palestinians whose parents fled or were exiled with only the shirts on their backs. As a result, I, we, have become masters at reconstructing memory, not through the presence of objects, but rather through their absence. After our exile, I spent the first ten years of my remembered life in Saudi Arabia, a desert country with endless sand dunes, listening to stories and poetry that described what my parents had left behind in Palestine. These stories and poems fed my imagination and my yearning for a place I did not live in, but one that I remember. A place I know. Most vivid in my constructed "memory" is our garden in Palestine. My parents spoke about the pomegranate tree, the jasmine bush, the thorny cactus that birthed the sweetest fruit, the sycamore

---

www.abc.net.au/news/2015-08-28/lapkin-palestinian-national-identity-and-the-roadblock-to-peace/6732462

tree, the vegetable garden … a life that seemed so beautiful and full of color against the backdrop of a Saudi desert city where nothing grew. But this stark contrast only added to the pain of exile, the trauma of a life disrupted, a family uprooted and grandparents that were left locked behind high walls. Forgetting is not an option. Only through remembering is our life worth living.

We cannot move on while our loved ones are under falling bombs, under siege and under Occupation. So we do not. And we pass this on to our children. This blessing and curse. And they pass it on to theirs. We pass on the guardianship of Palestine through songs, stories and poetry and we know that generation after generation of Palestinians will fill in the blank spaces of erasure. We saw this during May of 2021, the Unity Intifada. We saw a young generation of Palestinians from around the world, born and raised in exile, lead protests calling for unity and solidarity and resistance. My WhatsApp notifications were going through the roof and my heart brimmed with pride when I discovered that, in my circle of activists who were doing the things that mattered, I was one of the oldest. Most of them were in their twenties and thirties, born and raised outside the homeland. This is Generation Exile and they are writing their stories with ferocity into the blank spaces of erasure; together they will break through the boundaries of the "moral communities" of the world. I can still hear them chanting, as I did decades ago, "from the river to the sea, Palestine will be free." Such incurable hope and determination can never be defeated.

## The Path Forward

When Zionism began to grow as a political movement in the late 19th century, the representation of Palestine without its indigenous inhabitants was a "trademark of the Zionist imagination."[39] By the early 1900s, the Zionist movement adopted the slogan, "A Land

---

39 I. Nassar, "Remapping Palestine and the Palestinians: Decolonizing and research," *Comparative Studies of South Asia, Africa and the Middle East* (2003) 23 (1–2), 149–151.

without a People for a People without a Land."[40] This striking ability to see the land and not its people is not unfamiliar in the history of imperial wars and conquests. In fact, in Australia, a similar phrase had been used—*Terra Nullius*—meaning "a land that belongs to no one," to justify the British invasion and dispossession of the indigenous Aboriginal population.[41] How do we move past that?

Truth-telling and acknowledgment of past atrocities and wrongdoings are foundational blocks for reconciliation, and I need to reconcile my identities, my Palestinian and my Australian selves. While I listen to the voices of the indigenous peoples of this land, I can imagine a future where Palestinians and Israelis can co-exist in peace. However, this is not going to happen any time soon, because peace cannot be founded on injustices and denial of past crimes. First, there needs to be a complete collapse of the structures of apartheid and oppression, before we can get to the next sweet phase, one of truth-telling and reconciliation.

Archbishop Desmond Tutu, former Chairman of South Africa's Truth and Reconciliation Commission in the post-apartheid era, points out that the process of forgiveness "requires acknowledgment on the part of the perpetrator that they have committed an offense."[42]

But Israel has not offered any acknowledgment; instead, it continues on the path of more discrimination, oppression, human rights violations, ethnic cleansing and apartheid without any accountability. This is why the Boycotts Divestments and Sanctions movement is a necessary tool of resistance. Much like South Africa, Israel, too, needs to feel the pressure of the international community to stop its crimes of ethnic cleansing and apartheid. Israelis have to recognize that they have colonized all the land of Palestine, and that this colonization needs to end. Ethical decolonization is the only way

---

40 Edward W. Said, *The Question of Palestine* (New York: Vintage, 1992).

41 Henry Reynolds, *The Other Side of the Frontier: Aboriginal resistance to European invasion of Australia* (University of New South Wales Press, 1981).

42 Desmond Tutu, *The Forgiveness Project,* https://www.theforgivenessproject.com/desmond-tutu

forward to usher in an era of freedom, justice and equality, in a one secular democratic state on all the land of Palestine.

As for me, I believe we all wage resistance using our best skills. Mine is writing. So, I will continue to write. I write the names of the nameless and tell the stories that are deliberately untold. I write to counter the Zionist erasure and, while I do that, I am mindful of my privilege as an exile whose homeland is colonized and who lives on colonized land. I write with the awareness that here, in Australia, and there, in Palestine, our struggle is one. For me to find peace on this stretch of earth, I must open my heart to the truth of its history and its violence against its indigenous people. I write with that Palestinian incurable hope, and I feel the ground swell with the energy of the Palestinian youth from around the globe, chanting in one voice "from the river to the sea, Palestine will be free!"

# SECTION II

# THE MANY FACES OF RESISTANCE

FATHER MANUEL MUSALLAM *is a Catholic priest, political activist and writer. He is iconic in his native Palestine. Born in 1938, in the town of Birzeit in the central West Bank, Musallam studied philosophy and theology to become a priest in 1963. He has served various parishes, from Jordan's Zarqa and Anjara in the 1960s, to Palestine's Jenin (1970–1975), Zababdeh (1975–1995) and finally Gaza (1995–2009). Father Musallam chaired the Palestinian Department of Christians, the Palestinian Independent Commission to Pursue Israeli War Criminals in 2002, and Gaza's Islamic-Christian Forum, among various peacekeeping roles which, ultimately, earned him the Catholic title of Monsignor in 2006. Father Musallam retired to his birthplace, Birzeit, in 2009. His fierce pro-Palestinian advocacy continues to this day.*

# BLESSED ARE THOSE WHO RESIST
# A Christian Vision for Liberation[1]

*Father Manuel Musallam*

A STORM OF METEORS rained upon Palestine by the British Mandate has burned everything sacred in our Holy Land. Church and mosques, these holiest of spaces, were burned. The olive trees, the holiest of trees, were burned. White phosphorus struck our towns, villages and refugee camps. Humans, the holiest of creatures, were burned. Children, the holiest of humans, were burned. The very dignity of the Palestinian Arabs—estranged from their land and their people—was burned. Truth and justice, too, were burned when the land was supposedly "promised" to those from the far ends of the globe, but not to its own inhabitants. In fact, our very humanity was burned, when the Israeli army and armed Jewish settlers preyed on us like wolves.

I was only nine years old when Zionist gangs invaded our Palestine.[2] The Haganah, Irgun, Stern Gang and Palmach took over our land by force, massacring our people, and burning our fields, orchards and homes. They demolished, killed and expelled as many as they could of our people. Instead of punishing the perpetrators, the United Nations offered the invaders, who then owned only 7%

---

1 This essay was originally written in Arabic and was translated by Nahed Elrayes.

2 Saleh Abdel Jawad, "Colonial Anthropology: The Haganah Village Intelligence Archives," *Palestine Studies,* Issue no. 68, 2016, https://www.palestine-studies.org/sites/default/files/jq-articles/Pages_from_JQ_68_-_Saleh_Abdel_Jawad_0.pdf.

of the land, 56% of Palestine, leaving us with the meager remainder. We refused. We had to refuse. Zionist leaders clashed; David Ben-Gurion accepted the offer while Menachem Begin declared the partition invalid, claiming that all of Palestine, including Transjordan, belonged to the Jewish people forever.[3]

Eventually, Israel was founded upon the ruins of our destroyed homeland.[4] Our properties were declared to be "absentee" property, illegally appropriated by the new state. The Palestinian refugees who were expelled and forced to flee their homes were and to this day are denied their right of return, although this right is enshrined in international law. Most of our villages were fully or partially destroyed. The season's harvest was left unharvested as hundreds of thousands of Palestinian peasants were never allowed to even salvage their crops. New Jewish settlements and towns quickly sprang up in place of our cities and villages.

The *Nakba* was upon us, a catastrophic event in our history, like no other. Our struggle with Israel had begun and continues to this day. For us Palestinians, it is a struggle for life or death, for survival or annihilation. It is not even a struggle for peace, but for the very preservation of our civilization and our existence; it is a struggle for our people's sanctity, their humanity and their inalienable right to justice.

## My Story

I was born amidst that Zionist-wrought chaos. I was surrounded by extreme poverty, real hunger and deprivation of all kinds. However, I was born into a family that also gave generously to the struggle and to those in need. Our olive trees, vineyards and fig trees were also generous, and helped my family uphold its dignity when so many families could not. At a young age, I was breast-fed with courage, patience, persistence, hard work, generosity and defiance. My mother

---

3 Jorgen Jensehaugen, "Terra Morata: The West Bank in Menachem Begin's Worldview," *Contemporary Levant,* 5:1 (2020), 54–63, DOI: 10.1080/20581831.2020.1710675.

4 Ilan Pappé, *The Ethnic Cleansing of Palestine* (Oxford: Oneworld, 2006).

and father raised me with the tools to confront the humiliation that awaited our people at every turn. Yes, I was born into hardship, but that very hardship taught me to be stubborn in my resistance.

I remember being only five years old when, in 1943, I saw a movie in Jerusalem about war. In the movie, I saw soldiers leaping from military vehicles and hiding in the trenches. I heard the sound of cannons exploding. It was my first experience with this kind of violence. I was afraid. I closed my eyes and eventually fell asleep in my uncle Yakub's arms. That was not a real war, but a depiction of events that were transpiring in Europe around that time. The movie, however still planted the first seed of war in my heart and mind. The 1948 war, though, was different.

The Zionist war against Palestine was all too real. Not even children could shut their eyes to avoid the horrors we experienced during those days. Refugees poured into my town of Birzeit, bringing with them awful stories of horrific massacres, of Deir Yassin, Qibya, and Kafr Qasim. When news arrived of the martyrdom of top Palestinian commander, Abd-al-Qadir al-Husayni, the entire town was devasted.[5]

Al-Husayni's death left a mark on me, though I was only ten years old. However, that was not the end of the terrible news. It was only the beginning of numerous tragedies that have never ceased.

When, in 1967, all of Jerusalem fell to the invaders, I remember banging my head against the wall. This feeling of despair has defined much of my life. The tragedy of the homeland awakened numerous feelings in me. It shook me, and it continues to shake me to my very core. Yet, I did not allow despair to define me. I had to take a stance. Numerous images of violence followed me, as they followed most Palestinians in, and sometimes out of, the Palestinian homeland. I remember watching Israeli bombs fall near the fedayeen and army base in Ajloun, Jordan, in 1967. As I ran towards the nuns in my parish to offer some help, I found them kneeling down, weeping in

---

5 "Fayṣal ibn ʿAbd al-Qādir al-Ḥusaynī," *Encyclopedia Britannica.* Accessed May 27, 2021 at https://www.britannica.com/biography/Faysal-ibn-Abd-al-Qadir-al-Husayni.

terror. Missiles began to fall all around us. Just meters away, trees were lighted on fire. A nearby orchard was completely obliterated. On that day, we, too, almost perished.

Similar experiences, though with different victims, accompanied me throughout the first uprising, the Intifada of 1987 and again, in the Second Intifada of 2000. During both popular revolts, I proudly played my part as a Christian Palestinian leader in the defense of my people.

Like millions of Palestinians in Gaza, I suffered the horrors of the 2008–09 war and massacre, but I never relented in speaking out against injustice. I turned the shrapnel of Israeli army missiles into a Cross. My struggle, my pain and my resistance have grounded me in my identity like nothing else:

I am a Palestinian Arab Christian. I know that the world has falsely robbed me of my land. I will struggle with the rest of the Palestinian resisters for the liberation of my holy home. I will resist from a religious standpoint, stemming from the theology of my church, and my strong conviction in this theology. I also fully comprehend the political reality that the Zionist entity represents a hybrid form of colonial conquest, with built-in political and economic interests, falsely dressed in religious garments. Therefore, as a Palestinian Arab, I will also resist from a patriotic standpoint. My patriotism is reinforced by my people's poverty, pain and humiliation, and their diaspora. This is my story, the story of my family, the story of my people.

## The Theology of the "Promised Land"

As a Christian, especially as a Palestinian Christian, I refuse to subscribe to the notion that Palestine was promised to the Jews at the expense of my people. From 1951 to 1963, I studied philosophy, theology and the sacred Testaments at the Latin Patriarchate Seminary in Beit Jala, Palestine. In deciphering these holy texts, I began to understand how the Zionist Movement manipulated biblical verses to lay a religious claim over my homeland. One of the most interpreted—or misinterpreted—verses is Deuteronomy 14:2,[6] which states, "For you are a people holy to the Lord your God. Out of all the peoples on the face of the earth, the Lord has chosen you to be his treasured possession." From these few words, the notion arose that the Jewish people are the "chosen," "holy" and "eternal" people of the promised land. For them, this meant that the fate of my people, marginalized and dispossessed, was sealed forever.

This notion persists despite the fact that, with the advent of Christianity, Apostle Paul had made it clear in Galatians 3:16[7] that God's promise was directed to Abraham and his seed, drawing attention to the singular: "Scripture does not say 'and to seeds,' meaning many people, but 'and to your seed,' meaning one person, who is Christ." Paul elaborated in Romans 9:6–9,[8] "It is not as though God's word had failed. For not all who are descended from Israel are Israel. Nor because they are his descendants are they all Abraham's children. On the contrary, it is through Isaac that your offspring will be reckoned."

As if this was not clear enough, Augustine further explained in Saint Augustine (Letter 196),[9] that "the Church is heir to the promises God made to Israel. Thus, it is the new Israel which eagerly seeks to reach the heavenly Jerusalem." Historical Christian doctrines have thus made it clear that the Promised Land is not for the Jews alone, but the children of God's Promise; that is, those who believe in the faith of Abraham.

Starting sometime in the Middle Ages, various churches became concerned with Millennialism: the belief, stemming from the Book of Revelation that, in the Apocalypse, Christ will return to Earth and remain there for a thousand years, until the Day of Judgement. These prophecies were centered largely around Revelation 20:1–3,[10] "And I saw an angel coming down out of heaven, having the key to

---

6 Deuteronomy, 14:2, NIV.

7 Galatians, 3:16, NIV.

8 Romans, 9:6–9, NIV.

9 Saint Augustine of Hippo (354–430), *The Works of Saint Augustine: A Translation for the 21st Century* (Brooklyn, NY: New City Press, 1990, 2019).

10 Revelation, 20:1–3, NIV.

the Abyss and holding in his hand a great chain; [he threw Satan] into the Abyss, and locked and sealed it over him, to keep him from deceiving the nations anymore until the thousand years were ended."

In the seventh century, these prophecies took on a political nature, one which morphed, many centuries later, into something else entirely. This is the genesis of today's notion of a Jewish return to Palestine, which has for long been championed by Christian fundamentalists and, eventually, Zionist Christians. For them, the Jews had to return as a prerequisite to the return of Jesus himself. The prophecy led to an even more sinister interpretation. According to Christian fundamentalist thought, the returning Jesus will lead a war against the forces of evil, one in which two-thirds of all Jews will perish and the remaining third converts to Christianity. Only then, can Christ rule the world as king for a thousand years.

Politicians seized on this Messianic notion. As early as 1655, English General Oliver Cromwell drew a link between Christian fundamentalism and Britain's strategic interests.[11] This connection would endure and would eventually lead to the Balfour Declaration in November 1917, which asserted that "His Majesty's government view with favor the establishment in Palestine of a national home for the Jewish people, and will use their best endeavors to facilitate the achievement of this object…"[12]

Despite the fact that politics and Millennialism were finding a common ground, the Catholic Church refused to accommodate what it perceived as a dangerous precedent regarding the status of the Holy Land. Though unofficially, the Catholic Church announced its position on Christian Zionism as early as May 1897—coincidentally, the year that the leader of the Zionist Movement, Theodore Herzl, convened the First Zionist Congress in Basel, Switzerland. This position was articulated in an article published by its official newspaper, *La Civiltà*

---

11 Jeffrey R. Collins, "The Church Settlement of Oliver Cromwell," *History* 87, No. 285 (2002): 18–40. Accessed June 13, 2021 at http://www.jstor.org/stable/24425701

12 Leonard Stein, *The Balfour Declaration* (Jerusalem: Magnes Press, Hebrew University, 1983).

*Cattolica,*[13] which asserted that "the rebuilding of Jerusalem as the center of a reconfigured Israeli state contradicts the prophecies of Christ himself, who told us that Jerusalem ['shall be trodden down of the Gentiles, until the times of the Gentiles be fulfilled.']"

The Catholic position became more pronounced in response to the Balfour Declaration. Then, Pope Benedict XV declared, "No to the supremacy of Jews over the Holy Land."[14] Furthermore, in 1944, the Congregation for the Doctrine of the Faith announced its explicit rejection of Millennialism—declaring that there would not be a 1000-year period between the age of the Church and the end of the world.[15]

## What Palestine Means

But as Palestinians, Christians and Muslims, we are not bound by the politicized manipulation of God's words. For us, this is an issue of a stolen land and a dispossessed people. Palestine is our mother, robbed of her children, and we are deprived of her tenderness. We, the people of Palestine, are one. We belong to one civilization and are united by one destiny. For me, Al-Aqsa is Christian and the Resurrection belongs equally to my Muslim brothers and sisters. Every martyred Muslim is a martyred Christian and every martyred Christian is a Muslim. Our youth are killed by the same Israeli occupier. Our homes are demolished by the same Israeli military bulldozer. Our land is stolen, holy shrines defiled, families separated, people ethnically cleansed by the same Israeli perpetrator.

Zionists often claim that Palestinian Arabs were never a cohesive people. Such fraudulent claims were designed to deceive

---

13 *La Civiltà cattolica. La dispersione d'Israello pel mondo moderno,* reviewed in *Rivista Internazionale Di Scienze Sociali E Discipline Ausiliarie* 14, no. 54 (1897): 221–22. Accessed June 13, 2021 at http://www.jstor.org/stable/41570188

14 Silvio Ferrari, "The Vatican, the Palestine Question and the Internationalization of Jerusalem (1918–1948)," *Rivista Di Studi Politici Internazionali* 60, no. 4 (240) (1993): 550–68. Accessed June 13, 2021 at http://www.jstor.org/stable/42737184

15 Cf Sant'Offizio, *Decretum de millenarismo* (19 luglio 1944): DS 3839.

the world into thinking that Palestine was an empty land. But the 500 destroyed towns and villages during the *Nakba* in 1947–48 were a testament to the fact that the land was inhabited.[16] Despite the dispossession of our people, the endurance of our language, identity and culture all refute the claim that we are anything other than a Palestinian people, grounded in history and spirituality. The earth and its people are one, just as the rose and its perfume are one.

However, in order for the earth and the people to unify once again, for the rose to acquire its perfume once more, we Palestinians, Christians and Muslims, must continue to resist. As a Christian, resistance for me is as much of a duty as it is for the Muslims. True, God has told me to "love your enemy"[17], but He has also told my enemy, "Do not kill."[18] God has taught me that "whoever asks for your garment, give him your garment," but He has also commanded my enemy, "You shall not steal" and "You shall not covet" the possessions of another.[19]

As a student of history and the Bible, I believe that justice is taken, not given. Justice for my people—the reclaiming of our stolen land, the Right of Return for our refugees, the freedom of all Palestinians—must supersede the unconditional existence and safety of Israel. This is true because Israel's position is not that of self-defense. It is merely defending its military Occupation of Palestine. Those who accuse us of terrorism must be reminded that we fight back, not to occupy cities, but to liberate them from the occupiers. We are the historical caretakers of this land; we are the holders of justice, history, and the civilization and heritage of Palestine. Israel is guided by an insatiable colonial appetite while we are guided by love, truth and freedom.

As a Palestinian Christian Arab, I feel the injustice hanging over me, over my people, but I will not let injustice reduce me into a state of despair, but rather strengthen my resolve in fighting for my

---

16 Ilan Pappé, 2006.

17 Matthew, 5:44, NIV.

18 Exodus, 20:13, NIV.

19 Romans, 13:9, N.

people's rights so that, someday, they may return from exile. We want our children to be set free from Israeli prisons. We want to build their future and, ultimately, develop a strong economy.

I do not resist for my own sake but for my earth, for my people, for my nation, for my holy city and my faith. Justice can never be truly attained without the soil of Jerusalem, the beating heart of Palestine, the true representation of its collective identity and the reservoir of its memory. We Palestinians, Christians and Muslims, are not against Jews or Judaism. Rather, we are the avowed enemies of Zionism, colonialism, Christian fundamentalism, and injustice in all its forms. Israel has subjected our people to mass murder, unrelenting theft and displacement. They have burned our mosques, our churches, our homes and even our children. This is why we resist Israel. If we do not resist, we sell our birthright, our civilization, our heritage, our Holy City of Jerusalem, the pain that our people have endured—in fact, our very sanctity.

Israel has snatched joy from our hearts. Joy is peace. Peace is stability, order and justice. If all these values are absent, law is also absent. Without law, we enter into an age of monsters. We, Palestinians, are fighting these monsters every day. One day, we hope to liberate our land, so that joy, peace, order, stability and justice can be restored. For as long as we are denied our rights, we intend to deny our occupiers their peace as well.

The world may have abandoned us. International law may have failed us. But divine law will not. O Palestinian brethren: live in a tent; dwell under a fig tree; reside under bare shelter; even live in a chicken coop, a cave or by an abandoned well. But do not ever give up. Roll up your sleeves. Build. Plant. Exist. Do not migrate. Do not cast your heart away from the ruins of your home. Do not divert your eyes from the roots of the vine your father planted by the door. Do not accept that your nose smells anything but the scent of your grandparents and your children in the stones and dust of your home. Do not accept the tickle of any breeze, but one infused with the fragrance of the olive, pine and lemon trees that sang to you as a child. This earth is yours. The soil and the stones are yours. And the wind and rain pouring over these ruins are also yours.

O Palestinians, plant your feet firmly in your land. Even when you die, let your graves feed and preserve your history, because even the dead and buried have a homeland. And remember these words in Matthew, 5:4,[20] "Blessed are those who mourn; for they will be comforted."

Also, be comforted by the fact that your homeland has defeated all the invaders that tried to conquer Palestine with swords and fire. Your ancestral tenacity crushed them all: Pharaohs, Assyrians, Babylonians, Greeks and Romans. Your civilization has defeated their barbarism. The Zionists will not fare much better. They, too, will be defeated. So, take heart and do not be afraid. Strive to always protect your homeland. Do not allow the Balfour Declaration, the Oslo Accords, the Arab normalization and spineless initiatives to define you. Do not lose sight of your resistance, do not let grief weaken you or shake your collective confidence.

To the Christians of the world, I would like to remind them of the saying by South African Bishop Desmond Tutu, "If you are neutral in situations of injustice, you have chosen the side of the oppressor."[21] If you show compassion towards Zionist criminality, then you betray the purity and innocence of Palestinians. In the Holy Land of Palestine, we are in desperate need of true justice and co-existence that is based on equality and togetherness, not racism, apartheid and ethnic cleansing. Those who strive for a just peace in Palestine are our true brothers and sisters in Christianity. They are the righteous ones, and the righteous ones shall always be rewarded.

"The fruit of that righteousness will be peace; its effect will be quietness and confidence forever."[22]

---

20 Matthew, 5:4, NIV.

21 Quoted in Susan Ratcliffe, Ed., *Oxford Essential Quotations* (5th ed.) (Oxford University Press, 2017), accessed 12/1/2021 at https://www.oxfordreference.com/view/10.1093/acref/9780191843730.001.0001/q-oro-ed5-00016497.

22 Isaiah, 32:17, NIV.

SAMI A. AL-ARIAN *is the Director of the Center for Islam and Global Affairs (CIGA) and public affairs professor at Istanbul Sabahattin Zaim University. He received his Ph.D. in 1986 and was a tenured academic in the United States for many years, receiving several teaching awards and grants. During his four decades in the US (1975–2015), Dr. Al-Arian founded numerous institutions and publications in the fields of education, research, religion and interfaith, as well as civil and human rights. He was a prolific speaker across many US campuses, especially on Palestine, Islam and the West, and Civil Rights.*

*In 2001, Al-Arian was named by* Newsweek *the "premiere civil rights activist" in the US for his efforts to repeal the use of Secret Evidence in immigration courts. In 2012, he was profiled by historians of the* Encyclopedia of American Dissidents *as one of only three Muslims in the US, out of 152 US dissidents and prisoners of conscience in the past century included in the two-volume series (along with Malcolm X and Muhammad Ali). His US story was featured in 2007 in the award-winning documentary "USA vs. Al-Arian," and in 2016 in the book* Being Palestinian. *Dr. Al-Arian has written dozens of articles and studies that were translated into many languages, focusing on US foreign policy, Palestine and the Arab Spring phenomena. His book of poetry on spirituality, Palestine, and human rights,* Conspiring against Joseph, *was published in 2004.*

# TOWARDS A GLOBAL SOLIDARITY MOVEMENT FOR A FREE PALESTINE

## Engaging Governments, Parties, Institutions, and Mass Action Networks

*Dr. Sami A. Al-Arian*

> *"The siege will last until those who lay the siege feel like the besieged."*
>
> —FROM A POEM BY MAHMOUD DARWISH

DESPITE NOT BEING born in Palestine, early on in my life I intuitively realized that I was Palestinian, and that being one meant that we had to struggle to survive. While I was born in Kuwait, grew up in Egypt and moved to the United States at the age of seventeen to pursue my college education, being Palestinian was an instinctive feature of my upbringing. To be a Palestinian in the diaspora is to be fully conscious of the historical struggle and grave injustices the people of Palestine have endured for more than a century—a history that I absorbed since childhood through the tragic experiences of my parents and grandparents.[23] Although I never lived in Palestine, throughout my life, Palestine has lived in me. Palestine was a present theme in my early attempts at writing poetry at the age of twelve. While Palestinian children learn about the history and tragedy of

---

23 Sami Al-Arian, In Yasir Suleiman (Ed.), *Being Palestinian: Personal Reflections on Palestinian Identity in the Diaspora* (Edinburgh University Press, 2016), 48–53.

Palestine at a very young age, we cannot help but be attracted to its beauty and majesty.

Even though I was born a decade after the 1948 *Nakba*, for my generation this trauma was not just a historical event that one might learn about in school, read in history books or hear from elders; rather, it was our personal story. Like for many others, every detail of it was etched in my parents' memory and subsequently implanted in me. On the occasions in which adults would gather together in a living room to sip coffee or tea, it was the norm to hear them discuss politics—almost always related to Palestine. Whether it was about the past, the present or the future, reminiscing about Palestine and talking about returning to it one day was at the heart of the conversation.

Just before I reached the age of ten, I had to witness a devastating ordeal and humiliating defeat, the June 1967 war. The rest of Palestine was lost and, with it, the illusion, as propagated by Arab leaders and their brand of nationalism, of defeating an elusive enemy. I can still see the silent tears my father shed upon learning that Jerusalem had fallen one night that June. From that moment, I realized that Palestine was not just a place to mourn and a distant home, but a defining cause for a just struggle.

To grow up Palestinian was to feel homeless, estranged and besieged, even in friendly environments. Wherever you might be, the struggle for truth, justice, dignity and survival was awaiting your presence and involvement. My father was deported from Kuwait—a country where he had worked tirelessly for eleven years to support his young family—because he refused to inform on the Palestinian community for the government. A decade later, I had to leave Egypt after being denied a proper education because I was Palestinian. Then, after four decades in the United States, once again, I was forced to move because I refused to be silenced as I was relentlessly targeted for my activism for Palestine—even after having spent nearly twelve years in prison and under house arrest.[24] Struggling for truth and

---

24 See *Shackled Dreams: A Palestinian's Struggle for Truth, Justice, and the American Way: The Story of Sami Al-Arian* (National Liberty Fund, 2004).

Also, for a synopsis of my trial, see the documentary, *USA vs Al-Arian,*

justice for Palestine was not really a choice, because abandoning it would have meant forsaking my soul, erasing my memory or negating my existence.

During my high school years in Egypt, my frequent conversations with my best friend at the time, another Palestinian, was not just about truth, justice or our common tragedy, but also about our path to recovery, return and redemption. Our search for answers necessitated extensive reading and understanding of history, philosophy, religion, politics, literature and the human struggle for freedom. Another important characteristic that defined me growing up was my early embrace of Islam, not simply as a religious belief to seek personal redemption, but more significantly, as a source of knowledge, empowerment and social change. My friend and I were asking hard questions regarding identity, purpose, history, politics, culture, social change, resistance, the struggle for justice and the future.

By the age of nineteen, I had studied various ideologies and political philosophies, including modern Western political thought. We felt that there was a dimension in Islam that was totally absent from Western ideologies such as communism, socialism, liberalism or secular-humanism. These dialectics and epistemological foundations were two dimensional, like a straight line with two end points. At one end is *Man* and at the other is the *Universe.* On the other hand, Islam's epistemological foundation is three dimensional, like a triangle with three indices: *God*, *Man*, and *Universe*. In the first model, man is at the center of attention and action, and the goal is to maximize the happiness and pleasure of "Man," regardless of the consequences, whether good or bad. In this paradigm, political power is used to subjugate the "Universe" and those who are weak and vulnerable to the will of the powerful and strong. It encourages conflict, corruption and exploitation. In the second model, however, God is at the center of the believer's life and activity. The purpose is, then, to please God to the best of one's ability by maximizing the best qualities one could

---

Jan Dalchow and Line Halversen Film production (98 min.), 2007. Link: https://vimeo.com/128413718

muster to attain God's favor. In this paradigm, political power is used to defend the venerated values and high morals that keep man from transgressing against God or His creation, including the universe and other beings. Such values include truth, justice, peace, wisdom, righteousness, kindness, mercy, compassion, respect, love, patience, humility, modesty, charity, cooperation and appreciation of beauty.[25] However, belief in these values is not enough; one should be willing to act upon them and, if needed, be ready to defend them.

Furthermore, with God being at the center and focus of the second model, one would find and utilize an essential source of knowledge, which is revelation, that unlocks as much of the universe's mysteries and discoveries, enabling us to use our minds and capacities to recognize and understand the potentials and limitations of our faculties and our realities. Consequently, we found that Islam, when interpreted in a dynamic civilizational context, provided meaningful answers to many of the questions we had. We believed that struggling for justice and changing the conditions of our society could not be undertaken without understanding our history and civilization, while realizing that consequential change occurs only when fulfilling its requirements of knowledge, determination, struggle and resistance. But more significantly, we believed that the endeavor needed to be guided by the Qur'anic principles of truth, patience, faith and virtuous acts. These were the bases for attaining righteousness and earning God's favor.

It was in December 1976 that I had my first introduction to the true nature and history of Zionism, after listening to a lecture by the late and notable Palestinian scholar, Ismail Al-Faruqi.[26] His presentation opened my eyes to the history of the Jewish European

---

25 For a more elaborate discussion on this topic see: Ismail Raji Al-Faruqi, *Al Tawhid: Its Implications for Thought and Life* (Herndon, VA: International Institute of Islamic Thought, 1994). See also my presentation, Sami Al-Arian, *Understanding Tawhid: The Basic Principle of Islam,* April 25, 2020 (95 min.), CIGA Ramadan Webinar Series #1, https://www.youtube.com/watch?v=nDX89EbxyiM

26 Ismail Raji Al-Faruqi, *Islam and the Problem of Israel* (TOP Publications, 2005).

experience and the Zionist enterprise, with a view to better understand our predicament and the challenges we face. I studied these topics through the works of many renowned scholars, including Abdelwahab Elmessiri, Alfred Lilienthal, Maxime Rodinson and Roger Garaudy, among many others. It was only a few years after this educational process began, that I shared a stage with al-Faruqi and another renowned scholar at the time, the late Ali Mazrui, at the University of Michigan in Ann Arbor in 1982, in which I lectured on the dangers of the Zionist threat. At the end of this educational journey, I concluded that our struggle is not only about recovering the land or the legitimacy of a particular narrative but more significantly, about the true nature of the conflict. If the essence of the struggle is not understood properly or defined correctly, there will not be a just and lasting resolution. It was quite clear to me that the ultimate goal of the Zionist movement is to negate the existence of Palestinians by denying their history, erasing their memory, destroying their future and degrading their humanity. Moreover, Zionism represented not only a grave and serious threat to Palestinians and their history and culture, but also to Judaism itself by redefining its essence, and undermining the relationship of its adherents with other communities and faiths, particularly Islam.

The summer of 1982 was particularly difficult for me, as I witnessed the Israeli army invade Lebanon, besiege Beirut and subject it to daily bombardment for 77 days, killing more than 17,000 Palestinians and Lebanese. The savagery of this onslaught continued with the massacre of over 2,000 Palestinians, overwhelmingly women, children and the elderly, in the Sabra and Shatila refugee camps near Beirut, weeks after PLO fighters had evacuated. It was further evidence of the vicious nature of the Israeli state that it empowered its Phalangist proxies to do its dirty work.

Living in the US and teaching at a university, as well as lecturing on dozens of campuses across the country over many years, allowed me to engage directly with a significant number of students and intellectuals on many important issues, particularly on Palestine. Furthermore, I spent several years meeting with the political class, including powerbrokers in Congress, policymakers and journalists, while working and lobbying on issues related to civil rights. Through these life experiences and direct engagement, it was clear that the Zionist narrative had significantly influenced politicians, journalists and was prevalent in popular culture—to the degree that the US, itself, has become a willing participant and partner in the crimes perpetrated against the Palestinian people.

My life in the United States taught me the importance of establishing institutions in order to deliver long-lasting impact and change. I established many institutions related to education, research, interfaith work, and civil and human rights advocacy. I also established two national organizations that focused on the Palestinian struggle.[27] Early on, I realized the importance of engaging the public, and the inevitability of clashing with staunch supporters of Israel. America has become the main, and sometimes only, sponsor and patron of the Zionist state's expanding enterprise.[28] In effect, that meant that the US had become a vital arena to litigate the future and fate of the Palestinian issue. Israel could not survive without US military and economic support, in addition to American political and diplomatic protection. And Palestine could not be set free without breaking that unholy alliance.

## Understanding the Essence of the Conflict

Many Arab and Western scholars argue that history has known two types of Jewish societies across the world: the Jews who lived in the Islamic world (the Jews of Islam), and the Jews who lived in Western Christian societies (the Jews of Christendom). However, the status of these two types of Jewish communities living in these two worlds was strikingly different. If a brief historical analysis is

---

27 The Islamic Association for Palestine (IAP) in 1981 and the Islamic Committee for Palestine (ICP) in 1988. I had to leave IAP in 1983 as a result of a dispute mentioned in this piece.

28 See my study, Sami Al-Arian, *Israel and the United States: From Enabler to Strategic Partner* (CIGA Publications, Istanbul Zaim University Press, 2019). Link: https://www.izu.edu.tr/en/ciga/publications/publications/geopolitical-strategic-studies

conducted, one would find that, since the Charter of Medina during the time of the Prophet Muhammad, the Jewish communities in Medina had lived as part of the Muslim community (the *Ummah*) and were recognized and honored as a distinct community within that city-state. For centuries, Jewish communities in Muslim lands were recognized and afforded their rights under successive Islamic states and empires in what the Jewish Encyclopedia would refer to as "the golden age of the Jews." These periods, especially in Andalusia, enabled the Jewish communities to flourish, with the rise of notable scholars and sages.

On the other hand, Jews who lived in the Christian world under the Roman umbrella and successive European empires, were subjected to all forms of oppression and persecution (when they suffered immensely in these countries, they found Islamic societies open for them to migrate to and settle in, as occurred during the Inquisition in Andalusia, during which many Jews were given the choice between converting to Christianity, or being exiled or even killed in the most heinous ways). The Jewish communities who resided in Europe for centuries had to live in ghettos, deprived of their most basic civil and legal rights. Despite their relative liberation after the Enlightenment and Renaissance era, as well as the French Revolution, racism and discrimination against them continued, examples of which are abundant, including the Russian pogroms at the end of the nineteenth century and the Holocaust in the twentieth century. Perhaps the most infamous incident that motivated the early Zionists was the Alfred Dreyfus case in France in 1894. This affair contributed enormously to the founding of the modern Zionist political movement. Because of the raw racism and hatred that the trial displayed, many Jews concluded that it was impossible for them to live among European Christians and began exploring the idea of establishing their own nation-state, most certainly influenced by European nationalism and their brand of settler-colonialism.

Thus, the Zionist movement was born out of a purely European experience. Within a few years, the early Zionists allied themselves with the leaders of the European powers, especially Britain and France, and to a lesser extent, the United States. The

Zionist movement found common ground with Britain in its attempt to divide and colonize parts of the Arab world. The 1916 Sykes-Picot agreement called for the partition and fragmentation of the Arab states of the Ottoman Caliphate. In 1917, the British government issued the Balfour Declaration, which called for the establishment of a Jewish national homeland in Palestine. The British hoped that having a Jewish settlement in the midst of the Arab and Muslim world would serve their strategic interests in the region. Similarly, the Zionist movement knew that, for its project to survive, it had to ally itself with a great power for legitimacy and protection.

Consequently, since the emergence of the Zionist movement at the end of the nineteenth and early twentieth centuries, its main goal has been the ingathering of the diaspora of the world's Jews in a national home modeled on the modern nation-state system in Europe. The Zionist movement implemented its program by mobilizing Jewish communities, first in Europe and then in the United States and beyond. This process underwent many stages, in which the Zionist movement established multi-faceted institutions, often in consideration of existing geopolitical realities, as its elites were constantly interacting with colonial powers, particularly Britain. In adopting the vision of a settler-colonial state in Palestine, the Zionist movement effectively served British strategic interests in dividing, weakening and colonizing the Arab and Islamic region, which had been dominated for centuries by the Ottoman Empire. During this period, the Zionist movement marshalled much of its resources in order to implement its vision. It also utilized all its capabilities to build alliances with colonial powers that could directly impact regional conflicts and influence the international system with a view to empowering the Zionist movement to impose its will on weak colonized peoples and regimes.

During the British Mandate, in the aftermath of WWI and the fall of the Ottoman Caliphate, Zionists started to vigorously implement their project in Palestine, triggering fierce resistance by the indigenous people. The Palestinians initiated multiple uprisings, demonstrating their complete rejection of what they perceived to be an aggressive encroachment on their homeland. They mounted a fierce struggle, despite their limited resources while under British occupation. Palestinian leaders had limited experience and a poor network of relations in the international sphere, which hindered their ability to seek independence and prevent the occupation of their land. This ultimately led to the 1948 catastrophe or *Nakba*. The *Nakba* resulted in the displacement from their homes, cities and villages of about sixty percent of the Palestinians at the time (about 800,000), as well as the occupation of approximately seventy-eight percent of Mandatory Palestine in what many, including my ancestors, remember as a dreadful, painful and dark moment in history.

While the conflict with the Zionist enterprise in Palestine has been a struggle over land and history, it is also a struggle over the future. Since it targets the Palestinians in order to take over their land, it is also a struggle for the existence and survival of the Palestinian people. Furthermore, the presence of an exclusivist Zionist state in the region has represented a great challenge and threat to the security and stability of Arabs and Muslims. The Arab regimes that faced Zionist militias in 1948 were weak, divided and mostly under the control or manipulation of foreign powers, which were working diligently to establish the Israeli state and provide it with the means of survival. The Arab regimes that were defeated in 1948 were mostly monarchic and embraced capitalist western-liberal values. They would eventually fall and be replaced by regimes that espoused left-wing or socialist ideologies, claiming to be revolutionary. In essence, the replacements were mostly military regimes that ruled and controlled their societies in an authoritarian fashion, trying to assert their legitimacy by merely claiming to confront the Zionist state.

This understanding coincided with one of my early influential readings that analyzed the political developments in the aftermath of the 1967 war. It was a short book that I read in the mid-1970s under the title *After the Two Nakbas* by Syrian author, Tawfiq al-Tayyeb.[29] It was a cogent and piercing analysis of the corrupt and incompetent regimes that lost Palestine, first in 1948 and then in 1967, and called

---

29 Tawfiq Al-Tayyeb, *Ma Ba'da Al Nakbatayn* (*After the Two Catastrophes*) (Germany: Islamic Center of Aachen, 1968).

for the importance and necessity of Islamic activists to be part of the struggle. After the 1982 invasion of Lebanon, I edited and published a study under the title *The Fall of the Third Illusion.*[30] It reiterated al-Tayyeb's argument about the first two illusions (the 1948 and 1967 regimes) and analyzed the consequences of the fall of the third illusion embodied by the Palestinian national movement, which was dislodged from Lebanon and scattered around the Arab world after the 1982 invasion, away from any border state. The study argued that the rise of the Islamic movements would ultimately necessitate their involvement in the Palestinian struggle. But it also questioned the nature of this engagement and whether it would end up as a fourth illusion. At the time, this study was heavily despised by many Palestinian Islamists because it raised the issue of the involvement (or lack of it) of Islamists in the Palestinian cause. A considerable number of Islamic activists dismissed the notion that the Palestinian cause should be central for the Muslim *Ummah*, as I and few others had been advocating. Advocating this slogan in those years brought me much grief and enmity from others.[31]

The centrality of Palestine for the Muslim *Ummah,* and the struggle for justice in Palestine have several dimensions: spiritual, political and civilizational. Palestine is at the heart of the Muslim

---

30 Mus'ab Al Zubeiri (pen name), *Suqoot Al Wahm Al Thaalith* (*The Fall of the Third Illusion*) (Islamic Association for Palestine, USA, 1982).

31 Most Palestinian Islamic activists in the late 1970s and early 1980s dismissed the notion that Palestine was the central cause of the Islamic movement or the Muslim Ummah. Some contended that it was God who was the central cause by seeking His pleasure. The majority, however, thought that the establishment of an Islamic state was the central issue. In 1982, I had a two-hour debate on the centrality of the Palestinian issue with another Islamic activist in an "invitation only" gathering that had over 120 people, the majority being Palestinian. At the end of the debate, not a single person in the audience supported my argument. However, by the late 1980s during the first Palestinian Intifada (1987–1991), the issue was no longer controversial and there was almost a consensus among Palestinian Islamic activists affirming the importance and centrality of the Palestinian cause. Another source of tension in the early 1980s was my advocacy to expand Palestinian activism, and involve non-Palestinian and non-Muslim activists.

world, where Jerusalem has been recognized in the Qur'an ever since the advent of Islam as a special sacred place and exalted land, next to Mecca and Medina. Throughout history, millions of Muslims visited and prayed in Jerusalem, fulfilling a prophetic saying that blessed those who prayed on its grounds. When the Crusaders occupied Jerusalem in the eleventh century, at a time of weakness and disunity for Muslims, its fall was considered a painful defeat and desecration of the holy land. During the time of the Crusaders, the Muslim holy places in Jerusalem were desecrated and defiled. It took almost a century to unite and mobilize the *Ummah* (Muslim community) under the leadership of Saladin, to push back the invaders, liberate Jerusalem and restore it to its majestic and revered status. Because Islam recognizes Christianity and Judaism and holds them in high esteem and great respect, the history of Palestine and Jerusalem was one of harmony and peace between the faith communities when foreign invaders were repelled.

People across the Muslim world recognize the symbolic significance of Jerusalem. Unlike any other place in the Muslim world (except Mecca and Medina), the status of Jerusalem is considered to be symbolic of the state of the Muslim Ummah: if occupied, it is seen as a sign of decline and weakness of the global Muslim community or, when liberated, a proof of its vibrancy and strength. Similarly, those who fought against Muslim powers had also understood the symbolic nature of Jerusalem. Upon entering Jerusalem in December 1917, British General Edmund Allenby remarked, "The wars of the Crusaders are now complete," while the French military general, Henri Gouraud, who conquered Damascus in July 1920, stood at Saladin's grave, kicked it, and declared: "The Crusades have ended now. Awake Saladin, we have returned. My presence here consecrates the victory of the Cross over the Crescent."

Another important dimension in this argument is the geopolitical aspect. The Israeli state that has occupied Palestinian land for decades is surrounded by millions of Muslims as well as Arab Christians—the majority of whom consider themselves part of the mosaic of Islamic culture and civilization. For Israel to survive, it must keep the states in the region divided, requiring it to ensure their weakness and vulnerability by colluding with colonial powers, as well as sowing war and discord on religious, sectarian, ethnic or other grounds. If anything, the history of the conflict in the past century has validated this equation: the survival of the State of Israel depends on the fragmentation, weakness and powerlessness of the Arab and Muslim states in the region. That's why Israel's geopolitical grand strategy is to be the region's hegemon, requiring it to maintain its aggressive military posture. Such a state of affairs is untenable for all parties, and casts uncertainty, instability and misery on the whole region. The examples of Israel's hands in the politics of the region that promote chaos, conflict, discord and wars are many.[32]

On the civilizational level, there are three main impediments to overcoming the deep civilizational decline facing many Muslim societies. They are: (a) the divisions among major countries and regions within the Arab and Muslim world; (b) their dependency on foreign powers, such as the US, in many spheres including security, economy, technology, culture, etc., while the US not only supports Israel in all aspects, but also adopts it as its client state that can be used as a club against any regime that may misbehave; and (c) the Westernization of societies through what Edward Said calls "cultural imperialism."[33] The record is quite clear regarding the destructive role Israel, the Zionist movement and its backers have played to impede any genuine political, socio-economic, scientific or technological progress across the Middle East, in general, and in the Arab world in particular.[34]

---

32 Some of the countries impacted by Israel's direct involvement to break them up, sow discord, encourage civil war, or face the wrath of its war machine since its founding include Lebanon, South Sudan, the Kurdish region in Iraq, Jordan, Syria, Egypt, and Iran, just to name a few. See also the *Oded Yinan Plan, The Zionist Plan for the Middle East,* translated and edited by Prof. Israel Shahak (The Association of Arab-American University Graduates, USA, 1982). Link: https://dokumen.pub/the-zionist-plan-for-the-middle-east.html

33 Edward W. Said, *Culture and Imperialism* (New York: Vintage, 1994).

34 See for example, David D. Kirkpatrick, *Into the Hands of the Soldiers: Freedom and Chaos in Egypt and the Middle East* (New York: Viking, 2018). In the book the author details how Israel and its allies in the State and Defense

After the 1973 war and the subsequent de-facto abandonment by the Arab regimes of the Palestinian liberation project, the PLO came to accept the Zionist state, starting with the declaration of the Ten Point Program in 1974, then with the recognition of Israel at the Algiers Conference and the Geneva declaration in 1988, and ending with the secretive talks that led to the 1993 Oslo agreement.

In the Oslo agreements, Israel insisted on postponing all issues that had any implications related to the legal or political rights of the Palestinian people. Referred to as final status issues, they included the status of Jerusalem, the Palestinian right of return, Jewish settlements on Palestinian lands, borders and sovereignty. With the return of the PLO leaders to the 1967 occupied territories in 1994, the bulk of Palestinian political action shifted, for the first time, from the outside to the inside. Still, the Israeli military Occupation was able to effectively control most Palestinian decision-making, setting up a system in which the so-called Palestinian Authority (PA) had limited political maneuvering insofar as it was shackled by economic agreements that heavily favored the occupier, and bound to a humiliating security coordination meant to keep any meaningful resistance under control.

After the Oslo process and the PLO leadership's recognition of the Zionist state, Israel had three strategic options for ending the conflict. If it chose to keep its Jewish majority and preserve the democratic façade of the state, it would have required the acceptance of what was called the two-state solution which, in essence, would have given the Palestinians a truncated state on roughly the pre-1967 borders. But if it chose to keep all the Palestinian land between the Jordan River and the Mediterranean Sea, while purportedly allowing democratic structures for all the inhabitants of the land, it would have meant accepting the so-called one-state solution, in which Palestinian Arabs would be granted equal civil and political rights to Israeli Jews. Of course, this option, which would have ended the Zionist dream of having exclusive control over the Holy Land, has so far been rejected

---

Departments, as well as its regional allies thwarted Egyptian democracy as they supported and defended the 2013 military coup.

by all Zionist parties, regardless of ideological or other differences, because the core of the Zionist ideology rests on the belief of Jewish supremacy and exceptionalism, and the refusal to grant equal rights to non-Jews. While the one-state solution was a Palestinian goal that the PLO had called for before it adopted the goal of the Palestinian state in 1974, the idea was vehemently rejected outright by all Zionist parties and their western allies.

The two-state solution, which was the goal of the Oslo process that many believed would end the conflict, has also gained the support of the so-called international community and great powers. However, with the continued colonization and expansion of Zionist settlements (colonies) during the post Oslo years, most international experts now recognize the impossibility of establishing a viable Palestinian state in the West Bank. The Israeli choice, as demonstrated by its strategy and policies, has been to maintain the occupation over all the historical land of Palestine and annex it, albeit gradually, and by establishing facts on the ground, either for religious, ideological, historical or strategic reasons, or through cost and benefit analysis against an opponent they consider weak, vulnerable and divided.

The path chosen by Israel has been clear: the complete rejection of both the one- and two-state solutions, in favor of an exclusionary Israeli Apartheid state. With this path, Israel is trying to convince the world that there is a fourth option: Palestine as a metamorphosed and demilitarized entity with limited sovereignty, not unlike the ten kingdoms of the Bantustans of South Africa. With Israel's decision to kill the prospect of a negotiated settlement with a feeble PA, whose legitimacy is already questionable, the latter has reached its tragic end as the decades-old political process has resulted in an abject failure, awaiting a slow death.

## Laying out a Vision

As a consequence, the logical response of the Palestinian national project must now be to return the Arab-Israeli conflict to its crux, by realizing the paradox of the Zionist project and its refusal to accept the Palestinian Arab existence in the land, recognize Palestinian rights or coexist on an equal basis. Therefore, the strategic goal of the Palestinian national project must be to dismantle the Zionist project with all its institutions and manifestations. In short, the goal is to completely de-Zionize Palestine. Some may say that this is unattainable due to the massive imbalance of power between the two sides. But the Zionist project, like any human project, has certain characteristics and features that must be analyzed and synthesized in order to understand its disposition, and to identify its strengths and weaknesses, capabilities and shortcomings. Thus, for the Palestinian national liberation project to realize this objective, it must provide a complete and comprehensive understanding and deconstruction of the nature and evolution of the conflict with Zionism. My vision for the just resolution of the struggle is predicated on the following:

1) The full right of return to the historical land of Palestine of the Palestinian people everywhere must be recognized and accepted. Since the Zionist project is based on the denial of the Other, there is no way to recover these rights except by dismantling it once and for all on the grounds that it is a danger, not only to the Palestinians and the people of the region, but also to Judaism itself. Zionism has defined itself as an ideology that ties Judaism and its adherents to a territory rather than to a belief system. This concept is dangerous to the Jewish identity and those globally who identify as Jewish, because it makes them complicit in crimes they may actually oppose or towards which they are at least apathetic.

2) This conflict is greater than the capacity of the Palestinian people to resolve on their own with their limited means or capabilities. Had it not been for the steadfastness, persistence and endurance of the Palestinian people to continue their struggle for more than a century, as well as the inability of the Zionist movement and its regional and international supporters to eradicate them or force their surrender, this conflict would have ended a long time ago. The Palestinian people were—and will remain—the spearhead in this conflict and will continue to pay the heaviest price for their sacrifices, and the sacrifices of future generations. This is their destiny. They either live under occupation, subject to the will of their enemy with humiliation and disgrace, or they remain defiant with their resolve, honor, resilience and continued resistance until their goals are achieved.

Their goals are to liberate their land, return their people to their towns and villages and defeat their enemy's plans to destroy them. However, despite all this, the Palestinian people are only a part (even if an essential one) of the power equation. The equation is simple: the Palestinians' efforts—on their own—will not be enough to resolve this problem, but the problem cannot be resolved without them.

3) The Zionist project was a dream of the early fathers of the project who wanted to solve the "Jewish problem" in Europe. Their leaders argued that they could solve this problem at the expense of the Palestinians and the Arabs. Therefore, the Zionist movement harnessed all its resources and capabilities, established international alliances, built institutions and used all tactics and mechanisms to achieve its goals. Similarly, the Palestinian national project must be liberated from its confinement to just the Palestinians and transformed into a global and human liberation project that mobilizes all energies and capabilities, not only within the Arab and Islamic contexts, but across the whole world. It is a just liberation struggle against a racist, aggressive and ruthless settler-colonialist movement. Such a struggle requires the establishment of a global solidarity movement with the Palestinian struggle for liberation. It will also transform the Palestinian cause from being a local or regional struggle to become a universal one at all levels, including the enlisting of global leaders who assume their role and earn their legitimacy in the struggle through their efforts, commitment and sacrifices.

4) With the fall of the Oslo process and the end of the illusion of the two-state solution, sooner or later the center of gravity of the Palestinian cause, with its various manifestations, will move abroad again. This, of course, does not mean the end of the role of the struggle of the people inside the Occupied Territories, but rather its transformation after ending the role of the Palestinian Authority as a partner and collaborator of the occupier (by limiting and suppressing the resistance, as well as reducing the cost of the occupation). It will also result in the emancipation of the cause from the shackles of being merely local or regional to becoming part of the universal struggle for justice and freedom. In addition, this will allow those inside to take a more global leadership role to continue

their resistance and shake up the occupation. Today, the Palestinians abroad represent more than half of the Palestinian people, while the other half is under occupation, siege or living under racist domination and a discriminatory system. Consequently, the logical result of this transition and transformation in the clash with the Zionist project is the rise of activities and the intensification of direct actions targeting the Occupation and its institutions and tools at all levels, in all fields and across all geographies.

The task of the Palestinian national project, then, will not be limited, as it was in previous decades, to the issue of establishing a demilitarized mini-state that, in reality, would continue to be under military occupation and oppression, as is the case of the vanquished and defeated. Thus, there will be two main missions for this project. The first is to support the Palestinian people in Palestine and in the refugee camps so that they continue their resistance and existence until they gain their full rights. The second mission is to engage and expose the global Zionist movement and its powerful backers worldwide at all levels and in all fields, economically, politically, legally, socially, culturally, academically, artistically, on human rights, in the media and in the courts. Not a single sphere or geography where myths and lies are propagated should be spared.

5) Like any political entity or social movement, the Zionist state, since its inception, has factors, components and strategic imperatives that guarantee its survival and continuity. Therefore, the strategic task for the Palestinian national liberation project will be to identify these factors and imperatives and exert all efforts to undermine, weaken and end them by all means available. Because many of these imperatives may be outside the control of direct Palestinian action, this reinforces the call for an effective global solidarity movement that may include states, governments, institutions, movements, parties, celebrities, as well as popular and mass action networks that utilize strategic plans and integrated efforts to undermine these factors and weaken these imperatives. This strategy, in turn, will gradually lead to the dismantling and collapse of the Zionist project just as other aggressive or racist regimes had fallen in the past, such as the apartheid system in South Africa.

6) The people must play an enormous role at the heart of this project not just the elites. Other people everywhere will see that they can play a major role in confronting the Zionist project and in supporting the Palestinian people until apartheid ends. This act of solidarity and engagement will not be limited only to the political, media or legal spheres, but will include everything that weakens the Zionist project. Resistance against it and the struggle against its colonization, expansion and racism will be the major mantra of the global liberation movement.

7) When the Palestinian cause becomes a requisite part of, if not at the center of the global struggle against injustice, occupation, oppression, racism, tyranny and exploitation, then the conflict will become not just global in its outreach but humane in its essence. It will transcend other conflicts and empty them of their destructive characteristics (be they sectarian, ethnic, tribal, class or ideological conflicts) that have preoccupied many parts of the region and the developing world for decades. At that time, Palestine will provide the scale, the compass and the rule, not because its people are more oppressed or their suffering is greater than others, but because of the nature of the conflict and the Zionist challenge that targets geography, history, the future and what it means to be a dignified human being.

8) As the Palestinian national liberation project realizes its universal appeal after the colossal failure of Oslo and, after it becomes the symbol for fighting for justice and freedom worldwide, and identified as the leading struggle against oppression and hegemony, it will become an indispensable partner for liberating the weak and poor of the world, like many global liberation and human rights movements that have struggled against exploitation, racism and enslavement.

9) This project, after adopting its strategic plan, establishing its institutions and activating its operational plans (many of which already exist but need activation and networking), will represent the core of all direct actions against the Zionist project, its institutions and its regional and global sources of strength.

10) With the escalation of all forms of resistance that would collectively weaken the strategic imperatives of the Zionist project,

a certain historical moment would arise in which a strategic change will occur where the balance of power would shift, and where the aggressive, racist project would disintegrate and collapse after the factors for its survival and the imperatives of its continuity have been eliminated or greatly diminished.

In a previous presentation, I had outlined twelve main imperatives for the survival and continuation of the Zionist project on which it depends for its existence, expansion and control within the global political scene. Some of these imperatives are already beginning to erode.[35] The global project for Palestinian liberation, then, must intensify its efforts and action, and focus on the mechanisms, tools, and tactics necessary to weaken all or most of these imperatives that will, eventually, lead to the dismantling of the ever-present racist and aggressive Zionist project. The main point of the vision here is that achieving the goal of dismantling this project as an end to the Israeli-Arab or Palestinian conflict is closely linked to the end or collapse of most, if not all, of these strategic imperatives.

## Conclusion

This essay has briefly presented a grand vision about the liberation of Palestine from a racist colonialist enterprise. It can be summarized as follows. There are crucial imperatives that guarantee the existence and survival of the Zionist project. When all, or most of the aforementioned strategic factors are challenged, weakened and become inoperable, this would, in turn, weaken the Zionist state, jeopardize its existence and force its disintegration and collapse over time. Therefore, those who care about the Palestinian cause or work for its liberation at all levels must examine these imperatives and deal with them accordingly, in order to revitalize the struggle against the Zionist project.

In addition, the Zionist project will also be greatly weakened when structural and strategic changes take place in the not-too-distant

---

35 See my presentation, Sami Al-Arian, *Ending the Israeli-Palestinian Conflict: A Geopolitical Analysis,* May 15, 2020. Link: https://www.youtube.com/watch?v=ZaNW9AH6uVo

future, whether internationally or at the regional level, which are based on many geopolitical factors related to the gradual transformation of the world into a multipolar system. These changes will force Israel to make massive concessions by eliminating or lessening its deep-rooted racist policies. In addition, there are many internal fault lines within Israeli society that will lead to its destabilization and significant weakening over time (Arab vs. Jew, Mizrahi vs. Ashkenazi Jew, secular vs. religious, rich vs. poor, settlers vs. city dwellers, old vs. young, etc.)

Furthermore, strategic shifts in the balance of power can be achieved when a consensus of vision, will and action are developed wisely, collectively and simultaneously. Additionally, shifts in allies and foes are part of the strategic power equation and are gradually shifting in favor of Palestinian rights. Half a century ago, Turkey and Iran were considered in Israel's camp, as parties with whom the Zionist state would collaborate, ally and coordinate against their Arab neighbors. Today, Israel and behind it the Zionist movement and its allies consider these countries to be in the camp of their opponents. This strategic change in the balance of power is the best evidence that strength and weakness are not inevitable constants, but rather variables as long as the struggle continues, carried forward by believers in the vision, who have a determined will and strive with all their utmost efforts until their goals are achieved.

Finally, one must emphasize the importance of creating a global solidarity movement that seeks to end the Israeli apartheid regime by activating and employing many tactics including those of the Boycott, Divestment and Sanctions (BDS) movement. The objective of such tactics is to isolate the Israeli apartheid state and force its racist-colonialist system to eventually disintegrate or collapse. This vision will lead to the increasingly vital role of people outside Palestine in the struggle against the Zionist project, after an absence of more than three decades. But this time, the struggle is not just a Palestinian struggle, carried out by Palestinians for a limited objective. It will be a universal struggle across the world, carried out by every person who cares about justice, freedom, equality and truth. This, of course, does not mean dwarfing the role of the Palestinian struggle inside, but rather their integration as they complement each other, with the realization that a large part of the struggle will become global, touching everyone and everywhere.

Naturally, many Palestinians abroad as well as activists for the Palestinian cause worldwide will spearhead this endeavor, implement this vision and execute its action plans. They will propel it forward by creating or activating all needed institutions to carry it out. This Palestinian act of resistance must also be complemented and shared in action, commitment and engagement by international solidarity movements, working side by side in all places and at all levels and in all fields, to invigorate the struggle, not for the sake of demarcation of borders or the creation of a truncated state, but rather for the sake of dismantling a racist colonialist ideology and its global manifestations.

While the Zionist settler-colonial state targets the land and the human being, the end of injustice and racism in Palestine will not only lead to the restoration of justice and freedom for the Palestinian people but will also save Judaism and its adherents from the racist doctrines of Zionism. In essence, this vision seeks not only to liberate Palestinians, but also to prevent the desecration of the great prophetic tradition of Judaism. The West, because of its racism, xenophobia, and anti-Semitism, has been unable to solve its "Jewish problem" (as they historically characterized it). However, the history of the Arab and Islamic world demonstrates that any Jewish person oppressed or persecuted in the West or elsewhere is welcome to migrate, and to live safely with dignity, to wherever he/she wants in the vast Islamic world, from Morocco to Indonesia, but without the exclusivist mentality and racist ideology that comes at the expense of the Palestinian people.

HANADI HALAWANI *is a prominent Palestinian activist in the Old City of Jerusalem and a Quran teacher at Al-Aqsa Mosque. Despite living within walking distance from Al-Aqsa, the Israeli Occupation authorities have barred her from entering or praying there for years, due to her political activism and advocacy of Palestinian rights in occupied East Jerusalem. In June 2021, she was awarded the International Solidarity with Palestine Award from the Center for Islam and Global Affairs (CIGA) at Istanbul Zaim University.*

# WE ARE THE MURABITAT
# Planting the Seeds of Resistance in Occupied Jerusalem[36]

*Hanadi Halawani*

I WAS BORN IN 1980, in Wadi Al-Joz, in the city of Al-Quds, Jerusalem, and that was where I grew up. I received my elementary and middle school education at the Arab Children's House, which was established in the year 1981 by Hind al-Husseini to look after Palestinian orphans who survived the Deir Yassin massacre. After I finished, I joined Al-Ma'munia School, where I completed my high school education, before enrolling at the Al-Quds Open University from where I graduated with a degree in Social Development. Currently, I am finishing a Master's degree focusing on Democracy and Human Rights at Birzeit University.

I spent most of my childhood living with my family in my grandmother's house in Jerusalem. I am filled with gratitude for the love and attention bestowed upon me by my parents. They guided my feet on the right path. Both of them lived their lives in accordance with high principles. Much of the morality that guided my every step is the morality I inherited from them. However, it was my grandmother, Katiba, who, in particular, influenced the choices I made regarding my relationship with the Al-Aqsa Mosque and my beloved city, Jerusalem. My early memories have often centered on her, as she took me with her everywhere. My grandmother is a survivor of the 1948 *Nakba* and the 1967 *Naksa*. In her heart, she carried a great deal

36 This essay was originally written in Arabic and was translated by Ramzy Baroud.

of sadness and so much resentment for the Israeli Occupation. She always looked at the Al-Aqsa Mosque in the hope that, one day, it would be liberated, as part of the liberation of the whole of Palestine. I remember her many stories about war, always rife with a mixed feeling of agony and hope of an assured victory.

She always took me with her to Al-Aqsa. First, we would rest in the shade of her favorite tree. Then, when we stood up, she would hand me an empty bag so I could walk around the large vicinity of the holy shrines and collect every speck of garbage I would come upon. I did so with much enthusiasm, though she would remind me, now and then, that sanctifying the Al-Aqsa compound is not just about cleansing it of trash but also of the violent settlers and armed soldiers who would raid the space so very often, fire at will and disturb the serenity of the otherwise peaceful place.

My grandmother's love for Al-Aqsa seemed to balance out her many fears about the fate of Palestine. For her, Al-Aqsa was not just a holy place, but a symbol of something much larger and more profound. She once heard me singing. She stared at me with teary eyes, saying, "I pray that, one day, I'll hear your melodious voice reciting the Quran at Al-Aqsa Mosque." I inherited my love for Al-Aqsa from my grandmother. She passed away, but she left us with that deep sense of responsibility for Al-Aqsa and for Palestine.

I was only 17 years old when I married Yasin Makawi, a young man from Jerusalem, whose roots hail from the historic city of Nablus. He, too, had inherited a legacy of love and warmth but also suffering. Together, we raised a family which, one day, will carry on with our mission in this life.

I was still a student at Al-Quds Open University when I had my eldest daughter, 'Ala, and my son, Mahmoud. Managing two children and responding to the demands from school while living in an occupied city was not an easy feat. However, that period has taught me to be stronger, to manage my time and to cope with life while carrying heavy responsibilities. After that, my son, Ahmad, was born and finally, Hamza. By the time Hamza was born, I was fully committed to a life dedicated to the Al-Aqsa Mosque, first as a student, then as a teacher and an activist.

Linking my life struggle to Al-Aqsa began when I became intensely involved in acquiring high-level certificates in the recitation and teaching of the Quran. Initially, I was motivated by my grandmother's wish that, one day, my voice could resonate with the words of God throughout the Al-Aqsa compound. That wish came true when I learned that the Islamic Movement in Occupied Palestine intended to expand an existing program known as "Terrasses of Knowledge," which was initially limited to men only, but eventually expanded to include women. That was in 2010 and, despite my humble education and knowledge at the time, I still applied for the position.

I knew that my qualifications did not measure up to those of many of the women who applied for the position of a teacher in the program. One was a strong-willed woman, with a high level of education, who was also the wife of a Palestinian martyr; another had been a religious preacher for many years; a third had unmatched certifications and extensive experience. As for me, I carried the wish of my grandmother, her love—now my love—for Al-Aqsa. I was armed with hope as I attended the job interview. I told the person who interviewed me, "I know that my certificates and papers do not meet the minimal requirements for the job, but I have something unique to me and that is my desire to turn words into action, for the sake of Al-Aqsa and our beloved Palestine." Hours later, I received a telephone call advising me that I had been selected as a teacher in the "Terrasses of Knowledge" program. My job description included the teaching of the Quran to young children.

I began my new role as a teacher at the beginning of June 2011. Little did I know that this was not just the beginning of a teaching career, but the threshold of a long road that would eventually designate me as a *Murabita*—a steadfast woman—whose main mission in life is to stand guard against all attempts to denigrate Al-Aqsa and to deny Palestinian rights in the occupied city.

It was the start of a very long and arduous journey that would have never been possible if it were not for the love, support, protection and loyalty of my husband, Yasin. He stood by me, when many others did not. He defended my choices, giving me the time and space to fight for a cause that is so dear to my heart. Still, it is not easy for a mother to be involved with an initiative that begins at 7:30 in the morning and carries on for much of the day. This hardship became more pronounced when such a mother would have to pass through various Israeli military checkpoints that are intentionally designed to keep us out. Yet, it was only a matter of time before the female component in this project became a dominant one.

In the beginning, I taught a small circle of students that eventually grew in number, compelling us to divide it into two. The number of students, however, continued to grow and, along with it, the circles of knowledge. Israeli soldiers watched us with alarm and began a campaign of harassment that lasted for years. They would come into our classes and would zoom their cameras into the faces of teachers and students, taking photographs all the while. Then, for no reason, they would collect the ID cards, hold them for a while and write down the names of the attendees.

Some of the women involved in the program were beginning to worry. Some wanted to leave because they could not predict the ferocity of the Israeli response. I remember standing amongst them once and saying this: "Let's imagine ourselves all in a bus that is taking us on a journey to a place far away. As we get fatigued by the arduousness of the journey, some of us may choose to leave. The ones who leave first pay the smallest of price, but by choosing to abandon the rest of us, the journey becomes harder for everyone else. If we stay together, we can share the hardship until we reach our final destination. Sisters, this journey we have embarked on is our path towards liberation. If we choose freedom for all of us, we have to share all the hardships equally." Thankfully, we stuck together.

Hundreds of children were registered in the various programs. It was a beautiful sight just watching these promising young faces learning about their religion, their culture and their identity, standing up for one another, especially when the soldiers decided to bully, deny entry or arrest any one of them. They would all gather around the checkpoint and chant for the soldiers to let them through; at times, the soldiers, overwhelmed and bewildered, would release the detained children.

Sometimes, mothers and children would attend school together, some learning how to read and write, and others taking on more advanced subjects and areas of knowledge. With time, I became the Director of the entire program, and began to seek young, energetic girls to help me in the project. When we would gather at Al-Aqsa, we would be as busy as a beehive, each teacher or volunteer dedicated to a specific subject and a specific circle of knowledge. At times, my job would entail my circulating from one circle to another, directing, encouraging, consoling and leading. The girls then called me "the butterfly of Al-Aqsa." I liked that nickname!

Parallel to our struggle for knowledge, there was another ongoing battle with the Israeli Occupation. Whenever the soldiers tried to make life difficult for us, we would find ways around these restrictions; when they tried to scare us, we remained fearless and steadfast. When they tried to threaten us, we would not budge an inch. Nothing they have done has ever changed our commitment to the educational program. Fear could not find its way to my heart, because in my heart I had my love for Palestine and for my grandmother—her resolve, her hope and her determination.

In 2013, I was banished from Al-Aqsa following an Israeli court order. The banishment order was for two months. I saw, in that unwarranted action, an opportunity to acquire yet more knowledge. So, I traveled to Jordan where I undertook several programs and obtained several certifications related to my field. Shortly after I returned to Al-Aqsa, I was banished again for fifteen days. Yet, I returned once more, this time with greater awareness that the reason behind all of these restrictions and banishments was to ensure armed Jewish settlers, who constantly raid Al-Aqsa, did not meet any resistance on their abrasive and often violent journey. Therefore, this is what I did: I changed the location of the knowledge circles to dot the path of the armed settlers.

The settlers, who raid Al-Aqsa under the protection of heavily armed soldiers, began their so-called tours at the Moroccan Gate (Bab Al-Magharib), before proceeding to the Al-Musalla Al-Qibli, then to the Marwan-e-Masjid, before proceeding to the Mercy Gate (Bab Al-Rahma) in their hope of reaching the Fountain of Qaitbay

(Sabil Qaitbay) to drink from its water. Finally, they often left using the Chain Gate (Bab Al-Silsila). Following my rearrangement of the knowledge circles, wherever they went they found a group of Palestinian women studying, reading and writing, reciting Quranic verses and chanting against the Israeli military Occupation. The Mercy Gate, which up to this time was somewhat abandoned—having been unsupervised, it had allowed the armed settlers more space to gather and organize—became a space for Palestinian Muslim women to learn and teach. If the armed settlers decided to go to the holy Dome of the Rock to pray at the Muslim religious sites, we would line up in front of them like a wall. We would raise our holy books in unison and chant, together, "God is greater." Frankly, we knew that many of these religious Jewish men believed that the sight of women would violate their prayers. Therefore, intentionally, we would stand in full view in front of them as they attempted to desecrate our holy shrines.

For a while, they employed the tactic of stealing our chairs. We then replaced the chairs with rugs. They stole the rugs, too, so we sat on the bare floor. The effort of these *Murabitat*, these steadfast women, forced the extremists to change the route of their raids by conducting only symbolic visitations, where they would enter from the Moroccan Gate and quickly leave from the Chain Gate without desecrating much of the compound, as they had always done.

A more serious crackdown began in 2014 where many of the *Murabitat* were violently arrested, some jailed and others deported for long periods of time. Instead of giving up, we moved our mobile school outside of the Chain Gate. I would gather the women around me, follow up on their studies and we would finish by reading the Quran together. Whenever the settlers triumphantly exited through the Chain Gate, we would be waiting for them, chanting "*Allahu Akbar*," raising our holy books in their faces, completely unafraid of their automatic rifles and unintimidated by their obscene language.

As I watched more and more women being denied access to the Mosque, we decided to reach out to the tourists who visit Al-Aqsa in large numbers on a daily basis. All of us wore similar colored t-shirts with the following words printed on placards: "Do you know why we are here? Ask us." We explained to them, in both Arabic and English, why the soldiers had denied us the right to pray, learn and teach in the holiest of our religious shrines. Eventually, the soldiers attacked us, confiscated our placards and forced us to pay a large fine for wearing our t-shirts. Still, we kept coming back, talking to everyone who was willing to hear about the injustice of the Israeli Occupation. Frustrated by our relentlessness, the soldiers began attacking us with unprecedented violence, beating us with heavy sticks, throwing teargas in our midst, spraying us with gases that burned our eyes, throats and irritated our skin. They punched and kicked women, young and old. They dragged us down the street, they stepped on us, they spat and used all kinds of obscenities. Yet, we kept coming back.

In 2015, the Israeli military released what they called the "blacklist." This contained the names of women who were no longer allowed to enter Al-Aqsa Mosque compound. My name was the first on the list, and everyone else who was "blacklisted" received all kinds of harassment, arrests, various types of punishment, including house arrests and, at times, torture. I told the women on the list that this was a "golden list," as it contained the names of the most powerful and most effective of all women, whose work and activism had scared off the supposedly "invincible army." That year, I was told that I could not set foot in Al-Aqsa during the holy month of Ramadan. Considering the significance of this holy Muslim month and the historic importance between Ramadan and Al-Aqsa, this decision was meant to break my will. My response was to break the fast outside the Chain Gate in a Ramadan *Iftar* like no other.

The sisters and I cooked a massive amount of *Maqluba*, an unrivalled Palestinian dish, loved by all. The entire meal was prepared on the street, and it was not only meant to serve the *Murabitat* who were deported from Al-Aqsa but was also smuggled to those who were inside. It was the first, but definitely not the last, time that the *Maqluba* feast became a regular occurrence in and around Al-Aqsa. Understanding the significance of our national dish to our collective identity, the soldiers would interrogate us about the reasons why we were always preparing this specific kind of food. Within weeks, we were making court appearances, as we were literally investigated for making *Maqluba*.

2015 was a particularly difficult year for the women of Al-Aqsa. We were treated with the same kind of violence and subjected to the same kind of torture to which Palestinian men were. We began spending long, painful nights in the dungeons of occupation. This suffering continued until an Israeli court decided, by the end of the year, to ban the Islamic Movement altogether, both in occupied Jerusalem and in Palestine '48. Their aim was the destruction of the "Terrasses of Knowledge" program, which had strengthened the relationship between Palestinian youth and Al-Aqsa; in fact, all of Jerusalem's holy shrines. Unfortunately, the program itself had to stop. This was not the end of the road for me. Guided by my grandmother's love and wish to never abandon Al-Aqsa, I continued to find ways to empower women so that we could continue to play our critical role in the struggle for freedom.

The Israeli Occupation continued to target me despite the violent closure of our educational program. In 2016, I was arrested during the trial of one of the teachers involved in the "Terrasses of Knowledge" program. They interrogated me for seven days, during which time I was mostly in shackles, being transported in the *Bosta*—the armed prison vehicle—between my prison cell and the interrogation room. These were days of constant humiliation, which included the insistence on degrading searches where one would have to be stripped naked every time. This was not the first, nor the last of my detentions. At times, they placed me with convicted Israeli criminals to scare me and to break my spirit. At other times, they placed me in solitary confinement, a tiny cell that felt as if it was a filthy toilet. My interrogators seemed to enjoy humiliating me, making fun of me and even calling me crazy. They often pulled off my *hijab* and forced me to attend court sessions without it. Once, and without any justification, they forced me to remove all of my clothes and sit in a small room surrounded by cameras. This lasted only 15 minutes, but it felt as if it was a lifetime.

In the following months, the Chain Gate itself was shut down with iron bars and barbed wire, so the women and I relocated our protests to the Hitta Gate (Bab Al-Hitta). Inevitably, our numbers began to dwindle. By Ramadan 2017, I was the only woman still protesting. I eventually relocated to a new spot, between the Hitta Gate and the Lion's Gate (Bab Al-Asbat). This new spot still exists, and the number of protesters is growing once more.

True, our educational program had been disrupted and many of the women were, once again, preoccupied by their own challenges in life, but my message and my mission did not stop. I then took the message of Al-Quds, Jerusalem and the struggle of all the *Murabitat* to many countries around the world, beginning in Jordan, then Kuwait, Indonesia, Bahrain, Turkey and elsewhere. Wherever I went, my audiences were always worried about the fate of Jerusalem, and every time, I would reassure them that we Palestinians will continue to stand at the frontlines of resistance against Israeli military occupation.

Upon my return to Jerusalem, I contacted many of my students, teaching them what I could and whenever possible. This, too, from Israel's perspective, was too dangerous, so the Israeli Occupation continued to make my life difficult, limiting my movement and denying me the right to travel. First, I was blocked from traveling for three years but, as soon as I regained that right, an Israeli court imposed it again in 2020. My family and I are denied health insurance and constantly forced to pay heavy fines for things that make no sense, simply to punish me. On any given day, I am denied entry, either to the West Bank or to Jerusalem's Old City, or placed under house arrest in lieu of prison time. However, the most painful of all punishments is when Israeli soldiers would break into my home and savagely begin to destroy everything in their way: my children's computers, desks and beds. With every break-in, they would confiscate my papers and my certificates, and they would drag me in handcuffs, often late at night, to an Israeli prison. On one of these occasions, I cast a glance on the street only to see a seemingly endless stream of Israeli vehicles, police cars and Special Forces. The military caravan that took me to be interrogated was so loud and massive, as if I was a dangerous criminal. In the interrogation room, I asked one of the Israeli officers why it was necessary for them to deploy such a large force to arrest an unarmed woman. He answered with a smirk, "But you deserve more than this, you are the most dangerous woman to Israel's security."

But I am going nowhere. Our rightful struggle cannot be negotiated, and it will continue, no matter the passing of the years. If we cannot fulfill our mission in this life, another generation of Palestinians will. I know the price will always be high because dignity, freedom and victory are precious. Now, I am back at the University, studying Democracy and Human Rights. I want to take my message, the message of the *Murabitat* in the streets, to every international forum that is willing to hear our pleas. I try to take every opportunity to address the world, whether online or whenever I am allowed to return to my spot outside the Al-Aqsa compound. My message to the Israeli Occupation is that we will never give up and my message to the new generation of Palestinian *Murabitat*, "Do not be scared, but carry on with your noble fight for freedom."

Sometimes, I feel that my grandmother's heart is beating in my chest and that I am a mere messenger, carrying her message to the world. My grandmother's legacy has taught me that when you plant a seed, do not worry if you are not the one who eats from the fruits it bears. Our fight for freedom is inter-generational—my grandmother planted a seed in my heart, and I am planting the seeds in my children's hearts. The more I carry on with my fight for freedom, the more courageous I feel, the more unmoved, unafraid. I feel that God is always with me. He gives me courage and strength. Even when I sit alone outside the walls of Al-Aqsa, surrounded by hordes of soldiers, inside of me, I feel the power of Palestine, all of Palestine, and her people.

KHALIDA JARRAR *was born in the city of Nablus in the northern West Bank on February 9, 1963. She has a Bachelor's degree in Business Administration and a Master's degree in Democracy and Human Rights from Birzeit University. She served as a Director of Addameer Prisoners' Support and Human Rights Association from 1994 to 2006, when she was elected to the Palestinian Legislative Council (PLC)—the Palestinian Parliament. She now heads the PLC's Prisoners Commission, in addition to her role on the Palestinian National Committee for follow-up with the International Criminal Court.*

*Khalida Jarrar's high profile as a Palestinian leader dedicated to exposing Israeli war crimes to international institutions has made her a target of frequent Israeli arrests and administrative detentions. She has been arrested several times, first in 1989, on the occasion of International Women's Day. She spent a month in prison for taking part in the March 8 rally.*

*In 2015, she was detained in a pre-dawn raid by Israeli Occupation soldiers, who stormed her house in Ramallah. Initially, she was held in administrative detention without trial but, following an international outcry, Israeli authorities tried Khalida Jarrar in a military court, where 12 charges, based entirely on her political activities, were made against her. Some of the charges included giving speeches, holding vigils and expressing support for Palestinian detainees and their families. She then spent 15 months in prison.*

*Khalida Jarrar was released in June 2016, only to be arrested again in July 2017, when she was also held under administrative detention. The Israeli raid on her home was particularly violent, as soldiers destroyed the main door of her house and confiscated various equipment, including an iPad and her mobile phone. She was interrogated at Ofer Prison before being transferred to HaSharon Prison, where many Palestinian female prisoners are held. She was released in February 2019, after spending nearly 20 months in prison.*

*Once more, Khalida Jarrar was arrested from her home in Ramallah on October 31, 2019. During her latest imprisonment, one of her two daughters, Suha, passed away at the age of 31. Despite an international campaign to allow Khalida to attend her daughter's funeral on July 13, 2021, the Israeli government rejected all appeals. However, a letter by Khalida was smuggled out of prison to serve as a farewell to Suha. In the letter, she wrote:*

> "Suha, my precious.
> They have stripped me from bidding you a final goodbye kiss.
> I bid you farewell with a flower.
> Your absence is searingly painful, excruciatingly painful.
> But I remain steadfast and strong,
> Like the mountains of beloved Palestine."

*Khalida Jarrar is one of many examples where Palestinian resisters have taken their steadfastness and resistance with them inside Israeli prisons, finding opportunities to fight back, despite their confinement, despite the physical pain and the psychological torture. Moreover, instead of seeing prison as forced confinement, Khalida Jarrar has used it as an opportunity to educate and empower her fellow female prisoners. In fact, her achievements in prison changed the face of the Palestinian female prisoners' movement.*

# FASHIONING HOPE OUT OF DESPAIR
## How to Resist and Win Inside Israeli Prisons

*Khalida Jarrar*[37]

PRISON IS NOT JUST a place made of high walls, barbed wire and small, suffocating cells with heavy iron doors. It is not just a place that is defined by the clanking sound of metal; indeed, the screeching or slamming of metal is the most common sound you will hear in prisons, whenever heavy doors are shut, when heavy beds or cupboards are moved, when handcuffs are locked in position or loosened. Even the *bosta*—the notorious vehicles that transport prisoners from one prison facility to another—are metal beasts, their interior, their exterior, even their doors and built-in shackles.

No, prison is more than all of this. It is also stories of real people, daily suffering and struggles against the prison guards and administration. Prison stakes out a moral position that must be renewed daily and can never be put behind you.

Prison is comrades—sisters and brothers who, with time, grow closer to you than your own family. It is common agony, pain, sadness and, despite everything, also joy at times. In prison, we challenge the abusive prison guard together, with the same will and determination to break him so that he does not break us. This

---

37 This essay by Khalida Jarrar was first published in Ramzy Baroud's book, *These Chains Will Be Broken: Palestinian Stories of Struggle and Defiance in Israeli Prisons* (Clarity Press, 2019). Though Jarrar had agreed to contribute an essay to this volume, her prolonged, unlawful detention by Israel made it impossible for her to do so. The manuscript of the book was completed before her release on September 26, 2021.

struggle is unending and is manifested in every possible form, from the simple act of refusing our meals, to confining ourselves to our rooms, to the most physically and physiologically strenuous of all efforts, the open hunger strike. These are but some of the tools which Palestinian prisoners use to fight for and earn their very basic rights and to preserve some of their dignity.

Prison is the art of exploring possibilities; it is a school that trains you to solve daily challenges using the simplest and most creative means, whether it be food preparation, mending old clothes or finding common ground so that we may all endure and survive together.

In prison, we must become aware of time, because if we do not, it will stand still. So, we do everything we can to fight the routine, take every opportunity to celebrate and to commemorate every important occasion in our lives, personal or collective.

The individual stories of Palestinian prisoners are a representation of something much larger, as all Palestinians experience imprisonment in its various forms on a daily basis. Moreover, the narrative of a Palestinian prisoner is not a fleeting experience that only concerns the person who has lived it but is an event that shakes to the very core the prisoner, her comrades, her family and her entire community. Each story represents a creative interpretation of a life lived, despite all the hardship, by a person whose heart beats with the love of her homeland and the longing for her precious freedom.

Each individual narrative is also a defining moment, a conflict between the will of the prison guard and all that he represents, and the will of the prisoners and what they represent as a collective—capable, when united, of overcoming incredible odds. The defiance of Palestinian prisoners is also a reflection of the collective defiance and rebellious spirit of the Palestinian people, who refuse to be enslaved on their own land and who are determined to regain their freedom, with the same will and vigor carried by all triumphant, once-colonized nations.

The suffering and the human rights violations experienced by Palestinian prisoners, which run contrary to international and humanitarian law, are only one side of the prison story. The other side can only be truly understood and conveyed by those who have lived through these harrowing experiences. Quite often, missing from the story of Palestinian prisoners is the inspiring human trajectory of Palestinian men and women who have persisted through defining moments, with all of their painful details and challenges.

Only by delving deeper into the prisoners' narratives can you begin to imagine what it feels like, while being confined to a small cell, to lose a loving mother, to deal with a broken leg, to be left without family visitation for years at a time, to be denied your right to education and to cope with the death of a comrade.

While it is important that you comprehend the suffering endured by prisoners, such as the numerous acts of physical torture, psychological torment and prolonged isolation, you must also realize the power of the human will, when men and women decide to fight back, to reclaim their natural rights and to embrace their humanity.

Fighting back can take on many forms. Throughout the various stints of imprisonment as a political prisoner in Israeli jails, I, too, took part in the various forms of resistance within the walls of the prison. For me, education for Palestinian female prisoners became an urgent priority.

Female prisoners in Israeli prisons are treated somewhat differently than males, not only in terms of the nature of the violations committed against them, but also in the degree of their isolation. Since there are far fewer female prisoners than males, it is easier for Israeli prison authorities to isolate them completely from the rest of the world. Moreover, there are only a few women prisoners with university degrees; the level of education among these women is alarmingly low.

I was already aware of these facts when I was detained by Israel in 2015, spending most of my detention in HaSharon Prison. Therefore, I decided to make it my mission to focus on the issue of education for women who were denied the opportunity to finish school, whether as children or those who were denied such a right due to difficult social conditions. The idea quickly occupied my mind: if I could only help a few women achieve their high school diplomas, I would have made good use of my time in detention. These diplomas would allow them to pursue university degrees as soon as they were able to and, eventually, achieve a level of economic independence. More importantly, armed with a strong education, these women could contribute even more to the empowerment of Palestinian communities.

However, there are plenty of obstacles facing all prisoners, especially women. Israeli prison authorities place numerous restrictions on prisoners who want to pursue formal education. Even when the Israel Prison Service (IPS) agrees, in principle, to grant such a right, they ensure all practical conditions required to facilitate the work are missing, including the availability of classrooms, blackboards, school supplies and qualified teachers.

The latter obstacle, however, was overcome by the fact that I have a Master's degree, which qualifies me from the viewpoint of the Palestinian Ministry of Education to serve as a teacher and to supervise final high school exams, known as *Tawjihi.* Just seeing the excitement on the faces of the girls when I floated the idea by them inspired me to take on the daunting task, the first such initiative in the history of Palestinian women prisoners in Israeli jails.

I began by contacting the Ministry of Education in order to fully understand their rules and expectations, and how they would apply to female prisoners who want to study for their final exams. My first cohort of students consisted of five women, who so giddily took on the challenge.

At that early stage, the prison administration was not fully aware of the nature of our "operation," so their restrictions were merely technical and administrative. The experience was, in fact, new to all of us, especially to me. I must admit that I may have exaggerated my expectations in my attempt to ensure a high degree of academic professionalism in conducting my classes and the final exam. I just wanted to make sure that I did not, in any way, violate my principles, because I truly wanted the girls to earn their certificates and expect more of themselves.

We had few school supplies. In fact, each class had to share a single textbook that was left by Palestinian child prisoners before they were transferred by IPS to another facility. We copied the few textbooks by hand; this way, several students were able to follow the lessons at the same time. My students studied hard. A single class would, at times, extend to several hours, which meant that they would willingly lose their only break for the day when they were allowed to leave their cells. We had so much to cover and so little time. In the end, five students took the exam, results of which were sent to the Ministry of Education to be confirmed. Weeks later, the results came back. Two of the students passed.

It was an extraordinary moment. The news that two students had earned their certificates while in prison spread quickly among all the prisoners, their families and organizations that champion detainee rights. The girls celebrated the news, and all of their comrades felt truly happy for them. In no time, we mobilized again, getting ready to produce yet another cohort of graduates. However, the more media attention our achievement garnered, the more worried the Israeli prison authorities became. I was not at all surprised that the IPS decided to make it difficult for the second group, also consisting of five students, to go through the same experience.

It was a real battle, but we had every intention of fighting it to the end, no matter the pressure. The prison administration informed me officially that I was no longer allowed to teach the prisoners. They harassed me repeatedly, threatening to send me to solitary confinement. But I know international law well, and I repeatedly confronted the Israelis with the fact that I understood the rights of the prisoners and had no plans to back down. Despite all of this, I managed to teach the second group of girls, preparing the exams myself, in coordination with the Ministry of Education. This time, all five students who took the exam passed. It was a great triumph.

After what we achieved, I realized that there is a need to institutionalize the educational experience for female prisoners, and not to tie it to me or to any single person. For this to succeed in the long term, it needed to be a collective effort, a mission to be championed by every group of women in prison, for years to come. I placed much of my focus on training qualified female prisoners, by getting them involved in teaching and by familiarizing them with administrative work required by the Ministry of Education. I set up the apparatus to ensure a smooth transition for the third group of graduates, as I was anticipating my imminent release.

I was freed in June 2016. Although I returned to my regular life and professional work, I never ceased thinking about my comrades in prison, their daily struggles and challenges, especially those who were keen on getting the education that they need and deserve. I was thrilled when I learned that two female prisoners took on the final exams after I left, and successfully graduated. I felt as happy as I did when I was freed and reunited with my family. I was also relieved to learn that the system I put in place before my release was working. This gave me much hope for the future.

In July 2017, the Israeli military arrested me again, this time for 20 months. I returned to the same HaSharon Prison. There were many more female prisoners than before. Immediately, with the help of other qualified prisoners, we began preparing for the fourth group to graduate. This time, nine female prisoners were studying for the exam. There were more volunteer teachers and administrators. The prison had suddenly bloomed, turning into a place of learning and empowerment.

The prison administration went crazy! They accused me of incitement and began a series of retaliatory measures to shut down the whole schooling process. We accepted the challenge. When they closed our classroom, we went on strike. When they confiscated our pens and pencils, we used crayons instead. When they hauled away our blackboard, we unhooked a window and wrote on it. We smuggled it from one room to another, during the times that we had designated for learning. The prison guards tried every trick in the book to prevent us from our right to education. To show our determination to defeat the prison authorities, we named the fourth group "The Cohort of Defiance." In the end, our will proved mightier than their injustice. We completed the entire process. All the girls who took the final exam passed with flying colors.

I cannot describe to you in mere words how we felt during those days. It was a huge victory. We decorated the prison walls and celebrated. We were all happy, smiling and jubilant because of what we managed to achieve together, when we stood united against the unfair rules of Israel and its prison administration. The news spread beyond the prison walls and celebrations were held by the families of the graduates throughout Palestine. The fifth group was the crowning of that collective achievement. It was the sweet reward following months of struggle and hardship that we had endured, while insisting on our right to education. Seven more students are now studying for the final exam, in the hope of joining the other 18 female graduates who obtained their certificates since the first experience commenced in 2015.

The aspirations of female prisoners evolved, as they felt truly capable and empowered by the education they had received, especially as they had endured so much to obtain what should be a basic human right for all. Those who have obtained their *Tawjihi* certificates are ready to progress to a higher level of education. However, since the Ministry of Education is not yet prepared for this step, the prisoners are creating temporary alternatives.

Since I have a Master's degree in Democracy and Human Rights, and also have lengthy experience in this field through my work with Addameer and the PLC, among other institutions, I offered my students a training course in International and Humanitarian Law. To teach the course, I managed to bring into prison some of the most important and relevant texts pertaining to international treaties on human rights, including the Arabic translation of all four Geneva Conventions. Some of these documents were brought in by the Red Cross, others by family members who came to visit me in prison.

Forty-nine female prisoners participated in the course, which was divided into several periods, each consisting of two months. At the end of the course, the participants received certificates for having completed 36 hours of training in International and Humanitarian Law, the results of which were confirmed by several Palestinian ministries. While we celebrated in prison, a large ceremony sponsored by the Ministry of Prisoners' Affairs was held outside, where the families and some of the freed prisoners attended, amid a huge celebration.

In the end, we did more than fashion hope out of despair. We also evolved in our narrative, in the way we perceive ourselves, the prison and the prison guards. We defeated any lingering sense of inferiority and turned the walls of prison into an opportunity. When I saw the beautiful smiles on the faces of my students who completed their high school education in prison, I felt that my mission has been accomplished.

Hope in prison is like a flower that grows out of a stone. For us Palestinians, education is our greatest weapon. With it, we will always be victorious.

JAMAL JUMAA *was born in Jerusalem. He has a Bachelor's degree in Arabic Literature from Birzeit University in the West Bank, and an MBA from City University in London. Through his work and activism, both in civil society organizations and grassroots movements in Palestinian society for the past thirty years, together with many colleagues and starting from small initiatives, he was able to contribute and build, starting significant organizations and grassroots movements, most of them still in operation and having an impact on Palestinian civil society and the Palestine cause. Most of these initiatives arose from a serious need for the services provided, or as a response to critical situations that were created as a result of occupation policies.*

*He co-founded many civil society organizations such as the Palestinian Agriculture Relief Committees (PARC), the Palestinian Association for Cultural Exchange (PACE) and the Palestinian environmental NGOs Network (PENGON). Through his work at PENGON, he contributed towards the establishment of the Popular Campaign against the Wall and Settlements (STW) in 2002.*

*Within his work in the grassroots campaign and as part of the urgent need to organize international support for the Palestinian struggle, he contributed within STW efforts to the foundation of the National Committee for BDS in 2005 and he is still a member of the secretariat of the Committee on behalf of STW. In 2013, he worked with activists and grassroots organizations on the establishment of the Land Defense Coalition (LDC) to function as an umbrella for a number of grassroots movements, initiatives and organizations to enhance coordination and cooperation among them and work to expand the popular grassroots base.*

*At the same time, and as part of these efforts, STW and LDC—in collaboration with colleagues and the Popular Committee in the Jordan Valley—founded the Popular Council for the Protection of the Jordan Valley as a framework for the unification of the efforts of the Jordan Valley residents, especially the targeted communities, to meet the challenges they face.*

# ON POPULAR RESISTANCE AND BDS
# The Future of the Palestinian Struggle[38]

*Jamal Jumaa*

The signing of the Oslo Accords in 1993 has had an impact far worse and more dangerous on the Palestinian people than the Israeli incursions into the West Bank in 2002. This is because the Accords reversed the values and principles of the Palestinian Revolution, reduced the map of Palestine into shrunken and fragmented territories, and distorted the Palestinian educational curricula and inalienable national ideals instilled into the Palestinian consciousness over decades. The Accords effectively ignored key events in the Palestinian struggle: the *Nakba* of 1948, the *Naksa* of 1967, in addition to countless other massacres and displacements of the Palestinian people. Palestinian cities like Haifa, Acre, Nazareth, Jaffa, Lod and Ramle suddenly ceased to exist as Palestinian, and the term "the Israeli enemy" was rendered mute.

Even the Left could not act as a safety valve to rescue the sinking ship of the PLO. Instead, they sank into an identity and existential crisis. After the collapse of the Soviet Union and the socialist camp, the Palestinian Communist Party (PCP), to which I belonged, entered a major crisis that resulted in abandoning the party's ideological identity and changing its name to the Palestinian People's Party (PPP). Subsequently, many of the Party's members left. A similar storyline can be told about the Popular Front for the

38 This essay was originally written in Arabic and was translated by Ahmed Almassri.

Liberation of Palestine (PFLP) and the Democratic Front for the Liberation of Palestine (DFLP).

The extent of the crisis resulting from the Oslo Accord is clear to us, Palestinians. Instead of ending the occupation, the Accords institutionalized it by not reaching a final settlement on key issues, including the administrative division of the Occupied Territories into "A, B and C." This has allowed Israel, among others, to maintain—and even strengthen—its colonial project in Jerusalem and Area C, both making up over 60% of West Bank areas.

Like most Palestinians, especially First Intifada activists, I expected that the next popular uprising would inevitably be against the PA and in protest of the Oslo Accords. The Second Intifada of 2000, however, worsened an already horrific reality on the ground.

In truth, the PA has failed to preserve the Palestinian national project. Coupled with its poor governance practices, are its corruption, nepotism, bribery, silence over Israel's actions in Jerusalem and the West Bank, its suppression of the Palestinian resistance, especially members of Hamas, the Palestinian Islamic Jihad (PIJ) and the PFLP, its control over the judicial system and over people's lives. Crony capitalists have also emerged because of the alliance between businesspeople and the PA's security services, institutions and political elite. This, in turn, has led to the rise of a bourgeois class whose interests are linked with the occupation system and who, thus, became threatened by the Palestinian national project. They did so by strengthening economic dependence on Israel and eradicating what might be called the *resistance economy* developed during the First Intifada. As a result, the middle class shrank and a wide segment of people living below the poverty line was formed.

Following the Benjamin Netanyahu-led Likud Party's rise to power between 1996 and 1999, a freeze on settlement activity ended, and the pace of settlement expansion increased. I noticed, at the time, that an undeclared war was being waged on the Palestinian environment. Most of the wastewater from settlements poured through Palestinian agricultural lands, destroying lands, crops and polluting spring water. The West Bank ended up being a disposal site for solid and hazardous waste, including wastewater coming from pre-1948 Palestine (Israel). Israel's destruction of the Palestinian landscape and environment includes the cutting down of trees, mostly under security pretexts, as in Gaza's buffer zone. Israeli bulldozers destroyed most of the orchards there, from where hundreds of tons of citrus had been exported to Jordan and other Arab countries during the 70s, 80s and earlier.

In 1999, I began coordinating with the Palestinian Hydrology Group (PHG) to establish a Palestinian Environmental NGOs Network to confront Israel's systematic environmental destruction of the Palestinian environment. I enjoyed a cordial relationship with the Group's managers and the directors of other institutions by virtue of my work in agricultural relief in the early 90s. The Network included 12 NGOs operating in the Occupied Territories in 1967; the challenge was to advance its work despite the lack of an allocated budget. The PHG provided the location and logistical support for the Network, and my battle with funding began.

This was my first exposure to the dynamics of NGO work, the means for securing funding and the conditions set by international donors to allocate funds. It helps one understand local interactions with international bodies, usually with underlying conflicting ideals. One dangerous aspect to this interaction is the relationship between NGOs and the parties they are affiliated with, and how these NGOs' influence has become stronger than that of the parties they represent because of the financial resources at their disposal.

These service-based popular initiatives represented the civil branch of the political parties, the key link between the parties and their people, as well as a strong means of attracting people to join the ranks of political parties during the period leading up to the Intifada. Most of these NGOs, if not all, were affiliated with the Left. Another type of NGOs emerged against the backdrop of promoting the peace process and co-existence between the two peoples. The goal of these NGOs was to normalize relations between the Palestinians and Israelis, at local or regional levels.

My first task was to design a webpage for the Network and produce material on environmental issues, the project being funded by UNDP/PAP. On completion of the webpage design and content, the NGO had one condition: to acknowledge them as the sponsor for this work. However, when they discovered the content of the designs, they declined association with the webpage because of its "national" orientation. Is it a sin to talk about the Israeli violations committed against our people and the destruction of our country's environment?! All I did was to address the crimes committed by illegal settlements against the environment and the future of Palestinian life on this land that were contrary to international law, but I excluded any mention of either armed or peaceful resistance. This exemplifies how the war we face seeks to curtail our awareness, distort our national culture and sever our association with Palestine. Obviously, this NGO then terminated funding.

The environmental destruction was enormous during the first year of the Second Intifada from September 2000 until the incursions into the West Bank in March of 2002. Thousands of perennial olive trees were cut down along the main roads under the pretext that they would be used as shields for anybody shooting at army and settler cars. Entrances to cities were closed and garbage trucks were denied exit from Palestinian cities, leading to mountains of waste accumulating in the cities.

During my work at the Network during this period, I focused on two key issues: exposing, on a global scale, Israel's destruction of the Palestinian landscape and environment, and achieving the dismissal of two NGOs in the Network that promoted normalization and were members of the Friends of the Earth Middle East (FoEME). I also wanted to have the organization removed from Friends of the Earth International, the largest environmental umbrella in the world. FoEME has claimed to represent Palestine, Israel, Jordan and Egypt in this global network, this being made possible in 2004 after lobbying, pressure and forging alliances in the Network that lasted over two years with groups from the South. The two groups promoting normalization were eventually expelled from the Network at the beginning of 2002.

The Second Intifada (or Al-Aqsa Intifada) began as a popular uprising similar to the First Intifada. I recall how when we went out by the thousands for the funeral of a martyr to the Al-Bireh Cemetery, we would return with more than one martyr. The Israeli Occupation government unleashed its forces, authorizing them to repress, kill, abuse and exercise outright collective punishment to break the uprising since the Intifada erupted on September 28, 2000.

The Intifada was met with Israeli forces' repression, abuse and killing, leading up to its militarization, which was exactly what Israel wanted. Palestinian armed groups and faction brigades then began attacking settlers and army patrols on the main roads, with operations later striking inside Israel in response to the crimes committed daily by the occupation forces. This led to Israel's invasion of the West Bank under Ariel Sharon's orders. At the time, I was working with foreign journalists, mainly facilitating their meetings with political leaders and civilians. I hoped that the Palestinian factions would end these operations immediately after the September 11 attacks in 2001, especially following George Bush's declaration of his war on terror campaign. I expected that Israel would take advantage of this campaign to slap us with that label to stigmatize our struggle and to isolate us internationally.

Using tanks, the Israeli army invaded the West Bank on March 29, 2002, bombed the headquarters of the Palestinian Authority, bulldozed streets, razed entrances to cities and villages, besieged the West Bank, cut off cities and villages from each other, invaded the camps and committed a massacre in every city and village they entered. The most horrific of these massacres was the infamous Jenin refugee camp massacre.

Nobody realized that Israel's so-called Operation Defensive Shield was carried out purely to strike the Palestinian Resistance and re-occupy the West Bank in preparation for the construction of the Wall (the Apartheid Wall). Two months after the start of the Operation in June, while the West Bank was still under siege by tanks, nearly 250 vehicles began razing agricultural lands in the northwest of the West Bank along the Green Line, labelled as the first phase of building the 145 km Wall from Salem, north of Jenin, to Mas-ha, southwest of Qalqilya. Simultaneously, they started to bulldoze many areas around Jerusalem.

Here, the Israeli plans seemed clear, as it symbolically declared the Oslo phase and negotiations with the Palestinians dead. It then began dictating and forcing its vision for the future of the geographic area and for the relationship with the Palestinians through a colonial apartheid regime, starting with the unilateral disengagement plan. It is based on the ideology of the Zionist project, where Greater Israel is seen as stretching from the "River to the Sea," with as few Palestinians as possible within its borders.

The project was based on the administrative divisions set out in the Oslo Accords. Therefore, Israel planned to build the Wall around areas A and B of the West Bank, hence isolating 62% of West Bank area for illegal settlement expansion. Here, Yasser Arafat should have dissolved the Palestinian Authority, withdrawn recognition of Israel and let Israel, as the occupying power, take responsibility for the entire population under its rule, as was the case prior to the First Intifada. However, Arafat was not going to live for long, and was under immense American and Arab pressure—he was surrounded by tanks at his HQ—to abandon his responsibilities in favor of Mahmoud Abbas as Prime Minister and Salam Fayyad as Minister of Finance. The two were imposed after Yasser Arafat passed away in 2004.

## Starting the Grassroots Popular Campaign

Palestinian farmers in northern West Bank began to raise their voices over a potential third *Nakba*: the destruction of agricultural lands, greenhouses, irrigation networks, wells and water tanks. Movement between the cities and towns was very difficult, as there were still tanks on the streets, with military barriers erected in every corner. I consulted my connections and representatives of the Network in the northern governorates of the West Bank to arrange a meeting with the farmers, organized for the end of August in the Asla village in Qalqilya, two months after Israel began to raze their agricultural lands. Those who could, attended from the villages of Qalqilya and Tulkarm. I accompanied colleagues from some NGOs. The meeting was stormy, attended by nearly forty farmers and activists. The cries of some of them still ring in my ears: "This is a third *Nakba*. It seems the PA has agreed to the building of the Wall; they ruined everything for us, they plundered the land."

Shocked, we returned to Ramallah. The next day, we, the Network's coordinating committee, decided to launch a campaign to expose the scheme. Some of the NGOs donated to help facilitate the work. The PHG arranged for the work to take place in the Qalqilya Governorate from nearby Jayyous village, in addition to the Agricultural Relief in the Tulkarm Governorate and the Medical Relief in the Jenin Governorate. I left Ramallah and traveled between the governorates in coordination with active colleagues in these NGOs and their affiliates. We held meetings in the villages affected by the Wall and formed popular committees in each village, selecting representatives of affected farmers, village groups and local leaders. The idea of popular committees goes back to our experience in forming unified leadership committees in the First Intifada. These committees were then known as the "Popular Campaign Committees" or "Popular Committees." Each popular committee bore the name of the village it was representing.

Farmers from different villages unanimously agreed about the Wall: they saw it as an attempt by Israel to separate their villages and homes from their agricultural lands as well as to isolate entire villages from one another. In other words, Apartheid. The campaign we launched was called the "Popular Campaign to resist the Apartheid Wall." There were two factors behind this designation: the nature of the Wall project and its consequences, which is on a par with colonial apartheid practices. The second factor was farmers' spontaneous accurate description of the project as an Apartheid Wall.

The challenge for popular resistance was to organize civil demonstrations and get people to join, despite the bloodshed and killing of Palestinians every single day. It was also equally challenging to keep the protests 100 percent peaceful. The use of firearms by one person could derail the peaceful movement. The committees started to organize daily demonstrations in many locations in areas of Jayyous, Flamiyya, Qalqilya, Baqa al-Sharqiya, Far'un and *Al-Ras* in Tulkarm, in addition to Zabouba and Anin in Jenin and other areas.

All of these protests were committed to traditional popular rallies, and we did not have to stress the need for the protests to remain peaceful.

Demonstrations often took place in the early morning at the sites where bulldozers worked in order to disable them. On the first day, the bulldozers' work was successfully disrupted. The people's connection to the land in the north was organic; fertile agricultural lands were the main source of income for farmers and their families; hence their activities were being carried out daily. People were ready to sacrifice to protect their land from bulldozing and confiscation.

There is a very important dimension to popular resistance that was quite influential: international solidarity. In response to Israeli crimes, international solidarity began to re-emerge with the Second Intifada, with solidarity delegations arriving in Palestine. During Israeli invasions, groups of them formed human shields in some camps and in the HQ with Yasser Arafat. As Israel began constructing the Wall, we drew the attention of solidarity activists to it, and the International Solidarity Movement (ISM) began to form, in parallel with the *Ta'ayush* (or co-existence) movement (which included Jews from the Israeli Left and Palestinians from 1948 areas). What is unique here is that solidarity activists participated in popular activities at the Square.

The participation of foreign and Israeli solidarity activists in demonstrations, sit-ins and tents, such as the *Mas-ha* tent in 2003, created a kind of confusion and added a new dimension that required defining the nature of their participation. One of the female protesters arrested by Israeli intelligence was investigated by an Israeli officer who pretended to be part of the solidarity group and was present in the tent. Another problem was the direct interaction and contact they had with the village residents, which also began to create some social problems. Namely, some people involved in the solidarity movement exceeded their mandate as members of the solidarity committees and began to dictate the form of resistance which they perceived to be acceptable and the kind of slogans that should be used. This was unhealthy and unsustainable for the popular resistance, affecting its popularity among the Palestinian public.

To discuss this issue, I initiated a meeting for the representatives of the popular committees in Tulkarm, Qalqilya and Jenin. This was necessary to resolve several issues, the most important of which were: restructuring the committees to facilitate the process of communication with solidarity groups as their numbers increased, and determining the kind of relationship to be established with *Ta'ayesh* and other Israeli groups and the international solidarity movement. The second issue was the dispute concerning the use of terminology relevant to the Wall, and the underlying understanding of the nature of this project and its objectives. This would determine the nature of the work strategy that we would adopt during the next stage. There was constant debate within the Network's coordinating body (the umbrella of the popular committees' campaign). Some of the members objected to calling the Wall the "Apartheid Wall." The Palestinian Authority also rejected this label, calling it the "Wall of Annexation and Expansion," instead. The NGOs' premise in opposing the label has to do with the sources of funding: they feared that, insofar as European institutions do not accept this label, they therefore would not provide the necessary funding, taking us back to the risks of conditional international funding. The PA, in my opinion, viewed the "Apartheid" label as suggesting extremism and, hence, felt it would anger the Europeans and Americans.

We held the meeting in Tulkarm at the end of June 2003. This meeting was crucial for determining the campaign conditions and its political affiliations and relations. Undoubtedly, I was apprehensive about the direction the meeting would take, especially because of the relationship of some activists with certain NGOs. The meeting began with an analytical introduction about the Israeli plans for building the Wall and its repercussions, in addition to how that would determine the nature of the resistance strategies at the local and international levels. I also spoke about the popular resistance, the set of values and principles that should govern our work and the need to control and regulate the committees' relationship with villages, on the one hand, and with the Israeli and foreign solidarity committees, on the other. At the end of the meeting, the committees adopted the following detailed points:

1. Focusing on decentralizing the relationship with the committees and working to integrate the people's committees in each governorate into a single committee that represents all the villages in the governorate, in addition to forming a coordinating committee in each governorate that would be responsible for communicating with the village committees.

2. Placing an emphasis on the popular campaign's comprehension of the nature of the Wall and the political meaning behind it, as it is an apartheid wall that forms the framework for the colonial apartheid project, which aims to end the Palestinian cause and eliminate the Palestinian struggle and inalienable rights.

3. Placing an emphasis on the leadership and decisions of the popular committees being *Palestinian*, and that the role of *Ta'ayush* and the ISM being limited to solidarity to support the Palestinian struggle and to change the Israeli and international public opinion. At the end of the meeting, we agreed on a program of activities until the end of the year.

In light of this decision, we requested a meeting with the Israeli *Ta'ayesh* movement and the ISM to agree on the principles of work. The meeting was arranged in al-Jawarish village in Tulkarm and attended by me and two representatives of the committees, where we presented our position to them. They requested some time to reflect before they answered, but we never received any response to our suggestions. Following this, we decided to organize their participation through the committees.

The first phase of building the 145 km-long Wall from Salem village, north of Jenin, to Mas-ha village, east of Qalqilya, was completed in mid-2003, i.e., within a year. At the time, we issued the first book in Arabic and English documenting this phase, an important document of which more than 20,000 copies were distributed, mostly to parliaments, international institutions and embassies.

In September 2003, I received an invitation from the United Nations to talk about the Wall. The invitation's proposed title for the topic was "Does the Wall constitute an obstacle to peace?" Personally, I found this headline provocative and disgusting—the United Nations was still asking whether the Wall is an obstacle to peace. I am not sure what kind of peace they were talking about.

I accepted the invitation and prepared the summary of the book as a video presentation, showing the first phase of the Wall building, supported by maps, pictures and analyses. My speaking slot at the conference was for ten minutes but I spoke for about twenty minutes without interruption. Clearly, the information I provided shocked the audience and as soon as I got off the stage, I spoke to our Ambassador to the United States, Nasser Al-Kidwa, who assumed responsibility to take this file to the General Assembly and, from there, to the International Court of Justice. After the Conference ended, a tour of several US states was arranged to talk about the Wall.

That visit marked the beginning of the campaign's work at the international level, after which it participated in many conferences and tours to talk about the Wall and its political and economic ramifications on the future of the Palestinian people and their struggle for freedom. During these interactions, I encountered a painful reality, especially in Europe: that at any conference or workshop, there had to be a "good" Israeli sitting by my side. I saw in this approach an implicit racist discourse and a colonialist view of the Palestinian people as they live under a settler-colonial occupation. Expressly, for a European to believe what you say, there must be a white Israeli at your side to give you credibility, which led me to challenge this approach. We are the ones whose suffering from the occupation will require generations to overcome, after liberation. We are the ones in the position to talk about our pain and the meaning of being robbed of freedom and dignity. At first, I refused to have any Israeli on the stage, even if he or she was anti-Zionist, leading to several disputes in this regard with our friends in European institutions and solidarity committees.

With the growing work of the popular campaign internally and of the Network's external relations, differences were deepening between me and the coordinating committee of the Network. The popular campaign was emerging as a popular movement. The requirements of its work differed from the work of the Network. The latter is limited to coordinating the efforts of groups and organizations in relation to environmental issues, and the former is a popular political action and a form of resistance that is not compatible with the administrative or strategic work of civil society organizations. Hence, we decided on the Network's coordinating committee to separate the popular campaign from the Network, and to change the administrative structure of the campaign so that representatives of the popular committees in the governorates form the coordinating committee to manage the campaign. The Network's organizations requested that a place for representatives of the Network remain in the committee.

Following the death of President Yasser Arafat in November 2004, his opponents in the PA replaced him, supported by the Americans and the Israelis. The first is Mahmoud Abbas, who was one of the founders of the PLO, who has been a strong proponent of achieving peace through negotiations with the Israelis since the 70s and was the architect of the Oslo Accords. The second is Salam Fayyad, a distinguished World Bank employee. This is how a new phase in the Palestinian life and struggle was ushered in. It was based on first restructuring and forming the Palestinian security services with a new security doctrine, supervised by US General Keith Dayton. Among Palestinians, this is referred to as the "Dayton Doctrine." The doctrine is also overseen by American, European and Israeli intelligence. Secondly, the new phase included the adoption of neoliberal policies and economic openness aimed at changing the economic lifestyle and attitudes of Palestinian society. In 2005, the PA realized that the popular movement to resist the Wall had begun to affect Palestinian and international public opinion, and the political discourse it presented embarrassed its political system and its orientations. Its work was only confined to the cycle of negotiations and the strengthening of security coordination with the Israeli Occupation, regardless of the fundamental changes that Israel was making on the political map on the ground, and the consolidation of its apartheid regime, in which Israel bypassed the issue of establishing a Palestinian State. In 2007, in an attempt to co-opt the work of the committee, Salam Fayyad twice offered to open a bank account for popular resistance activists from all over the West Bank and to deposit 6,000 shekels per month to support committee activities. We coordinated with Fatah activists in the popular resistance and caused the meeting to fail, twice.

The destructive effects of the post-Oslo era were not limited to the Palestinian struggle on the ground, but also affected international solidarity. In the 1970s and 80s, and up until the First Intifada, international support for the Palestinian cause came from the countries of the South and the revolutionary movements in the world. During the First Intifada, support expanded to the formation of solidarity committees with Palestine in Europe and America. But during the 1990s, the form of solidarity changed and became limited to Europe and America, led by civil society organizations in coordination with Palestinian NGOs. This support was framed within the scope of what is permitted under international law and official international institutions such as the European Union and the United Nations. The demands sought to put pressure on Israel without putting enforceable and effective means in place to hold Israel to account. The unions and popular movements were largely absent from the scene.

The Palestinian Grassroots Anti-Apartheid Wall Campaign was among the first to begin to restore international solidarity to its rightful place. First, it had a clear vision and demands from the international community; second, it had laid the foundations of solidarity within the framework of mutual solidarity based on the common enemy of peoples, represented by the alliance of imperialist and capitalist forces, including Israel, which aim to drain the wealth of peoples and perpetuate colonialism. Two examples of the latter stand out: Transnational Corporations (TNCs), and Israel's arming and training of dictatorial regimes and militias that companies and regimes use to suppress revolutions and carry out assassinations of resistance leaders. The third point pertains to the active participation in large international social forums such as the World Social Forum, which includes thousands of institutions and movements from different countries and holds its annual conference for a week. We became members of the International Preparatory Committee for the Conference after a year of active participation. Our inaugural participation in the forum was in India in 2004, where Palestine was mentioned in the final statement as one of the places of conflicts in the world. In 2005, there was a paragraph in the final statement on Palestine and, in 2012, the International Social Forum devoted its conference to Palestine under the name of the "Social Forum Global/ Free Palestine." Fourth, the committee launched joint solidarity campaigns shedding light on the suffering and common struggle of peoples. In 2017, we started an international campaign alongside indigenous movements, human rights groups and coalitions in Mexico, Brazil and America in the name of "A World Without Walls." The campaign has now spread across more than 30 countries in the world, highlighting the impact of walls of colonialism and oppression on peoples and immigrants in Europe, America, Latin America, Kashmir and the Arab world.

## Starting the BDS Movement

In 2003, we began a number of international conferences and meetings, raising the issue of boycotting Israel with foreign delegations. Our position was based on our struggle against the Apartheid Wall and on our understanding of Israel's institutionalization of a dangerous apartheid regime in the West Bank, akin to that of Apartheid South Africa. We then initiated an immediate discussion with the Academic Boycott movement and BADIL Resource Center for Palestinian Residency and Refugee Rights. We discussed the founding statement of the Boycott, Divestment and Sanctions (BDS) movement in depth, which would then develop into a document representing its set of founding principles.

We worked on the document for an entire year, which included discussions and brainstorming with figures and institutions inside and outside of Palestine. The biggest challenge was to find a comprehensive discourse that all Palestinians could agree upon, to be the basis for their demand to boycott Israel. Completing this task on the discursive and referential levels was the most important factor contributing to the success of the BDS movement. Therefore, it was impossible for the movement to adopt in its discourse a political solution based on the two-state solution or the one-state solution because the Palestinian people do not agree on either of them.

Any solution to a legitimate struggle must ultimately achieve the demands and rights that the peoples struggle for. The Palestinian issue is one of rights, against the injustices and violations they are subjected to. The solutions presented are complex. Realizing absolute justice for our people, given the extent of the historical injustice that has befallen them, does not seem possible in the near future. Therefore, talking about one or two states becomes a political luxury and privilege in light of the great imbalance of power in favor of the colonizer that is using the most advanced modern technology to subdue, oppress and displace the colonized.

Therefore, it was agreed that the movement's statement should be based on comprehensively addressing human rights, over which neither the Palestinians nor international solidarity activists would dispute. The statement adopted three basic rights and, to realize these rights, we demanded the boycott of Israel and sanctions enforced on it until it respects international law. These basic rights are the right of return for Palestinian refugees who make up 50% of the Palestinian people; ending racial discrimination and inequality for Palestinians living in pre-1948 Palestine (now Israel)—who make up 12% of the Palestinian people—and, finally, ending the occupation of Arab territories, including the occupied Syrian Golan Heights, which has gone on since 1967.

The statement was signed by 171 Palestinian groups and bodies inside and outside Palestine, whose representatives formed the movement's general body which, in turn, forms the movement's secretariat, where membership is voluntary. Its decisions and leadership are established by consensus.

Thus, the BDS movement restored Palestinians' sense of unity, united international solidarity and provided activists with effective and influential tools for solidarity. Accordingly, the Palestinian people have strengthened the concept of the internationalism of human struggle, inspired by the exceptional experience of the people of South Africa.

The greatest achievement of BDS is restoring hope to the Palestinian people, making them realize that they are not alone in their struggle. The movement's leadership style has become a shining Palestinian model of purity in an atmosphere where conspiracies against the Palestinians never stop.

As I write the last lines of this essay, the Bedouin families of Humsa are still living in tent-like shelters on the ruins of their homes, pursued by the occupation forces from one site to another, just like dozens of other Palestinian communities that continue to be uprooted by Israel. Sheikh Jarrah and Silwan neighborhoods are still being forcibly cleansed of their Palestinian population by gangs imbued with hatred and terror, armed with bulldozers and trucks to uproot and displace, while the world is still watching.

RAJI SOURANI *has been dedicated to the promotion and protection of human rights in the Occupied Palestinian Territory throughout his professional career, despite the personal and professional sacrifices he has been forced to make in the process. He has been an active lawyer since qualifying in 1977 and has represented a wide range of victims of human rights abuses. He has received many honors during his career, the most recent of which is the "Right Livelihood Award" for 2013.*

*Despite periods of political imprisonment in Israel, years of harassment and violence from the Israeli military, and harassment from the Palestinian Authority and other Palestinian groups, Sourani has maintained an unwavering commitment to human rights. He has been an advocate for basic human rights standards, both at a domestic and international level, and has refused to curtail his outspoken criticisms of failures by Israel, the Palestinian Authority, political groups and other states to adhere to human rights standards.*

*Despite the obstacles faced, Sourani continues to promote and protect human rights through the Palestinian Centre for Human Rights, which he founded in 1995 with a group of fellow lawyers and human rights activists in the Gaza Strip. Sourani has spearheaded this award-winning center since its establishment and continues to ensure the center provides legal and other services to victims of human rights abuses in the Gaza Strip, thus enabling them to seek justice and reparation.*

*A committed family man, Sourani has been blessed with an equally committed and understanding family, providing love and encouragement through the worst of times. Sourani's wife, in particular, has proved to be the strongest source of support, despite the often great sacrifices that his work has brought into their lives.*

*Throughout the recent challenges presented during the years of the Second Intifada and during the Israeli offensive on the Gaza Strip (Operation Cast Lead), Sourani has remained stalwart in his determination that the center will continue to provide services to the maximum number of victims. He has managed to achieve this aim and the center continues to respond effectively to the challenges faced in the Gaza Strip and throughout the Occupied Palestinian Territory.*

# PURSUING PALESTINIAN RECOURSE THROUGH INTERNATIONAL LAW

*Raji Sourani*

FOR OVER SEVENTY YEARS, Palestinian life has been characterized by widespread and systematic violations of international law. Since the creation of the State of Israel and the mass displacement of Palestinians—a disaster we know as the *Nakba*—we have endured annexation, military occupation, apartheid and oppression. Our life as Palestinians is marked by forced displacement and the violation of virtually every human right, from the right to self-determination, the right to health and the right to freedom of movement, to the prohibition of discrimination, the prohibition of torture and the right to life itself.

We know of international law through its violation.

Every Palestinian, even our youngest children, is all too familiar with war crimes. From the theft of our land and resources for the construction of illegal settlements that prevent our growth as an independent and viable State, to indiscriminate attacks and willful killings. We have even become accustomed to attacks on our hospitals, our health workers and volunteers, journalists, disabled people and children. Entire families have been erased. For us, witnessing a war crime is nearly as normal as taking a breath.

The world knows this. Our suffering has become a staple of prime-time TV, an ever-present news item. Everyone is familiar with the sight of white phosphorous raining down on Gaza, of the complete destruction of entire neighborhoods like Shuja'iyya, or the murder of unarmed protestors for the crime of demanding a better life, for demanding a future.

In the face of this reality, it is legitimate to ask why we put our faith in international law, and why we see international law as providing the roadmap for our future.

For me, turning to international law and seeing its possibilities, was a gradual process. I come from a family of lawyers, judges and prosecutors and, when I started my career in the late 1970s, it was natural for me to visit political prisoners. My own brother had been one of the "early birds" of the prisoner population after the Occupation of Gaza in 1967. I was naïve at the time. I used to go to prisons and ask "Have you been tortured?" If I could not see physical damage, I thought that torture had not occurred, and I moved on. I had no idea what psychological torture was, or how deep its scars ran.

Then I was arrested myself and lived through my own personal experience of it. I realized what "moderate physical and psychological pressure" really meant. Even though this was not the worst form of abuse, as I lived through it, I wanted to die fifty times a day. I also saw first-hand what "justice" under occupation meant. During interrogation I would be coerced to sign a false statement and returned to torture when I refused. Repeatedly. I saw the reality of kangaroo courts, where prisoners were detained or sentenced in minutes. I knew that this law under occupation was not the law I was trained in, that it was not the justice I believed in.

Over time, I began to understand just how miserable life was for prisoners, and I began to pay serious attention to international law. Israeli law offered no accountability for Palestinians, and so there had to be another way. I developed a close relationship with the International Committee of the Red Cross and while I was in prison, they brought me copies of the Geneva Conventions. I started to see a language we could use. These were laws ratified by every country in the world that were designed specifically for situations like ours. They regulated our reality.

After I left prison and developed my own private legal practice, I decided to devote some of my time to representing prisoners. I knew that the prisoners could not be abandoned, that we had to try to challenge the military orders and do what we could to stop the kangaroo courts and introduce a semblance of due process. I did not have any illusion of justice under occupation but decided that we should do our best to minimize the damage, and to fight for whatever victories we could achieve. I soon became overwhelmed. What was supposed to be minor work on the side of my practice soon became my entire work, and I bore witness to a dirty era.

I realized that the proper documentation of cases and the use of international law was a powerful tool. It allowed us to move beyond rhetoric. No longer were we "just" making demands. We had international laws and standards that we could use, which could not be dismissed as "political" claims. I started to engage with international organizations, with Amnesty International, the International Bar Association and the International Commission of Jurists. I also started to develop real relationships with lawyers and human rights organizations in Israel, both Jewish and Palestinian. This was our connection to the "other side" and our work together and friendship were a daily reminder of our shared humanity.

International law gave us a common language and a framework for engagement. We went to work and invested all our time and efforts fighting in the Israeli legal system and its courts. We tried to use the system, and to introduce international humanitarian law and the Fourth Geneva Convention into our language before the courts. Gradually, we came to the conclusion that pursuing justice in Israeli courts was not going to be sufficient on its own.

In the '90s, I took over the Gaza Center for Rights and Law, and we started to build the team that would later go on to become the Palestinian Centre for Human Rights. We built a team of lawyers and advocates, and started to make connections throughout the community. We also made a deliberate effort to reach out internationally. We painstakingly documented the violations of international law that were occurring in Palestine and brought our work to the international community.

The relationships that we had started to develop in the '80s really started to pay off. The International Commission of Jurists was hugely important to us, as was our relationship with Al-Haq in the Occupied West Bank. Over time, I became a member of the Executive Committee of the International Commission of Jurists, and the Vice President of the International Federation for Human Rights (FIDH). This international platform allowed us to start taking our message to the world. We started to participate in events at the United Nations and to build relationships with grassroots organizations from South Africa to South America. We shared our experiences in fighting oppression and learned from each other. This solidarity is so important. It is a reminder that you are not alone. A reminder, too, that, no matter how different we are, we are all united in a shared struggle for justice.

Importantly, however, while we engaged internationally as much as we could, we always had our feet planted firmly on the ground in Gaza. This is where our work really is, and we never stopped working in the Israeli legal system. We do not do this because we feel that real justice under occupation is possible. We do it because we must. We have to pursue every avenue possible for our clients and we have to be eyewitnesses to injustice. We have to document how the courts and the legal system itself actually work. We have to record our experiences. It is important that we show the world the reality: that from the military courts right up to the Israeli High Court of Justice, the entire Israeli system provides full legal cover for the systematic commission of war crimes and crimes against humanity. It is also required in pursuit of international legal redress to show that we have "exhausted" the Israeli justice system, and that justice has been denied. This allows us to turn to international mechanisms, whether it is the International Criminal Court or universal jurisdiction.

No one would believe us if we simply said that justice under occupation is no justice at all. We would be dismissed out of hand. Many people believe that the Israeli court system is one of the best in the world. But if so, insofar as Israeli law is like Roman law—one law for the masters and another for the slaves—it only applies to the former. Without our legal work, our criticisms would be pushed aside as political. People would think that we are "just being Palestinians."

However, we do not ask to be judged on the strength of our word. Judge us on the strength of our work. Our documentation and our use of international law give us the language to clearly depict the reality of the situation in normative, legal terms. People might want to dismiss us as politically motivated Palestinians, but it is impossible to dismiss well documented cases and clear and sound legal analysis. For those who do not believe us, we suggest they consult a lawyer for verification of our work.

In the late 1990s, we started to more actively seek out possibilities for international justice. From the outset, we have been supporters of the International Criminal Court. This has always been the beautiful but seemingly impossible dream: the hope that the law would be applied equally to everyone, without discrimination, and that those responsible for the most serious international law violations would be finally held to account.

It was only months after the final adoption of the Rome Statute of the International Criminal Court in 1998 that news of the arrest of General Augusto Pinochet in the United Kingdom, based on the principle of universal jurisdiction, hit us like a bolt of lightning. This was a revolution. The possibility that an individual could be arrested and held to account in another country for torture or war crimes was music to our ears. While it would take years for the International Criminal Court to get up and running, universal jurisdiction was something that we could pursue immediately. This gave us a new focus and energy, and we put a huge amount of effort into preparing cases and monitoring the movements of our list of war crimes suspects.

We brought our first universal jurisdiction case in England on 29 October 2002, seeking the arrest of Shaul Mofaz. Mofaz had been Chief of the General Staff of the Israel Defense Forces, from 1998 until July 9, 2002. The complaints lodged covered a broad range of serious violations, including grave breaches of the Geneva Conventions, war crimes and crimes against humanity. At the time, Mofaz was Minister of Defense, and as such was provided personal immunity. However, the Crown Prosecution Service noted that the case could be revisited once his term in office ended.

This gave us hope and, over the next few years, we built an excellent legal team, bringing together committed lawyers and human rights activists from all over the world. I am proud of this work. Among the universal jurisdiction cases we brought: in September

2003 two complaints were submitted to the Swiss Military Attorney General in Berne on behalf of Palestinian victims and relating to the extensive destruction of Palestinians homes, and five counts of torture. The suspected were Benjamin Ben-Elizer (former Israeli Minister of Defense), Shaul Mofaz (former IDF Chief of Staff), Doron Almog (former Commander IDF, Southern Command), and Avi Dichter (former Director, Israeli General Security Services). The complaints were brought against the defendants pursuant to their individual criminal responsibility, in light of the principle of command responsibility. However, the Swiss Military General Prosecutor decided not to prosecute the case, as none of the accused was on Swiss soil at the time the complaints were brought, in what is a procedural, rather than a substantive ground for dismissing the complaints.

Following these outcomes, we did not give up. To the contrary, we have stepped up our efforts to bring war criminals to account and restore the rule of law and the rights of the victims.

Not all of our cases are made public, and we are still waiting for some suspects to travel to countries where they might be apprehended. That said, we have secured arrest warrants for Tzipi Livni in England, for Moshe Yaalon in New Zealand and Ami Ayalon in the Netherlands. Dramatically, in 2005 we secured an arrest warrant for Doron Almog, former Commander of the Southern Command, as he was flying to London. The moment his flight landed on 11 September 2005, he was liable to arrest. However, British police refused to board the aircraft—rumor had it that Almog's bodyguards were armed—and, following a tip off from the Israeli embassy, he never left the plane, flying straight back to Tel Aviv.

One of the greatest, most hopeful moments, was on January 29, 2009, when a Spanish judge ruled that the Israeli authorities were not willing to properly investigate the Al-Daraj massacre in 2002 in which an Israeli strike on Gaza killed 15 people. and opened a universal jurisdiction case. This came just days after Operation Cast Lead, which was—at that time—the most brutal and deadly offensive in the Gaza Strip. It was a clear reminder that Israeli officials suspected of international crimes could be held accountable and that they were not above the law. In those dark days, as Gaza lay in ruins, it gave us hope.

Some people have criticized our universal jurisdiction work, saying we never achieved any actual prosecutions and were wasting our time. But in actuality, we did two really important things. First, we convinced judges in some of the most respected legal systems in the world that we had an actionable case. While this did not lead to a conviction, it did clearly show that the judges believed in the evidence sufficiently to necessitate a prosecution. That cannot be lightly dismissed. Second, we reminded Israeli military and government officials that they are not above the law, and that we will not play good, docile victims. We will not stop in our fight for justice and accountability, and we will follow them around the world.

However, in recent years, pursuing universal jurisdiction has become nearly impossible. There has just been too much political interference to make this a viable option. In England as an instance, the law, itself, was changed following pressure from the Israeli government.

The International Criminal Court became our only option. The year 2015, when Palestine joined the Court, marked a new era after years of frustration. We had supported the International Criminal Court from the outset and had been fighting to find a way to seize the attention of the Court for years. We faced huge pressure, threats, and at times, it seemed like mission impossible. Israel´s Operation Protective Edge, the 2014 war on Gaza, was a turning point, and it finally looked like the Palestinian Authority in Ramallah might ratify the Statute, but they would not do it without the support of the de facto government in Gaza. We played a key role in bringing all the groups to the table, including Hamas and Islamic Jihad. In 2021, the opening of an investigation by the Office of the Prosecutor of the International Criminal Court was a huge leap forward. We hope that it is the start of a new era of accountability for crimes against Palestinians. Needless to say, we are well aware that powerful political pressure will seek to obstruct access to justice for victims. We all remember the attacks and the fact that in 2020, former US President Donald Trump went so far as to place sanctions against Ms. Fatou Bensouda, former Prosecutor of the International Criminal Court, and other Court officials (and family members, alike).

Now we have two fights. We continue to represent our clients before the Israeli courts, to fight for whatever victories we can achieve and we are fully engaged with the investigation at the International Criminal Court.

The pressure we have faced because of our work at the International Criminal Court has shocked me—but it is only a testimony to how important this work is. We have been accused of misusing international law. It is claimed that we are agents of terrorist organizations. The Israeli Ministry of Strategic Affairs and Public Diplomacy circulated a document internationally, called "Terrorists in Suits," where we are named as individuals and organizations. The former Israeli Prime Minister, Benjamin Netanyahu, considered opening an investigation against us as a strategic threat to Israel. It is claimed that we are engaged in "lawfare" against Israel.

Why is the State of Israel so worried about a small group of Palestinian and international lawyers working at the International Criminal Court? We do not use any magic formula. We legally document facts, we apply international standards, the same as do other international litigants. In our view, our case files show that Israel has systematically committed war crimes and crimes against humanity. But Israel will not join the International Criminal Court. They have some of the best lawyers in the world and vast resources. But they boycott the Court. Why? If they disagree with our findings, why not face us across the court?

I have lived my entire life under occupation. I am 67 years old, and this is my life story. I do not have a nationality. I am totally under Israeli control. However, I do believe in the rule of law and our shared dignity. We are romantic revolutionaries. I firmly believe that we are on the right side of history, that justice will be achieved, but the road is not easy.

So now, looking back, what do I think about international law? Has pursuing this path been worth it?

The Oslo Accords were a major lesson. We opposed them and came under huge pressure for doing so. But we opposed them because they did not properly reflect international law. How can there be peace without human rights? How can you build a future that is not based on human rights? We cannot victimize the rule of law, democracy and human rights for the sake of security. This was the logic of the US and the EU in supporting the Oslo Accords and, in doing so, they effectively legitimized all of the human rights violations that followed. We were accused of being anti-peace, but we knew that this flawed agreement would only create a new brand of apartheid. What has happened in the years since then are a daily reminder of what happens when politics trump international law. The Oslo Accords remind us of the importance of staying true to our belief in our rights and of speaking truth to power in their pursuit.

We did not invent international humanitarian law or international human rights law. These laws emerged from the horrors of war, and they offered a shared hope for a better future. The Geneva Conventions have been ratified by every single country in the world. We cannot be dismissed as political voices for using them. Such charges are only to be expected from the parties that are the abusers. The legal cogency of our cases has been proven by the arrest warrants we have secured around the world and the role that we have played in ensuring the International Criminal Court began its investigation.

International law is a way of demonstrating that we are equal. What we are asking for is the equal application of the law, so that we are treated the same as everyone else, that we enjoy the same rights under law as everyone else. Indeed, including that we be held accountable, just like everyone else. This is why we work on two strands. We work to hold Israel accountable for the crimes of the occupation, and we work to hold the Palestinian groups to account as if there was no occupation. There is no other way.

Sometimes our legal analysis is ahead of its time. At the 2001 World Conference against Racism, we issued a statement accusing Israel of the crime of apartheid for its treatment of Palestinians in Israel and occupied Palestine. This conclusion was shocking to many people at the time and caused huge controversy. Twenty years later, first B'Tselem, an Israeli human rights organization, and then Human

Rights Watch reached the same conclusion. This is a reminder to stick to our principles and our belief that we are entitled to our rights.

We are living in the rule of the jungle. What we demand, what we fight for, is simple. We want the rule of law. We are committed to justice and dignity for Palestinians. This is why accountability is essential.

We will not play "good victims." We are in this work knowing that it is a long fight, but we have no right to give up. Tomorrow will be ours.

# SECTION III

# ON LIBERATION, CULTURE AND EDUCATION

GHADA AGEEL *is a visiting Professor in the Department of Political Science at the University of Alberta, and the editor of both* Apartheid in Palestine: Hard Laws and Harder Experiences *and* Women's Voices from Gaza *series. A third-generation Palestinian refugee, Dr. Ageel holds a Ph.D. and MA in Middle East Politics from the University of Exeter/UK and a BA in Education from the Islamic University/Gaza. Her research interests focus on rights-based approaches to forced migration, Palestinian refugees in comparative perspective, oral history and the Arab-Israeli conflict.*

# "NEXT YEAR IN BEIT DARAS"
# Reclaiming Our Narrative, Telling Our Stories

*Ghada Ageel*

I LOVE LISTENING TO and sharing stories. I owe that love to my grandmother, Khadija, who, each night, used to tell her grandchildren stories from real life and from fiction, too. Stories of the former include the tale of our village, Beit Daras, prior to its destruction, in the 1948 *Nakba* and the loss of the homeland. These stories recount the *Badrasawi* traditions that we need to preserve. When asked where we are from, we will state proudly that we are from Beit Daras. My grandmother narrated her story, the Palestinian story, with passion and love. To this moment, I can repeat these tales with the same facial expressions and body movements, while telling the stories to my children. These stories shaped my life and, to a large extent, my vision and even my future. My grandmother's storytelling became the recipe for my life of storytelling. Her narrative was not metaphoric or abstract but embodied and physical; she was reliving the story which had occurred in reality, not as myth. As listeners, we responded in kind: when her voice creaked or broke, so too, did our hearts. Thus embodied, she narrated both the personal and the political. The ingredients of her life fill the pot of our national story: one spoon of happy, two spoons of sad.

In this short essay, I will share part of our story/history, which stands as a counter account to mainstream narratives, hoping that such a small part of an individual account can convey a clear picture of the communal one, a representation of the collective Palestinian struggle for rights and freedom. The chapter also aims to invite readers in, at both the moral and epistemological level, and to open new venues for conversation which break the intellectual apartheid imposed on Palestine. This account, as the rest in this volume, attempts to offer a vision for decolonization and contribute to de-colonial scholarship by centering the lives positioned on the margins at the heart of the conversation and research.

I am a third-generation Palestinian refugee from a village, Beit Daras, a place that no longer exists on the world map. I inherited the genes of a refugee from my father, Abdelaziz, the eldest son of my grandmother, Khadija, who was expelled from her home and land during the *Nakba*. She lived a harsh and often cruel life, struggling through poverty, misery and the humiliation of losing everything overnight. Growing up in a refugee camp in the Gaza Strip, decades after the destruction of Beit Daras, my grandmother told me the story of our village. At this time (the late 1970s), it was too dangerous to even mention the word "Palestine." We were denied the right to study, read or possess anything related to our homeland. My grandmother stepped in to fill that gap of historical denial by passing on her story. Our land was in her memories every day.[1] The story of our lost village was, in the words of Ramzy Baroud, "a daily narrative that simply defined our internal relationship as a community" (2009). Telling the story of her village, Khadija knew, would not bring back the dead from their graves nor would it return Beit Daras to existence, but telling the story would help to prevent Beit Daras from being exiled from human memory and history. It would also help us—the new generations born in the camps—to learn and preserve our history. That was her mission and, to a large extent, she succeeded in it (Ageel 2016).

The Khan Younis refugee camp is the place my grandmother and my parents called their temporary home while waiting to return to their original home in Beit Daras. Khan Younis is also the place where I was born, raised and educated. It is also the place where my

1 Contrary to the prediction of David Ben Gurion that the old generations would die and young generations would forget (Ben Gurion 1948, cited on *Al-Awda* website, https://al-awda.org/).

grandmother, my father and I, like every other Palestinian in Gaza, were imprisoned in our houses every night when the Israeli military imposed a shoot-on-sight curfew from 8 P.M. until 6 A.M. throughout the six years of the First Intifada, 1987–1993. This is the place into which I was pushed and squeezed, leaving me feeling like an exile in my own land. This is also the place where I will always think of Beit Daras and Palestine and of my grandmother, a grand tower of resistance who passed away in 2016 and was buried in the family cemetery in the camp (not in Beit Daras, the village from which she was expelled, 71 years ago.[2])

To make a hole in the wall of poverty, to secure a place under the sun and to be able to shorten the distance between ourselves and Beit Daras, we, the generations born in the camps, were taught from a very young age that education is the way forward.[3] Education was both part of our national story and also a methodology for imparting it. The annual *tawjihi* exams (high school graduation exams) are a key moment in the Palestinian calendar for liberation. Even during times of war, exams are rarely canceled, only postponed or deferred. The euphoric release of exam results is a moment of enormous celebration, where the nation marks the ability of our students to overcome whatever has been thrown at them.

So, as with others in Gaza's camps, my parents invested heavily in educating us. Despite the curfews, school closures and the ongoing attacks and harassment during (but also prior to) the First Intifada, I studied tirelessly, and it was no surprise that I obtained the high marks required to join a good school—in Palestine this typically means to study medicine or engineering. My family was very proud when the

---

2 Ageel, Ghada, *Apartheid in Palestine: Hard Laws and Harder Experiences* (Edmonton, Alberta, Canada : The University of Alberta Press, 2016).

3 In the mainstream Israeli narrative Palestinian education is described as a methodology of hatred. Our school texts come under scrutiny from foreign governments and funding institutions and media. But, for Palestinians, education is a form of liberation. Thus the highest status job among the prisoners is the librarian, the holder of stories, the passer of secret messages. And the highest accord one offers a friend upon greeting them is not "sheikh," a religious title, but "ustaaza/ustaaz," teacher, professor, friend of wisdom.

*tawjihi* results were announced. To celebrate my achievement, my father, Abdelaziz, made a big pot of tea and bought a box of Salvana chocolates and rushed to the family *Diwan* where our *Mukhtar*, Salah Aqil, prepared the Arabic coffee.

Happiness, alas, does not last long in Gaza. Israel's decision to close all the Palestinian universities in 1988 deprived me, as well as the 18 thousand students who finished *tawjihi* that year, from pursuing higher education. That short-lived joy was snatched in an instant. The occupying power's decision shattered my dreams and left me in a state of deep despair. I had to wait for six full years, dreaming of the day that I could join university in order to continue my education. During those years, I kept clutching tightly to my dream and never let it fade away. Mahmoud Darwish was right: Palestinians are diagnosed with an incurable disease called hope. Yet, for me, the spark of hope took an entire month to get ignited. During that month, I could not comprehend my situation. For me, the sky had crashed. 1988 became like 1948, the *Nakba* year, my own *Nakba* that struck at my ability to think or even engage in a rational conversation.

"*Fi el harakeh barakah,*" my grandmother would tell me when she saw my tears. Yes, I know our proverb "In moving there is blessing," I would reply, angrily. Then my father would gently remind me of one of the proverbs that I had learned and liked when I was preparing the school morning program, "'From the very small window of their cell, two captive people gazed out: one looked at the sky and the other looked at the mud under his feet.' We still have the choice of where to gaze," he would say, when he entered my room and saw me looking at the floor. I had little to no response to my family's constant attempts to get me out of the state of loss and limbo that I found myself in. I spent that month in my room/bed crying, unable to deal with my *Nakba*.

Then one morning, I woke up feeling sick and tired of crying and sleeping. I was weary of gazing at the ceiling of our room and its floor. My body was aching, and I needed to move. I felt I was suffocating, and I needed a bigger space to breathe. I missed looking at the sky. I waited until everyone went to sleep, then left my room at around midnight and sat in the small yard gazing at Gaza's vast, clear sky. It was so beautiful and full of stars. Without doubt, Gaza's sky is the most beautiful sky I have ever seen. I kept gazing for hours, absorbing deeply the beauty and greatness of our sky. Suddenly, something clicked inside me. I started to think of my dad's and grandmother's words. Then I heard the voice on the army megaphone, announcing that the curfew on the camp was lifted. Neighbors started to wake up and move into their homes. Because the houses are so close to each other in the camp, I could feel them moving about. The *Imam* called for the *Fajr* (morning) prayer, and I went to pray. I felt an inner peace inside me; I felt I was back on track. Like the people around me waking for a day of activity, I, too, needed to move.

During the Intifada, young people had a lot of time on our hands. Paradoxically, the very restrictions of the occupation created a fertile ground for activism and community work. So, the following week, I joined the Intifada volunteer team that managed the camp's social affairs and became involved in the educational committees that helped young students during closure of schools. We gave lessons at mosques and homes, and sometimes we had to jump from wall to wall to reach students at their homes to avoid arrest by soldiers for breaching the curfew.[4] Two years later, I found myself a job as a teacher in a kindergarten in the eastern part of Khan Younis town. I was paid $8 a month, of which $4 went for transportation. In the following year, 1991, I also registered to take Hebrew classes which were offered in the evening. Many Palestinian men knew Hebrew because they worked in Israel as laborers, but very few women could speak it. I felt that communication with the occupation soldiers who bombarded the camp daily, chasing children who threw stones at them, was a necessity. During the Intifada, curfews were imposed often. Men between the ages of 16 to 64 were regularly ordered to leave their homes and head out onto the streets to be searched,

---

4 This is an echo of Freire who argues that through education and the relationship with action liberation is uncovered. "As critical perception is embodied in action, a climate of hope and confidence develops which leads men to attempt to overcome the limit-situations." (Freire, 1970, p98 as found at https://envs.ucsc.edu/internships/internship-readings/freire-pedagogy-of-the-oppressed.pdf )

interrogated and possibly arrested. At the same time, soldiers would conduct house-to-house searches, rampaging through our homes. Language seemed to be a way to help in some way. Knowing Hebrew would not result in different treatment, but it could serve as a bridge. Sometimes, it was the Palestinian sense of humor that enabled the expression of our common humanity, and this helped.

This was the case for my relative, Ahmad. One day the curfew imposed on Khan Younis was lifted for a couple of hours. Only women were allowed out to buy necessities. Ahmad did not care. He put on his *Jalabiya* (traditional Arabic dress), took his donkey and his cart and went out to buy a sack of flour for his family. He was caught by soldiers, who started attacking/beating and threatening him for breaking the orders. They reminded him that only women were allowed in the streets. Ahmad answered, "Who told you I am a man? I am a woman today. Look at my dress...We swap in my home," he continued. "One day I am a woman, one day I am a man. Luckily, today I am a woman. And so, I'm out. Do you want me to break my word before my wife?" The soldiers laughed and sent him back home!

At the end of 1992, and during the early days of the peace process, the so-called Israeli civil administration in Gaza, a body that oversaw education, health and social affairs, announced four scholarships to study Hebrew in the Akiva Language Institute, a language boarding school in Natanya city. At that time, I had finished three courses in Hebrew and so filed an application. I was over the moon when I won one of the scholarships. The problem now was how to convince my family to allow me to study inside Israel for a year. My grandmother and mother immediately rejected the idea, and so did my uncles. "What could we learn from those who destroyed our society and stole our land?" my grandmother said. My mother's main concern was about the dangerous environment that her eldest but still young and single daughter would live in. She was concerned that I would be mixing with strangers, the settlers and newcomers who came to occupy our land. Each one of our extended family and neighbors had their own fears and worries. Despite the risk and the fears, my father saw it as an opportunity. Driven by my passion for education and excited by the possibility of securing a job after graduation, he talked to my mother for a good part of that rainy night. I could hear their voices breaking the silence in the camp and I was praying that my mother would reconsider her decision. The fears of my family started to find a place in my heart, too. I slept very little that night and, in the morning, my mother woke me up. Placing her faith in me, she told me that I could go. Feeling relieved but at the same time aware of the huge responsibility this put on my shoulders, I packed my bag and left.

The very minute I left the Strip, passing through the Erez Crossing which separates Gaza from Israel and stepping into the Palestine of my grandmother's stories (now Israel), I felt like I had traveled through time and space. I felt like I had moved thousands of kilometers away from my camp—as if it was to another planet. It was hard to believe that I was less than an hour's distance from Khan Younis. I remembered my grandmother's words when she was exiled from Beit Daras. She told me that the minute she stepped into Gaza, she felt as if she was thrown from paradise into hills full of sand. (Khan Younis' topography, at that time, was sandy hills.) For a short time, I felt that I was thrown from the hills of sand back into the lost paradise that my grandmother described.

Yet, that feeling was short-lived. In everyday conversation, I came to recognize the sheer levels of injustice, inequality and racism. I still remember the story of an Israeli student who came late to class because he enjoyed having his regular ten minutes' shower. For the teacher, class time should be respected. For me, the issue was more about inequality and less about time. How can one individual consume, in a single shower, the same amount of water that is allocated to an entire family? Yes, each home/family in the Gaza camps—including ours—was allocated 15 minutes of water a day. It was also an awkward and painful experience to share classes with white foreign settlers coming from eastern Europe, mainly Russia, who possessed no connection whatsoever to my land, but enjoyed the privileges to study, live and gain citizenship. Yet we, the indigenous people of the land, still battle in our refugee camps. I started to imagine how my life might have been, had I not been thrown into the hills of sand that became Gaza's refugee camps.

A month after I finished my study, I got a job as a teacher in one of Gaza City's schools. Securing a job was (and still is) a far-fetched dream that everyone in Gaza prays for.[5] My worried family became happy. Now, I could help my father, my siblings and myself.

The following year, 1994, was an eventful one in my life. Besides getting a job, I also got my driving license, got engaged and started to work as an interpreter for a Japanese journalist. Studying Hebrew for a year had also helped improve my English and I learned a bit of Russian, too, as I needed to communicate with foreign students coming to learn Arabic in Gaza. In that same year, the Palestinian Authority was created as a result of the Oslo agreement between the Palestinian Liberation Organization and Israel. The Israeli authorities began to relax some restrictions and reopened the Palestinian universities, allowing my five siblings and I to join schools! What a tough year for my father to suddenly support this army of students! By the end of the year, I also got married. We moved from the camp and rented an apartment in Gaza City.

Because of my work and the new horizons offered to me, I encountered many interesting people over many years. Many years into the future, one such encounter was with a British judge who commented on a visa application I helped a relative obtain. His words have added to my understanding of disenfranchised groups:

Life is full of challenges and one's color, citizenship and, possibly, some luck would determine the amount of hardship people may endure and the efforts needed to invest to succeed. When one is a Palestinian, they need to double those efforts.

So often we, the wretched of the earth, need to exert double, or even triple, the efforts compared to privileged groups. In the words

---

5 Gaza's unemployment rate continues to impose a massive impact on society at large (43.1% in December 2020) and for women in particular as high as 60.4%. See Gisha, "Gaza's workforce continues to shrink, 43% unemployment in the last quarter of 2020," April 13, 2021, https://gisha.org/en/gazas-workforce-continues-to-shrink-43-unemployment-in-the-last-quarter-of-2020/.

of my youngest brother, Fahed, we need to exert 180 percent effort to be able to get normal things done. Or, in the words of my brother, Manar, who studied engineering in Germany, our efficiency should exceed that of a machine.

This was exactly my situation from 1994 to 1999. I was teaching at one of Gaza's schools in the morning, studying at university in the afternoon and, in the evening, teaching Hebrew to Palestinians and Arabic to foreigners at a language center in Gaza; meanwhile, I also acted as an interpreter whenever an opportunity arose, all the while leading a family and raising a daughter, who was born in 1996.

Although Gaza was being opened with the arrival of Arafat and the Palestinian Authority, it was envisioned to become the Singapore of the Middle East. Yet for myself, leading the life of a young mother, activist and educator still had many of the features of a life under the thumb of another. We were still an occupied people and, although my life was full, it was still not free. In Gaza, even under the Oslo period, only the birds remained free. Our water still only ran for limited periods. Our movements were still subject to suspicion and scrutiny. The underlying structure of occupation remained ever-present: although we were allowed out of the cages, we were still kept as if on safari where, at any moment, the occupier could return us to them. I graduated in January 1999 with a GPA that offered me a springboard to dream further and to look for opportunities beyond Gaza's sky. Education was the path. I started applying to universities outside Palestine to do my Master's degree. To secure acceptance and possibly a scholarship, I needed a good TOEFL score. The language proficiency exam was offered twice a year, but I had already missed the first one. I studied hard, filled dozens of applications with the help of my foreign students who joined my Arabic classes at that time. In July 1999, I got an acceptance letter and a scholarship from the political science department at the University of Exeter in the UK. That September, I boarded a plane and headed to the UK, leaving my three-year-old daughter, behind, although we were all to be reunited in Gaza a year later, when I finished my degree.

The Second Intifada erupted in September 2000 while I was finishing my thesis and nursing my two-month-old son, Tarek. Yes, I planned to have my second child while doing my MA! The joke was, if I could not pass the exams, then at least I had a ready-made excuse!

I submitted my work in early October and, on the same day, flew to Gaza. It was just days after the murder of Mohammed Al-Durra, a young child who was shot and then bled to death in his father's arms. Gaza's population and infrastructure were under full-scale assault by the American-made Apache helicopters and the F16. This raised the violence to a new level which I had never experienced before. When I stepped into the Strip, I did not recognize the area: everything was wiped off the map. The level of destruction was beyond my imagination. I was interviewed by the late Bob Simon who was in Gaza for 60 Minutes, and I spoke about the pain of encountering this new reality.

Upon my return to Gaza, I found myself at a crossroads with little direction about where to go and how to help. The situation was like that of 1988, during the First Intifada, when I felt/got lost. It did not take much time, though, to get back on track and to find in education the way forward and the source of empowerment. I was better educated now than I was in 1988, but how could I utilize this education to better advance both myself and the cause? I was no longer willing to return to my old job to teach and manage the language center. I felt, as many of my generation in Gaza, powerless and helpless while seeing our homes being bombarded, destroyed and our men and young people assassinated, shot or in chains.

Despite the intensive coverage by the western mainstream media of the situation in Palestine, our story was always, somehow, missing. Even when it was covered, it had little resemblance to our reality. There is a huge gap between the Palestinian lived experience and what is reported in the media about it. I felt the same gap in academia and in literature when I was doing my MA in the UK. Both my study and work with media exposed me to the prevalent narratives that bear little resemblance to our lived experience, and which serve to defame Palestinians as a group and, in addition, to exclude their voices from international discourse. This exclusion is further complicated by narrative deformation. As pointed out by Ramzy Baroud, Palestinian discourse has largely been supplanted by an assertive narrative representing Palestinians as irrationally angry, reactive actors, hapless multitudes of passive victims rather than having the ability to act as agents. Additionally, whatever (little) knowledge exists of Palestinian life before the foundation of the state of Israel is largely determined by mainstream media coverage, Western and Israeli academic research and Zionist-oriented narratives, commonly reducing Palestinian history to a collection of stereotypes.

The more I read about and watched our story screened on TV, the more exasperated I became. This feeling was shared by an Australian friend, Barbara, who was working in Gaza and joined one of my Arabic courses back in 1998. Barbara was amazed at the rich history, generosity and beauty of Gaza and its people—one that clashes, to a large extent, with what she learned in school and from the media. She conceived the idea of conducting an oral history project, recording and publishing the authentic version of the Palestinian story in English. As a Palestinian, born and raised under occupation, and who had never had the chance to learn our history, I became very enthusiastic about the idea. I saw in this research project a way to place our story at the center when talking about Palestine. Research emerged as a further methodology to break down the superimposed narratives which keep us in the frame developed by the oppressors. Research itself became a way to contribute to the struggle.

We started the project, and in no time, I gained back some of the energy and motivation I have always enjoyed. The oral history research was my way forward out of the state of powerlessness and a source of empowerment and enlightenment. It also offered an attempt to create and project an alternative approach to communicating the history of the Palestinian people and as such, a step towards decolonization. Adopting the discipline of "History from Below" and "Herstory," a term often used by feminist historians and activists telling the untold life stories of women, particularly marginalized women, over a period of two years we interviewed seven ordinary women, but especially sought those with a variety of experiences and a good memory who were, thus, capable of conveying the depth, diversity and richness of Palestinian life. The life-stories of each and all these women highlight everyday experiences in Palestinian villages and towns in pre-1948 Palestine and the Gaza Strip as well as their experiences of war and exile, of two Intifadas and their thoughts on the future. In 2020, the first story, *A White Lie*, came to fruition. The second, *Light the Road for Freedom*, followed in 2021, while the rest of the series will be released in the coming years.

Barbara and I became the midwives of these voices. In so doing and joining other academics and activists who preceded us (of whom I knew little in 1999), we acted against the "voice-cide" of established patterns of academia and media by assisting indigenous Palestinian voices to have their own space, which, in itself, is a revolutionary strategy of resistance which has the power to topple oppressive discursive regimes. Across walls in Gaza and the West Bank, the phrase "to exist is to resist" is written in simple black letters. These stories become acts of resistance by virtue of their sheer existence. They add drops to the ever-growing sea of knowledge which washes Gaza's shores. They place Palestine in the context of other global struggles against colonialism, racism and apartheid because, with a human lens, they demonstrate the impact of such policy on the lives of people.

The 2021 attack on Gaza was also a turning point in the journey along the freedom highway. When I visited Gaza in the summer of 2021, I witnessed how young people, in particular, were countering the narrative of Palestinians as mere supplicants to the aid industry or as grim statistics in a war between two sides of equal status. Instead, this summer of 2021, again the boxes of chocolates and the tea were distributed in the streets and *Diwans,* celebrating the achievement of Gaza's students who occupied the majority of the top ten places in all Palestine, despite the brutal Israeli attack that ripped through the ravaged and besieged Strip just weeks before the start of the exams.

These young people were/are not the helpless and hopeless Palestinians who are often presented to the world through grim statistics or chronicles of events. These young people were successfully molding the concept of hope into a revolutionary tool in the battle for dignity and freedom. They were equipped now with a story: a story of brutality and ugly violence by an occupying power and of life lived in response. With this powerful tool in their hands, like each preceding generation, they would send this story into the world for all who had ears to listen.

The fragmentation and separation which is endured by Palestinians should have been intensified by this war on civilians but instead, the collective resolve was strengthened with a message of its unity.

As I was packing my bags to return to Canada, I said a tearful goodbye to my family. Rafah Crossing was a short drive away and, on the other side, would be a journey into the pain of separation from my homeland. As I said goodbye, my family tried to lighten the load with some smiles and humor. (Naturally but ironically, the ones staying in Gaza were bringing the laughter!) Playing on the old prayer of the Passover Seder, their words echoed in my ears "Next year in Beit Daras." Insh'Allah!

JEHAN ALFARRA *is co-chair of the Palestinian History Tapestry Project. She is a Palestinian writer, multimedia journalist and producer, covering Middle Eastern affairs and specializing in Palestinian political news and social issues.*

JAN CHALMERS *is a nurse and embroiderer who worked for UNRWA in Gaza in 1969 and 1970. She founded the Palestinian History Tapestry Project in 2011. Her idea for a Palestinian history tapestry was prompted by her experience in working with South African village women to create the Keiskamma History Tapestry. With Palestinian colleagues, Jan coordinates the Tapestry panel production.*

# THROUGH THE EYE OF A NEEDLE: Stitching the Palestinian History of Resistance and Sumud

*Jehan Alfarra and Jan Chalmers*

## INTRODUCTION

Oxford is one among many places around the world which have special relationships of various kinds with Palestine and Palestinians. The Oxford-Ramallah Friendship Association (ORFA) was formed in 2002 after volunteer observers from Oxford had witnessed Israeli military assaults in Ramallah. The relationship between the two cities has grown stronger over time. It was formalized in 2019 when the Lord Mayor of Oxford, Colin Cook, welcomed the Mayor of Ramallah, Musa Hadid and the Palestinian Ambassador, Husam Zumlot, to Oxford Town Hall. A twinning agreement was signed, celebrating many years of grassroots friendship between people in the two cities.

Another link between Oxford and Palestine was established in 2009 in response to a devastating Israeli assault on Gaza. It was met with a very muted response from the UK government. To remind people in Gaza that they had not been forgotten in Britain, a group of individuals in Oxford raised money to initiate an annual postgraduate scholarship scheme at Oxford Brookes University. The scheme has resulted in Master's graduates in development and emergency practice, e-business, engineering, human rights law, computing and public health.[6]

A couple of years after the Gaza-Brookes Scholarship had been established, the "Palestinian History Tapestry Project" was initiated in Oxford.[7] The result was the creation of a substantial history tapestry stitched by Palestinian embroiderers in Palestine, Lebanon and Jordan, telling the story of Palestine and Palestinians. In this chapter, we provide two personal accounts of the evolution of the "Palestinian History Tapestry Project."

## BROUGHT TOGETHER BY THREADS
### *Jehan Alfarra*

It was 1988. The First Palestinian Intifada was in full swing. My mother, an ambitious young woman, had recently returned to Gaza from Soviet Russia where she had studied for a medical degree. She started working at the Shifa Hospital, only meters away from where she lived in Gaza City. It was there that she met my father, also a doctor, for the first time. By January 1989, they were married. Due to a night curfew imposed by the Israeli Occupation forces in the city of Khan Younis, my parents' marriage ceremony was a small, muted affair held at home.

I was born the following year. I was too young to remember the events of the First Intifada, but I vividly recall the Second Intifada in 2000. We awoke to the news that Ariel Sharon, Israel's Prime Minister at the time, had entered the Al-Aqsa Mosque. There was widespread outrage. Mass Palestinian protests and a general strike quickly followed.

I remember, one day, I was on my way back from school and crossing the road when a tank approached from a side street. The

---

6 "Gaza Scholarship," Oxford Brookes University, accessed September 30, 2021, https://www.brookesalumni.co.uk/support-us/gaza-scholarship

7 *The Palestinian History Tapestry,* last accessed September 30, 2021, http://www.palestinianhistorytapestry.org

sheer size of its gun pointing towards me brought me to my knees in fear. That was one of the first and most unforgettable moments I had to process as a young child. By that point, I was already familiar with the sight of Israeli watchtowers at checkpoints and Israeli soldiers with their crackling radios, loaded rifles and armored jeeps. To this day, in fact, boxy SUVs remind me of Israeli jeeps and soldiers and bring back memories of the Intifada. However, finding myself that close to a moving tank—it must have been just a meter or two away—filled me with dread I had never known before.

By the time I was a teenager, I had grown accustomed to the sounds of bullets and shells. I had seen young men shot by armed soldiers in green uniforms. I had learned what death sounds and smells like. Running out of school wrapped in a blanket of smoke from burning tires became a standard occurrence.

In 2005, the Second Intifada was over and Israeli troops had "disengaged" from Gaza. Israeli settlements were dismantled. For the first time, I was able to visit the beach of Khan Younis, which had been used exclusively by Israeli settlers. Previously, I had only been able to see the beach from rooftops overlooking the coast in the distance. Now, I no longer had to pass through an Israeli checkpoint to go from Khan Younis to Gaza City to visit my grandmother, my aunts and cousins.

Except Palestine was still occupied. The Israeli military still exercised full control. Like many other Palestinians in Gaza, we had a picture of Al-Aqsa Mosque at home, but I had never actually seen the mosque. The idea of visiting Jerusalem was a dream. An impossible dream. Being from Gaza meant that any visit to the West Bank or Jerusalem came with conditions, ones I did not meet. However, something unexpected happened in 2006. I won a scholarship to study for a year of high school in the United States as an exchange student. It was a program funded by the US State Department. To apply for a student visa to visit the US, I was granted a special permit to apply in person at the US Consulate General in Jerusalem.

As part of a group of students on the same program accompanied by US officials, a van took us from Gaza through the Erez Crossing to the Consulate office in Jerusalem, and back. We were allowed out of the van only once, to buy some souvenirs from a shop. I could not simply go out and explore this mesmerizing city of which I had often dreamed, nor speak to fellow Palestinians who lived there. It did not matter that it was part of my homeland, I could only see the holy city from the windows of the moving van. Suffice to say, that was the extent of my experience of Palestine outside of Gaza.

Less than a decade later, I found myself sitting around a dinner table halfway across the world in Oxford with two other Palestinian women, Yasmin from the Naqab and Jumana from Bethlehem. We were nibbling delicious *sfeeha*, a traditional Palestinian meat pie that our hostess, Yasmin, had prepared, as we shared stories of home and the future. We were joined by Jan and Iain Chalmers, friends of Palestine since the 1960s.

As Jan recounted one of her many stories about Palestinian embroiderers she had met in Palestine, Yasmin brought out a beautiful calligraphy tapestry she had embroidered. It was a verse from a poem by the Palestinian poet, Lutfi Zaghloul. It translates as: "You have a great place in our hearts. Oh Jerusalem, you are beloved."

It was perfect. There we were, three Palestinian women from Gaza, the West Bank and the Naqab casually sharing a flavorsome Palestinian meal and talking Palestinian embroidery with British friends. We did not have to worry about checkpoints or permits. Now Jerusalem was also present through this beautiful artwork, which was Yasmin's contribution to the "Palestinian History Tapestry Project."

It was a truly surreal moment for me. I could not help but think how impossible this would have been to achieve in Palestine, our shared homeland. I know I would have probably never been able to meet these women or learn about their lives.

I had been awarded a scholarship to study for an MSc in Computing at Oxford Brookes University and was hoping to develop a web-based business solution to the land, sea and air blockade that Israel had imposed on the Gaza Strip since 2007. However, after I came to Oxford, I found more than that. Apart from being home to the oldest university in the English-speaking world, this charming city was also the birthplace and home of the "Palestinian History Tapestry Project," which I now co-chair.

I could feel right away how this tapestry project brought Palestinian women together. Despite our geographical fragmentation and our different experiences of the occupation, we were piecing together the story of Palestine through the ages, one panel at a time. It is fitting that these stories and interpretations of different experiences and moments throughout Palestinian history would be articulated using the embroidery stitches that have long been central to Palestinian culture and which are familiar to us all, wherever we may be.

That is the essence of the Palestinian History Tapestry. It is a battle against the fragmentation of Palestinian society and the Palestinian experience imposed by the Israeli state or, as some of the Palestinian embroiderers have put it, the project serves as a *lam shamel* (Arabic for family reunification) through art. Whether living under direct military occupation in the West Bank or a suffocating blockade in Gaza, facing displacement in the Naqab and Jerusalem, or in isolation as refugees in Lebanon and Jordan, simple threads have managed to weave us together in a shared manifestation of resistance. The power of thread and its use as a means of resistance is not a novel notion, and I have long been fascinated by the effects of conflict and war on dress and textiles.

Threads have immense power. They certainly have the capacity to shape a nation's perception and standing. To Palestinians, threads are that, and much more. They embed our identity, heritage, unity and resistance. These effects are not confined to embroidery. The Arab *kuffiyyeh*, for instance, with its chequered black and white patterns, has morphed over time into a fundamentally Palestinian symbol, deeply associated with the national struggle for liberation.

The historical significance of traditional cross-stitch (*tasliba*) and the Bethlehem couching (*tahriri*) embroidery, passed down from one Palestinian generation to the next, lends this artistic needlework a special place within Palestinian culture and heritage.

For centuries, Palestinian women have donned meticulously hand-stitched *thobes* (traditional dresses) that proudly and distinctly reflected their cultural and regional roots. The style, stitching method and colors of a local Palestinian woman's dress often identified her status and place of origin within historic Palestine itself. Many of the motifs featured in Palestinian embroidery, traditionally comprised of geometric designs, are indicative of the long and diverse history of the land. Some of them bear names inspired by various periods of Palestinian history, such as the "Canaanite Star" and "Tents of Pasha."

However, the style of embroidery employed in the panels of the Palestinian History Tapestry marks a shift from the traditional designs. These usually rely on traditional patterns and motifs incorporated in *thobes* and other household linens and personal items, such as cushions and handbags. The Palestinian History Tapestry Project required that traditional embroidery designs should be used to capture stories and recount historical events, making the Tapestry an extension of the legacy of the traditional Palestinian dress and its great social and symbolic value.

Since the *Nakba* of 1948 and the establishment of the Israeli State, embroidery has been widely used to visualize symbols and icons of the Palestinian struggle for independence, thus becoming a valuable way of keeping Palestinian identity and heritage alive. It would not be uncommon to find embroidered tapestries hanging in the homes of Palestinians within Palestine as well as in the Diaspora, displaying the map of Palestine or an image of Jerusalem's Al-Aqsa Mosque. Another commonly stitched image is that of the "Key of Return," which symbolizes the UN-declared right of Palestinians to return to their pre-1948 homes in historic Palestine, which they were forced to leave in order to make way for the establishment of the State of Israel.

Beyond these national symbols, other folkloric scenes and depictions of everyday Palestinian life before the Zionist Occupation are also commonly stitched. These include the traditional Palestinian wedding and the pre-wedding henna party.

The Palestinian History Tapestry embroiderers have embraced and developed this practice of illustration.

Palestine's history, since the assault of the Palestinian homeland by Zionist forces in 1948 and the subsequent and ongoing dispossession of Palestinians, currently accounts for a large segment of the Tapestry. Events and accounts since that critical juncture are represented under the theme of *sumud*—"steadfastness"—a concept that has come to define the current stage of the Palestinian struggle for liberation.

The Tapestry project continues to grow and evolve as present-day events unfold, with the Great March of Return and the Unity Intifada being two of the most recent episodes in the Palestinian struggle to be represented. Every panel of the project is a compelling piece of art in its own right, recording and interpreting a specific event, place or symbol that tells a story.

Most of the Palestinian women who stitched these panels have never met, except through their embroidery and contributions to the Tapestry. Their embroidery highlights their individual styles, experiences and impressions all of which blend effortlessly. As one of the embroiderers remarked, "Each woman's special touch and unique character becomes evident in the finished panel." Many of them proudly "sign off" their panels, leaving their names forever embroidered in the Tapestry's artistic chronicle of Palestinian history.

Some of these women are remembered in an entirely different way. Samar Alhallaq is one such woman. She was introduced to Jan and the Tapestry Project when she visited Oxford in 2013, when her husband was studying at Oxford Brookes University. She stitched a panel based on an image widely used on social media to express solidarity with Palestinian hunger strikers in Israeli jails. The panel reads: *Samidun* (Arabic for "steadfast").

Samar, her two children and unborn baby were all killed, a year later, during Israel's 2014 summer onslaught on Gaza, which killed over 2,200 Palestinians (UN-OCHA).

Her panel, though originally created in solidarity with Palestinian women prisoners and their steadfast determination to attain their rights, now also evokes memories of one of Israel's most brutal offensives against the besieged Gaza Strip and the hundreds of innocent women and children who lost their lives.

Every thread and every stitch by Palestinian embroiderers tell a piece of the story of Palestine. Every panel narrates a tale of joyous celebrations or of sorrow and struggle but, ultimately, it speaks of our collective hopes and dreams of freedom and justice. This is why the Palestinian History Tapestry Project is critical for us. This project has been a labor of love and solidarity between Palestinians and British friends of Palestine.

Since its inception in 2012, the Tapestry has been widely promoted through its website[8] and in talks, publications, and exhibitions. Fifteen eminent Patrons have endorsed the Project. Most important of all, 100 meticulously embroidered panels have so far been created, illustrating the long and diverse history of Palestine and the tribulations of Palestinian life under Israeli occupation.

The current leadership of the Project, with two co-Chairs from Gaza, will increase awareness about the Tapestry and the history of Palestine and Palestinians, and help to turn it into an iconic national treasure. Unlike the "Keiskamma Tapestry" which proudly hangs in the South African Parliament Building, at present there is no such possibility to permanently exhibit the Palestinian History Tapestry in occupied Palestine where it would be vulnerable to damage and perhaps destruction. Today, in 2021, as it continues to grow, the Tapestry remains in Oxford, in the hope that, one day, it will be on display in a free Palestine and stand as witness to the record of a rich and turbulent past.

---

8 *The Palestinian History Tapestry,* last accessed September 30, 2021, http://www.palestinianhistorytapestry.org.

# Selected Embroideries

# THE PALESTINIAN HISTORY TAPESTRY PROJECT

Photography by Theo Chalmers

1. Birth of Jesus in Bethlehem, using Tahriri embroidery

DESIGN: Hamada Atallah [Al Quds], Al Quds, Palestine
EMBROIDERY: Suhair Handal, Bethlehem; Marcel Rabie, Randa Abu Ghattas, Beit Jala, Palestine

*The birth of Jesus of Nazareth in Bethlehem. "And so it was…that Mary gave birth to a son in a stable. She called him Jesus and wrapped him in strips of cloth and laid him in a manger of hay."*

ERA: Roman Period (63 BCE–325 CE)

## 2. Godfrey de Bouillon and Crusaders

Source of image: Bridgman Images, Bibliotheque Nationale, Paris

Embroidery: Dowlat Abu Shaweesh [Ne'ane], Ramallah, Palestine

*The First Crusade began in 1099 when Pope Urban II called for a military expedition to help the Byzantines take control of the Holy Land. This inaugurated a period of two centuries in which Christians and Muslims often fought one another.*

Era: Crusader Period (1099–1291)

3. "On this Land," Mahmoud Darwish, Palestinian National Poet

SOURCE OF IMAGE/DESIGN: Ibrahim Muhtadi [Al Quds], Gaza, Palestine

EMBROIDERY: Hekmat Ashour [Gaza], Gaza, Palestine

*"We have on this land that which makes this life worth living."*
—Mahmoud Darwish, Palestinian National Poet

*Palestinian national poet Mahmoud Darwish is renowned for his poems about Israel's occupation of Palestine and the struggle for freedom and liberation for the Palestinian people.*

## 4. Olive Harvest

DESIGN: Hamada Atallah [Al Quds] Al Quds, Palestine

EMBROIDERY: Dowlat Abu Shaweesh [Ne'ane], Ramallah, Palestine

*Olives and olive oil symbolize Palestinian land, identity and culture. The olive tree is seen by many Palestinians as a symbol of nationality and connection to the land, particularly due to the slow growth and longevity of the tree. The destruction of Palestinian olive trees has become a feature of the Israeli occupation, with regular reports of damage and destruction by Israeli settlers.*

## 5. Faris Odeh, Standing Alone, 8 Nov 2000

SOURCE OF IMAGE: Laurent Rebours, Associated Press

EMBROIDERY: Nawal Ibrahim al Ahmed [Tabariyeh], Ain al-Hilweh, Lebanon

*On 29 October 2000, during the second month of the Second Intifada, a French photojournalist photographed 15-year-old Faris Odeh from the Zeitoun quarter in Gaza City confronting an Israeli tank with a stone at the Karni crossing into the Gaza Strip. Ten days later, on 8 November, Odeh was again throwing stones at the Karni crossing when he was fatally wounded by Israeli troops. The boy and the image subsequently assumed iconic status as a symbol of opposition to Israel's occupation of Palestinian land.*

ERA: Sumud – Steadfastness (1948 onwards)

## 6. Destruction of Bedouin Villages

SOURCE OF IMAGE: Painting by Bashir Abu-Rabia'

DESIGN: Bashir Abu-Rabia (Naqab)

EMBROIDERY: Naama al Awawdah [Es Samu], Khalil District.

*This panel draws attention to the cycle of destruction and reconstruction of many Bedouin villages, including Al-Arakeeb, Um El-Heran, and threatened Khan Al-Ahmar in the Jordan Valley. These villages have been destroyed by the Israeli Army in a policy of further ethnic cleansing to establish Jewish-only settlements. The panel is inspired by a painting by Bashir Abu-Rabia',the first Bedouin artist in the Negev, who began featuring Palestinian embroidery in his paintings in 1969.*

ERA: Sumud – Steadfastness (1948 onwards)

## 7. Sumud (Steadfastness)

Source of image: Samar Alhallaq [Majdal], Gaza, Palestine

Embroidery: Samar Alhallaq [Majdal], Gaza, Palestine

*Palestinian prisoners in Israeli jails use hunger strikes to protest against prolonged administrative detention without trial. This embroidery is based on an image by an unnamed illustrator, which was disseminated widely among activists on social networks in an expression of solidarity with the mass hunger strike. The image endeavoured to raise awareness of the suffering of Palestinian women prisoners and their steadfast determination to attain their rights. The Arabic lettering reads "Samedoun" ("We are steadfast"). The Hebrew lettering reads "Shabas," the Israeli Prison Service. The panel was stitched in Oxford by Samar Alhallaq in 2013.*

*She and her children were killed by Israeli shelling in Gaza in 2014.*

Era: Sumud – Steadfastness (1948 onwards)

## 8. Palestinian Henna Party

SOURCE OF IMAGE: Traditional design

EMBROIDERY: Ruba Al Behery
[Bir Seb'a], Gaza

*Palestinian wedding ceremonies start the night before the wedding day, when women from the bride's family and her friends gather to sing, dance, and apply temporary tattoos with henna, a plant dye. Older women decorate the skin of the bride and her guests with designs that often take hours to complete. Decorations put on the bride's legs represent the return of the dove to Noah, as evidence that the flood's destruction was over. The women wear traditional, hand-embroidered dresses, with that of the bride being the most beautiful.*

9. Palestinian Wedding

Source of image: Traditional design | Embroidery: Mothers' Embroidery Group, Al Deheishe Refugee Camp, Bethlehem, Palestine

*This panel displays a typical Palestinian country wedding with its rituals, Dabke folk dance, the bride on a horse, and traditional music. The Dabke dance is characteristic of the whole of the Levant, with the music and the dance steps differing slightly from place to place. Palestinian cuisine is the cuisine of the Levant—msakhan, maftoul, kibbeh, hummus, and mansaf, for example—which have become very widely known and appreciated.*

## 10. Tahriri Embroidery

Source of image: Traditional design

Embroidery: Amari Women's Group Ramallah, Palestine

*An example of tahriri embroidery with traditional cross stitch. This tahriri sample has been stitched by the Amari Women's Group in Ramallah. The Women's Child Care Society in Bet Jala is maintaining the traditional Bethlehem tahriri stitching by training local women to produce embroidered items for the tourist market, providing income for women working from home. Tahriri stitching is also known as couching, and is used to preserve golden threads used in the decoration of church raiments.*

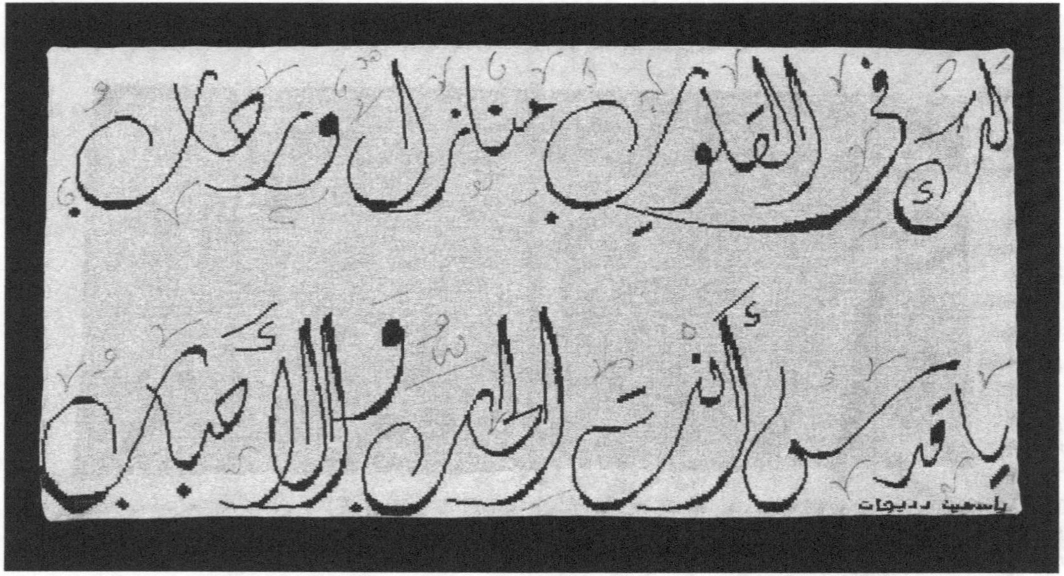


## 12. "Jerusalem, you are beloved"

Design: Haroon Haj Amer, Drejat, Naqab

Embroidery: Yasmeen Haj Amer, Drejat, Naqab

*"You have a great place in our hearts. Oh Jerusalem, you are beloved."—from a poem by Lutfi Zaghloul*

Era: Sumud—Steadfastness (1948 onwards)

## 11. Check Point, 1967–

DESIGN: Based on tapestry created by Hannah Ryggen (Norway)

EMBROIDERY: Karema Nasser [Barbara], Gaza, Palestine

*During the 1967 war, Israel occupied what remained of Palestine. Hundreds of military checkpoints were established in the West Bank and East Jerusalem, and in Gaza. These are used to entrench Israel's occupation of all of historic Palestine. Movement of Palestinians is restricted within the occupied Palestinian territory, with dire consequences for access to education, health care, and the economy. The design of this panel is influenced by "The Death of Dreams," a tapestry woven by Hannah Ryggen at the time of the German occupation of Norway during the second World War.*

ERA: Sumud—Steadfastness (1948 onward)

## WHAT IS THE PALESTINIAN HISTORY TAPESTRY PROJECT

*Jan Chalmers*

I am a British nurse from Oxford, and an amateur embroiderer. In 1969 and 1970, I lived in Gaza and was employed by the UN Relief and Works Agency (UNRWA) for Palestine Refugees. I worked as a maternal and child health nurse in the refugee camp in Jabaliya, at the northern end of the Gaza Strip. There, I got to know the local women very well and enjoyed a gossip over coffee most days. I learned about their traditions, rituals and beliefs. I also experienced and shared the community's feeling of terror when Israeli army halftracks trawled the camp, as they often did. It was a life-changing experience. I made close friends in Gaza and visited most parts of Palestine and I have returned there on several occasions.

During my two years in Gaza, I became an admirer of the very high quality and longstanding traditions of Palestinian embroidery. The UNRWA embroidery center on Omar Al-Mukhtar Street was a favorite place for me, not only to purchase embroidery, but also to watch the women stitching and to learn the names of some of the traditional designs. Most Palestinian embroidery is used to decorate women's clothes, handbags, cushions and other items. It has only rarely been used to illustrate scenes from Palestinian life.

Tapestries have had significant impact as treasured markers of momentous historical events. One such very celebrated use of embroidery to illustrate life is the Bayeux Tapestry, which provides a pictorial account of the Norman invasion of England in 1066.[9] I remember learning about the Bayeux Tapestry at school, but I never thought I would become deeply acquainted with its stitches, colors and story. This familiarity happened because, in 2002, I was invited to help with an embroidery project in a village on the Eastern Cape of South Africa, where the Keiskamma River flows into the Indian Ocean. The Xhosa women living there used colorful beads to decorate

9 "The Bayeux Tapestry," Bayeux Museum, last accessed September 30, 2021, https://www.bayeuxmuseum.com/en/the-bayeux-tapestry/

clothing, but they were not embroiderers. Introducing the women to the Bayeux Tapestry showed them how stories could be illustrated using embroidery. They were excited at the prospect of using threads to illustrate the history of their people. I was asked to teach them embroidery to create a history tapestry. This led to the now-famous 126-metre Keiskamma History Tapestry, a national treasure that hangs permanently in the South African Parliament Building in Cape Town.[10]

After a ten-year association with the Keiskamma Art Project, I wondered how I could make use of the experience I had gained through my association with the Keiskamma History Tapestry, specifically. A remark by my husband (who had also lived in Gaza in 1969/70) led me to consider whether the celebrated embroidery skills of Palestinian women could be used to create a tapestry illustrating the history of Palestine and Palestinians. This history is insufficiently known, and Britain's disastrous role in it—promising the Palestinian homeland to foreign colonists and failing to protect the rights of indigenous Palestinians—has never been adequately acknowledged.

As a British citizen, I felt shame at Britain's betrayal of the Palestinian people. I felt that working with Palestinian embroiderers to create a tapestry illustrating their history would be a new way of expressing solidarity with them. In 2012, I invited two British friends, one of them married to a Palestinian, to join me in establishing a Palestinian History Tapestry Project. We agreed that such a tapestry would not only record an insufficiently appreciated history of Palestine and Palestinians but would also extend the traditional craft of Palestinian needlewomen to illustrate this history, as well as generate income for them and their families. These remained the Project's objectives throughout its first decade.

But how do you cover a history that spans thousands of years, I wondered, and where do you begin? Two professional historians prepared a historical chronology to help the Project select images to be used in the Tapestry. It was decided to start with an illustration of

---

10 Keiskamma Trust, last accessed September 30, 2021, http://www.keiskamma.org/

the walled city of Jericho during the Neolithic era, and to continue into the 21st century.

Deciding which images should follow Jericho was not an easy task. I assembled the sketches and photographs that had been collected and Ghada Karmi, our Founding Patron and an historian, came to Oxford one Sunday afternoon to help with the selection. It was evident we needed more input, so an image selection subcommittee with wholly Palestinian membership was established, particularly to select images for the years following the 1947–49 ethnic cleansing.

The initial challenge I faced was how to recruit Palestinian embroiderers from within and outside Palestine: how to maintain contact with them, how to choose and distribute the images to be embroidered and how to pay for the work done. The Palestinian Diaspora presented a challenge. I began by visiting places where I already had Palestinian friends—the Gaza Strip, the West Bank and East Jerusalem, Lebanon and Jordan. Many of the Palestinian embroiderers I met were impressed by the Keiskamma History Tapestry and excited about the idea of making something so significant in addition to traditional uses of embroidery. We connected on a more personal level as well. I remember one woman I met near Hebron who asked me why I left my hair so white. There was mirth when I told her it was a color from God, not from a bottle.

I built many great relationships with the Palestinian embroiderers but, sadly, I could not return as often as I would have liked—especially to Gaza, which has been under siege since 2007. It was evident that I needed locally-based coordinators to help grow the Project and liaise with the many embroiderers who expressed interest.

The first Field Coordinator—Jamila—volunteered to coordinate Project work in the Gaza Strip. I knew Jamila well because she had been a Gaza Scholar in the scholarship scheme run by Oxford Brookes University. On returning to Gaza on completion of her Master's degree, she soon recruited some embroiderers for the Palestinian History Tapestry Project. As I am familiar with Gaza and still know many people living there, it was easy for Jamila and me to discuss how coordination between Gaza and Oxford could be facilitated.

Importantly, it was through Jamila that I was introduced to Ibrahim, a Gaza-based designer, whose contributions became indispensable to the Project. He was an important source of encouragement and guidance for me and became a key influence in organizing the Palestinian History Tapestry Project, later becoming a co-Chair. During my visit to Gaza, I met Ibrahim for the first time in his workplace, Atfaluna Society for Deaf Children, in Gaza City. He was the manager of an enterprise in which young people with hearing disabilities produced handmade arts and crafts. I also visited embroiderers at Albeit Al-Salaam. They went on to stitch the henna party panel, which later became the Tapestry's flagship image.

After coordination arrangements in Gaza had been shown to work, other women we knew volunteered to be Field Coordinators in Ramallah, the Naqab, Jordan and Lebanon. It has been a joy to collaborate with the five Field Coordinators, even though there have been times when it has been difficult for them and their embroiderer colleagues—skirmishes within Ein el-Helwe refugee camp in Lebanon, repeated Israeli assaults on Gaza, and Israeli destruction of Palestinian homes and villages in the Naqab. Against the odds, production of tapestry panels continued.

Although those developing and implementing the infrastructure for the Project were (like me) unpaid volunteers, funds were needed for designers and embroiderers. My fundraising skills were nil, but nonetheless sufficient money was raised to support the work, thanks to over 100 donors, many of them my friends and relatives. I and others sold Palestinian embroidery at charity events and also to those attending our talks about the Project. We invited donations on these occasions, as well as through our website and in letters to groups known to support Palestinians.

The first ten years of the Project culminated in one hundred colorful, moving, tapestry panels, each as unique as the embroiderer who had stitched it. The embroiderers took on the work of the Tapestry Project with enthusiasm. Some were interested to know more about their history and their forebears and others who had settled in the country hundreds of years before.

The conclusion of the first phase of the Palestinian History Tapestry was marked with two public exhibitions and Tapestry launches at the end of 2018, coincident with the 50th anniversary of UN Resolution 194, which asserted the right of Palestinian refugees to return to their homes. St Antony's College at the University of Oxford hosted the first of these launches, and Middle East Monitor and the P21 Gallery in London hosted the second, with the Palestinian Ambassador in attendance.

The end of the Project's first decade marked a milestone at which the Project Committee agreed that its future should be conceptualized and led by Palestinians. Everyone associated with the Project was delighted when Jehan Alfarra and Ibrahim Muhtadi agreed to co-chair the Palestinian History Tapestry Project going forward. Palestinian embroiderers and designers will continue to be commissioned by the Project to stitch additional panels illustrating past and current events and themes.

TERRY BOULLATA *is a proud Jerusalemite who served on the boards of Jerusalem Cultural and Women's Centers (the Palestinian National Theater—Al-Hakawati, and the Women's Studies Center and a member of the general assembly of the Palestinian Art Court—Al-Hoash) in defense of cultural and women's rights. She remains an active volunteer in conducting activities that aim to encourage the city's development, preserve its rich cultural and tourism resources and protect its Palestinian national identity. Exposing violations of human, socio-economic and political rights of Palestinians remains a haunting mission, on which she focuses most of her efforts.*

*During the First Intifada, Boullata was detained four times between 1987–1989. Following her release, she graduated from Birzeit University and pursued her defense of Palestinian human rights, including women's rights. Through her work, she came in touch with the suffering of her people, which she tried to voice through the production of two films:* The Iron Wall, *which documents the Israeli land-theft policy and segregation of the Palestinian people in the occupied Palestinian territory and* Jerusalem: The East Side Story, *which voices the suffering and aspirations of her Jerusalem community.*

# CULTURAL TOURISM AS A MODE OF RESISTANCE

## Preserving Cultural Heritage While Promoting Development

*Terry Boullata*

I WAS BORN in East Jerusalem in 1966. Despite growing up in a very protective middle class, city-dwelling family with minimal exposure to life in rural Palestine or to the politics of resistance, it was impossible not to hear my mother's stories about her family—the Freij family—stories that often centered on the dispossession of their houses, family library and shops in West Jerusalem.

The details of my family's plight in 1948 were well-drawn in my imagination: how the family escaped the bombing of their homes in Baqaa by Zionist military groups, forcing them to walk all the way to Bethlehem for refuge, but how they then returned to the Old City of Jerusalem to establish a new family business in the production of lemonade; how my Aunt Jamileh insisted on not registering her firstborn son in Bethlehem, but waited three months to return to register him within Jerusalem's registrar.

The stories of cultural life before the *Nakba* were always nostalgic moments for our elderly, when they described how the cultural life then was so rich, rife with cinema houses, with theaters receiving famed Arab singers like Um Kulthoum, Abel Wahab and others in the YMCA Jerusalem or in Jaffa. The stories of Nabi Moussa Festival (Mawsim Nabi Moussa),[11] in particular, dominated the

---

11 Since Salah Eddin Ayyoubi, who defeated the Crusaders in 1187, and throughout the period of Ottoman rule, the Nabi Musa festival emerged as the

Boullata family conversations, considering my family's generations-long residence at the House of the Flags—Dar Bayrak[12]—of the Husseini Family complex in Aqabet Taqiyeh, the oldest street of the Muslim Quarter in the Old City of Jerusalem. Unfortunately, the Nabi Mousa Festival stopped around 1948 and never resumed, neither under Jordanian rule nor under Israeli occupation since 1967.

Such stories are never unique to one family or a community. Every family or community has its own stories left in the corners of centuries-old historic buildings, or in the *Zaffa* tradition at weddings, *Thobes* and dresses, or around a *Maqam*—or a shrine—or on the peaks and ranges of mountains throughout the West Bank. These sites are traditionally sanctified by Palestinians as pilgrimage sites for holidays and religious occasions (*Mawassem*) for prayer, religious ceremonies and rituals, circumcision celebrations and weddings, public and private occasions, and simple outdoor family recreation. All of these cultural ruins should be searched and restored, but with a new approach in order to galvanize a process of reconciliation with a broken history; to plumb the depths of history and culture that express and preserve the landscape and spaces, our cultural way of life, the Palestinian cultural identity—inclusive of the different

---

largest Islamic festival in the region, consisting of a one-week celebration and pilgrimage to Moses' tomb, southwest of Jericho. It culminated in a gathering at the shrine on the Friday preceding the Greek Orthodox Easter weekend. Salah al-Din invented the phenomenon of religious "seasons," distributing them geographically at a specific time that falls between March and April of each year to cover entire Palestine, around the period when the Christian pilgrims came to visit the holy places; keeping the country in a state of full alert, to prevent the exploitation of pilgrimage through aggression. However, the festival evolved into an active element in the formation of Palestinian nationalism and a resistance mobilizing event against the colonial British where political riots erupted in April 1920 and in 1921.

12 The house of Hajj Amin Al-Husseini was the home of flag until they decided to gather at Haram Sharif Square in 1937. Women participated in this occasion by ululating to greet the masses or spraying rose water and dressing specifically for the procession. The delegations of the procession would arrive from the neighboring villages of Jerusalem carrying their banners. The daluna, the folk dabkes were all part of the procession together with traditional food.

passing civilizations—and to safeguard the outstanding universal values of our *indigenous cultural heritage.*

As the original people of historic Palestine, we have underestimated the value of taking positive control of our lives as families and communities, of building on our cultural identity despite all the injustices to heal the losses suffered through colonization by seeking collective self-determination. It remains imperative that the Zionist narrative, which has falsely maintained that Palestine is "a land without a people, for a people without a land," be challenged.

Following years of direct political resistance, including imprisonment, and feeling constrained with family responsibilities, in addition to facing many health problems, I came to discover the value of reviving our culture and cultural heritage as a core avenue through which I could continue to contribute towards my country's decolonization efforts.

Our heritage has always been the central pillar of our cultural identity and the emblem of our pride. It is a fount of inspiration and a vital source of creativity. Strengthening our heritage means reviving the past which lives within us and pointing us towards a future that will embed new concepts of Palestine on the global cultural map. Our heritage, the living memory of individuals and our society, is an authentic bedrock that carries the features of our people through history, confirms its treasures, voices our concerns and daily suffering, and expresses our common hopes and optimism. In the dire period of upsurge in violence and colonization, culture has the power to transform and cohere entire societies, to promote citizenship, to connect people individually and collectively, and to sustain social and economic development for future generations. The loss of our cultural heritage would mean not only the loss of our historical memory and of our cultural traditions and festivities (*Mawassem*), but also the loss of economic opportunities for sustainable development. Comprehensive development based on the country's abundant heritage strengthens its rural and urban towns and cities and encourages the use of the country's natural and cultural resources, as well as unleashing the energies of local youth and women.

Hence, it has been important to connect all the cultural activities, whether through the promotion and development of folk *Dabke* and *Dabke* groups, cultural songs, the rehabilitation of historic centers, *Maqams* and shrines and even the drive to change the status quo around our religious and cultural heritage sites, which were taken over and destroyed by Israeli settlers and to transform them into comprehensive Palestinian cultural icons of decolonization. It is important to connect the different dots, merging them towards a sustainable Palestinian cultural identity that reflects, not just the *sumud* (steadfastness) of the people, but also spurs them to a development process that benefits them and rewards their resilience over decades of dispossession, fragmentation and oppression.

Community-based eco-tourism has been the flagship of several cultural organizations and networks such as the Rozana Association for the Development of Architectural Heritage, Palestine Heritage Trail and the Network of Experiential Palestinian Tourism Organizations (NEPTO). They are involved in designing, delineating and leading a number of thematic tours and trails (the Nativity trail, Masar Ibrahim and the Sufi trails). Their core focus is to advance community encounters and explorations of ecological, cultural, historic and solidarity tourism based on empowered and welcoming local communities. Experiential cultural tourism benefits communities and helps to protect the natural and cultural heritage of the local people. Their programs employ the rehabilitation of historic centers to foster modern functions that serve the entire community, or rehabilitating historic *Maqams* or shrines, building the capacities of youth with trek guiding skills, encouraging women with hospitality skills to establish homestays and promote art, crafts and artisan works. Their programs also advance fair trade, environmental and wildlife protection and the organizing of cultural, heritage and agricultural festivals. The resultant cultural interaction with local and foreign visitors fosters harmonious relations among peoples, promotes acceptance of diversity, and enriches people's lives, simulating their creativity to respond to new challenges. It is not the denial but rather the recognition of differences that keeps the world together.

Since 2007, my daughters and I have spent our summers volunteering at the annual iconic event, The Birzeit Heritage Week, which encourages a variety of cultural activities from across all of historic Palestine to take place in the partially rehabilitated historic area of Birzeit town. It is a model of what the Birzeit historic area (old town)—with its flagged stones of the Mamluk and Ottoman era and houses and attics—could become 365 days a year: a vibrant community and cultural zone that will draw visitors from near and far. It engages the local community, civil society organizations and businesses in a dynamic, holistic process of activities and programs that seeks to foster contemporary functions for the old houses and spaces in the historic area, illustrating the value of culture, cultural heritage and architectural heritage and capacities in the ensuing development of rural Palestine. It aims to engage the local communities, including both youth and women in a dynamic process, drawing their attention to planning and protection requirements in order to safeguard the outstanding universal values of our indigenous cultural heritage and the potential values and benefits it produces to galvanize and encourage local production, hence enhancing our awareness of our common identity and its expression through food, storytelling, folklore, culture and handicrafts.

Every year, aside from my small family, a number of young Palestinian men and women are also involved in the organization as well as in the designing of the festival. Their participation is channelled through different committees where they lead, organize, design, prepare and implement the master plan for action. Their dedicated participation primarily ensures establishing lifelong connections and friendships, gender-equal opportunities for participation and, subsequently, an accumulation of leadership skills which are indispensable in generating awareness, commitment and capacities in the fields of promoting culture and cultural heritage. It is also a platform that seeks opportunities for exchange with world cultures, expanding, diversifying participation and completing the cultural mosaic. The flags of participating countries are raised on top of Birzeit municipality, creating a first-hand encounter with the Palestinian community and breaking the isolation matrix of colonial control, of its fragmentation by checkpoints and walls. Needless to say, the heritage week has also been instrumental in promoting the role of Palestinian women in protecting our heritage, preserving it and transmitting it from one generation to the next. This is particularly highlighted through the Flower of the Countryside Tradition where each year, a group of young female contestants from the countryside, aged between 16 to 18 years, compete while wearing the traditional bridal dresses of their villages and families as were worn before the *Nakba* in 1948. The winner is chosen by leading Palestinian cultural experts and arbitrators, including historian Dr. Sharif Kana'neh, Sonia Nimmer, Ph.D., Nabil Alqam and Munir Nasser, Ph.D. The competition is based on several standards, including 1) the bridal village parade (*zaffa*) singing traditional songs, 2) the contestant's knowledge about her village, including the roots for its name, 3) details of the traditional dress, its function and the accessories she is wearing and 4) her knowledge in reciting a folk story from her village. Three times, female contestants from Palestinian towns in 1948 areas won these contests celebrating a commitment to Palestinian culture that goes beyond the imposed colonial borders.

In 2010, the same model was implemented within the Old City of Jerusalem that possesses a fascinating array of authentic local cultures and cultural communities due to its important religious, cultural and architectural heritage. Indian, Moroccan, African, Coptic, Assyrian and other diverse cultures have settled inside the city, reflecting its rule by various dynasties such as the Romans, the Arabs, the Crusaders, the Muslims and others who over the past 15 centuries have left abundant traces of their cultures and heritage throughout the different corners and communities of the city. However, these rich varieties are not reflected in the current cultural and tourist programs due to Israeli policies of neglect, de-development, brain-drain and disenfranchisement of the Palestinian cultural and tourist sector, as well as by the inability of Palestinians to control the political, economic and urban processes that shape their lives.

As a Jerusalemite, I did not think twice about volunteering, with my daughters, at The Jerusalem Tourism Cluster (JTC), a Jerusalem-based NGO working to design and coordinate networking of cultural and tourist activities in order to benefit local businesses and communities in Jerusalem. I contributed to their diligent work to re-introduce the city in its different historic periods reflecting all the cultures, the heritage, the religions and the architectural mosaics it has acquired over the centuries, while aiming to benefit the surrounding local communities as deemed possible through special events, tours and. trails. I introduced their mission and their cultural ideas to several expatriate communities residing in Jerusalem as well as to local schools. My family and I, again, became attached to their key event entitled, the Nablus Road Open Days event, created and implemented for three consecutive years.

To reverse the marginalization and impoverishment of East Jerusalem City due to the systematic Israeli colonial policies which were designed to accelerate Israeli-Jewish development while obstructing, cutting off and detaching the Palestinian population in Jerusalem from its natural hinterland and historic markets, *al-Hoash* began to implement a number of donor-funded projects and activities to develop cultural-tourism sectors in East Jerusalem. These included Palestinian Jerusalemites who were with key civil society organizations, led by Jerusalem Tourism Cluster, including the Arab Hotel Association, al-Ma'mal for Contemporary Arts, the Palestinian National Theater and the Palestinian Art Court. A key figure for such activities was Mr. Raed Saadeh,[13] a Jerusalem hotelier and cultural activist who led different cultural organizations.

Although, many of the programs were funded by foreign donors, yet the core ideas, the efforts and the objectives were all Palestinian. Many might debate the impact of donors' funds, but should be reassured by the fact that there was no conditional funding attached or interference from donors in any phase of implementation. Seed funds to jump-start cultural programs have been of major

---

13 Raed Saadeh is the co-founder and chairman of the Jerusalem Tourism Cluster and the co-founder and chairman of Rozana Association for Rural Tourism Development, based in Birzeit. Mr. Saadeh is also the owner and general manager of the Jerusalem Hotel, a boutique hotel in Jerusalem, a former president of the Arab (Palestinian) Hotel Association (AHA), and the co-founder of the Network for Experiential Palestinian Tourism Organizations (NEPTO).

importance to cover those crucial expenses within activities that voluntarism could not cover. Writing proposals, preparing ideas for the media, organizing the volunteers to build booths or to secure the safe flow of participants and people were all excluded from any cultural expenses. This is where several volunteers and I stepped in, working energetically, including working through long sleepless nights.

The key event that reflects the culmination of cultural resistance in East Jerusalem was the Nablus Road event. Nablus Road Open Days was initiated in 2016. It required that we organize a variety of decentralized activities to reflect the richness of this historic road, thereby promoting networking among participating institutions. The history that this street represents with its many institutions and historical buildings is tremendous. Nablus Road is one of the important streets in East Jerusalem, connecting the Old City from Bab Amoud/Damascus Gate towards the north and includes a number of important religious, tourist, cultural and sports institutions with beautiful, secluded gardens, monasteries, hotels and institutions that provide a good sampling of the myriad worlds to be found only in Jerusalem. The event aimed at providing an opportunity to revive Palestinian cultural identity in the area around the walled Old City, *through converting the historic Nablus Road into a Palestinian cultural-tourist destination,* providing a bridge between cultural diversity, identity and economic prosperity while capitalizing on and promoting existing services along Nablus Road.

Under the management of JTC and the Arab Hotel Association, together with hundreds of volunteers, I immersed myself in long months of preparations to install a number of exhibits, displays and performances targeting children and families in the variety of spaces available within the different institutions along Nablus Road. For three days, Nablus Road was bustling with thousands of families and visitors bringing life to the heart of East Jerusalem.

We also ensured the creation of opportunities for local artisans, artists, producer groups and other suppliers to promote and sell their work, bolstering local businesses and income generation. Children walked round with painted faces and balloons, teenagers met and fell in love with their city, families were proud to walk through their street while taking ownership of their own space. The event was conducted for three continuous years until the COVID-19 pandemic hit the country. Some love stories were celebrated with marriage a few years later, like Ghassan and Rania, who met as volunteers at the event.

The event managed to bypass several Israeli obstacles through mobilizing and networking among the diverse cultural, sport, religious and tourist organizations and being based on an identified diverse heritage. Insofar as all activities were conducted within the participating institutions along Nablus Road, whether a Nuns' convent or the Dominican Church or the Anglican Church, a hotel or a school, we were able to bypass the entire Israeli colonial system that demands permits for events in the public arena. Thousands of people would walk along the road as passers-by while the actual events were only conducted indoors, with each activity conducted inside its specialized organization. Theater performances were conducted at the Palestinian National Theater—al Hakawati—while children's inflatable castles and slides were installed on the grounds of St George School. English literature exams were conducted at the British Council and artisan booths were all installed in the big yard of the Dominican Church, while other arts exhibitions and singing performances were under the Church's protection. We were able to evoke pride and enthusiasm among the thousands of local and foreign visitors, not only for our ability to defy Israeli policies, but also for our ability to create a successful cultural tourism model in the heart of our city, based on steadfastness, on networking and coordination among the different institutions and organizations existing along the Road, and on the readiness to defy the abyss that has been imposed on us for so long.

Like many Palestinians, the stories of *Nakba* and my family kept digging at the depths of my soul. When an Israeli-Dutch filmmaker and friend, Benny Bruner, with whom I worked in covering stories of Palestinians around the Wall, contacted me to present an important film project about the private libraries stolen from Palestinian homes during the *Nakba*, I jumped on the idea and simply opened channels for him to a trusted European donor that provided the required seed funds to initiate his important film. I also helped him to connect with elderly Palestinians who had witnessed the theft of their libraries. *The Great Book Robbery* was broadcast in 2012 on Al-Jazeera TV. It unraveled the systematic theft of hundreds of Palestinian private libraries by the Israeli army and its precursor, the Haganah, in cooperation with the Israeli National Library. The books included priceless volumes of Palestinian Arab and Muslim literature, including poetry, works of history and fiction. Thousands of the books were destroyed and recycled for paper, while many others remain in the Israeli National Library, designated as "abandoned property," although many of the Palestinian owners are still suffering through the atrocities of their losses.

All the above modest personal stories that I have lived through with my family are nothing compared to the Israeli revenge policies faced by many of the cultural organizers and activists. I was just a volunteer in all these creative cultural events. Israeli police and tax agents' raids on hotels, restaurants and shops in Jerusalem, or the several police orders to close the theaters just one hour before the performance, as well as Israeli army destruction of rehabilitated *Maqams*/shrines, the arrest of tour guides and hikers in the West Bank, were all but a small price that had to be endured following the evident success of the cultural events. No regret or complaint was ever expressed, as we all understand well that fighting for our Palestinian cultural identity and heritage is priceless and remains an important pillar for the decolonization of our beloved country. Tomorrow will definitely be a better day as we remain armed with the inspiring heritage of our ancestors and the dreams of our beloved children.

Our national poet, Mahmoud Darwish, has said it all:

*On this land, we have what makes life worth living,*
*April's hesitation*
*The aroma of bread at dawn*
*A woman's beseeching of men*
*The writings of Aeschylus*

*Love's beginning*
*Moss on a stone*
*Mothers standing on a flute's thread*
*And the invader's fear of memories*
*We have on this land all of that which makes life worth living...*
*On this land*
*The lady of our land*
*The mother of all beginnings*
*And the mother of all end*
*She was called Palestine*
*Her name later became Palestine*
*My lady ...*
*Because you are my lady*
*I have all of that which makes life worth living.*

REEM TALHAMI *is a Palestinian artist, largely involved in the Palestinian cultural performing arts scene as a singer and actress. She was born in the city of Shafa Amr, north of Palestine, and graduated from the Music and Dance Academy. She currently lives in Palestine.*

*Despite her western classical academic study, Talhami sings in different styles. She has several music/songs releases, both locally and internationally, albums and singles as well as partnerships. The essence of Reem`s work involves the struggle of her people. In her work, she speaks out about injustice, hope, sorrow and the search for freedom as part of the Palestinian dream for freedom and salvation. Her works in theater include "Jidariyah," "Blood Wedding," "Half Sack of Bullets," "Khail Tayha," "The Sea is West," "Kalila wa Dimna," "Green Salt," and others.*

# WARS WITHOUT BLOODSHED
## Songs of Liberation[14]

*Reem Talhami*

EARLY 1987, I applied for law school at the Hebrew University of Jerusalem. A relative, whose enthusiasm made me suspicious, said, "You have leadership qualities and courage. You are worthy of the legal profession and should not consider any other!" My family wanted me to steer away from art and singing and get an academic degree and have a proper profession. I consoled myself, vowing that if I got accepted, I would follow the steps of advocate Felicia Langer. I would devote my time to defend those who have no voice: Palestinian political prisoners of Israeli occupation.

Langer's book, *With My Own Eyes,* caught my attention from the moment I first spotted it in my father's library, where it sat among countless books of all genres. My father built the library shelves with his own hands and infected me with a passion for reading and a love for books. I remember how my sisters and I would gather around him, with braided hair, in clean pajamas, to compete in a game of "Find that country on the map." He was never satisfied with only teaching us the location of a country; he would often add his commentary and analysis on world events that shaped it, the wars it suffered, its historical and archaeological landmarks and its language. My father was a man of a few words, except when it came to explaining historic events. I wondered if his obsession for reading might explain his quiet nature, or if reading and silence were his inevitable refuge from the constant setbacks his generation of Palestinians had endured.

---

14 This essay was originally written in Arabic and was translated by Samah Sabawi.

When the Zionist entity was established on the ruins of our lands, my family, like other Palestinians, found themselves under Israeli Occupation. Never in my father`s worst nightmares could he have imagined all the restrictions the occupiers would impose on us, under its military government.

I was born and raised in Shafa Amr, northern Palestine. My family roots (Al-Bandak) of the Al-Anaterah branch go back to the fourteenth-century city of Bethlehem. I am the eldest of four daughters. I grew up in a multi-faith town and received no official musical education outside of the primary and preparatory classes, where my teachers paid attention to my voice and performance skills. I attended public schools run by the Israeli Ministry of Education which was subject to the state agenda. I joined all the usual school activities; choir, *Dabke* and girl scouts. Our principal and teachers were under constant supervision of school inspectors, also known as Israel's law enforcers, who ensured full compliance with the orders of the Ministry. One of these orders was for all Palestinian public schools to participate in Israel's official ceremonies. I remember being punished for refusing to raise the Israeli flag and sing on Israel's day of "independence," a day that marks our catastrophe and the destruction of our way of life. Even with my simple, naive understanding at the time, I knew perfectly well that something must be wrong if I were to hold the Israeli flag and sing the Israeli "Tikva."

In the '70s, I was part of a young generation severed from our natural Arab environment, living in a controlled reality designed to impede our awareness of what it meant to be an Arab-Palestinian, especially as we became known as "Israeli Arabs."

Identity is not a blue document.[15] Identity is a calm certainty that grows through thoughts, feelings and convictions. My identity is part of the spirit of this place; my place of origin, where I was born, and is part of the people I belong to and the language I speak.

---

15 The Israeli official identity card certificate that was given also to the Palestinian citizens inside Israel. The colors of identities given to the Palestinians vary according to their geopolitical position.

* * *

My application to law school was quickly rejected and, just as quickly, I was accepted to the School of Social Work. I consoled myself once more: "This too, would enable me to help those who have no voice." I moved to the big city of Jerusalem, excited to start my academic journey, which lasted not more than two and a half years.

At university, my political awareness grew as I connected with my brothers and sisters in Jerusalem, the West Bank and Gaza. The "new" Occupation of '67 had just reached its twentieth year, and the Palestinian people were about to begin a new phase of resistance, later named the "Intifada of Stones." Twenty years separated the year of the great catastrophe in 1948 and the year of my birth in 1968. Now, another twenty years later, in 1987, my life in Jerusalem and the Occupied Territories began! It was then that I made the decision that would change the course of my life.

During the years of the First Intifada, I began to explore new ways of singing, similar to, yet distinct from, traditional nationalist songs that were popular in Egypt and the Levant, coming to us through Jordan. These new themes of songs were inspired by protest chants: angry, loud and powerful. The first time I heard Kamilya Jubran's voice,[16] it made me wonder why I had not heard it before. Her voice, and the songs she sang with the band Sabereen,[17] touched my heart and soul, and impacted my style of singing for years to come. I was amazed by Kamellia's unique oriental voice movement, melody and rhythm, which were different from anything I had ever heard before. Moreover, the lyrics of her songs captured the Palestinian Arab experience that belonged to and spoke to us.

---

16 Kamilya Jubran is the lead singer of the Palestinian group Sabreen. Born in the village of Rama in the Galilee in 1966

17 The Sabreen group was founded in Jerusalem in 1980 by composer Said Murad, in an effort to develop the modern Palestinian song.

*"Some songs are a cry you cannot sing*
*So if my songs provoke you, be angry*
*O builders on the ruins of my house*
*Beneath the ruins a curse will turn*
*If my trunk is a victim of the axe*
*My roots like a God in the clod they turn*
*This is me naked, clad only in tomorrow*
*Either rest in its show, or be crucified*
*For his eyes and for the eyes of my brothers*
*I walk and give the path what it demands*
*This is me, have saddled all my troubles*
*My blood is singing on my palms,*
*So go on and have a drink!"*[18]

*"Silence is dishonor, fear is dishonor*
*Who are we? Lovers of day*
*We live, we cry, we love*
*We fight with ghosts*
*We live in waiting*
*We keep on digging through the wall*
*Either we open a hole for the light to come through*
*Or we die on the wall*
*Our shovels do not despair... and we do not tire or break*
*When the clouds of autumn dry up*
*And the summer train passes by*
*Our spring clouds are pregnant*
*With an abundance of rain*
*And tomorrow will be our victory"*[19]

*"Sleep, love of my eyes*
*This is how the nightingale slept*

---

18 Palestinian poet Samih Al-Qasim, featured on *Dukhan al-Barakin* (*Smoke of the Volcanoes*) album (Sabreen, 1984).

19 Yemeni poet Abdulaziz Al-Maqaleh, featured on *Dukhan al-Barakin* (*Smoke of the Volcanoes*) album (Sabreen, 1984).

*Sleep son, a good night's sleep*
*Are these your milk or your adult teeth?"*

*"Why be patient my love?*
*Above the hardships we are*
*Why are eyes so blind?*
*When justice is in our hands?"*[20]

These were the songs that transcended their eastern form and refined my vocal skills during the initial phase of my singing career. I found the beauty of the Palestinian dialect as powerful as classical Arabic. I began to imagine protest chants and daily Palestinian street talk, then composed and sang them. This set me off on a quest to find words that could satisfy my hunger.

I met Ibrahim Khatib, a nursing student and a guitar player. Ibrahim was an aspiring writer and composer, who was about to change the course of his life, too. However, my hastened return to northern Palestine delayed my creative quest. I regressed to singing other people's songs, lyrics that I did not examine or choose, melodies that did not reflect my personal thoughts. Songs I loved and with which I resonated, but they were not mine.

Ibrahim had written *Ya Mhajer weinak,* "O Migrant, Where Are You?" and that was the first original song I performed. We presented the song for the first time at a celebration held by the Arab Students Committee at the Hebrew University. The reaction of the audience exceeded our expectations. News of our performance spread, and we began to receive invitations from the Arab Student Committees in other universities. This opened up space for us to create our own Palestinian sound, one that is both original and authentic to the experiences of our predecessors. Between Shafa Amr, Tamra and Nazareth, in the north of Palestine, the *Gh'orbah* band (Alienation) was born. The work of *Gh'orbah* lasted for only one year, from 1988 to 1989. The vocals, as well as the lyrics, melody and instruments

---

20 A mother's lullaby by the Palestinian poet Dr. Husein Barghouti, featured on *Dukhan al-Barakin* (*Smoke of the Volcanoes*) album (Sabreen, 1984).

took on new shapes. Our work in *Gh'orbah* resulted in a collection of original songs, as well as compositions of poems written by well-known Palestinian poets. None of *Gh'orbah*'s works were recorded due to the scarcity of resources, and the fact that we had no time to complete the journey which ended in its infancy. The band was dismantled and all its members, including myself, moved back to Jerusalem to study music at the Academy of Music and Dance.

*Gh'orbah* reflected our courageous persistence in creating original songs. The poems we chose were close to our hearts and expressed our sense of alienation in our own homeland; poems like Mahmoud Darwish's "Soft Rain in a Far Autumn," "A Stranger in a Far City" and "How Alone You Were." Being a collaborative partner in making a choice, in owning an idea, and for the ability of that idea to reflect us, both as young individuals, and as part of a collective—that might be called a Nation.

I was accepted into the Academy of Music. The great musician and composer, Khaled Jubran (Kamilya Jubran's elder brother), led me by the hand on my first visit to the Academy and had me sing to the voice teacher available on that day, who accepted me on her team. It was then that Khaled advised me, on a serious note, to put away all the Arabic music cassettes that I had. "Close the box well, and don't open it until the day you graduate from the Academy," he said.

An Eastern classical music education department had not yet been established at the Academy; therefore, western classical music and operatic voice development techniques were my only choice. Years later, I would shy away from the classification of Opera singer, and I would also refrain from restricting my voice to one vocal field.

In any case, I took Khaled Jubran's advice partly for the first year of study, and I mastered operatic singing and graduated from the Academy in 1996. I did not open the box during the years of my studies, but I did collaborate with musicians and composers, amongst whom was Suhail Khoury. Suhail and I, with other musicians who joined later, established "Washem" (Tatoo) band. In 1993, the band released their first and only album, *"Ashiqa" (Woman in Love)*, written by Palestinian poet, Waseem Al-Kurdi, and composed by Suhail Khoury.

*The hero never dies*
*Because he is life*
*Because he is its air and clouds*
*Because he is its soil and wheat*
*Because he is the eternal willow*
*Giving shade to the spaces*
*Covering the horizon*
*With his voice.*

*"Oh Jerusalem, where is the soul, where is the open range?*
*This space is desecrated"*

*"Gaza who is walled by radiant Children*
*who throw defeat behind and one brother holds the other."*

This musical experience was more timely than others that followed; the lyrics were written during the simmering of the Palestinian street in its First Intifada, and were released as a cassette, almost two years later. *Washem* and Ashiqa were fundamental blocks in my musical journey. My performances were in their heyday in the years 1992 and 1993.

In 1992, I was thrilled to be invited by the Al-Kasaba Theatre in Jerusalem to perform with the great Greek composer and pianist, Sarandis Kassars; then together, we toured Palestine. Subsequently, we were invited to perform together in Cairo.

That was the first time I visited Egypt or any Arab country. My joy was overwhelming. We presented two musical performances at the National Theater, which were positively reviewed in the media. That same year, I received an extraordinary invitation to sing at the Carthage International Festival in Tunis on the 25th anniversary of the occupation of Jerusalem, conducted by the great Tunisian conductor, Mohammad Al-Garfi.[21]

---

21 Tunisian Maestro Mohammad Al-Garfi conducted Voices of Freedom (singers and orchestra) at the Carthage International Music Festival, 1992.

I was in seventh heaven, aware of the weight of responsibilities, as I stood on the rocks of Carthage. Behind me, Palestinian children stood on a high stone ledge, carrying Palestinian flags and wearing *kuffiyyes.* I was told later that they were the "children of Yasser Arafat"; some were orphaned refugees who came to Tunisia with Arafat when the PLO was exiled from Beirut in 1982. Meeting Arafat, himself, was magical. The man`s name and actions preceded him back home and neither the news nor my father could stop talking about him. My tears would not stop while he fed me with watermelon at his residence in Almanzah, Tunis. I was impatient to share this with my father, while my father was anxiously worried about my return and feared my being arrested.

Historical junctures sculpt and shape us. Moving from northern Palestine to Jerusalem held so much meaning; the First Intifada, and the way in which Jerusalem, the West Bank and the Gaza Strip connected to me like we were parts of one Palestinian body. Patriotic sentiments I grew up with were challenged every day in confrontations with the Occupation. Taking part in protests calling for an end to the occupation and the establishment of a Palestinian State. A rebellious love story. Marriage. Graduation from the Academy of Music. Motherhood. Postponed projects. Successive disappointments, both in art and life. Peace negotiations. Signed agreements. Round table. Peace treaties. Pens and papers. Second Intifada. The brutal separation wall. Oppression. Death, hanging over our heads daily at checkpoints. The nightmare of proving residence in Jerusalem. Dabbling in theater. Performing theatrical plays. Touring music and theater outside of Palestine. Awards and honors. New songs. Albums. The siege on Gaza. Continuous bombings. Martyrs. More death. Refugees aching to return. Palestinians in Diaspora. Dispersal. Alienation. And tiny Palestinian dreams.

All of this became, eventually, my inspiration to write new songs. It was important to keep my art away from cliché political discourses and their many profiteers. Tracking and finding the words that would capture reality without falling into the trap of sloganeering was not an easy task.

Songs reflect various moods that need to be deeply explored. That is why I confront the song, and direct it towards areas and details that are not necessarily categorized into a specific genre such as arabesque, classical singing or jazz. I am guided by the text. Lyrics confront events with literary linguistic vocabulary, far from the slogans that characterize them, much like describing a terrestrial event in celestial terms. This idea embodies my work and my partnership with the Palestinian musician, Habib Shehadeh Hanna. Our partnership consisted of special lyrical works, in addition to the songs of theatrical works and films in which I participated as a singer/actress. Habib wrote the musical compositions of "Jidariyyah" ("Mural") by the poet Mahmoud Darwish, "Ors al Dam" ("Blood Wedding") by Federico Garcia Lorca, as well as the documentary film *Jerusalem Back and Forth* by Akram Safadi, where the song "Ya'lou" ("Rise") described, in summary, the experience between Habib and I, up to this day. "Ya'lou" presents the transition of singing in different vocal spaces: head, chest and throat, and a great sensory accumulation and a prominent escalation in the music.

*"He rises, rises in space*
*He passes by the sun between two clouds*
*behind the wind*
*He blinks maddened by love*
*dances in front of his shadows*
*Butterflies and dolls make fun of him*
*Inside a suitcase"*[22]

The same idea was reflected in lyrics also, in 2013, in my album, *Yihmilni e leil* (*The Night Carries Me*), ten songs written by Khaled Juma, and composed by Said Murad. The album was inspired by and dedicated to Gaza. The songs did not include words like destruction, bombing, missiles, blood, siege, division or any of the

---

22 Lyrics from "Ya`lou," written by Akram Safadi for the documentary film, *Jerusalem Back and Forth* (2005), Habib Shehadeh (Composer), Reem Talhami 2015.

buzz words often heard in news reports about Gaza. The songs used a different language to tell the same story.

*"My homeland is in the empty plains*
*And I am estranged from myself*
*And I call out to you,*
*But the echo returns to me"*[23]

*"Walk on my eyelashes*
*Drape the sound of a flute and my madness over you*
*Sleep in the warmth of my gaze*
*On my shore*
*Your footsteps are the melody of night*
*And whispers of a star that sing to me*
*It softens the cruelty of darkness*
*Inscribes a word across the morning*
*My chest is filled with papers I write*
*And my blood is ink to my writing."*[24]

*"Strong like hope*
*Thoroughbred like a mare*
*Between sleep and drowsiness*
*Her eyes dream of the ways*
*The sun shining on her*
*When it kissed her, shy ... she melted."*[25]

Looking back, I wonder what value was accomplished. I think of the young woman from the north of Palestine with a burning fire in her soul, her ideas and dreams that were waiting to be fulfilled and her intense passion for stage. What did that strong urge to sing

23 Khaled Juma (Poet) and Said Murad (Composer), "The Night Carries Me," title song of the album, Reem Talhami 2013.

24 Khaled Juma (Poet) and Said Murad (Composer), "Step on," *The Night Carries Me* album, Reem Talhami 2013.

25 Khaled Juma (Poet) and Said Murad (Composer), "Samra" *The Night Carries Me* album, Reem Talhami 2013.

on the stage before an audience mean? How ready can one be for this exposure? And what power does the exposure have? Is it just a group session for venting? Or a one-person sensory therapy, with a few short interventions by others? Sometimes, I wonder about the fine line between a heavenly gift and a satanic curse! There are those who produce wars and those who produce songs! Which category would one prefer?

The thought of the price I pay as an artist who had chosen her path a long time ago, when I tirelessly decided, time and again, to produce a new song, or to take part in a new theatrical production, even when I know that it would only be staged five or ten times at most—and I think, maybe, that the whole thing is a curse. Despite the constant bleeding in art, the restlessness, the anxieties, the sweat and the few visible scars, they lead into the joy of launching new works and the ecstasy of a premiere! People's attachment to songs, the way they memorize them by heart, their glorious attendance at live performances and their awaiting new works, their observations and impressions, these are all heavenly gifts! Exposure makes you as vulnerable as if naked, but yet powerful; you take on the art of disclosure, of speech and movement and relieve the audience from the arduous task of speaking for a while. All they need to do is watch, observe and listen in order to feel liberated.

Here and now, the artist is the maker of joy, the speaker of words, and the proprietor of ideas. That is a force to be reckoned with! You own the stage, so you own the world.

Songs bring us together as if we are one, accompanied by our applause and the movement of our bodies. Songs free us from burdens we can no longer bear. They make us lighter and fill us with life.

Those who know the Palestinians well know the extent to which they relate to traditional songs. If you see the tight-knit Palestinians stuck together in a *Sahja* or a row of *Dabke*, you will know beyond doubt how free they are. No one can resist the temptation and the infectious joy, courage and ecstasy that are transmitted to Palestinians when they hold a vigil or protest against their occupiers. With songs, we wage wars without shedding a single drop of blood. A battle, whose weapon is beauty, language and music, and in which we do not mourn a single martyr! How can anyone think this could be a curse?

Once I settle into texts that speak to me and express my feelings and ideas, I begin to explore the theatrics of sound and space. Theater plays a very important and influential role in my psychological and artistic formation and voice. The characters I play on stage are a part of me. Theater opens new doors and outlets for my voice. The songs are dramatic scenes, and the hero of each song is a character in their own right. Since 2004, I have wandered the dynamic space between singing, theater and voice. My voice reached into areas that I once feared and refrained from, thinking I could not belong there. Theater contributed to the liberation of my voice far more than any vocal lessons I received at the Academy of Music ever could.

My artwork reflects Palestinians, wherever they are, with poetics and renewed vocabulary, despite the risk of rating scales and reviews. I deliberate on finding new angles, sometimes small ones, within the great and unending conflict on the ground.

The Palestinian reality demands resistance and freedom fights on a daily basis, while the Occupation with all the tyrannical power that they have, is quick to provoke, escalate and sow oppression and death in our land. On the other hand, with every disappointment, ongoing frustration, lack of vision, loss of direction, the alienation status of Palestinians grows wild and legitimate fatigue afflicts the steadfast in their own country.

We, Palestinians, are caught between daily resistance and steadfastness, and the hammers of the executioner multiply and branch out. It feels as if the Palestinian people have been abandoned to face their fate alone.

> *"When your lamp lights your night*
> *When you rise above your wounds*
> *When your madness pulls your fear*
> *When your voice falls from you,*
> *Strengthen your heart and get angry"*[26]

26 Arafat Al-Deek (Poet) and Ibrahim Najem (Composer), "Rebel," Reem Talhami 2014.

*"Where is your neighing, mare?!*
*Your echo used to travel far*
*You used to jump carefree*
*Trample on the borders of the guards*
*Where is your neighing, mare?"*[27]

*"I heal in him the neighing of the horses,*
*I heal him after he stopped talking*
*I pour him into the cupboards of the night*
*I pour him into my weeping eyes*
*I give him clouds and feathers,*
*Come back*
*Bring him to me,*
*I'll hold him in my bosom*
*and he will come back to life."*[28]

*"When our homeland chants, its people join in chanting*
*When our homeland falls into fatigue, its people stand guardian*
*A starry soul is jubilant, a loving heart with feeling thumps*
*The teary-eye wells with a longing, on heartache it stomps*
*Should our homeland make a wish, we grant its wishes*
*We embrace its breeze as by nightfall it swishes*
*How beautiful is its crazy breeze! This homeland is not to be forgotten."*[29]

I got married to Kamel Al-Basha in 1995 after a stubborn battle that lasted four years because of mixed religions. We have three daughters, Mona, Mariam and Marwa. I chose to live between Jerusalem and the West Bank. This prompted some of my friends residing inside historical Palestine to ask, "Why did you choose the

---

27 Arafat Al-Deek (Poet) and Basil Zayed (Composer), "Where is Your Neighing, Mare?," Reem Talhami 2017.

28 Khaled Juma (Poet) and Moneim Adwan (Composer), "I Heal in Him," Reem Talhami 2018.

29 Waddah Zaqtan (Poet) and Moneim Adwan (composer), "Elna Balad," Reem Talhami 2021. Translated originally by Alice Yousef.

hardest life where there are daily confrontations with Occupation, when you could have lived in a house overlooking the coast of Haifa or the coast of Acre?" "The uprising of Palestinian citizens of Israel in the 2021 Unity Intifada, confirmed that they are part of the Palestinian people, and that efforts to integrate them into Israel and to erase their identity have failed. The uprising showed a deep and strong commitment to the cause of Palestine. Israel will double its efforts using the carrot and stick approach and will re-evaluate its methods in order to subjugate or integrate them, but this only means that the uprising of 2021 will not be the last, nor was it the first."[30]

With every new Palestinian outburst, new songs are born. Contemporary political and artistic Palestinian songs that reflect the dreams of Palestinians. The song is an instrument and a language. It is a tool, like all other tools Palestinians have invented, to confront their occupiers who have usurped their souls, their sky and their future, their land and their sea, and who think they can determine their fate.

In choosing this strenuous, rebellious, revolutionary path, songs, music, theater and all kinds of art carry in their folds important and great messages to describe a people and a homeland, each with its own style, method and choices. Purposeful arts vs commercial art. Thrust of words that are honest, real, which reflect us with all the diversity of Palestinian society.

I am reminded of a question a friend once pointed to me: "To what extent do you think that Palestine and the cause has become a burden on songs, poems and novels?" I was amazed at the sincerity of the question by my friend, writer Ziad Khadash. The question was deep and complicated. Yes, it is a dilemma but it is a choice as well! I would think of myself as more of a rock star than an opera singer, and I would find the way to speak up about Palestine and its people in any music genre that I would choose, or in any sound, but I would also go far and switch on and off between all genres and sounds—but what really matters are, those thrusts of words!

Art for the sake of art, or art for a purposeful cause? My answer was simple and short: There is no other way for me but this way! Purposeful art.

---

30 Quote of Anthony Shalat.

FARAH NABULSI *is an Oscar Nominated and BAFTA Award Winning Palestinian British filmmaker and human rights advocate. She uses the power of storytelling, her films, social media and the online platform* www.oceansofinjustice.com *to share the Palestinian experience with Western audiences. Learn more about her work at* www.farahnabulsi.com

# LIBERATION THROUGH CINEMA
## On Power, Identity and Art

*Farah Nabulsi*

*"Until the lion learns how to write, the story will always glorify the hunter."*
—AFRICAN PROVERB

FOR MORE THAN 100 years, the Palestinians have suffered oceans of injustice. We are the victims of a relentless ideology, the ultimate goal of which is to ethnically cleanse us from our land. This enormous crime against humanity continues while Western democracies ignore or even support it. They can afford to either ignore or support it because their citizens do not pressure them sufficiently and, therefore, fail to make democracies work the way they are supposed to. Citizens do not pressure their governments enough because most do not understand the realities or context of the conflict, what role they are playing in it and, most notably, they do not empathize enough with the Palestinians. They do not *feel* our pain enough with us.

As with Apartheid South Africa, it is only through grassroots efforts in the West that we can stop the final ethnic cleansing of Palestine. However, it is not enough for people of goodwill to be mentally engaged in this struggle; they must also be emotionally engaged in order to feel compelled and galvanized into becoming active supporters and members of those grassroots efforts to move their governments to action on our behalf.

Khalil Gibran wrote, *"In battling evil, excess is good, for he who is moderate in announcing the truth is presenting half-truth. He conceals the other half out of fear of the people's wrath."* I am afraid that, in the struggle for Palestine, we have been rather "moderate" in announcing our truth. Understandably, we have been so busy putting out fires, dealing with relief and always reacting from a defensive position, that our narrative has fallen to the wayside. It has, therefore, by and large, not been presented sufficiently, effectively or extensively to the outside world. Without a truthful, evocative, more complete and widely disseminated narrative, how else can we expect to rally people of goodwill to our cause? How can we hope to shift consciousness and consciences, build and scale solidarity, encourage meaningful BDS and achieve a full-scale global movement for freedom, justice and equality? The cause itself is a worthy one by default, so that part is beyond contention.

We, Palestinians, have ended up in this terrible situation for many reasons but a core explanation for its duration and scale, despite our having truth, right and international law on our side, is that political Zionism is a colonial, settler enterprise. It is no secret that all colonists throughout history work extremely hard to ensure the indigenous populations they are colonizing are first dehumanized, then branded as barbarians or terrorists if they resist, and eventually are claimed not to even exist. This is done for both foreign and domestic consumption, so that people of goodwill, worldwide, will not empathize with those populations or will think the issue has ended, following which any and all violations, abuses and atrocities can be carried out against them with neither any recourse for the victims nor punishment for the perpetrators. We know this process has been systematically and meticulously carried out against Palestinians. For our liberation to have a fighting chance, it requires engaging people on a large scale in ways that reverse this dehumanization, arousing their empathy and from that empathy, drawing them into action. Another major requirement for the struggle to succeed is to place our situation in its rightful and actual context. We need to inform and educate people so that Palestinian resistance, revolt, aggression and even violence can no longer be framed as terrorism, barbarism and baseless hatred, but actually be recognized and respected for its decades-long struggle against illegal occupation, its protest against a 14-year siege on Gaza, its outrage against a system of apartheid, its rejection of ongoing war crimes, home demolitions, child arrests, checkpoints, daily humiliations and so much more.

*"Until the lion learns how to write, the story will always glorify the hunter.*" When I came across this African proverb, I immediately and instinctively thought of Palestine and I knew that, unfortunately, we were the lions in this equation. If we want the true stories of Palestinians to be heard and felt and for people to take action with us and for our cause as a result, then we must tell our stories creatively, authentically, evocatively and certainly beyond our echo chambers.

This is not to say that we do not have, or have not had, our own accomplished, brilliant and esteemed storytellers: our writers, poets, artists, filmmakers, orators and commentators. Rather, we don't have enough of them. Many have been silenced, killed or have passed away, while others have been forced to dwell in an environment that has not allowed them to flourish. Frankly, our narrative has been hijacked for decades now. If we are not actively and continuously telling and funding the telling of our own stories, then our oppressor and its cronies will exercise control over all narratives, theirs and our own. But today's new technologies can bypass the traditional gatekeepers of false narratives and project the works of our storytellers much further across the globe than was previously possible.

We will come back to this later. Let us start at the beginning.

I was born, raised and educated in London, but my heritage, my blood is Palestinian. What that means exactly is for another essay in another book ... Growing up in the UK, I was never confused about where my family came from or who I was. I was British, born and raised, but my heart and body were pumping with the blood and genes of an Arab—a Palestinian. I knew the plight of the people of Palestine, their struggle for freedom against a relentless colonizer. At the same time, while I have always understood and empathized with the helplessness and victimhood of Jewish people over the centuries—which explains the psychological reasons why some felt the need for a "Jewish homeland"—it has never justified the dispossession and ethnic cleansing of the innocent Palestinians that was involved in creating one. It certainly does not excuse the ongoing oppression, injustice and apartheid that Israel inflicts on Palestinians in order to keep and continue expanding this homeland. Simply as a human being, of this, I am sure.

Throughout my teenage years, I rode my bicycle around Hyde Park in support of medical aid for Palestinian children, participated in Palestinian cultural events and promoted Palestinian charities at my Church of England school (I am Muslim, by the way!). I have held the microphone at rallies and protests at the top of High Street Kensington, and recall smiling and waving at "government" agents hiding on nearby rooftops while taking pictures of us! The chant back then was "1, 2, 3, 4—Occupation No More! 5, 6, 7, 8 Israel is a Terrorist State!" and still is, at protests today. It was also "Sharon, Sharon, what do you say, how many babies have you killed today?" (A chapter about chants and messaging at protests for another day in another book, perhaps!). Despite the occasional protest, charity and sympathy, I went on to become an investment banker and then set up and ran a business for several years.

Fast forward more than 25 years later. I am often asked how I ended up changing the trajectory of my life entirely from the banking and business world to becoming a filmmaker. The short version of the story is simply that I went home.

Growing up in London, I knew what was going on in Palestine or, at least, I thought I did. I had visited a number of times as a child, but from around the age of 10 to 35, not a single visit! We stopped going around the time of the First Intifada and, somehow, I found myself in my mid-thirties having never gone back. It was preposterous, given the privileged position I was in, being able to freely travel to Palestine, unlike the millions of Palestinians who, to this day, still remain in squalid refugee camps, unable to return home. So, I decided to visit.

The deep connection I felt to my ancestral land, coupled with the injustice I was witnessing there, first-hand, hit me, simply as a human being, like a ton of bricks. Whether it was the Israeli checkpoints, their apartheid separation wall plowing through Palestinian lands, towns and villages, the refugee camps, the separate road systems, the watchtowers and illegal colonies on all the hilltops—or the first-hand conversations I was having with mothers whose teenage sons had been taken into Israeli prisons under military detention or sipping tea with families on the ruins of their demolished homes—this first-hand experience literally changed me!

My initial trip was followed by a number of subsequent trips. Though initially not so obvious, a major revelation I had from these visits was that it was crucial to bring people from the West to Palestine to enable them to witness with their own eyes what was really going on. I was certain that this would lead them to finally understand and care about us. This is what ultimately changed the trajectory of my own life and, when I have met Westerners who are active, committed and passionate for Palestinian freedom and rights—sometimes even more so than some Arabs or Palestinians I have met—it is usually because they went and saw the facts on the ground for themselves. In fact, their reactions are usually so overwhelming because they never fathomed such blatant and institutionalized injustice. They are shocked by the extent to which they had previously been un- or misinformed about the cruel reality. For this to really work, though, it would need millions upon millions of people to visit Palestine and see it for themselves. I did the math. For only 20 million people to visit Palestine at, say, $2,000 a person for, say, a flight and one week's stay, it would cost over $40 billion. For 40 million people—$80 billion! It would take decades to actually accomplish, and they would need to willingly want to go there, in the first place—an urge that itself would have to be created, even before that. Realistically, it would be a financial and logistical impossibility—at least from my point of view!

However, what was a feasible and more economical, intelligent, effective, powerful and achievable alternative was to bring Palestine to them. In their tens of millions all around the world, only asking for, at most, two hours of their time—while packing a huge emotional punch and eye-opening experience through beautiful, powerful cinema! Equipped with a deep desire to express myself creatively, to tell these human stories and a love for film and theater from a young age—my mind was made up. I would become a filmmaker.

Some time ago, I read the following words penned by an art critic that resonated with me and made complete sense: "*You cannot make art without a sense of identity, yet it is identity you seek in making art.*" Certainly, I chose the art of film as a means of seeking my identity further, but I also chose it because it can serve as the master of advocators.

There are, of course, various forms of advocacy that we should be supporting and doing more of, including but not limited to: political advocacy, media, human rights, BDS and academic advocacy. In my opinion, though, one of—if not *the*—most important forms of advocacy, because it essentially ignites all those other forms, is artistic advocacy. Artists are able to engage us through film, video, audio and visual installations, poetry and theater, using the full array of human emotions from deep pain to humor. This is because art speaks to the heart and is the medium through which you can humanize and draw empathy. It also paves the way for all other forms of advocacy to be more willingly received.

You need only look at Hollywood and the way Muslims and Arabs have been portrayed in film, for the perfect example of how film can influence people's perceptions all over the world. Or consider how resistance theater has been cited as a major and powerful factor in influencing the court of public opinion and activating audiences around the globe which, in turn, contributed to marshalling pressure from world governments that ultimately brought an end to apartheid in South Africa.

Take myself as a case study. I chose artistic advocacy in the form of live-action narrative cinema because I knew that I could bring to people's attention all the facts and figures, truth and proof, maps and international laws under the sun but, unless I had opened people's hearts, I would not be able to access their minds or activate their ability to reason.

Studies have shown that, even when you provide absolute factual proof to people, if it contradicts what they have been repeatedly told or made to believe, a deep inertia remains. Even in the face of evidence and facts, not only do people still stick to their beliefs but, sometimes, they become even more entrenched in their attitudes and perspectives. However, those same studies have shown that, when you can bring those same people to empathize, if you can address them through their hearts regarding the same topics, views or beliefs, they become far more receptive—and it is *empathy* that ultimately changes their minds or moves them away from their original positions.

So, speaking to someone's heart gives you a much better chance of influencing them to understand your perspective and your cause.

Dale Carnegie, the author of *How to Win Friends and Influence People.* said, "*When dealing with people, remember you are not dealing with creatures of logic, but with creatures of emotion.*" Referring to UN Resolution 282, 1397 and Resolutions 2254, 2334 and the 4th Geneva Convention, Article 49 is all well and good and very important, but it will only go so far. What really galvanizes people is information that hits them on an emotional level and this can be done effectively through stories. People love stories. We are all attracted to them as human beings. It is in our nature. It is why people enjoy good books or films. It is why we pick up the newspaper every day, watch the news, go on social media or come together for meals. Stories are the currency of life, and with art, there is no limit to the stories you can tell or the ways you can tell them.

My experiences have shown me that people around the world are genuinely open and interested in understanding the plight of Palestinians and our struggle when we speak to their hearts. Whether at film festival Q&As, panel discussions or at universities, people have been welcoming and intrigued by my films. They have not only appreciated the art, but also the truth and reality in which it is laced. They ask questions about the what, why, where and how. When conducted engagingly and resonating on an emotional level, to a standard they are accustomed, attracted and can relate to, audiences and the industry will even award and distribute it. Take our short film, "The Present." This 24-minute film not only won a BAFTA and was nominated for an Oscar, but on its journey to the pinnacles of the film industry, it received dozens of awards at international film festivals, was distributed on major streaming platforms, was shown on television stations around the world and screened at many cinemas in countless languages. A simple, short film about a Palestinian man and his daughter going to buy a gift in the West Bank but having to grapple with the humiliation of Israeli checkpoints, garnered the attention and coverage, not only of all the major entertainment publishers, but also the likes of CNN, Sky News and the BBC, to name but a few. This included an opinion piece penned by former CIA Director, John Brennan, published in the *New York Times* and a discussion on CNN with Christiane Amanpour. The film has been distributed across the globe, including with Netflix Worldwide, iTunes and Amazon Prime. Numerous international public figures, celebrities, musicians, fashion models, politicians, academics and beyond, have publicly endorsed the film. As I write these words, over a year and a half since "The Present" premiered in France, the film continues to be shown and pick up awards at festivals and we are still receiving requests to screen and discuss the film nearly every other day. From Brown and Colombia University in the USA to top schools, fundraisers and public events in the UK and beyond, the artistic advocacy continues. It was even used as a film work case study in the educational curriculum across the entire State of Ohio. (Since there are always naysayers, I want to highlight that Netflix and most distributors took on the film months before we were nominated, or even shortlisted, for the Oscars or the BAFTAs). The reason I mention all of this is not to blow my own horn, but to illustrate the power of artistic advocacy. The trajectory of "The Present" is proof to me that there *is* a space for our bold and authentic stories to engage and flourish in the world arena, and to overwhelm the presently dominant mainstream narrative.

So, back to the lion learning to write—we need to become relentless, fearless lions who become masters of our own narrative, telling our own stories, of which there are so, so many. We do not need to deceive, sensationalize or create melodrama—all things the oppressor has often engaged in—because we have truth and right and international law on our side. We also have a plethora of absurd, engaging and incredible stories you could not make up, even if you tried—decades upon decades of them but, ultimately, the onus is on us to tell them!

Art alone, of course, cannot free Palestine, but I believe that without it, Palestine will never be free! It is the pillar of advocacy upon which all others stand. Films alone cannot *change* the struggle, but they have their important role *in* the struggle. They engage and ignite. They have the power to transcend borders, tear down stereotypes and overcome misconceptions and misperceptions. They can garner interest and intrigue, encourage research and further understanding. They pave the way so that people can ultimately "feel" with an oppressed people and be galvanized to take action to end that oppression, for and alongside the oppressed. Of course, a powerful, clear, unified social movement needs to be in place to liberate Palestinians but, for it to grow and build momentum, you need people to feel compelled to join that movement and this requires engagement. Film, in my opinion, is possibly the most powerful, far-reaching artistic medium for engagement and meaningful human communication the world has known.

Retrospectively, many might read this chapter and think that what I have written/expressed here is obvious but, regretfully, it is this very element of soft power that is often left as an afterthought when it comes to investing in the struggle for Palestinian freedom. I also believe, given all the oppression and pressure that Palestinians within Palestine are enduring, that the onus is on Palestinians in exile, and our allies, to carry out the "lion's share" (pun intended) of this ongoing and growing endeavor, while supporting those Palestinian artists within.

Palestinians will be free one day. I truly believe this. If you look back at the last 50, 20, 10 or 5 years—even the last 12 months—the strides are evident. While on the ground, the situation is truly desperate for Palestinians living under occupation and apartheid, in the court of world opinion, things have never been better. Tipping points are always potentially around a corner. Persistent action towards a united movement is the main ingredient, but a bucket of hope and a large dollop of art complete the recipe. If you have creative talent and a deep sense of justice, I encourage you to apply them towards Palestinian freedom and equality—or be sure to support those who do. I have no doubt that, together, we *can* make a difference.

SAMAH JABR *is a Palestinian psychiatrist and psychotherapist living in East Jerusalem. She serves as the Head of the Mental Health Unit at the Ministry of Health in Ramallah, Palestine, and maintains an office practice for children and adults. Dr. Jabr is widely published in scholarly journals and the popular press on the themes of psychological well-being, and the intersection of political, social, and clinical dynamics. She speaks nationally and internationally on issues related to Palestine and is well-recognized as a thought leader in human rights. Author of the book* Beyond the Frontlines, Derrière les fronts: Chroniques d'une psychiatre psychothérapeute palestinienne sous occupation, *published by PMN in 2017, which appeared in French and Italian, and the book* Sumud, resistere all'oppressione, *published in Italian by Sensibili alle foglie in 2021. Dr. Jabr is also a founding member of the Palestine Global Mental Health Network.*

# LIBERATION PSYCHOLOGY

## Therapy, Awareness and the Development of Critical Consciousness

*Samah Jabr*

I CAME TO LIFE with an injury and pain. I weighed 5300 grams at birth, which took place through an ordinary vaginal delivery. However, because of my large size, the delivery was so difficult that, in order to save my life and that of my mother, the doctors had to break my clavicle. This caused permanent injury to the underlying left brachial plexus—the nerves connected to my supposedly dominant arm. For years afterwards, my parents used to carry me, as they went on foot from Shufat to the French Hill so that I could receive physiotherapy sessions at an Israeli medical center. I continued that treatment well into the time that I developed the capacity to remember what I experienced.

I remember Riva, the practitioner who was taking care of me—an Israeli woman, whom I now recognize as a religious Jew on the basis of her appearance. I remember the yellow ladders I had to climb to strengthen my atrophying arm. This was a difficult exercise, and I undertook it only to receive the chocolate I earned when I finished all of my training for the day. I also remember very well how exhausting this trip was for my parents, who did not have a car or speak Hebrew, and were apprehensive about the dominating Israeli presence in the center. These trips were especially hard on my mother, who would return home tired and sunburnt after the morning's journey; I remember her making a yogurt-based emulsion to ease the sun's effect on her face.

I had been the fourth girl in a row. My sisters were closer to one another in age; my mother had given birth to a stillborn baby boy just before me, and then had to cope with my difficult delivery and injury. I highly suspect that she suffered from post-partum depression after my birth. I also know that I was given the name “Samah,” meaning “forgiveness,” to make up for the disappointment of a fourth baby girl.

In primary school, I was overweight and myopic, with thick corrective eyeglasses. I was a “clumsy” child and therefore not a great physical play partner. When I joined play, I was often blamed for the team losing the game. The weakness in my arm and its limitation of movement caused me frequent injuries and led to the formation of multiple scars on my forehead and scalp. Perhaps, this early experience as a bit of a misfit made me sensitive and empathic to other people who have difficulty integrating—such as classmates with learning disabilities and students who come from a difficult social background.

On the other hand, my subtle physical weaknesses gave me a strong motivation to develop my brain muscles. I was very good at playing with words and stood out as a popular and reliable colleague and friend. I was labeled “the advocate” by schoolmates who sought my help when in trouble, and who asked me to write letters on their behalf to the teachers and administration. Likewise, I was labeled an “argumentative troublemaker” by the adults, albeit still esteemed as a wise child. As one might have anticipated, I was punished several times for standing up for my rights and the rights of others in the face of strong and powerful adults.

My adolescence, during the collective experience of the First Intifada, accentuated these early childhood traits. I was aware of being viewed as part of a broken, dysfunctional, defective community, and this interaction between the personal and the collective accelerated my development of a sophisticated understanding of politics and power dynamics. I developed hypertrophic qualities of openness, authenticity and autonomy, to the point that my friend, Betsy Mayfield, used to tell me, “You are embracing the world with one arm." My mother used to warn me in a similar vein, "You can't hold a big watermelon under one arm and not expect it to fall down."

As a wise adolescent, aware of my parents' anxieties, societal prohibitions and political oppression, I was keen to calculate risks so as to avoid putting them, or myself, in danger. The courage, caution and critical thinking I developed during my adolescence have helped me walk the narrow alleys and navigate a path to love and freedom through many subsequent dangers: the Israeli occupation, the oppression by Palestinian institutions, societal corruption, patriarchy and sexism and, as my world got bigger, to also deal with Western Islamophobia and complicity in the oppression of my people. My adolescence equipped me for a long journey in pursuit of well-being and liberty for myself, for my loved ones and for the injured Palestinian community.

I armed myself by studying and working hard in the field of medicine, followed by a specialization in psychiatry. Several theories of psychotherapy seemed appropriate for the mission of healing the traumatized individuals whom I encountered in clinical settings. Yet, I had to find "treatment" for the ill relationships caused among individuals, which weakened the cohesion of a community under military occupation. Our tendency to collaborate with Israelis, our pervasive distrust in ourselves and our collective sense of inferiority and helplessness are just a few of the symptoms typical of an oppressed community. I found it equally important to maintain close observation of the direct experience of people. I learned to draw my conclusions from the ground up and to seek remedies for historical and collective trauma by promoting agency, self-direction and wellness within individuals, within community development and through social and political action.

My work has been extremely varied. It has included policy-making and the development of national strategies, such as a national suicide prevention strategy and a national mental health response plan to COVID-19, etc., as well as extensive involvement in providing training and supervision for doctors and mental health workers, an area of involvement that contributes to building professional capacities and liberal and ethical attitudes in future mental health practice in Palestine. In addition, I have had a wide range of clinical experience with patients suffering from psychosis and other severe mental disorders, families with battered women in shelters, civil law prisoners, political prisoners, juvenile offenders and victims of trauma due to political violence and torture. In all of these groups, I see how political violence interacts with the individual's bio-psychosocial vulnerabilities to provoke illness and impede recovery.

I also support the struggles of those whom I encounter outside the clinic—demoralized people oscillating between survival and surrender under oppression and enduring social ills, such as patriarchy, gender-based violence, corruption, nepotism, institutional hypocrisy and the subtle pernicious way of flattening and evacuating the values and belief systems of Palestinians and imposing false values on them by oppressive political powers.

When people protested against the death while in custody of the Palestinian opposition activist, Nizar Banat after his arrest by Palestinian security forces, official media diffused the situation, claiming that those demonstrators have an "external agenda," that the women who participated in the demonstrations have no "honor" and that their slogans "scratch the purity" of the Palestinian society. The mobile phones of the women participants were confiscated, and their content was used as a subject to blackmail, silence and render them invisible. Like Israel's agents who pose as Palestinians to assassinate activists in our markets and camps, Palestinian official security agents sneaked into opposition demonstrations wearing civilian clothes and started attacking the demonstrators with stones in order to break their bones, in images that remind us of the behavior of soldiers following the orders of Yitzhak Rabin to break Palestinians' legs and arms. All of the above Israeli tactics are now copied by the Palestinian security system that not only identifies with but is also fascinated by the aggressor.

Activism through writing, public speaking, mobilization and networking with friends, colleagues and comrades, and advocacy for social and political justice have also served as medical-psychological interventions to heal the social ills burdening the occupied Palestinian psyche. I engage in this work as a conscientious citizen, pressured by the heavy weight of crushing oppression, affording me deeper analytical experience and understanding than an external expert looking on from afar.

Like many other Palestinians, my life is characterized by the theft of both space and time. In Jerusalem, where space is shrinking for its Palestinian residents, neighbors can kill each other for a parking spot for their cars or for an empty space on the roof of their shared buildings. I am aware of these strangulating constraints, as I live through the resulting aggression of this reality. My personal survival strategy includes hyper-functioning and politically analyzing this reality, as I live at the crossroads of the two worlds of Jerusalem and the West Bank. I feel that the chronic lateness and deliberate slowness of the bureaucracy and administration are yet additional tools to suffocate the people of Palestine. Liberation must mean taking possession of both our space and our time, and using them wisely, an issue that I struggle to explain to friends outside Palestine.

Generating local knowledge of Palestinian experience and sharing it with the world is another battlefield for me and other Palestinian scholars. Our special relationship with time, the lack of appropriate budget and appropriate personnel, are just a few of the obstacles on the pathway to generating knowledge in mental health. Scholarly writing takes endless effort in footnoting, proofreading and formatting, and often requires authors or readers to pay to have the journal or its articles forwarded to colleagues. Conferences are expensive to attend, even when one is presenting at them.

While I rely on confident colleagues to help me co-author academic papers to transmit Palestinian local knowledge and expertise, I also try to simplify and explain relevant international academic knowledge to Palestinians. The abstruse lingo of much academic writing can be above the heads of many of the people who are involved in social and political change. Instead, I would rather spend my time rendering the sophisticated language of academia intelligibly and popularly. I prefer to draw applicable points and bring take-home messages to ordinary people who can benefit from it.

With my growing reputation and authority as a leading Palestinian and regional mental health professional, comes pressure to write ambiguous medico-legal reports that are dictated by powerful authorities and serve their specific interests—another challenge which eats up into my physical and mental health. A hard-won reputation and financial independence have been my route to standing up to and resisting this kind of seduction and pressure.

I use my authority as a professional to advocate for an increase in staff and budget in mental health, to oppose stigma, ignorant myths, discrimination against patients, women, queer and fragile people in the community. I try to promote psychiatric treatment outside the psychiatric hospital and integrate mental health into primary health care and general hospitals.

I try to encourage the contextualization of Palestinian psychological thinking, questioning the Western concept of PTSD, exploring important notions like "jihad," "*shaheed*," "sacrifice," "betrayal," "honor," "*sumud*," "resistance," "homeland," "solidarity" and other influential concepts that are relevant to the Palestinian vision for liberation. I see the work of clarifying and validating the medical consideration of these concepts as a contribution to dismantling established and entrenched systems of injustice.

I have no illusions as to the extent of my influence or impact, but I will try to live long enough to leave behind a meaningful contribution in the liberation project of Palestine as enabled by and needed in my professional field. I find that the liberation of the mind, through therapy, awareness and critical consciousness ais fundamental to both my discipline and to the Palestinian project writ large, and that this is the area where I can contribute the most.

This day marks 45 years of holding a weak and painful arm to my body, as well as a partially weak and painful representation of Palestine in my mind. My physical experience has taught me something about asymmetry, power imbalances and tilting. Nevertheless, I know how to get around the weakness in my arm whenever I wash my face, cut my steak, drive my car and give a big strong hug to my loved ones. I use this experiential knowledge and understanding to undertake counter-maneuvers during moments of weakened morale, and I continue to wrestle with power relations and fight for the liberation of Occupied Palestine.

MAZIN QUMSIYEH *is founder and volunteer director of the Palestine Institute for Biodiversity and Sustainability (PIBS) at Bethlehem University (http://palestinenature.org). Qumsiyeh published over 160 scientific papers, over 30 book chapters, and several books on topics ranging from cultural heritage to human rights to biodiversity conservation to cancer. He serves on the board of a number of Palestinian youth and service organizations (see also http://qumsiyeh.org) and oversees many projects related to sustainability of human and natural communities. A 2020 laureate of the Paul K. Feyerabend Foundation award (which acknowledges and encourages remarkable accomplishments that represent a true source of inspiration), and the 2019 recipient of the Takreem award that honors Arab leading accomplishments (for environmental work).*

# A PALESTINIAN REFLECTION ON WHAT WE LEARN

*Mazin Qumsiyeh*

WHAT WE LEARN in childhood shapes our future. Every day, this simple fact is emphasized to me because the experiences of my childhood have made me who I am today. It was the kindness of my mother, who is now 89 years old, to strangers, that taught me the real meaning of philanthropy. It was the commitment and hard work of my father that taught me not to waste time. It was accompanying my uncle, Sana Atallah, the first Palestinian zoologist, to the fields that taught me the love of nature. My maternal grandfather taught me to value and love books. All of these influences were there, even when I was 6–7 years old. I did not always appreciate how lucky I was to be born into a family of educators.

Let me tell you about just two of those people. My maternal grandfather was born in our small village of Beit Sahour, like his ancestors and most of his descendants. Located in the hills halfway between the Mediterranean and the Dead Sea, Beit Sahour was the "Shepherds' Field" mentioned in the Bible where the shepherds, who some two thousand years ago saw a star and walked up the hill to Bethlehem where Jesus was born. My grandparents' and my parents' homes are literally down the hill from the Church of the Nativity, where tradition holds that Jesus was born. On my way back from school in Bethlehem, I would often stop by and look at the candles in the grotto of the Church, then go to visit my grandparents. My grandfather, or *Sido,* loved to tell his story of hardships during WWI, when he lost all his immediate family and how, as an orphan, he built himself up.

At times, a group of us children would head to the nearby hills for adventure. We would eat wild roots, the fruits of the *za'roor* (the hawthorn) and occasionally use slingshots to get a sparrow or a lark for meat. After these tiring trips, we could always count on a nice meal prepared by my grandmother who somehow knew when we would be stopping by. These visits were more frequent in the season of loquats, figs, apricots, grapes and almonds that were plentiful in the garden, which was so well-tended by my grandfather. My father and mother had no garden—we lived in a rented apartment—until after 1970, when we built our own house. I was 13 then. Thus, memories of my grandparents' garden flood my mind some five decades later, as I tend my own garden as well as the botanical garden at the Palestine Institute for Biodiversity and Sustainability.

*Sido* also occasionally grew Beit Sahour's most famous agricultural product, *faqoos*, a diminutive, sweet snake cucumber, that seemed to thrive in the rich red soil of the hills around Bethlehem. The townsfolk prospered on agriculture for more than 5,000 years, growing wheat, olives, almonds, figs, grapes and other assorted fruits and vegetables. Beit Sahour's inhabitants lived peacefully together but were not homogenous. The mosque and the church were—and are—right next to each other. Secular and religious people joked about each other but were best friends. We had leftists, even communists, including one of my uncles, and rightists, like my other uncle. I enjoyed the open debates among them that sometimes became heated, only to be followed, a few moments later, by even more heated quarrels over playing cards! There was at least one black family I knew of in Beit Sahour, an Ethiopian Christian family. Occasionally, there were issues, of course, though not between Muslims and Christians or over skin color. Rather, they were doctrinal differences between the majority Greek Orthodox and the Protestant denominations. These disagreements were more noticeable to us because my mother's family was Lutheran and my father's, Greek Orthodox. The nearby town of Bethlehem was even more diverse with Armenians, Sharkas, Copts and other religions and nationalities, all intertwined. Any family disputes were easily dealt with by wise and elderly leaders, whom only hot-headed teenagers like us dared to challenge.

Other occasional disputes occurred between the villagers and the nearby nomadic Bedouins, whose goats ravaged our crops. It was, thus, not unusual to have *natoors*—meaning unarmed guards—posted around fields for protection. Yet, we were also dependent on the Bedouin for milk, cheese and meat products, and they were dependent on us for agricultural products. Overall, harmony between humans and nature persisted there for millennia. Things began to change dramatically with the advent of Zionism in the late 19th century, accelerated in 1918–1948 under the British "Mandate" and peaked with the *Nakba,* or catastrophe, of 1948–1949. This seminal event made most of our people refugees and tore apart the ancient landscape. Palestine's vibrant multi-ethnic, multi-cultural, multi-religious communities, understandably, rejected the idea of a "Jewish state." (Qumsiyeh 2004). The Armistice line introduced in 1949, called the "Green Line," divided families from their lands and from each other. My grandmother, living here in Bethlehem, hails from Nazareth and longed to see that ancient town. My mother still recalls her friend, Hayah Balbisi, who was killed at the age of 16 in her village of Deir Yassin, one of 33 villages where massacres were committed during the *Nakba*. But our *Nakba* did not end in 1949. The new state of Israel occupied the rest of Palestine in 1967.

Immediately after 1967, Israel started to confiscate Palestinian land in the areas it acquired and to build Jewish-only colonies/settlements there. This was a settler-colonial project and not a mere military occupation. Israel was created to become a Jewish state and we, the Palestinians, were the unwanted "other." Thus, there are now over 7.5 million Palestinian refugees or displaced people and the other 6 million live in isolated ghettos/Bantustans like Bethlehem. Palestinians were mostly employed in agriculture. As their lands were taken, many were forced to find other jobs. Thousands were forced to work in building the Jewish settlements and the roads that now cover much of the West Bank and Gaza.

Thus, what shaped my childhood and views included both family influences and the bigger national influences. If I were to pick one seminal event that made me who I am, it would be the death of my uncle Sana in 1970, who had taught me the love of nature.

This was a turning point. Uncle Sana had just finished his Ph.D. and started teaching in Iran when his van, remodeled as a mobile research unit, was hit head-on by a truck that swerved to the other lane. Sana and his assistant were killed instantly. He was 27 years old. I, at 13 years old, promised myself and his father, *Sido*, that I would follow in his footsteps. Four years later, I graduated from high school and embarked on a long career of education in biology—I still consider myself a student of knowledge. This included a Bachelor's degree in biology (1978), teaching in schools in Jericho, Bethlehem, and Jerusalem (1978–1979), a Master's degree from Connecticut (US, 1982), then a Ph.D. from Texas (1985), followed by postdoctoral stints in Lubbock, Texas and Memphis, Tennessee (1986–1989), then at last faculty positions in medical schools and hospitals at the University of Tennessee (to 1992), Duke University (1993–1999) and Yale University (1999–2005). I also became board certified in medical genetics and ran clinical labs, both affiliated with academic hospitals and also private.

Starting up new enterprises and organizations actually became most fascinating for me. As noted, formal education and formal professional services were not the ones I consider to have most shaped my thinking, collective activism or entrepreneurship. It was the informal observations and role models of family members that shaped my future very early on in childhood. My father, a schoolteacher, had started at least two ventures totally unrelated to his background as an elementary school teacher: a children's toy shop and a factory for paint thinner. My maternal grandfather wrote books on subjects ranging from Arabic grammar to Palestinian proverbs, simply because he loved knowledge. This is why there is not a day that passes by without me thinking of these people.

Of course, there were people who influenced me as an adult, and I should mention some of them. My major advisors for the MSc and Ph.D. degrees were very kind and generous people. Ralph Wetzel was the Ph.D. advisor to my uncle Sana at the University of Connecticut 1966–1969 and my Master's advisor 1979–1982. I was his last graduate student before his retirement. He was such a kind and hard-working man. I lived in the attic of his house for a while and enjoyed the excellent cooking of his wife. My major advisor in Texas was Robert Baker, who used to challenge me. When I was faced with difficulties, he would tell me: "What does not kill you only makes you stronger!" This support was critical, for example, when I had a stroke that paralyzed my left side or when a disgruntled ex-student tried to defame me to get back at Robert. I was so distraught on some occasions that I even considered quitting science. Robert's wisdom and advice, and the help of fellow graduate students at the time, were critical to passing through that period and to coming even out stronger. Being away from home country, Robert and Laura were our family. Graduate students and undergraduate students from many parts of the US and the world melded together as a close-knit "mammalogy" family. I especially remember how some graduate students, with the help of Robert and Laura, took care of my wife as a new mom in 1985, while I was in Kenya for two months.

I tried to emulate these mentors in dealing with my own students. I endeavored to support them, not just academically, but in personal ways that are difficult to describe. As Robert Baker said to his graduate students, on several occasions: "The umbilical cord is never cut!" I knew that he meant that we should stay in touch, and that advisers are like parents who continue to care even after their children leave the house. Many years later, I also recognize that this "knowledge" umbilical cord transcends generations. Those who taught and shaped the lives of a previous generation have shaped our lives, even if they have never met us. This point is most evident to me now, more than ever. I have lost most of those good people to the inevitable death that stalks us all, and I lose friends and colleagues on a regular basis now that I am in my 60s. I have lost 19 close friends since I returned to Palestine in 2008, most of them killed by Israeli soldiers as they participated in non-violent resistance to the occupation. It is difficult, sometimes, to keep going, while facing so many challenges, especially when you decide to take on big challenges. However, the strength that those earlier generations gave us is the main gift in life, which goes on and on, generation after generation. Therefore, I spend most of my time now with young people and focus most of my new projects on empowering young people.

When I moved to the US, I had always planned to return to Palestine, to serve by empowering new generations there and, thus, repay some of the debt I owed to my own formal and informal teachers. Delays in returning occurred, such as getting married and having a son who needed to get a good education in the US, combined with great opportunities like positions at Duke and Yale Universities. These delays, though, were also my way of getting better prepared financially, socially, academically and emotionally for the move. The move back to Palestine in 2008 was the best move I ever made in my life. I left a well-paid career to teach one or two courses a year here and to focus most of my energy on service to the people, especially the youth. In the USA, I had been politically active, co-founding a number of organizations and movements like the Palestine Right to Return Coalition and Wheels of Justice Bus Tour. I had published three books in the US, including *Sharing the Land of Canaan.*[31] However, it was becoming clear that I could do more of service in Palestine, to more people. Thus, in 2008, I started a clinical laboratory here at Bethlehem University, and I started teaching, on a part-time basis at more than one university. I engaged in popular resistance and wrote a book on the subject.[32] I passed out copies of my book—the Arabic version—to young people and was happy to listen to their ideas and to learn from them. Some of the young people I engaged with stood out more than others. For example, Basil Al-Araj of al-Walaja, was especially keen to learn and try out methods of non-violent resistance.[33] He and a group of young people blocked a settler road. He and I, and four others, boarded a bus—one of the segregated settler buses—to highlight apartheid in an action we called Palestine Freedom Riders. During the many times that I was detained, it was always a pleasure to chat with fellow detainees, all of them less than

---

31 Mazin B. Qumsiyeh, *Sharing the Land of Canaan: Human Rights and the Israeli-Palestinian Struggle* (London: Pluto Press, 2004).

32 Mazin B. Qumsiyeh, *Popular Resistance in Palestine: A History of Hope and Empowerment* (London: Pluto Press, 2012).

33 Mazin B. Qumsiyeh, "Basil Al-Araj of Al-Walaja: RIP," March 8, 2017, https://peacenews.org/2017/03/08/basil-al-walaja-rip-mazin-qumsiyeh/

the age of my son. Basil taught me a lot. We miss him—he was killed by Israeli soldiers.

I have always believed that resistance is important, but that education, art, agriculture and hundreds of other forms of life's activities under colonialism are also resistance. It is called *sumud* in Arabic, which is a combination of resistance and resilience. Since returning here, I have always been looking for ways to use my somewhat privileged new status to help in this regard. I say "privileged" because I was economically self-sufficient, had a great educational background and even a US passport. So, all my actions were directed at helping people in *sumud*, whether by acquiring sheep to give to a needy family in order for them to build a source of income or paying for the tuition of needy students in the sciences or planting a few trees. To help young people, we established Master's programs in biotechnology at Bethlehem University and environmental studies at Birzeit University. In 2014, my wife and I donated $250,000 to start the Palestine Institute for Biodiversity and Sustainability and the Palestine Museum of Natural History at Bethlehem University. The Institute has a motto: "Respect—for ourselves, for others, for nature." These levels of respect help us achieve the vision of sustainable human and natural communities. The Institute's mission includes research, education and conservation, related to our cultural and natural heritage.

Jessie and I have been full-time volunteers over these seven years. With the help of other volunteers and later, a handful of staff members, we were able to do much in the areas of environmental education, research and conservation. Again, this is all a form of resistance, after all. Thousands of school and university students have benefitted from having this center in Bethlehem. The garden and facilities have become an oasis of refuge for people and wildlife, amidst the uncertainty, even outright mayhem, in Palestine. The botanical garden now boasts more than 380 species of plants. We have a good natural history museum and an ethnography exhibit. We have a library of thousands of books. There is a community garden, an exploration playground for children, an animal rehabilitation unit, research units, herbarium and models of sustainability—biogas, solar panels, a compost and recycling center, hydroponics and aquaponics, etc. Yet, all these "facilities" are small compared with the spark produced in one child or one university student who, like me so many decades ago, became hooked on knowledge with the aim to serve others.

The best form of flattery is, of course, imitation and I have tried to imitate those who preceded me and also influence the next generation. The memes generated do not need to be identified with their originator: who invented the wheel anyway? When my son, Dany, saw the map of a shrinking US after colonization and drew the map of a shrinking Palestine in 1998, I used it and then hundreds of thousands have used it, after—this is a ripple effect. Those who shaped lives are, essentially, immortal through actions of those they influenced, which shape other generations and so on, ad infinitum. We must not underestimate this ripple effect, the reality that small initial causes may have large effects, commonly referred to by scientists as "the butterfly effect," first voiced by Edward Lorenz, who contended that a butterfly flapping its wings in Brazil could set off a tornado in Texas. We vaguely know who influenced a previous generation and it is, sometimes, fascinating to speculate. If I were to go back in a time machine, would I be able to go back, generation after generation, to find, perhaps, that a spark that influenced my grandfather and, hence me, came from a disciple of Jesus here in Palestine? A more practical way to think about it is to decide how we spend our own time to help others. I am most proud when I see students whom I helped are now well-established and helping others. When I witness the passion of one of our volunteers or employees working with a child, I cannot help but become emotional. I recall the immortal words of Khalil Gibran, and wonder who influenced him and who he has influenced:

You give but little when you give of your possessions. It is when you give of yourself that you truly give. For what are your possessions but things you keep and guard for fear you may need them tomorrow? And tomorrow, what shall tomorrow bring to the over-prudent dog burying bones in the trackless sand as he follows the pilgrims to the holy city? And what is fear of need but need itself?[34]

If we are hopeful that humans will transcend the challenges of colonialism, racism, wars, technology, pandemics and climate change, then that success can only be attributed to such a ripple effect. If a candle lights another candle before it is extinguished, is it really extinguished? Further, it would be a cliché to say so, but the brightness of a light is only made more obvious and more appreciated in the darkness.

34 Kahlil Gibran, *The Prophet* (New York: Alfred A. Knopf, 1923).

SECTION IV

# ON LIBERATION, POLITICS, EMPOWERMENT AND SOLIDARITY

HASAN ABDUL-RAHIM ABU NIMAH *was born in 1935, in Battir, Palestine. He attended schools in Battir and Bethlehem and graduated from the American University in Beirut. He taught in UNRWA schools for four years, before joining the Jordanian diplomatic service from 1965–2000, serving in embassies in Kuwait, Baghdad, Washington and London. He was appointed ambassador to Belgium, the Netherlands, Luxembourg and the European Community in 1979 and, from 1990, served as ambassador to Italy and non-resident ambassador to Portugal and San Marino. In 1995, he was appointed as Jordan's Permanent Representative at the United Nations in New York and non-resident ambassador to Cuba. He was a member of the Jordanian delegation to the Washington peace talks in 1992–1993. Following retirement from the diplomatic service, he served as director of the Royal Institute for Interfaith Studies in Jordan (2004–2009) and director of the Regional Human Security Center in Jordan (2009–2011). He was a member of the Jordanian Senate from 2013–2020. He has been writing columns in English and Arabic for 40 years.*

# A PERSONAL JOURNEY THROUGH PALESTINE'S TRAGEDY

*Hasan Abu Nimah*

IT WAS IN 1940 when, as a small boy, I started to recognize the world around me in Battir.

The village of my birth has borne witness not just to ancient history, but to the consequences of the Zionist conquest and ongoing struggle over Palestine. It was through the experience of Battir that I formed my understanding of the personal and political dimensions of this struggle.

Located some six miles southwest of Jerusalem, there is evidence of human settlement in Battir at least since the Bronze Age. The village nestles on the upper part of a mountainside that faces west. The lower part was made up of neat terraces where villagers grew all kinds of produce—grapes, figs, olives, peaches, apples, pears, apricots as well as wheat and barley. The village was particularly known for *batinjan battiri,* a special variety of eggplant prized across Palestine.

The terraces were fed by springs bubbling out of the ground into pools and carefully maintained channels. This shared irrigation system is now recognized as a World Heritage Site by UNESCO, which calls it an "outstanding example of traditional land-use" that is "representative of many centuries of culture and human interaction with the environment." "The integrity of this traditional water system is guaranteed by the families of Battir, who depend on it," the UN body adds.[1]

---

1 "Palestine: Land of Olives and Vines—Cultural Landscape of Southern Jerusalem, Battir," UNESCO (https://whc.unesco.org/en/list/1492/)

In the valley separating Battir from the mountains opposite, the Ottoman-era railroad still runs. In those days it connected Jerusalem with Palestine's coastal cities, and then on to al-Qantara in Egypt. The first train stop after Jerusalem was Battir. It provided people in the village with a quick link to other parts of Palestine. Later, a train shuttled passengers and produce from Battir to Jerusalem and back, twice daily. It also brought people from the city, who would spend weekends picnicking in the shady orchards around Battir station. Parallel to the track ran an unpaved road used infrequently by vehicles, as well as by pedestrians.

Right by the station was the boys' primary school, where I was in my last year just as we had to flee the village in the spring of 1948. The school was partly shaded by lofty pine trees, which swayed pleasantly in the spring/summer breezes. There was enough land by the schoolhouse for students to learn basic agriculture skills, including keeping bees and chickens.

Life at that time for the 1,000 or so villagers in Battir—all Muslims—was simple, peaceful and safe. Order was maintained largely by tradition, interdependence and cooperation. As in rural communities all over the world, people depended on one another to help harvest the crops, build houses, deal with setbacks and celebrate joyous occasions. Everyone took turns to help their neighbors, and there was not much presence or need for government or a village council.

It was by no means a utopia. There were many hardships as well as the usual disagreements and rivalries. But generally, people respected each other, and the village notables had authority to settle problems amicably.

People lived in basic dwellings, often one room, with no electricity, running water or modern amenities. They cooked on open fires in front of their houses or beside narrow village paths. Some could afford Swedish-made Primus or Radius kerosene stoves to use indoors.

Many families owned animals which sheltered in the front part of the same room. Donkeys, mules and, rarely, horses were used to carry people and goods. Some kept a goat or sheep for milk or to slaughter on feast days.

Though religious and pious, people were tolerant. Women mixed with men and the veil was never known in the village. Separation of the sexes was impractical because in an agricultural community women bore many of the same burdens as men, and sometimes more. It was typically women who carried huge baskets of produce on their heads to the markets of Jerusalem, a two-hour journey they often made on foot.

This tranquil life, which must have existed for dozens of generations across Palestine, was not interrupted until world powers far outside our control decided to designate our homeland as the property of someone else.

Although Battir was somewhat isolated, people were fully aware of what was happening, and talked about the Zionist threat. They were concerned about the influx of Jewish colonists from Europe, land sales and the British commitment to help implement Balfour's promise to turn Palestine into a Jewish national home.

Although news sources were limited to one or two copies of the daily newspapers brought in from Jerusalem, people in Battir stayed informed. Many were illiterate, but when a newspaper arrived, they would gather around to hear someone read about the political events on which their future hinged.

There was one other major information source: A radio with a loudspeaker installed by the British administration, tuned permanently to the Palestine Broadcasting Service. The radio, which ran on two car-like batteries, was placed at my family's house. Twice a day, people would gather on the large open veranda to hear the bulletins.

Each week, a red post office car brought freshly charged batteries from Jerusalem and took away the depleted ones. The car, however, could only make it as far as the station. The batteries would be carried the rest of the way by donkey.

People were not fooled by assurances that the so-called Jewish national home would not affect their lives. They understood it, correctly as it turned out, as an existential threat. They talked proudly of the heroic Palestinian resistance against the Zionists and the British that began in the 1920s and continued to erupt until the end of the Mandate.

Even at school, which I entered in 1942, pupils whom one might assume knew little of such things, talked with apprehension and fear about the Jewish colonization of Palestine. I remember the reaction when the Arabs rejected the UN Partition Resolution of November 1947. Even children would say that the Zionists would only accept the portion of Palestine allotted to them as a foothold, until they could take over more territory.

This kind of talk—undoubtedly reflecting what they heard from adults—was explicitly exchanged among schoolchildren even though any involvement in politics was strictly prohibited by the British authorities.

The Zionist scheme in Palestine had the blessing of the British, who had taken Palestine over from the Ottomans in 1917. It also gained the blessing of the League of Nations, which bestowed on Britain a Mandate ostensibly to prepare the country for self-determination.

But the 1922 Mandate document did not mention the Palestinian people or their rights even once. Instead, one third of its articles related to Jewish colonization and the Jewish colonists, who at that time were less than 10 percent of the population.[2] The British commitment to Zionism would ensure that the only people whose desires should have mattered—the indigenous Palestinian people—were given no say in the future of their own country.

Obviously, Zionism was strongly rejected by the Arabs, particularly the Palestinians. It was also opposed by some British officials who warned of the dangerous consequences. Zionism was also inimical to the vast masses of Jews who viewed the "national home" idea as a threat to their own settled life in many countries around the world. It was precisely for this reason that Zionism ultimately gained the support of Nazi Germany, which saw it as a convenient means to transfer Jews out of Europe and, on that basis,

---

2 Joseph Massad, "Recognising the right of the Palestinians to surrender," *Middle East Eye,* July 30, 2021.

the Nazi government signed the 1933 Transfer Agreement with the Zionist Federation of Germany.

That anti-Semitic motivation for supporting Zionism was not exclusive to Germany, however. Lord Arthur Balfour was notoriously anti-Semitic. So was Winston Churchill, who viewed Zionism as a useful way to recruit Jews into supporting the British Empire, and as a means to fight communism.[3]

Having banned most Jewish immigration to the United Kingdom in 1905, the British government allowed mass migration of Jews from Europe to Palestine, ensuring that a violent struggle over the land would be inevitable. The British crushed Palestinian resistance with an iron fist, while giving the Zionist colonists every advantage, allowing them to set up a state within a state—and an army—that would be ready to conquer Palestine when the time came.

The British created an irreconcilable situation, though responsibility could not be shared equally. From the start, Palestinians sought a national government for Palestine, with a parliament representing Palestinian Arab Muslims, Christians, and Palestinian Jews.

The Zionists, by contrast, demanded that all of Palestine be exclusively Jewish, a program that has not changed one iota since the earliest settlers arrived. The Nation-State law, passed by the Knesset in 2018, makes clear that the goal of Zionism remains exclusively Jewish sovereignty in the whole of historic Palestine.

On November 29, 1947, the UN General Assembly adopted the recommendation to partition Palestine into a Jewish and an Arab state, with Jerusalem under an international regime. It was a nonstarter: the plan gave the Jewish colonists, who by that time were a third of the population, more than half of the country. The indigenous Palestinian majority would be relegated to a minority portion of their own country, and many would have faced removal from the putative Jewish state, which would otherwise have lacked a clear Jewish majority.

---

3 See: Joseph Massad, "The Balfour Declaration's many questions," *The Electronic Intifada,* November 8, 2017.

The Zionist leadership saw it as unacceptable as it gave them too little, but eventually accepted it as a base from which to expand. Arabs rejected it for the right reason. Why should anyone be forced to give up any of their country, let alone more than half of it, to European colonists?

In contrast to the strong support the Zionists received, the British brutally crushed Palestinian resistance, particularly during the great revolt of 1936–39. Possession of weapons was strictly prohibited and severely punished. Given this context, it is no surprise that the Zionists were able to quickly initiate their plans for ethnic cleansing as soon as the November 1947 partition resolution passed.

In the months before the British departure in May 1948, the carefully planned Zionist onslaught had already turned hundreds of thousands of Palestinians into refugees. The British barely intervened. Arab villages and communities were left defenseless in the face of Zionist attacks which—like that in Deir Yassin on 9 April 1948—were calculated to sow terror and precipitate the flight of the Palestinians.

Deir Yassin, the scene of a dreadful massacre, was only a few kilometers away from us. I remember terrified survivors arriving in Battir, seeking shelter. But our village was already host to many families ethnically cleansed from other villages that had fallen to the Zionist militias.

People were in disbelief, but there was a general feeling that the trouble would not last. They expected the UN to intervene and restore order and justice. They also pinned hopes on the arrival of the Arab armies, which were waiting for the official end of the Mandate on 15 May, so they could rescue Palestine, or what was left of the country, from the Zionist onslaught.

At that time, Zionist attacks accelerated, particularly in and around Jerusalem. We would hear radio bulletins and alarming stories from village men who spent whatever they had to purchase old-fashioned weapons and ammunition to defend their homes, the British restrictions on possessing arms having lapsed. Those brave men would also rush on foot to help repulse attacks on neighboring villages.

Small groups of fighters and weapons arrived from some Arab countries, including Syria, Lebanon, Jordan and Sudan. They did as well as they could, winning some battles, and their morale at the beginning was high. I remember a group camped in the abandoned buildings of the Battir railway station and organized training for the village men.

When the Jewish terrorist organizations turned against their British sponsors, they often planted explosives under the train tracks, causing serious damage and casualties. Cargo trains were repeatedly ambushed and goods looted. Every train had British guards on board, but they often surrendered without resistance. The line was soon blocked, and the entire railway paralyzed, when a heavy locomotive was blown up and burnt on the tracks close to Battir.

By early 1948 the situation had worsened and several villages surrounding Battir were overrun by Zionist militias. Many of their inhabitants came to Battir too, hoping they would soon return home.

But in the late spring, just as the British were completing their departure and the State of Israel was declared, Battir was exposed to heavy machine-gun fire from the slopes to its west, which were under Zionist control. We were terrified as hails of bullets struck houses and property. As we had no adequate defense, it was no longer safe to stay.

So, with the little that we could carry, all of us fled eastwards on foot. Some men remained behind in an effort to guard the village, but they could not stop Battir from being looted, with even doors and windows taken from their frames.

I remember we camped with many other families in a vineyard called Al-Qusayr that belonged to the village, about an hour's walk away. There was a small spring. We spent the night under the trees, still believing we would soon return home. But as Battir remained under constant fire, we built shelters from branches and prepared for a longer stay. Some people took the risk of sneaking back to the village to bring additional belongings. I tried once with some of my cousins, but I was terrified, as the Jewish militias seemed to fire at anything that moved. I decided to turn back without reaching our house.

In Al-Qusayr, we survived on minimal supplies of flour, baking bread on open fires, cooking local vegetables and lentils and drinking tea. Sweet tea with bread was a standard meal, although sugar was a precious commodity. We supplemented this with grapes and figs as summer fruit became available.

The town of Beit Jala was not far away and those who had money could walk there and get additional supplies. I was with only my widowed mother and younger sister, but many relatives, including the families of my married older sisters, were of great help. We were about 20 families, but people acted as if we were one. No one would allow another to starve or suffer.

We remained in that vineyard through the summer of 1948, but by the end of September as the weather started to turn cold, each family had to decide where to go next. Battir had not been occupied but remained vulnerable to fire from across the valley. No one felt safe to return. Some families joined the refugee camps, which were forming in the Bethlehem area and the Jordan Valley. Others went all the way to Jordan.

My mother, my younger sister and I, along with the family of my eldest sister—11 of us altogether—took refuge in an apartment that had been assigned to my older brother in the Tegart police building in Bethlehem.

My brother worked in the wireless communications section of the Palestine police. When the Mandate ended, like many of his compatriots, he joined the Jordanian police. The Tegart building—one of many identical fortresses built by the British throughout Palestine—was, at that time, being used by the Jordanian army.

My brother's rank meant that he was entitled to use one of the apartments that had formerly been assigned to British officers' families. Along with my brother's family, about 20 of us were squeezed into that small two-bedroom apartment. We slept on the floor and ate whatever was available.

My sister's family eventually managed to rent a place in Bethlehem. We stayed with my brother as we had nowhere else to go. During the day I would wander around downtown Bethlehem, which was bustling with activity. Displaced people from all over Palestine were engaged in street vending. Some re-established businesses they had been forced to abandon elsewhere, including restaurants selling hummus and falafel. Others looked for whatever work they could find.

In the Tegart building there were Egyptian and Sudanese soldiers, along with the Jordanians. My brother's ground-floor apartment had a veranda overlooking a large courtyard with a rectangular pool in the middle for horses to drink from. But there were no horses. During the day, I would play with the children of other officers, and we would entertain ourselves by climbing up the metal spiral staircase that led to the watchtower. Up there, we would spend time with the bored watchmen, who would tell us stories. We would sit on the veranda late into the night, listening to conversations in the different Arabic dialects and watching cars coming and going with supplies and soldiers.

We would also watch as soldiers on the building's external grounds practiced shooting rifles or Sten guns. I once dared ask an officer if he would let me have a go. He agreed and invited me to the position. He showed me how to hold the Sten gun which was light, but needed to be held firmly because of the recoil. Then I tried the rifle, which was too heavy.

In the spring of 1949, the fighting ended with armistice agreements between Israel and the four countries surrounding it: Egypt, Jordan, Syria and Lebanon. By that time, Israel had occupied 78 percent of historic Palestine, including western Jerusalem. The Egyptian army had to leave, as did the Syrian and Iraqi armies, which had operated in the north of the country.

Gaza remained under Egyptian control until 1967—save for the months Israel occupied it in 1956 during the Suez war. The Jordanian army kept control of the West Bank, including East Jerusalem, which they had managed to defend with the support of local Palestinian fighters.

At the Tegart police building that spring, I watched a very neat military ceremony in a spacious yard behind the fortress. It was the handover of the Egyptian garrison to the Jordanian army. The rows of soldiers on both sides were elegantly dressed and neatly organized.

When they exchanged the flags, I saw some soldiers crying. It was a very emotional moment. The Egyptians then got in their trucks and left.

Soon after, we received good news. We were told that the Joint Jordanian-Israeli Armistice Committee and the UN Armistice Committee were in Battir drawing demarcation lines.

Battir had never been occupied despite its evacuation during the war. So, the village notables who met with the committee insisted that it should not be included in the occupied part. However, because the railway—which Israel wanted to use—ran through part of Battir's land, Israel insisted on drawing the armistice line some 200 meters east of the track.

A barbed wire fence erected immediately after the agreement cut Battir in half. Two gates allowed people to cross to either side. The special arrangement meant that, despite shifting the line well into the village, the people of Battir would not be separated and would preserve their right to use their lands that lay west of the track.

According to the agreement, Israeli soldiers could patrol the area west of the fence, which included about half the village houses. My school, right by the railway station, also fell within the Israeli-controlled zone. Our house, still standing but abandoned, was just about 10 meters east of the fence.

With that arrangement in place, we and the other villagers returned home. Houses were repaired and life resumed. The school reopened with a Jordanian flag flying on top, though Israeli patrols went by daily. In 1950, the West Bank was unified with Jordan, creating a large country in which we were free to move about—even if we were cut off from the areas that became Israel. For Battir it was a period of relative prosperity.

UNRWA built an asphalt road connecting the village to Bethlehem, which was required after the link with Jerusalem was severed. UNRWA also established a school for girls, the first in the history of the village. People generally rebuilt their lives, and many young people were able to pursue their education in secondary schools in Bethlehem. But they still believed that the injustice done to the Palestinians had to be redressed.

The joint armistice committee used to meet in the school yard. General Moshe Dayan was often there, driving down in a convoy of jeeps from Jerusalem. The atmosphere was generally calm, but sometimes, Israeli patrols arrested or even killed villagers tilling their land on the western side of the fence, believing they were trespassing. The armistice committee would secure the release of detainees but could do nothing for those who had been killed.

When the school reopened, I was able to finish, as the only student in the seventh grade. We had only one volunteer teacher in the village, so I would help teach the lower classes. Later, the school would be better organized under the Jordanian education ministry.

I also finished my high school in Bethlehem, in the only private co-educational school in the country, Al-Ummah College, established by Shukri Harami, a visionary educator who had previously served in the Ottoman army.

The school defied norms by using English as the language of instruction, except for the use of the Arabic language where it concerned religion, and opened from Monday to Friday, with the weekend on Saturday and Sunday. I received my diploma in the summer of 1954 from the hand of Sir John Bagot Glubb, the British head of the Jordanian army at the time. From Al-Ummah, I went to the American University of Beirut on an UNRWA scholarship, becoming the second university graduate in the history of Battir.

When I returned home with my diploma in the summer of 1959, I was received with singing and dancing, and rooftops decorated with torches.

Following the 1949 armistice, Israeli forces continued their night raids on defenseless frontline villages, blowing up homes, killing innocent people and terrorizing the population. The villages of Husan and Nahalin, near Battir, suffered such attacks.

In 1953, an Israeli force led by Ariel Sharon massacred dozens of people in Qibya, in the northern West Bank, laying total waste to the village. Sharon would, of course, later gain notoriety as defense minister for the crimes committed during Israel's 1982 invasion of Lebanon, especially the massacres in Sabra and Shatila. All such raids were reported to the armistice committee, but it could do nothing. Israel never respected rules or obligations of any kind.

The raid on Husan in September 1956 took place as night fell. It was a was a major attack by a motorized brigade. The Israeli force destroyed a recently built Jordanian police station, killing around 10 officers. They continued along the road in the direction of Al-Khader, attacking a Jordanian army garrison, causing heavy casualties. Both the police station and the garrison were right on the road linking Battir to Bethlehem.

Israel claimed such attacks, which killed hundreds of people each year, were "reprisals" for armed "infiltrators." In fact, these "infiltrators" were, in most cases, simply unarmed Palestinians trying to return home to the lands and villages from which they had been ethnically cleansed just a few years earlier.[4] Despite such horrors, life in the West Bank under Jordanian rule achieved a certain stability until 1967, when Israel fulfilled its goal of conquering the whole of Palestine. That marked the end of my own time in Battir. Because I was overseas when the occupation happened, Israel denied me family reunification and I have only ever returned there once, for a visit in 1997.

The Balfour Declaration, the British Mandate and later, the UN Partition plan were all elements of the larger European imperial conspiracy to control the region. Yet, the loss of Palestine to the imperial-backed Zionist movement may not have been inevitable, had there been a serious Arab strategy to defend the country.

Ultimately, Palestine was lost on the battlefield, where the Arab states were bitterly defeated in almost all engagements with Israel. History tells us that it is the will of determined peoples, more than political declarations or decrees, that shape events.

Israel has always been the biggest violator of UN resolutions and international law, but has always acted by Ben-Gurion's maxim that what matters is not what the United Nations says, but what the

---

4 See Benny Morris, *Israel's Border Wars, 1949–1956: Arab Infiltration, Israeli Retaliation, and the Countdown to the Suez War* (Oxford University Press, 1993)..

Jews—by which he meant the Zionists—do. Israel disobeys any and all laws as it sees fit.

The Arabs could have confronted an aggression based on illegitimate imperial decisions without needing to disobey. But they barely did so. For a century, many Arabs have blamed Balfour for repeated defeats. But the Balfour Declaration would not even be remembered if the Arab states had effectively exercised their legitimate right to defend Palestine.

Founded in 1945, the Arab League always officially considered Palestine to be its cause and defending Palestine a collective Arab responsibility. The Palestinian struggle during the Mandate was supposed to be part of their greater struggle for independence.

Regrettably though, what were supposed to be assets—Arab states, armies and political weight—turned out to be a liability for Palestine. From November 1947 until the British departure in May 1948, Zionist forces had a free hand to ethnically cleanse the Palestinians.

The Arab armies belatedly joined the defense of Palestine only after the British departure and failed miserably in their mission. They lacked a joint strategy or command, each acting without coordination. Despite pretensions towards "unity," Arab relations were governed by competition, which reflected itself in their military performance.

Except for the Jordanian army, which managed to save the West Bank including East Jerusalem, the Syrian, Iraqi and Egyptian forces did not do well at all. The Gaza Strip was saved, but probably because the narrow territory was packed with refugees from the surrounding villages, rather than because it had been well defended by the Egyptian army.

Apparently, the other Arab armies entered the war as a mere fulfillment of duty. The Arab League had failed to come up with a coordinated war plan to defend Palestine, leaving each member state to act on its own, whether that was only because they went in out of duty or were incapable or had no genuine motivation to protect the land under attack.

The Palestinians, who rebelled during the Mandate and later fought in the war, showed all the determination one would expect of people defending their own homes and communities. However, having only primitive weapons, lacking training and without an organized army, their feeling was that they just had to hold on until the Arab armies arrived.

The Palestinians could have done better, had the Arab League and its member states helped by providing effective weapons, money, training and volunteers, rather than leaving them to face the well-organized and armed Zionist militias with scarce and obsolete weapons. That would have cost a fraction of sending in the Arab armies and might have been far more effective. But improvisation, fragmentation of responsibility and absence of strategy meant that disaster could not be avoided.

From 1949–1967, the Arab states' discourse was based on the notion that the existence of Israel was illegal. They asserted that the armistice was temporary, until they were ready to fight again and liberate all of Palestine.

Egypt under Nasser waged intensive propaganda campaigns, accusing Arab "reactionary" regimes of responsibility for the loss of Palestine and calling for their overthrow. Soon after the first Palestine war, the governments in Syria, Egypt and Iraq were overthrown by their militaries, who called on other Arab countries to toss out existing regimes.

Palestine was mostly a pretext for such actions. Ambitious military adventurers repeated the claim that the road to liberating Palestine started with liberating Arab capitals. But in most cases—and despite some investment in the needs of the people, in Egypt, for instance—military rule ultimately proved to be no less oppressive and corrupt than what came before or existed elsewhere.

At the very least, these revolutions failed to lay the ground for long-term development and prosperity of the people, as rulers focused solely on remaining in power. Neither national nor common Arab issues were of any significance on the agenda of the emerging revolutionary elements.

Declarations aside, the world, including the Arab states, began to view the 1949 armistice lines as permanent borders. But Israel's territorial ambitions had barely been met. While Arab states' rhetoric was not matched by actions, Israel was quietly getting ready for the next round and the opportunity it would afford to seize more land.[5]

The opportunity arrived when the Egyptian leadership was lured into escalating its threats after Israel shot down six Syrian fighter jets in a dogfight in April 1967. Nasser was bitterly criticized for not coming to Syria's aid. In response, Nasser mobilized his forces in Sinai in late May. Then, moving deeper into the trap, he ordered the United Nations UNEF observers to leave.

That was an historic blunder. Although within Egypt's rights, Nasser should not have made the demand. The move played well in Israel's favor as did Egypt's closure of the Straits of Tiran, virtually laying siege to Israel's Red Sea port of Eilat. Egypt, with half its army bogged down in Yemen, neither wanted a war nor was ready for one. Its leaders were simply hoping for a propaganda victory at no cost, and Israel knew it.

On June 5, 1967, Israel launched a massive surprise attack, destroying most of the Egyptian air force on the ground. The Israeli army quickly swept into Sinai, occupying Egyptian territory up to the east bank of the Suez Canal. Israel then moved to open fronts with Syria and Jordan. The quick collapse of the Egyptian front left political and military morale in Syria and Jordan low, and the war was over in days.

The Arabs suffered a resounding defeat, as Israel occupied the West Bank and Golan Heights, along with the Sinai—tripling the territory it controlled in the space of a week. Nasser took responsibility for what he called the "setback," and resigned. But following massive demonstrations in Arab capitals protesting his resignation, he reversed course and decided to stay.

Israel immediately began colonizing the newly conquered territories, as well as annexing East Jerusalem, totally belying its claims that it would only hold the newly occupied land until the Arabs recognized it and made peace.

---

5 See Ilan Pappé, "Israel's occupation was a plan fulfilled," *The Electronic Intifada,* June 6, 2017. Serge Schemann, "General's words cast a new light on the Golan," *The New York Times,* May 11, 1997.

In November 1967, the UN Security Council adopted Resolution 242, which would become the reference for subsequent diplomatic efforts. It called for "withdrawal of Israeli armed forces from territories occupied in the recent conflict," infamously omitting "*the*" before the word "territories." This meant that Israel could interpret the text to mean that any withdrawal would be enough to fulfill the resolution's terms. Indeed, that is exactly what Israel claimed when it withdrew from Sinai after its 1979 treaty with Egypt.

But ambiguity was not the main problem with the resolution. Even if it required Israel to withdraw from every inch of the land it had occupied in 1967, Resolution 242 granted Israel de facto recognition on 78 percent of historic Palestine—far more even than the 56 percent allocated by the already grossly unjust 1947 Partition resolution.

Acceptance of 242 was a massive Arab concession to Israel, one arguably borne from a lack of other options following the defeat. However, rather than salvaging what they could, the Arab states' diplomatic performance compounded their losses on the battlefield with even more political losses.

The "compromise" in 242 was that the Arabs would regain the lands they lost in 1967 in return for recognizing Israel as it was on June 4, 1967. But such a deal could only succeed if both sides comply. Strangely, however, the Arab states—as well as the Palestine Liberation Organization—have insisted on fulfilling all that was required of them without demanding that Israel meet its obligations. So, Israel ended up with the land as well as recognition.

Indeed, in the context of the 1993 Oslo Accords, the PLO explicitly recognized "the right of the State of Israel to exist in peace and security." Israel, by contrast, offered no such explicit recognition of even a single Palestinian right. Rather, Prime Minister Yitzhak Rabin only agreed "to recognize the PLO as the representative of the Palestinian people."[6] Far from being a concession, this suited

---

6 See: "Israel-PLO Recognition-Exchange of Letters between PM Rabin and Chairman Arafat-Sept 9, 1993," Israel Ministry of Foreign Affairs, https://buff.ly/3lByQ2X (last accessed October 12, 2021).

Israel's agenda: Israel wanted the PLO, which was about to surrender Palestinian rights and become Israel's security subcontractor, to be seen to be doing so *in the name of the Palestinian people.*

Nowadays, Arab and other governments still talk about a Palestinian state "based on the 1967 borders" with East Jerusalem as its capital. This vague language is meant to enable Israel to annex settlements illegally built in occupied territory under the land-swap formula already accepted by the Palestinians and Arab states.

When Israel began to colonize the lands occupied in 1967, Arab states made verbal protests which no one took seriously, but they never insisted they would not move one inch on the diplomatic front until Israel ceased building settlements. Rather than a deterrent, such hollow condemnations became an encouragement for Israel to carry on with its building plans.

It is not hard to see why the Arab states, including the PLO and later the Palestinian Authority, failed in their diplomacy, just as they did in war. States must be independent and free in order to take the decisions and actions to defend their rights. This has not been the case with respect to most Arab states, including the PLO and the PA. To be fair, there are not many states that are totally free to conduct their policies without external influences and pressures.

Still, most Arab regimes lack the legitimacy that comes from any sort of genuine democratic process. Thus, they rely on support and protection from foreign powers against any danger, foreign or domestic. The equation is well known: America is a staunch supporter of Israel, right or wrong. For any regime to gain American favor or avoid its ire, it must obtain and maintain Israel's approval and consent.

The road to Washington passes through Tel Aviv. For example, the Arab countries that scurried to normalize relations with Israel recently did so to satisfy President Donald Trump. These regimes were happy to help Trump exchange Palestinian and Arab rights for illusory political gains for Trump, his ally Benjamin Netanyahu and themselves. But even after those leaders leave the scene, Israel continues to enjoy the fruits of those normalization deals.

One can always argue that losers in war must make do with what they can get. But even the most disadvantaged person—think of a political prisoner hunger striking against his captors, as Palestinians jailed by Israel have always done—can find a way to defend their rights if the will is there.

There is no doubt that Israel, armed by the US and European states, is the stronger party. Yet, that is insufficient to explain the Palestinians and Arabs losses that have continued to mount since 1967. The responsibility also lies with the PLO, the PA and the Arab League and its members, who persistently undermined their own rights and interests in these major ways:

The Palestinians and Arabs failed to condition any negotiations on Israel first ceasing settlements and other illegal changes to the Occupied Territories, as required by international law. That transformed protracted sterile "negotiations" into time for Israel to create more irreversible facts on the ground.

Rather than insisting on the removal of all Israeli settlements from all Occupied Territories, as happened in Sinai and Gaza, the Arabs agreed on "land swaps" that would let Israel annex most of its settlements in the West Bank. Since the putative swaps were not limited to any area, this incentivized Israel to accelerate construction, anticipating that the thefts would later be legitimized in a "peace" deal.

Arab states followed Israel's lead in adopting the empty slogan of "peace" as the goal, rather than the restoration of Palestinian and Arab rights in accordance with international law. This meant that any refusal of "peace" on Israeli and American terms turned Arabs into the aggressors and Zionist colonizers into the victims. However, there is no such thing as "peace" without justice, equity and the restoration of usurped rights.

The question of Palestine was supposedly a pan-Arab issue and its defense a collective responsibility based on the notion that no Arab country would act alone, on its own. Yet even after 1967, Arab states failed to act together. In 1991, they went to the US-sponsored Madrid conference and later to negotiations in Washington, as separate delegations. There was coordination, though mostly formal and ineffective, but they did not have a united approach. This suited Israel well, as it always insisted, since the 1949 armistice agreements, on dealing with each Arab state separately, correctly understanding that this would strengthen its hand.

Even worse, the PLO undermined its own Washington delegation, ably led by Dr. Haidar Abdel Shafi, by secretly negotiating behind its back with Israel in Oslo. When the Oslo process was revealed in 1993, it rendered the Palestinian delegation in Washington redundant.

At every stage, Israel has opposed UN involvement. This is understandable since international law and countless resolutions render its usurpation of Arab and Palestinian rights illegal. What is not understandable, however, is how Arab states allowed the UN to be sidelined, for example by agreeing to deal with the so-called Quartet—an ad hoc committee of officials from the UN, US, EU and Russia. How could the United Nations, a body of more than 190 countries, reduce itself to a mere member of, and a fig leaf for, a US-dominated committee whose purpose was to sideline it? Arab states and the Palestinians should have refused to deal with the Quartet.

Zionist leaders hoped that once Israel was founded, the ethnically cleansed indigenous Palestinian majority would resettle wherever they ended up and melt away. Those remaining behind could be dealt with gradually and quietly. The Zionists have always believed that, once established, facts on the ground cannot be reversed.

In its early years, Israel dealt with the perceived threat from hostile neighbors by building a formidable military, including nuclear weapons. In addition to its dependence on the US, Israel sought alliances beyond its immediate neighborhood—Turkey, Iran and African states, including, of course, South Africa's apartheid regime.

But dashing Israel's hopes, none of this has been sufficient. Today, the number of Palestinians inside historic Palestine almost certainly outnumbers the Jewish population. Millions more Palestinians live just miles from their homeland, in Jordan, Lebanon and Syria, with more scattered around the region and the world.

Those who are in Palestine will not leave again. In May 2021, as Israel savagely bombarded Gaza and attacked Palestinians in Jerusalem, Palestinians rose up collectively across the whole country, perhaps for the first time since 1948. The protests and resistance from Gaza to Jerusalem to the Galilee proved that decades of Zionist efforts at colonial divide and rule have only strengthened the collective Palestinian national consciousness.

There is no military "solution" to this "problem" from Israel's perspective. Even if Israel can, through violence and force, suppress this population for a few more years, Palestinians will not forever agree to live under occupation and apartheid in their own country.

For now, Israel maintains the support of the US and EU, as well as of a few Arab regimes. But its former alliances with Iran and Turkey crumbled and even in the US there are dramatic political and demographic shifts that are undermining long-term political support for Israel. As the consensus around the world grows that Israel is indeed an apartheid regime, its remaining international political support will also erode.

Israel succeeded in neutralizing most Arab countries (and, of course, the PLO through the Oslo Accords) because these regimes do not, or have ceased to, represent their people. Just like Israel, these regimes rely on American protection and support. For none of them, including Israel, is that a viable formula for the long-term—especially as the US itself retreats in the wake of its own failures in Iraq and Afghanistan.

For Israel, too, the days when sweeping military victories could dictate regional politics are over. To many, Israel once seemed invincible as it won all its wars against the Arabs from 1948 until its invasion of Lebanon in 1982. But Lebanon was the turning point where Israel's military superiority turned out to be counterproductive. Early military "victories"—even besieging Beirut—failed to translate into long-term political gains and only spurred stronger and more capable local resistance.

Following Israel's successive defeats in Lebanon and its inability even to crush the resistance in isolated Gaza, the myth of the invincible Israeli warrior has been shattered. It is now Israeli soldiers who fear facing fighters in Lebanon and Gaza. Nor can Israel's nuclear weapons be used to defeat resistance in Gaza or southern Lebanon. Israeli strategists certainly know all this. For Israel, there is no viable strategy except to delay the end as long as possible.

In my many meetings with European ambassadors and officials in recent years, I often heard that Israel is happy to maintain the current situation forever. They told me Israel faces no major threats and its relations with the Palestinian Authority and Arab states are stable or growing. They did not want to hear it when I told them that whatever "stability" they thought Israel was enjoying was illusory. You cannot build sustainable peace or stability on top of such horrifying and escalating injustice.

Israeli leaders always used to claim that the "Palestinians missed no opportunity to miss an opportunity for peace." Yet, it is Israel that has missed every opportunity given by the Arabs and Palestinians to consolidate its ill-gotten games. Had Israel agreed to the 2002 Arab Peace Initiative, for example, it could have legitimized virtually all its territorial conquests, save for a tiny Palestinian state, and normalized ties with more than 50 Muslim-majority states. But, perhaps, we should be thankful for Israel's stubbornness now, because no "peace" deal that Israel would have agreed to, at any time in the last five decades, would have been just.

Palestinians have endured many decades of injustice and have not given up their determination to be liberated from Zionist rule. They have shown patience and steadfastness. But Israel needs an exit from the current impasse. True, fatal mistakes by Arabs and Palestinians were of great benefit to Israel—mistakes that helped Israel secure international legitimacy.

But Israel has, however, relied so much on the dysfunction of Arab and Palestinian leaders that it has taken the situation for granted. Why should it not, when even the Palestine Liberation Organization willingly transformed itself from an anti-colonial liberation movement into a police force working on behalf of Israel? And still, some Arab regimes are in a frenzied rush for normalization, even as Israel intensifies its oppression of Palestinians.

Israel may have succeeded in neutralizing the least dangerous parties but it underestimated the resistance. It was able to defeat every formal Arab army, but not the guerilla resistance. It is experiencing the same paralysis as the United States, whose post-9/11 military adventures have ended in humiliation.

Both the Israeli and the US militaries have tremendous capacity to destroy, but repeated experience shows that this is no guarantee of success or security, and only widens the circle of determined resistance. Israel has also relied on unconditional support and impunity from the UN and the so-called international community. Although too slow, that impunity too is starting to erode as the International Criminal Court takes up the case of Palestine, and public opinion—especially in the US and Europe—is turning sharply against Israel's apartheid regime.

Throughout my four-decade diplomatic career, representing my country, Jordan, in the United States, Europe and at the United Nations, and participating in the Washington peace talks of the early 1990s, I dealt with the question of Palestine almost every day. Yet I have never believed that Israel was serious about reaching a just settlement for its conflict with the Palestinians, simply because I knew that it could never meet the minimum conditions for such an outcome. That is why it refused all the generous offers repeatedly made by the Palestinians and the Arabs.

I see no sign that Israel will ever willingly change. But the world and the region are changing around Israel. Palestinians are, once again, the majority in historic Palestine and will never leave or accept subjugation. Just like white South Africans had, Israeli Jews face a choice of whether to remain an embattled, isolated minority trying to impose its will by force, or to seek a different path. But if they do not make the choice to change, it will eventually be forced on them through resistance and international pressure.

I remain convinced that the violent partition of Palestine that I witnessed as a child will end, and the country will be made whole again, with people free to live and move wherever they wish. There is no room for an apartheid regime in Palestine. Yet, there is enough space for all the people there to live in equality, justice and peace, regardless of their nationality or religion.

That must be the final destination of the terrible century-long journey Palestine has endured. The only question is how many more precious lives will be wasted before we get there.

JOHNNY MANSOUR *is a historian from Haifa. He is a lecturer in history and political science. He has published several studies and research papers, such as: "The Military Institution in Israel," "Israeli Settlements," "The Hijaz Railway," "Lexicon of Israeli and Zionist Personalities and Terms," "The Other Israel: A Look from the Inside," "Distance Between Two States," "Arab Streets of Haifa," "Haifa, the Word that Has Become a City," "Centenary of the Balfour Declaration," "Aqila Agha Al-Hassi," "Religiosity in Curricula and Teaching Books in Israeli Schools," among others. He has also published many referred articles in Arab and foreign magazines, as well as opinion articles in Arab and non-Arab newspapers and websites. He has participated and is still active in conferences related to history, politics and education in various locations around the world. He is a political and social activist in various frameworks, inside and outside Palestine.*

# RESEARCHING THE ENEMY MADAR as a Case Study[7]

*Johnny Mansour*

THE PRODUCTION of knowledge for the Palestinians under the circumstances of confronting the current colonial Israeli project is based on the power relations between the two parties. The knowledge that Palestinians accumulate about Israel can actually be employed as a tool of resistance.

Palestinian research and studies on Israel have undergone a strong shift in orientation as a result of the signing of the Oslo Accords in 1993, the subsequent formation of the Palestinian Authority in Ramallah and the return of many exiled Palestinians to the homeland. This shift coincided with the beginning of the establishment of administrative, economic, social and cultural institutions of governance, as well as various research centers focused either on Palestinian or Israeli affairs. Several centers for political and strategic studies in a number of cities in the West Bank and Gaza Strip were formed, but chief among them is The Palestinian Forum for Israeli Studies (MADAR) in Ramallah, established in 2000.

The post-Oslo period was marked by Palestinian research centers being continuously dependent on the capabilities and experiences of 1948 Palestinians. Their proficiency in the Hebrew language and, more importantly, their direct knowledge of Israeli society and politics at the internal and external levels and in various fields of life, have been particularly useful. Living within Israeli society, 1948 Palestinians are able to contextually analyze internal

7 This essay was originally written in Arabic and was translated by Ahmed Almassri.

events. That is, the essence of the conflict can only be understood from within it. Consequently, the participation and contributions of 1948 Palestinians are of great value to Palestinian research centers.

Unfortunately to date, these research centers study only Israel, but not other countries, whether Arab or Islamic, in the region or outside of it, while Israeli research centers in Israel study the Palestinians, Arabs, Muslims and other peoples.

While working as a freelancer at MADAR, I have learned that the Palestinian research centers are careful when dealing with sensitive political issues. This caution derives from their deference to the agendas of their donors, most of whom are from Western and some Far Eastern countries. While the political agendas of NGOs remain largely undeclared, they can still be deduced by reviewing the outputs of their projects, including research, seminars, lectures and reports. NGOs' funding of these centers enables their guidance of the research, which relates to the objectives of the donors, whether joint or separate. Therefore, researchers at these centers do not enjoy the freedom necessary to enable independent decision making. Given the current political and economic conditions, Palestinians' cumulative knowledge sometimes goes in a direction designed to satisfy their donors and, at other times, these centers can be absorbed in self-criticism and accountability.[8] In general, cumulative knowledge is a key element in developing the Palestinian capabilities and the capacities necessary to analyze situations and predict the future through a strategic vision, rather than speculation.

## What is MADAR?

On its website, MADAR defines itself as "an independent research center specializing in Israeli affairs, based in Ramallah, Palestine. MADAR was established in 2000 by a group of Palestinian intellectuals and academics." MADAR's goals include the following:

MADAR was created to meet the urgent Palestinian and Arab need for a research center that is dedicated to studying Israeli affairs.

---

8 K. Nakhleh, *Globalized Palestine: The National Sell-Out of a Homeland* (The Red Sea Press, Inc., 2011; First edition).

Its main goal is to produce solid and critical research and analysis about the Israeli scene. It aspires to make an avant-garde contribution and to provide Palestinian and Arab decision-makers and citizens with access to a comprehensive scientifically sound body of knowledge on the different aspects of Israel.[9]

These goals and vision are reflected in MADAR's publications, both in-print and digital. They also enable a deepening of understanding of the choices made regarding the topics presented for research and discussion. MADAR publishes an Arabic language newspaper titled *The Israeli Scene*, distributed bi-weekly along with the Palestinian newspaper, *Al-Ayyam,* published in Ramallah. In terms of research, MADAR has, so far, issued 24 research publications in Arabic on various policy/political issues, two studies on economics and one research on military/security issues. Another 12 studies have been published on social/sociological issues, in addition to three research papers on literature and two on theater. MADAR also published six studies on illegal Israeli settlements. In terms of content in Hebrew, MADAR has published 44 translations of such publications up to now.

As the numbers above clearly show, translations into Arabic of original Hebrew content, focused on political, historical and social areas within the Israeli society, are nearly double the number of research publications produced by MADAR. MADAR's administration deems these translations necessary to familiarize the Palestinians with Israeli research on the conflict and society in Israel. Not surprisingly, calls are being made for more Palestinian research on Israel, based on the Palestinian understanding of, and interaction with, the Israeli society and state.

MADAR also produces a quarterly Arabic language journal titled *Israeli Affairs*, of which 81 issues have been published so far. This quarterly journal is broader in terms of Palestinian participants from 1948 Palestine and elsewhere, as well as by those Israelis

---

9 MADAR Center, last accessed on October 9, 2021, https://www.madarcenter.org/en/about-us/an-up-close-view.

interested in presenting their ideas and visions in a Palestinian journal published in Ramallah, as part of their dialogue with Palestinians.

MADAR has issued annual reports since 2005. These address key political, military/security, economic, social, and cultural research on Israel including a detailed report on Palestinians in Israel. They are considered a year-long summary of the Palestinian vision towards events in Israel. The participants are mostly 1948 Palestinians familiar with life in Israel.

Reflecting on my decade-long freelance work experience with MADAR, beginning in the early 2000s, I can say that Palestinians, in general, and academics and politicians in particular, have a clear interest in Palestinian and Israeli affairs. The actual research, however, is conducted under abnormal political and administrative circumstances for two reasons. The first is the Israeli military presence and its ability to penetrate self-governing, semi-autonomous Palestinian areas. The second is the limited political-administrative Palestinian Authority overseeing the management of municipal, day-to-day Palestinian affairs. The Israeli military has, additionally, established an apartheid regime by locking up millions of Palestinians in the Gaza Strip and the West Bank, utilizing barriers such as the Apartheid Wall, settler-only roads, the confiscation of private lands and the building of settler housing units on Palestinian lands of private ownership, including in Area C of the West Bank.

Operating under a complicated set of contradictory realities, MADAR is, therefore, motivated to conduct multi-directional studies, some of which directly relate to Israel, while others are focused on the Palestinian question itself.

Research centers, whether MADAR or other centers, seek to establish the Palestinian narrative not only from the standpoint of confronting the misrepresentations in the Zionist-Israeli narrative, but also to form an independent Palestinian narrative. This enables actual confrontation and resistance to be directed towards a realistic forward-looking formulation of the Palestinian narrative in contrast to the Zionist-Israeli one, which denies the existence of the Palestinian people and their narrative, and is effectively working to impose its own, instead.

## My Story

I have always been concerned with the Palestinian narrative, not only because I am a historian and have a vested interest in the Palestinian cause, but also because I come from a home that was directly affected by the *Nakba* in various ways. My father was born in Haifa in 1928, to parents who migrated from the village of Jish (District of Safad) in 1920 to Haifa in search of a livelihood.

In Haifa, my father lived an intensely active life, studying at the Salesian Fathers School (a congregation of Italian origin). This school closed down during the Second World War and my father ended up working in the English army camps as a result. There, he met Arab and Jewish workers from all over Palestine. He learned Hebrew with the help of a Jewish worker, teaching him Arabic in exchange. By the end of World War II, my father was able to collect enough money to support his parents and brothers to buy a house for the family near the Bahai Temple. However, the family did not enjoy the house for long because of the harsh and painful battles for Haifa during the *Nakba*, resulting in the family being expelled, along with others. Immediately after the operations ended, a family of settlers occupied their house.

My father and his brothers fled to Lebanon. Later, he managed to return to the family home in Jish but could not readjust to village life. He tried to return to Haifa several times after 1948, but the Israeli authorities did not grant him a permit to do so until the early 1950s. Once granted the permit, my father immediately went to the family home, only to find a Jewish family had already taken it. The settler occupying the house kicked him out, and he later learned that an unfair law—called the Absentee Property Law of 1950—issued by the Israeli Knesset deprived him of his right to his home and property because he had left Palestine for a while and returned after this immoral law took effect.

My mother, born in 1934, hails from the displaced Palestinian village of Al-Mansura. This village lies on the Lebanese-Palestinian border. At the end of October and early November 1948, the family was displaced from their home and village and denied the opportunity to return. Half of the family went to the villages of Rmaych (or Rmeish) and Ain Ebel in southern Lebanon. The other half fled to the village of Fassuta. That is when the borders closed, so my grandfather and his brother could not meet their other brothers across the border. They died without fulfilling their dream of reuniting and bringing back the missing part of the family living in the diaspora. The trauma of expulsion and violence haunted my mother for a very long time. Only 14 years old at the time of the *Nakba*, she was separated from her friends and extended family, never to meet them again. My mother lived with her parents and brothers in a small room in Fassuta village for a long time until her father managed to arrange a larger house for the family to live in.

Years later, during my frequent travels from Haifa to Ramallah, I often thought of the stories of the *Nakba* that I heard of over the years from my parents and their families.

Indeed, I used to travel once or twice a month from Haifa to Ramallah, where MADAR is headquartered. I would be accompanied by the late writer, Salman Natour, who helped establish MADAR and edited its magazine. During our travels, we exchanged conversations about the importance of exposing our people in the West Bank to the internal dynamics of life in Israel so that they would be able to understand and interact with Israelis. However, our conversations were often cut short on these issues once we entered the West Bank areas under Israeli control and saw the settlements taking over Palestinian lands, including private lands. We saw the human suffering, especially at checkpoints, and the Israeli military occupation's brutal and unjust treatment of West Bank Palestinians—not that we 1948 Palestinians were treated any differently. Sometimes, we are subjected to intense interrogation and relentless questioning. Our vehicles are also routinely searched, while we endure long hours of humiliation at Israeli checkpoints.

This is when I most recall the stories of the *Nakba*, especially those related to Haifa. The stories about the city, recounted at home, had a profound effect on me. I decided to dig deep into the history of Haifa and its Arab identity. I followed how its Arab residents had labored tirelessly to develop the city and drive its urbanization over many decades. Their work now benefitted only those who had taken over the city by force and displaced its resident population. This scenario has left its mark on my writings on the history of Haifa and other cities in Palestine.

The trauma of the *Nakba* still lingers on, even persists in various forms, partly because the third generation of the *Nakba* survivors are still suffering from its effects and implications. The personal and the public have blended together, as did entire families' personal narratives and the general Palestinian narrative. This blend has affected the way the narrative is written and published and the way it is transmitted to the Palestinians and the Israelis, with the goal of offering an alternative narrative to the monopolistic and fabricated Zionist and Israeli narrative. Therefore, I published a number of books on Haifa's political, social and cultural history and its role over time. I believe Palestinian society needs to engage in a cultural dialogue concerning the history of their cities so that they are able to reconnect with their homeland and fight for its liberation. This dialogue would strengthen Palestinians' self-perception as well as their connection to and relationship with their land—as part of their Palestinian identity. The act of writing the Palestinian narrative is, in itself, a dialogue with Palestinian history, first and foremost.

However, I wonder what dialogue would be possible in the future between the two parties if Israel continues with its aggression against the Palestinians? A dialogue between the Israeli and Palestinian peoples, not just a dialogue between politicians.

## Limitations and Opportunities

Indeed, MADAR inevitably found itself in a state of dialogue with the Israeli narrative through its research projects, translations and reports of all kinds. However, this dialogue is quite limited. The political establishment, i.e., the Palestinian Authority, imposes caveats and restrictions on research centers, including MADAR, despite it being an independent center licensed and registered with official government departments. Its administrative board[10] accordingly

---

10 MADAR Center Administrative Board, last accessed on October 9, 2021 https://www.madarcenter.org/en/about-us/administrative-board

takes into account the policy orientation of the Palestinian Authority, albeit indirectly. What does this mean? A number of publications by international (European, American and African) human rights organizations and research centers have concluded that Israel is an Apartheid State. These NGOs have an impact on the political decisions of the governments of many countries, even though states themselves are yet to take declare that the regime in Israel, and its occupation of the Palestinian territories, constitutes an apartheid regime.[11] Such findings would not be directly addressed by many Palestinian centers, and certain related terminology would not be used. MADAR, on the other hand, has described Israel as an apartheid state that was established and maintained through settler-colonialism. Israel's discriminative policies were emphasized in various research about the apartheid in Palestine. This, however, is still limited to research only, and the political discourse of MADAR remains cautious when engaging in a normative approach towards the phenomenon of the Israeli occupation. Of note, translations and articles on this subject have, in fact, been issued regularly by MADAR, albeit under the names of their authors, with a disclaimer that they only reflect the opinions of their authors, not of MADAR.

Still, MADAR enjoys a more open space to develop political discussions and dialogues when compared with higher education institutions, namely universities. Palestinian universities that have departments for historical studies and/or political science are limited to providing education without producing any significant publications. This indicates how essential the role of research centers is in providing new, effective and efficient research on pertinent issues.

The absence of a critical academic, media and political movement places more responsibility on research centers to take on this mission. This does not mean that the research centers have resources at their disposal that universities cannot afford. Rather, while

---

11 J. Dugard and J. Reynolds, "Apartheid, International Law, and the Occupied Palestinian Territory," in *European Journal of International Law,* Vol. 24, Issue 3 (August 2013), 867–913.

universities are essentially institutions that produce knowledge, in the Palestinian context, they are establishments limited to coursework and teaching.

Most of the researchers at MADAR work part-time, and also work in other places to supplement their income in order to make a living wage. They do not enjoy the same work conditions and standards as Israeli researchers. Researchers in Israel are dedicated to their research and are paid well. Salaries at senior levels can be quite high, allowing researchers to expand and further improve their research and conclusions. This is not the only concern for Palestinian researchers; they are also constantly subjected to Israel's policies and practices of cognitive erasure. That is, Israel subjects Palestinians to an almost complete denial of their presence on their land. Therefore, the research practices carried out by the Israeli research centers go hand in hand with the Israeli practices on the ground. Research centers in Israel constitute a supportive machine for the Zionist-Israeli narrative being imposed by the Israeli political establishment, while excluding and denying the Palestinian narrative.

The ongoing Israeli Occupation makes life in Palestine under the Palestinian Authority unstable. Israel has sought to confirm its narrative by relying, among other tactics, on channels of biblical indoctrination. This is impossible except by reducing the existing human, spatial, cultural and civilizational Palestinian presence on the ground. This has also meant that Israel seeks to dismantle the Arab world and turn it into isolated states, scattered here and there, spreading crises in an effort to demonstrate that Israel is not the core reason for conflict in the region. This is exactly what Israel has done with regard to Iran; Israel demonized Iran and aligned countries in the Gulf with its anti-Iran politics under the claim that Iran is the enemy, not Israel. At the same time, the normalization of relations between Israel and a number of Arab countries, particularly Gulf states, reflects an effort to paint Israel as a stable State, creating a false image of the conflict as being neutralized or reduced. Every part of the process of dismantling the Arab world affects the Palestinian issue.

Palestinian research centers are aware of such transformations but cannot address them on a research level, because of issue related to funding, not only for the centers themselves but also for the Palestinian Authority. Rather than being confrontational, several of these centers tend to focus their work on historical and applied research in sociology and economics. Meanwhile, research addressing the outlook for the future remains constricted and limited.

Therefore, Palestinian research capacity and output remain in a constant state of catching up with Israel's research and studies while also remaining limited and confined to specific topics. There have been discussions and proposals to study and emulate some, or all, of the Israeli systems of governance. The discussions focus on this question: will we ever reach a level parallel to Israel's in its studies on Palestinians, Arabs and Muslims? I tend not to follow this line of questioning, simply because I believe that cumulative knowledge is sufficient, only when it is of high quality and when key issues are prioritized. Issues such as sports, health and education in Israel may attract Palestinian interest.

The role that 1948 Palestinians play in advancing such knowledge cannot be overlooked. Based on my experience, their contribution is not limited to their knowledge and proficiency in Hebrew, which is also essential. Their day-to-day interactions are intertwined with the Israeli (Jewish) society, even though many live in Arab neighborhoods separate from Jewish ones, or in Arab villages and towns independent of Jewish towns. Nevertheless, they share many of the common spaces with Israelis because of work, study and other activities deemed essential to daily life. These shared spaces enable 1948 Palestinians to palpably capture the pulse of the Israeli street in everyday life. Life in Israel is dynamic and active. On a daily basis, key issues are discussed by the media and social networks from all political orientations. The media outlets spare no effort in their discussions of key issues, with great accuracy and attention paid to detail, while incorporating diverse opinions. The public, broadly speaking, interacts with these issues. Sometimes, their interactions leave a profound impact on the political process and the practices of the government, its ministries and departments.

On the other hand, the cumulative knowledge that is collected by MADAR and published through various means (books, magazines, pamphlets and reports—digitally or in print) reflects the politics of 1948 Palestinians, who choose which topics need to be addressed and presented. Doing so helps Palestinians under Israel's military occupation understand the dynamics and trends in Israel. My role, along with other colleagues from 1948 Palestine, is not limited to helping Palestinians understand the nature of the political, economic, and social movement in Israel. Rather, it also includes spreading the spirit of solidarity among us, as one people under an occupation practicing two types of control. The first one is the 1948 Israeli occupation that displaced and expelled Palestinians from their properties and land, only to grant them an Israeli identity and render them as "citizens" of the State, the same state that caused their *Nakba*. The second is the 1967 occupation of the rest of the Palestinian territories. Under international law, this is a military occupation that oppresses Palestinians, tightens the blockade on them, renders their armed resistance unacceptable, and falsely portrays them as terrorists, murderers and criminals. Any sane person in the world understands that it is the legal and moral right of the Palestinians to resist the occupation.

## Research as Palestinian-Israel Dialogue

An important question in this context is: can research be considered a type of Palestinian-Israeli dialogue?[12] Certain trends indicate that research is a dialogue and discussion of issues that each party deems important. It does not necessarily mean imposing an opinion. Note that the Zionist-Israeli narrative is racing against time to impose itself as the standard, while denying the Palestinian narrative any legitimacy. However, the Palestinian narrative, unlike the Zionist one, is slowly and deliberately penetrating into various segments of Israeli society. The Palestinian narrative is taking over outside Israel, even though the process of making the Israeli audience

---

12 C. MacInnis and John P. Portelli, "Dialogue as Research," *Journal of Thought,* Vol. 37, No. 2 (Summer 2002), 33–44.

aware of it still faces several challenges—even huge impediments, and sometimes falling on deaf ears.

Over the course of two decades in particular, 1948 Palestinians have contributed to two scenes or situations: they have contributed to the Palestinian scene by introducing the Palestinians to events in Israel and by helping improve their knowledge about life and its dynamics in Israel. 1948 Palestinians have also contributed to converging intra-Palestinian dialogue among educated and academic Palestinian segments. In this context, MADAR's experience demonstrates the opportunity for such convergence between the two scenes through dynamic research and dialogue.

There are several ways of dialogue on central issues, especially when talking about conflict between two or more parties, as in the Arab-Palestinian and Israeli case. One of these methods is found in political, military, social, economic, and cultural research that becomes part of the landscape of competition and the race for expansion and domination in politics, culture and others. Research dialogue does not necessarily mean relying on the amount of research, as much as it is focusing on how this research is conducted and who its audience is.

I saw in the Palestinian Forum for Israeli Studies (MADAR) a model for such a dialogue. A research center's dialogue should not mean its acceptance of the opinions, directions and recommendations of other centers, especially when they are from their enemy (considering that Israel is a persistent enemy, for the Palestinians and the Arabs, in general) or affiliated with it. The accumulation of knowledge in MADAR creates a certain type of connection between the reader and the main issues discussed in Israel. This connection contributes to the deconstruction of the Israeli-imposed reality from a progressive research identity and is essential to the decolonization of the Israeli settler-colonialist regime.[13] The way MADAR works, and its vision, both reveal shifts in its conduct of research and studies and even its choice of translations of Israeli publications. After a

13 Based on a conversation with Honaida Ghanem, the director of MADAR, May 10, 2021.

decade of work at MADAR, it has become clear that independent research centers enjoy dynamism and space wider than that available for, and in, Palestinian universities. However, the issue of funding and meeting donor expectations is yet to be addressed, and still has a negative impact on these research centers. Their ability to expand and reach a larger audience through various topics remains limited, and is heavily connected to the donors, their ability to fund the centers and their will to help them in their organizational aspirations. This is clearly a rich avenue for future pursuit in the Palestinian struggle.

HANEEN ZOABI *is a political activist, a member of the National Democratic Assembly (NDA) of Tajamoa, a political party which was established in 1995, to counteract the Oslo Accords. She is the first Palestinian woman representing a Palestinian party in the Israeli Knesset 2009–2019. Zoabi joined the Gaza Freedom Flotilla, the "Mavi Marmara," in 2010, to break the international silence on the inhumane Israeli siege on Gaza, which was imposed since 2007. She has an MA in Communication Studies from the Hebrew University in Jerusalem, and a BA in Psychology and Philosophy from Haifa University.*

# IN PURSUIT OF THE "NORMAL"
# Palestinian Citizenship within the Zionist Colonial Framework[14]

*Haneen Zoabi*

WHILE I WAS the first Palestinian woman to represent a Palestinian political party in the Israeli Knesset, my story is not one of the upholding of Israeli democracy, liberalism, feminism or justice; rather, my story is that of renewed conflict and dissonance between ourselves, the Palestinians, and the State of Israel. My story centers on the struggle between erasure and visibility, between silence and speaking out.

I am descended from those Palestinians whom Israel did not expel in 1948, a group often seen as the weakest link in a people dismembered, torn to pieces and scattered far apart. I grew up in Nazareth, a town that was described in the first deliberations held by the Israeli Government as "occupied," because it fell outside the UN Partition Line. In fact, 30% of the new state that was established in 1948 was, in Israel's own terminology, "occupied territory." In its early years, Israel grappled with the basic question of to whom to grant its citizenship. A minority in the government believed the new state should consider the Galilee, the north of Palestine, an occupied area, exclude the Palestinians who remained there from Israel's official census, and deny them the right to vote. However, Israel's first Prime Minister, David Ben-Gurion, had other ideas. It was clear

14 This essay was originally written in Arabic and was translated by Samah Sabawi.

that the demographic reality on the ground was not conducive to the creation of a Jewish state with a durable Jewish majority. Ben-Gurion, therefore, moved to seize all land occupied by the Zionist militia and expelled the entire Palestinian population, aware that the very existence of the Jewish state was predicated on the erasure of our own. The resulting military operations succeeded in expelling as much as 85% of the Palestinians living within the 1948 borders in the Palestinian *Nakba*, or catastrophe.

In the aftermath of the devastation of the Palestinian cities of Jaffa, Acre, Haifa, Lydda, and Ramle, and following the inflow of internal refugees from surrounding villages terrorized by the Zionist militia, our small town of Nazareth became the largest Arab city within the 1948 borders. Ultimately, Israel succumbed to pressure from the UN to grant citizenship to the Palestinians who remained inside the declared borders of 1948. However, we were not party to the process of decision-making; it was taken out of our hands. According to whom did we even desire to become Israeli citizens? And why did the UN believe that the Jewish state, which expelled the majority of our people, would treat us better as citizens than it had done beforehand? According to whom were we willing to exchange our land, homes, orchards and trees for alien citizenship in a state in which we had played no part in founding or shaping? According to whom did we wish to be deposited in what was supposed to be an outpost of "developed" Europe within the surrounding "backward" Arab region? According to whom did we want our history to be erased and replaced by an artificial, falsified historical narrative? And who expected us to express thanks and gratitude for any of it?

* * *

In 1948, 21 years before I was born, we, the Palestinians who remained in what was now termed Israel, were forcibly severed from 85% of our people. More than 570 Palestinian villages and towns were destroyed by the Zionist militia during the *Nakba*. They ripped apart our social fabric, destroyed the emergent middle class, together with civil society, the agricultural and industrial sectors, as well as the theaters and the sports clubs that Jaffa was famed for. It was in the aftermath of this horrendous violence that 150,000 Palestinians, members of a people catastrophically deformed and beaten, were ushered, through the gates of the military, into the politics of the newly-established State of Israel.

Our induction into citizenship came via military rule. Israel placed us, the Palestinians who remained inside its 1948 borders, in a ghetto under explicit military rule from 1948 until late 1966, cutting us off from our own people, as well as from Israeli Jewish society. It thereby denied us the opportunity to play any part in defining our new "citizenship." We knew nothing of the state but its military, its police, its intelligence agencies, and its engineering officials, i.e. the state's advisors for Arab affairs, responsible for crafting the new "Arab Israeli." Losing memory and identity is no less devastating than losing a homeland and accepting one's inferiority.

Military rule also embodied the logic of that citizenship; it made use of the military tools with which we were already familiar, now transformed into police repression and intelligence surveillance, through which the state interfered in our day-to-day lives and routinely denied us our political and individual rights. Israel's laws, and the so-called democratic tools of its citizenship, proved to be no more than an extension of our *Nakba*, our dispossession.

Instead of being born into my homeland as a Palestinian citizen, then, I was born into a homeland that told a narrative that contradicted the truth of my existence. A sense of alienation from the violent entity that excised Palestine was to come to define my relationship with the Jewish state. The central question I grappled with became how I, gripped by a growing sense of alienation, could build a "political" relationship with such an entity?

The Jewish state, like all settler colonies, fortified itself by creating an intermediary class between itself and the indigenous population, in this case the Palestinians. It manipulated the selection process of Arab Members of Knesset to advance representatives who were more palatable to Israel than they were to their own people. It forged strong ties with what remained of the Palestinian leadership, including the *mukhtars*, or local chieftains. The appointment of school principals, teachers, and other employees was conditioned on the candidates' approval by the Shin Bet intelligence agency, which blocked the appointment of anyone who participated in a demonstration or who was suspected of holding any affiliation to their Palestinian national identity. Today, the Israeli intelligence apparatus is still one of the main tools employed by the government in maintaining its control over Palestinian "citizens" of Israel.

* * *

We entered into politics defeated and prepared to come to terms with our defeat. Hassan Jabareen warns of the dangers of polarizing the political conditions to welcome a defeated entity into a political and victorious one. He writes, "we agreed to participate in the first Israeli Knesset elections, quickly adopting the language of rights, duty and loyalty to Israel."[15] Our participation in the Israeli political system was, in fact, participation in a colonial project, with all that entails in terms of submission and animosity, and was not based on the application of genuine liberal principles, either by Israel or by ourselves.

It might be surprising and, yes, reprehensible, to think that when I was in the fourth grade of primary school, along with my classmates I held aloft the Israeli flag and sang the national anthem. The school informed us that the Education Department would be sending an inspector to the school on Israel's Independence Day, and that we would festoon the classroom with flags for the occasion. So that is what we did.

Two years later, I watched news reports on the massacres of Sabra and Shatila with deep shock. I understood that something significant had happened that was somehow related to my own existence but was not yet able to fully comprehend it. A short time later, I watched a large demonstration of Palestinians go by beneath the balcony of my grandmother's house in the eastern neighborhood in Nazareth with great interest. Awareness began to take shape within

---

15 Palestine Forum, last accessed October 1, 2021, https://rb.gy/ufbsmv

me, an altering of my perception of reality. A deep feeling, older and greater than Palestine, was developing within me, a form of rebellion stemming from a profound sense of injustice.

Five years after I sang the Israeli national anthem, and two years after the massacres of Sabra and Shatila, I began listening to the *Al-Asheqeen*, singing along with Marcel Khalifa, and reciting the poetry of Mahmoud Darwish.

After 12 years of protesting in demonstrations and non-partisan political activism, I committed myself fully to the field of politics. In general, my own generation was less politicized than its predecessors, who in the 1970s established the multi-party Arab political apparatus that endures today.

Listening to Azmi Bishara speak about citizenship and nationalism during the Madrid negotiations in 1991, I felt that I had found the answer to the question that had long been occupying me: how to maneuver between the world of politics, which requires a deep dive into reality, and my feeling of alienation, which drives detachment from that reality.

Several years later I joined the Arab-founded *Tajamoa* (NDA, the National Democratic Assembly, Balad in Hebrew) political party, in 1998. Three years thereafter, I ran for membership in its Central Committee, and subsequently in its political bureau. It took only a few years for *Tajamoa* to be identified as a strategic threat to Israel. By 2008, Yuval Diskin, then head of Israel's intelligence services, placed it on a list of strategic threats that also included Iran and Hezbollah.[16] We took this designation as confirmation that we were on the right track.

The *Tajamoa* party was established as a response to the Oslo project, which demoted the Palestinian cause from one of liberation and freedom to one of border disputes. The rights of our people were written off: the Right of Return, the dismantling of the settlements in

---

16 "Back to Basics: Israel's Arab Minority and the Israeli-Palestinian Conflict," *Middle East Report* 119, March 14, 2012, last accessed October 1, 2021, https://www.ecoi.net/en/file/local/1048334/2016_1331806197_119-back-to-basics-israels-arab-minority-and-the-israeli-palestinian-conflict.pdf

the 1967 Occupied Territories, the questions of Jerusalem, borders and Palestinian sovereignty were all left off the table in the Oslo Accords. All the root causes of Palestinians' suffering, all Israel's means of control and abuse, were relegated to the sidelines of the negotiations. What, then, did the parties agree on? They agreed to contrive a new false narrative with which to rebrand our reality. From the Oslo Accords onwards, the world spoke of two equal parties to the conflict. The asymmetry of the equation was brushed over and, with it, the historical context. Also excluded from the Oslo Accords were the Palestinians living inside 1948 borders, whose plight was categorized as an "internal Israeli matter." Oslo constituted a whitewashing of Israel's crimes, not a means of resisting them, and it was the Accords that set the *Tajamoa* Party in motion, as the only political party in the Knesset that was prepared to vote against them.

* * *

It was through *Tajamoa* that I manage to preserve my sense of alienation while engaging in parliamentary politics. Alienation arguably creates a "noble state of hostility" towards an unjust reality, hostility which, I argue, is necessary when confronting hegemony. However, our lives are defined by what we do, and action requires goals, strategy, and practical tools that a state of alienation cannot generate, but rather impedes. Political involvement without alienation, on the other hand, runs the risk of normalizing a reality in which a liberal discourse of rights and citizenship is used to mask the underlying colonial context. Thus, the fundamental question becomes how we can engage in politics, using the context of citizenship and a discourse of rights, while also nurturing, through this engagement, consciousness of our colonial reality. How do we make political gains as Palestinians, in an environment in which dozens of political participation laws aim at extricating our political action from its Palestinian context?

*Tajamoa* offered an answer. It was the first Palestinian political party to tackle the schizophrenic gap that occupies the space between the Israeli reality and the Palestinian "truth," and to suggest a possibility of Palestinian political action within the context of Israeli citizenship. It did so by simultaneously rejecting and accepting this citizenship: rejecting its Zionist character but accepting its formalism. *Tajamoa* proposed a radical alternative, based on absolute national and individual equality. The "State of all its Citizens" became the official slogan of *Tajamoa*, threatening the very idea of Zionism. Since we could not envision making any real political progress without placing our work within a narrative of historical injustice, we emphasized the fact that this is our homeland, and that we are called on to make a compromise to live alongside those who choose to come here as settler-colonialists. This compromise, however, requires the latter to abandon their colonial ambitions.

We were convinced that any political action on our part that does not create a Palestinian political narrative rooted in our own history is destined to fail, not only morally, but also politically. While the political platforms of other Palestinian political parties active in Israel required them to separate identity and belonging from "pragmatic," everyday political action, *Tajamoa* believes that pragmatism should not controvert our "truth" as Palestinians. Thus Azmi Bishara, the party's intellectual founder, differentiated between "equality" (*musawa* in Arabic), and "integration" (*indimaj*); *Tajamoa* wants equality for Palestinian citizens, but not if it means being subsumed by Zionism, i.e., not by becoming part of the Israeli State, but rather by opposing the Zionist-colonialist logic that underpins it.

Other Arab political parties have and continue to endorse the "preservation of national identity." However, unlike *Tajamoa*, they refuse to politicize identity and insist on containing it within a separate sphere from politics. Such was the political formula adopted by the Arab-founded Israeli Communist Party (or Maki; the choice of name here is significant, as is the rejection of the obvious alternative, the "Palestinian Communist Party"), for example, and subsequently the Democratic Front for Peace and Equality (Hadash).

In *Tajamoa*, we believe that there is no separation between the Jewish state and the Zionist project. We therefore understand Israel as an ideologically-based entity, in which Zionism looms above everything else: the state, history, geography, international law and human rights. As a Palestinian with Israeli citizenship in the Zionist state, one is not permitted to object to or even question the ideological basis of the state. This dictate is understood not only by state institutions, but also by Israeli society at large: 67% of Israelis believe that issues of peace and security must be decided upon by a Jewish majority, and that there is no contradiction between Israel's "democracy" and Jewish privilege within the state.[17]

Under Israeli domestic law, Israel not only stands above international law and human or democratic values, but it also redefines and subverts these universal concepts. Section 7 of the Jewish Nation-State Law, as well as dozens of land and housing laws that preceded it, legitimize the state's promotion and establishment of exclusively Jewish towns and cities. Its citizenship laws are designed not only to bring in Jews, but also to keep out Palestinians, while allowing even the entry of non-Jews in the effort to limit the Palestinian presence within the state.[18]

*Tajamoa* set out to decouple the idea of the state from the idea of citizenship in order to make the most of the margin of freedom afforded by the state, and to expose the contradiction between what the Israeli State offers on the one hand, and the requirements of natural citizenship on the other. Azmi Bishara emphasized the fact that the rights of Palestinians predate the creation of the State of Israel, and therefore that these rights are grounded firstly in our connection to our homeland, not in our connection to the Jewish state. One can draw from this argument the conclusion that the pertinent question is not whether or not to "enter into" this citizenship, but rather how to shape it. As Palestinians, we believe that the Palestinian narrative should form the basis our citizenship; otherwise, we will be unable to reconcile ourselves with it.

---

17 "New Polls On Israeli Public Opinion - December 2012," it.scribd.com, last accessed October 1, 2021, https://it.scribd.com/document/118421778/New-Polls-on-Israeli-Public-Opinion-December-2012

18 The State views the development of Jewish settlement as a national value, and shall act to encourage and promote its establishment and strengthening. Basic Law Nation State, https://main.knesset.gov.il/EN/activity/Documents/BasicLawsPDF/BasicLawNationState.pdf

Thus, while *Tajamoa*'s concept of "the State of all its Citizens" first took shape as a project that was liberal in its language and goals, it was never at odds with or indifferent to the Palestinian conscience and historical narrative. Indeed, it could more accurately be described as liberational than liberal. *Tajamoa* exposed the colonial nature of Zionism without initially using the term "colonialism," though it gradually began to employ more radical and nationalist rhetoric after the Second Intifada.

*Tajamoa* was the youngest Palestinian parliamentary party and the first to include women on its parliamentary list, with women holding at least one-third of its seats. I entered the Knesset in 2010, after Azmi Bishara's term in the Knesset, which revolutionized politics and parliamentary representation for Palestinians within the 1948 borders.

*Tajamoa* advanced the idea that the Palestinians inside Israel's 1948 borders must create their own national political center. Building such a political center was imperative given that the alternative was Israelization, or the deformation of our identity and political failure within the trap of citizenship.

When I entered the Knesset in 2009, the first piece of advice I received was: "Don't be like Azmi Bishara. Be like Ahmad Tibi" (an Arab MK who peppers his speech with nationalist rhetoric in an artificial and superficial manner). The Knesset was laying down the conditions for my acceptance in the Knesset, for my domestication. "In this home" was a phrase I often heard Palestinian Members of the Knesset from other parties insert into their speeches. The word "home," however, jarred sharply with the sense of alienation I felt within the Knesset.

Following an interview that I gave to Channel 2, Israel's most popular television network, in 2014, I was told that I came across as a rejectionist. As I was speaking out against Israel's acts of aggression, rights violations and repression of the Palestinians, the host interrupted with the question, "Is there anything you like about Israel?" I swiftly responded with, "No, nothing."[19] Even those closest

---

19 Larry Derfner, "The Most Hated Woman in Israel," *Foreign Policy,*

to me criticized my performance in the interview, for what they saw as its "over-intensity" and "negativity." They asked why I could not have said something more agreeable, something that did not mark me out as a rejectionist. They wondered why I could not have cited the high-tech sector, for example, or the weather, or even the anti-Zionist movement. However, my priority was to convey the true nature of my relationship with Israel, and what it represents for me personally, namely alienation and rejection.

* * *

Even if we want to move on from the politics of recognition towards the politics of liberation, we must ask ourselves whether it is possible for us to engage in a fruitful dialogue with Israeli society when 70% of it believes that the Jews are God's "chosen people,"[20] when 57% are disturbed by the large number of Arab doctors working in hospitals, 40% of Jewish Israeli youth support denying the right of Arab citizens to vote,[21] 73% support politics of the far-right (compared to just 19% who identify as "leftists"), and when 73% support placing Arab citizens in concentration camps in the event of a war between the Jewish state and an Arab country—all percentages that are increasing over time. We must recognize that the hostility and fascism of Israeli society has surpassed that of even its most racist laws. In contending with this kind of society, the politics of recognition must play a central role.

While the Zionist state has undergone change in the decades since its establishment, it has always been in the direction of consolidating its colonial nature. Israel succeeded for the first 50 years

---

January 11, 2013, https://foreignpolicy.com/2013/01/11/the-most-hated-woman-in-israel/

20 Nir Hasson, "Survey: Record Number of Israeli Jews Believe in God," *Haaretz,* January 27, 2012, https://www.haaretz.com/jewish/1.5175991

21 Or Kashti, "'Map of Hatred': Half of Israeli Religious Teens Would Strip Arab Right to Vote, Poll Finds," *Haaretz,* February 19, 2021, https://www.haaretz.com/israel-news/.premium-israeli-religious-teens-would-rescind-arab-vote-poll-1.9551732

of the state to market itself as a liberal democratic state rather than a colonial project. However, the Oslo process and the policies of the Zionist left, who, after Camp David II declared "there is no partner for peace," led to the abandonment of their classical separationist solution of two states. That then paved the way for the emergence of a fascist state that has not even troubled itself to hide beneath the cover of liberal democratic rhetoric over the past decade.

Hence, Israel made the transition from an entity that was run by an elite group of liberal Zionists—who hid behind a veneer of democracy while steadily erasing the Palestinian presence—into an entity run by an elite group of right-wing religious-nationalist settlers. The latter have scant regard for democratic principles, and their response to the "demographic threat" posed by the Palestinians is, simply, Apartheid. The demand that Israel has made since 2003 to be explicitly recognized as a Jewish state was designed to counter any political demands by the Palestinians and led to general disillusionment with the Oslo ideal of peace and equality. The Second Intifada cemented the demise of the discourse of "coexistence" that had prevailed amongst Palestinians inside the 1948 borders, led by the Communist Party and the Democratic Front for Peace and Equality (Hadash).

In the aftermath of the Second Intifada, Israel resumed and refined its policies of erasure and social engineering. It did so under the direction of the ascendant Israeli right, and their proposed Apartheid-based solution: to absorb the Palestinians, on both sides of the Green Line, while also mitigating the impact of their existence.

Ilan Pappé unearthed the memories of a Jewish immigrant who, after arriving in Palestine, wrote in a letter to his beloved in Europe, "I arrived in Jaffa and found many strangers there." That immigrant still lives among us. After 70 years, our land, homes, orchards, and cuisine are no longer "strange" to the immigrants. They liked it all. They took it all. But they still see us as "strangers." In 70 years, these invaders have not bothered to learn our language or get to know our history or culture. After 70 years, they demand that we lower the sound of the call to prayer, as they do in Europe. Here, "as in Europe." Are we not still regarded as strangers here?

* * *

Initially, Israelis viewed me as harmless, innocuous. To them, I was merely a woman who made a few headlines as the first woman to enter the Knesset on a Palestinian party list. This public perception changed dramatically when I joined the Gaza Freedom Flotilla in 2010, in the hope of breaking the inhumane siege on Gaza. There were 730 passengers on board the Freedom Flotilla, including parliamentarians, journalists and human rights activists. I was on the largest ship, the Mavi Marmara, when Israel intercepted the flotilla in international waters, and Israeli commandos killed nine activists and seized our vessels. As these events demonstrated, Israel is determined not only to besiege Gaza, but to besiege and kill, "if necessary," those who act to demand its freedom. Terrorism is not Israel's biggest threat; its biggest threat is, in fact, freedom.

During a tumultuous Knesset session held on Wednesday, June 1, 2010, I was attacked and labeled a traitor to Israel. For me, however, the greatest act of treachery I could have committed would have been to shirk my responsibility to defend my own people under siege. As a result of my participation in the flotilla, I was barred from attending Knesset sessions for six months, placed under surveillance, stripped of some of my parliamentary rights, and even faced demands for the revocation of my citizenship. These demands were not only on the agenda of the Minister of the Interior and voiced repeatedly in the Knesset, where they were followed by attempts to prevent me from running in the Knesset elections held in 2013 and 2015, but a poll revealed that as much as 38% of the Israeli public supported the revocation of my citizenship. Thus, a significant portion of the Israeli public view Israeli citizenship as a "reward" to be bestowed on those who swear their loyalty to the "Jewish state," a state which places itself above humanity, above rights, above history and above the law. I should stress that what was at stake was not the loss of my Israeli citizenship per se, but rather the loss of my homeland; stripping Palestinians of their citizenship is but one weapon in Israel's arsenal, used in pursuit of its long-established policy of expulsion.

By becoming involved in the Freedom Flotilla, I confounded early expectations that I would be the "Arab liberal feminist" in the Knesset, and that I would spend my term preoccupied with the projected backwardness of my own society, perhaps taking some interest in the more mundane and "acceptable" issues of budgeting and service. Why, then, did I subvert these expectations by joining the Mavi Marmara? Why do I demand that Israel lift its siege on Gaza? What possible affiliation could I, a petite feminist who speaks of freedom, have to Gaza, a place full of "terrorists" who "force" women to wear headscarves?

Israeli "liberals" sneeringly told me, "Go to Gaza and see for yourself how Hamas treats a single woman in her forties like you." "You spinster," Yohanan Plesner remarked. "No man wants to touch you." Plesner was later to become the President of the prestigious Israel Democracy Institute; his words to me speak volumes about the true nature of so-called "progressive" liberal-Zionism.[22]

What surprised me most during my time in the Knesset was not the attempts made by some MKs to physically attack me, nor the ferocity of their attacks. What surprised me was their astonishment that I had participated in the Gaza Freedom Flotilla, and at my advocacy work to break the silence surrounding the criminal siege of Gaza. What to me seemed intuitive and self-evident, for them was incomprehensible: I belong to my people, I belong to my history, I belong to Gaza, and to all of Palestine.

In addition to a series of incitement campaigns against me, and my total of five suspensions, for a collective total of sixteen months, the Israeli Knesset passed legislation to impose new restrictions on the political activities of Palestinian Members of Knesset in response to my actions. Amongst these pieces of legislation was the 2016 Expulsion Law, more commonly known as the "Zoabi Law."[23] This law allows a majority of 90 Knesset Members to oust a serving

---

22 YouTube, last accessed October 1, 2021, https://www.youtube.com/watch?v=8uZ1SUREOOQ

23 Adalah.org, last accessed October 1, 2021, https://www.adalah.org/ar/law/view/603

MK for their political actions. It allows an elected representative to be suspended by their peers on ideological grounds, in a clear undermining of the democratic process. In other words, the Knesset granted a majority of its members the authority to expel their publicly elected peers.

My experience is a living example of the impossible nature of the practice of citizenship for Palestinian citizens in Israel. By refusing to normalize Zionist citizenship—even while we are locked in it—and by fostering our alienation from it, Israel has made visible the political situation of Palestinians inside the 1948 borders in its full complexity. Our insistence on the duality of our presence in Israeli politics as Palestinians, and our alienation from the colonial hegemony, is a political act of the first degree. It serves to empower the generations of Palestinians who have not lived through any victories against Zionism.

In conclusion, Israeli citizenship was not granted to Palestinians as a means of integrating them into Israeli society on an equal status basis; rather, it was the manifestation and exercise of Israel's victory over us. Palestinians engaging in Israeli politics must preserve the clarity of the inherent contradiction between justice and colonial citizenship. We must use the tools of citizenship in order to demonstrate the colonialist essence of this citizenship, and offer an alternative, decolonized version of it. I believe that this is our strategic mission and would be our most valuable contribution to the Palestinian struggle. It is our strategic asset. And it was in recognition of the value of this asset that former Shin Bet chief Yuval Diskin said in 2008 that, "Israel faces three strategic threats: the Iranian nuclear program, Hezbollah, and every citizen who opposes the Jewish Democratic State."[24]

---

24 International Crisis Group, "Back to Basics: Israel's Arab Minority and the Israeli-Palestinian Conflict," *Middle East Report* 119, 14 March 2012, last accessed October 1, 2021, https://www.ecoi.net/en/file/local/1048334/2016_1331806197_119-back-to-basics-israels-arab-minority-and-the-israeli-palestinian-conflict.pdf

Israel cannot escape its own truth (its racist, colonialist function). Seventy years after its establishment, that truth has caught up with it, and is now on full display for the whole world to see with the legislation of the Jewish Nation-State Law. The law was officially enacted in 2018—though Israel has been implementing its provisions on the ground for decades—in an attempt to legitimize the state's racist colonialist nature, its ethnic cleansing and regime of Apartheid.

However, it is not enough for the world merely to know Israel's truth. What is needed now is for the latent Palestinian liberation project to regenerate and bloom. There are generations of Palestinians ready to nurture and propagate it. Just as the Jewish Nation-State Law exposes the true nature of Israel, so in turn must the Palestinian national project reveal the truth of the Palestinian people's struggle for liberation.

Palestine has changed, and so have the Palestinians. The stranglehold of the old political guard is waning, and with it the old mentality and ways. Demands for new leadership have taken center stage. The Palestinian struggle today can be characterized as liberating and liberational. Palestine's truth is rooted in justice, and it requires liberation of thought and imagination to balance the asymmetry of power. Such a reimagining was what we witnessed with the advent of the Uprising of Dignity (*Hibat Al-Karamah*) of May 2021. The uprising is a movement that embodies justice and truth through the revolutionary nature of its acts, and thereby creates the means to redress the imbalance of power.

The new Palestinian struggle must be a struggle for the new Palestine.

AWAD ABDELFATTAH *is the Coordinator of the One Democratic State Campaign (ODSC). He is the former Secretary-General of Balad/Tajamoa party. Abdelfattah is a prominent political analyst and a speaker in various international forums.*

# FROM SHAM CITIZENSHIP TO LIBERATION DISCOURSE

## The One Secular Democratic State Campaign[25]

*Awad Abdelfattah*

IN THE EARLY EIGHTIES, an elderly Israeli man came into the office of *Al-Fajr English Newspaper* where I worked in East Jerusalem and introduced himself as a journalist from the Israeli *Maariv* newspaper, Israel's second most widely circulated paper at the time. He said he was investigating what he described as the "phenomenon" that drives Palestinian citizens of Israel into relocating to East Jerusalem, which was occupied by Israel in 1967. He told me he read a story in *Haaretz* about the time the Israeli forces stormed into our newspaper offices to hand me an order forbidding me from going into the West Bank and the Gaza Strip for "security reasons." That time, they brutally beat me up inside the police vehicle before they took me to the wretched Al-Maskobeyah Prison in Jerusalem, where they beat me up again. In the *Haaretz* article he had read, I was described as an "Arab-Israeli Journalist."

"Arab-Israeli" is the way Israel describes those Palestinians who have survived its crimes of ethnic cleansing elsewhere in historic Palestine, whom it had forced into Israeli citizenship as part of its colonization scheme. Calling us "Arab-Israeli" is a deliberate act that aims to sever us from our Palestinian people's history and culture. This is how they sought to render our national identity invisible and

---

25 This essay was originally written in Arabic and was translated by Samah Sabawi.

replace it with a hybrid identity that is loyal to the Jewish state. For decades, our particular segment of the Palestinian people has been subjected to media blackout and to marginalization by all international and regional powers, including Arab ones.

The story of my arrival from one of the small villages of Galilee, Kaukab Abu al-Hija, in the north of Palestine/Israel, where I was born and raised, to my employment at the newspaper is an interesting one, as it illustrates the doctrinal application of Israel's oppression and control over our lives. I was called to work for the paper after I had sent an article explaining Israel's manipulation of education in Arab schools as an instrument of control and suppression of the Palestinian narrative. The Israeli Intelligence that controls the Arab section of the Israeli Ministry of Education did not like my political views and my opposition to the educational curricula imposed on Arab schools, which completely excludes and distorts the Palestinian narrative. I was fired from my job as an English teacher, but that was not enough to satisfy the Israeli authority; they continued to harass me in my new job as a committed journalist, and accused me, ironically, of betraying the State of Israel by working for a Palestinian newspaper because I was "an Israeli citizen," even though the newspaper itself was licensed by Israel. This demonstrates the kind of convoluted situation that continues to reproduce itself inside Israel, which leads those of us who are committed and belong to the Palestinian people to search for a counter equation to confront the system of oppression that we live within.

In truth, since I was fired from teaching in 1980 only four months after I was employed, I have been involved in what is a steadily growing national political movement that places the Palestinian national identity at its core and calls for the establishment of a democratic secular state in all of historic Palestine. It is a movement of the *Abna'a al-Balad,* the "sons of the country." Along with my comrades, I contributed towards its reconstruction and to the formation of its central leadership committees and was elected as its Deputy Secretary-General.

Back to the Israeli journalist: he continued his interview with me, which lasted about two hours. His central question to me was

"How do you accept, as an Israeli citizen, living in the Occupied Territory?" He identified himself as a liberal Zionist who does not accept settlements in the territory occupied in 1967. Nonetheless, the interview turned into a tense political debate and a heated confrontation between two people with contradictory narratives. Mine was the story of a people exposed to the largest robbery in broad daylight, dispossessed of their homeland by invading foreign aggressors. His was an account about a people who claim that, after 2000 years, they have returned to their land. The next day, the interview ran under the headline "Settler Awad Abdel Fattah is calling for Yasser Arafat's State of Palestine!" The title was not a complete surprise, given his proactive questions during the interview, but I did not expect him to make up such a provocative and ludicrous headline, describing me as a "settler."

This gave me a good insight into the mindset of liberal Zionists and the Israeli labor movement, and their moral schizophrenia towards the Palestinians. They—who occupy our land, kill and persecute our people, take our homes and villages and populate them with Jews from outside Palestine—are still able to claim that theirs is a democratic state. The headline linking me to Yasser Arafat, the leader of the Palestinian revolution, viewed by Israel as a murderer and a terrorist, not as a fighter for the freedom of his dispossessed people, was intended to be inflammatory—to Israelis.

During the interview, I had conceded that advocating for one secular democratic state is perceived by Israel, and amongst large sections of Palestinian society, as unrealistic and risky. At that time, those who dared speak of it suffered a great deal of persecution and abuse. I also conceded that some Palestinians, who were made citizens of Israel, support equality and the two-state solution as espoused by the Israeli Communist Party, the majority of whose members are Arabs. However, there were others, who have been domesticated by the policies of intimidation, containment and the push for Arab citizens to vote for the Zionist parties, for whom adapting to colonization was the only way to survive.

* * *

My early political awareness came from two sources. The first was my parents, who spoke of the brutal ways our village was occupied. My father repeated, with great sadness, the story about the martyrdom of his brother, who was part of the Resistance. My mother wept whenever she was reminded of her uncles and aunties who were forced to flee when the Zionist gangs conquered our village. Like hundreds of thousands of our people, they fled to surrounding Arab countries, seeking refuge, only to live and die in exile without being allowed the right to return. All they left behind is their story to fuel the struggle for their children and grandchildren, so they may return.

My second source of political awareness came from a Socialist Zionist Kibbutz built with modern infrastructure on land belonging to our village. It had running water and electricity when our village did not. In fact, it took thirty years of hard work by the people of the village to finally get Israel to connect us to the grid. My father, like the other villagers, would look at the Kibbutz and sigh in pain at the accelerated expansion of settlements, wondering how did they rob us of our land? How can it be that they cultivate fruit on our land and force us to pick the fruit for low wages as if we were strangers, or even slaves?

Our village is a microcosm of how looting took place by way of settlements and expulsions. Our village extended over 20,000 acres of land before 1948; today all that is left is 2,000 acres. It is now surrounded by four settlements, whose total population is not up to half of the population of our people in the village. What remains of land for Palestinians who are citizens of the State of Israel, is now less than three percent[26] of their original land, the result of the looting, confiscation, settlement and Judaization activity.

Western governments have glorified Israel as a "democratic, enlightened" country even as it was imposing a repressive military rule that infringes on the freedom of its "Arab" citizens, allowing

---

26 Kaminitz Law (Draft Planning and Construction Law) (Amendment 109) 5776-2016, Position Paper, last accessed October 1, 2021, https://law.acri.org.il/en/wp-content/uploads/2017/02/2017.2.5-keminitz-law-position-paper-eng.pdf

the confiscation of Palestinian land and the destruction of our socio-economic fabric. This is the Israel that prevented the implementation of United Nations Resolution 194 on the Right of Return. This is the Israel that killed more than 5,000 Palestinians who tried to return to their homes in the early years after its establishment, without any accountability to the international community which continued to grant it legitimacy.

After the aggression of 1967, Israel widened the discriminatory policies it implemented against the Palestinian citizens of Israel to cover its newly occupied territory—the city of Jerusalem, the West Bank and the Gaza Strip. However, an unintended outcome of its brutal occupation of the remainder of our historic homeland was that Palestinians on both sides of the Green Line were able to connect once again. This ushered in a new phase of political and cultural interaction that was open to all Palestinians in historic Palestine.

Since the mid-seventies, Palestinians inside Israel reclaimed their identity as a part of the Palestinian people, contrary to the perceptions abroad that we are submissive, have accepted our inferiority and political marginalization and have dissolved into the Jewish state. The transformation of our people was marked by the latest four decades of struggle, organization and development of educational and cultural training. The first outcome emerged during the unrest and strikes on Land Day in March 1976,[27] and the street confrontations that erupted against the Israeli forces. The second was in 2000, when we joined the Second Intifada together with our brothers and sisters in Jerusalem, the West Bank and the Gaza Strip. In this Intifada, as well as the First Intifada of 1987, several Palestinian citizens of Israel, were martyred and many wounded.

Since then, we have passed through deep transformations, both internally and with Israel, as well as with the Palestinian people and the national cause. This was reflected in the third uprising which swept Palestine from the river to the sea, *Intifadat al Amal*, the "uprising

---

27 "Land Day, 1976: A Turning Point in the Defense of Palestinian Lands in Israel," *Palestinian Journeys,* last accessed October 1, 2021, https://www.paljourneys.org/en/timeline/highlight/14509/land-day-1976

of hope and dignity," of May 2021, where we actively participated through massive demonstrations and street closures. Palestinians, who were made citizens of the State of Israel, presented themselves in the conflict as a living and dynamic force, after decades of neglect and underestimation of both their orientation and commitment.

## *Abna'a al-Balad:* A Secular Democratic State in Historic Palestine

In 1972, a local national movement appeared in the Palestinian city of Umm al-Fahm, situated within the 1948 Israeli borders. At the time, the Israeli Communist Party was the only party legally permitted to run, and many Arab intellectuals and nationalists found within it an outlet to express their feelings and political positions, even though they did not support its Marxist ideals and its legitimization of the State of Israel. After the strikes on Land Day, the *Abna'a al-Balad* movement emerged, a new central national movement, with a large presence of Arab students from five Israeli universities.

The *Abna'a al-Balad* movement affirmed that we, the Palestinians inside the 1948 border, are a part of all the Palestinian people and, like the rest of the Palestinian people, we were under occupation and that the national movement of the Palestinians that grew up and crystallized in exile, led by the Palestine Liberation Organization, represented our aspirations. *Abna'a al-Balad* believed that the PLO had a legitimate right to all forms of resistance. However, due to the different political circumstances that Palestinians inside the 1948 borders encountered, we felt the need to adopt a mode of civil, cultural, and legislative resistance. Therefore, we set up organized branches of the movement in Israeli universities, as well as in some Arab towns adopting a political, ideological, and confrontational discourse against Israel, regarding it as an aggressive colonial settler entity.

We adopted the program of the Palestine Liberation Organization, which at that time sought the return and liberation of all of Palestine and the establishment of a secular democratic state, where Palestinians and Israeli Jews could live in equality. The movement also adopted the principle of a boycott of Israeli elections as an exercise in refusing to accept the legitimacy of the settler entity. Not surprisingly, most of the leaders and cadres of the movement were subjected to various forms of persecution, including repeated arrests, torture, being fired from work, having university enrolment terminated and our newspapers shut down, but there was never an official ban on our activities. I, myself, was arrested for a few days several times, and three of my brothers served prison sentences of between two to three years, each.

The collapse of the Soviet Union, the US Iraq invasion, regional wars, Israeli aggression, the disintegration of the Arab countries and the fall of the PLO leadership through the signing of the Oslo agreements, forced us, *Abna'a Al-Balad,* and other progressive groups, to come up with a new national and political strategy, which we summed up in the slogan of "national identity and full citizenship."

## Confronting Zionism from Within

The Oslo agreement caused a deep fracture in the course of the Palestinian struggle. It reduced the Palestine issue to the establishment of a Palestinian state on 22% of our historic homeland, in the West Bank and the Gaza Strip. The issue of refugees, a core Palestinian issue, disappeared. As for us—the one and a half million Palestinians inside the 1948 borders who constitute 20% of the population of Israel—we were expunged from the conflict. This reflected an acceptance of the abuse, subjugation, level of discrimination and injustice we encounter under the rule of what is now Jewish state. This surrender to Zionism was a repudiation of the continued existence of the Palestinian people on this land, their legitimate resistance, and their enormous sacrifices for over a hundred years of fighting for their freedom and justice. That is why most Palestinian factions initially opposed the Oslo agreement, only adapting to it later as it became a reality.

The Israeli leadership, and to some extent the Palestinian leadership, were shocked by the strong opposition to Oslo by national Palestinian movements inside Israel, especially by *Abna'a al-Balad* and by other Palestinians who withdrew from the Communist Party of Israel that supported the Oslo agreement. We decided to regroup, establish a new political party, and take our fate into our hands, as we refused to appear to have bene taken out of the conflict and its resolution. The party was named the National Democratic Assembly- (*Tajamoa*). A strong momentum was building, and within a short period, thousands of people came to support it. *Tajamoa* ran for seats in the Knesset for the first time in 1996, after a long boycott of these elections by those who are now its members. It achieved an important representation, and I served as the Secretary-General of this Party until I resigned in 2016.

The *Tajamoa* party represented a new popular political and intellectual force—not only in its response to Oslo, but mainly in its call for a State of all its citizens, thus challenging the Jewish characterization of the State of Israel as a Jewish State, re-emphasizing the national and collective identity of the Palestinian citizens.

We continued to adhere, though implicitly, to the principle of liberation and the establishment of one secular democratic state in all of historical Palestine, even at a time of deep transformations marked by a retreating revolutionary climate. As agents of change, our isolation from society—which was undergoing profound socio-economic and cultural transformation—meant losing the ability to influence or worse, vacating the floor for Zionist parties and Arab parties that, exploiting the climate of defeat that was evident in the Oslo agreement, were oriented toward assimilation. We called for equal citizenship and pride in our Palestinian identity as an essential requirement to improving our living conditions, and to sustaining our existence as a national and indigenous minority.

This development in political thinking manifested itself in a remarkable proposition put forward by a new generation in a climate of revolutionary retreat and misleading campaigns and defeatism. We aimed to expose the contradictions inherent in the definition of Israel as a Jewish and democratic State, and to show that without the abolition of the "legal" structure of racism and colonialism, Israel would never be a secular democratic state and, consequently, Palestinian citizens would remain inferior citizens, oppressed and discriminated against, forever.

The transition from the discourse of colonialism to one of citizenship rights and challenging the Jewish nature of the state by participating in the elections to the Knesset to address our people and Israeli and global public opinion, required a great deal of intellectual courage, and, perhaps, risk. However, our deep understanding of Zionism, and of intellectual and moral standards and universal values, protected us against being co-opted politically, keeping a window open to development of a just, comprehensive vision of liberation that extends to all of Palestine. These political and intellectual experiences reflected the maturation of the collective, and its ability to be responsible towards the greater good. This resonated with the general Palestinian public and elite class, quickly making our party one of the three central Palestinian parties in Israel.

Over time, the party's demand for "a state for all its citizens," which presented Palestinian society with an alternative to the Jewish state, became the prevailing discourse. As a result, the party and its leaders suffered. Its President, Azmi Bishara, a member of the Knesset at the time and a renowned intellectual, was subjected to a campaign of incitement that included repeated attempts to remove him from the Knesset, and trials against him for denying the right of Jews to a state, as well as for building connections with the Arab world. There were a few courageous and principled Israeli academics and intellectuals who defended the party and saw it as the only real democratic party in Israel, as it called for a state of all its citizens, Arabs and Jews, and for justice for the Palestinian people, as stipulated by international laws and resolutions. In fact, over the course of two decades, the party won hundreds of Jewish votes in the electoral battles for the Knesset.

In response to the Second Intifada, and in the face of a growing national movement of Palestinians inside Israel with the *Tajamoa* party at the helm, Israel escalated its hostility, racism and settlement expansion against the Palestinian citizens of Israel. The differences between the ways in which Israel treated us and the way it was treating our brothers and sisters under military occupation in the land occupied in 1967 became blurred. Israel developed formal policies, using legal and administrative tools to counter the possibility of achieving equality between Palestinians and Jews. It became increasingly clear that all Palestinians were living under one oppressive regime. Many inside and outside the *Tajamoa* party began to realize that the discourse of citizenship and equality had reached a dead end, and it was time to begin new initiatives with our Palestinian brothers and sisters outside the Green Line and in the Diaspora. This culminated in a return to the discourse of colonialism, and the struggle to dismantle the apartheid regime through the unification of the Palestinian people via a shared vision of national liberation and comprehensive democracy.

It must be said that the discourse of equality and full citizenship within the State of Israel and the challenge it presented to Zionism was not a failure, as it brought to light the structural contradiction between Zionism and equality in an unprecedented way, and this contributed to highlighting the just cause of the Palestinians in Israel, as well as of Palestinians everywhere. To some extent, this was our main objective. We were determined not to succumb to the asymmetric balance of power and pressures that had pushed the leadership of the Palestine Liberation Organization into signing the defeatist Oslo agreement by using the citizenship that was imposed on us—with full awareness of the contradictions inherent in this approach—as a tool to fight the Zionist apartheid regime and expose its structural racism from within. The *Tajamoa* party filled an important political vacuum after Oslo, producing a modern political vision based on universal values such as democracy and social justice, individual and collective rights, imbued by thousands of activists, a large number of whom have become leaders at the national and local levels. It also contributed to the shift of the debate towards democratic citizenship in all of historic Palestine, within one single political entity.

Many in the West do not know that the One Democratic State solution is not a new proposition or a deviation from the Palestinian people's national liberation, nor is it a movement against the Jews. Historical documents indicate that in 1919, Palestinian Islamic and Christian institutions rejected the Zionist project and called on the British Mandate authority to declare the independence of Palestine as a democratic state for all its people. In the late twenties, a small Jewish group called Brit Shalom—made up of a number of prominent Jewish intellectuals, including the President of the Hebrew University, Judah Magnes—called for a bi-national state, and rejected the idea of a Jewish state. In addition, the modern Palestinian national movement, represented by the PLO, officially adopted this solution in the late sixties, before retracting it in favor of the two-state solution.

## From Citizenship Discourse to Colonialism and Apartheid

A new Israel is emerging; one that is more polarized and aggressive, blatant in its attack on free speech, equality and equal citizenship, unapologetic about its inability to reform itself from within, more Jewish and less democratic. The latest manifestation of this shift was the Nation State Law of 2018, which limited the right to self-determination only to the Jewish people, and deleted the word "equality."[28] It also shut the door on the possibility of stopping the settlements, withdrawing from Palestinian territories occupied in 1967 and the establishment of a Palestinian State. As for the right of return, laws prohibiting family unification were enacted to end, once and for all, the issue of return.

Against the backdrop of these explicitly fascist Israeli developments, and the impotence and erosion of Palestinian leadership over two decades, the Palestinian arena witnessed the growth of a multitude of diverse grassroots movements that advocate for alternative solutions centered on the unity of the Palestinian people, their land, their cause and their destiny. These movements and initiatives have not yet been transformed into being organized and united around one agreed-upon vision, due to objective and subjective obstacles. Amongst them is the One State movement that calls for a single secular democratic state which has attracted a growing number of activists, including distinguished Jewish academics. The One State movement has produced a great deal of

---

28 "Basic Law: Israel—The Nation State of the Jewish People" (Unofficial translation by Dr. Susan Hattis Rolef), *The Knesset,* last accessed October 1, 2021, https://main.knesset.gov.il/EN/activity/Documents/BasicLawsPDF/BasicLawNationState.pdf.

important literature exploring its vision, its founding principles and logic, and addressing the theoretical obstacles and challenges that stand in its way.

However, despite the expansion of the debate into larger circles, it has not yet managed to critically impact public opinion. There are objective factors behind this failure. The first is Israel's rejection of any initiative that recognizes the Palestinian people's right to self-determination. There is also the failure of the Palestinian factions and political parties to adopt this option: even though they agree with the principle, they argue that the two-state solution enjoys international legitimacy. Of course, there are also subjective reasons why the One State movement has not reached its watershed moment, which relate to the inability of the movement to campaign and organize effectively. The majority of initiatives are issued by Palestinians in the diaspora, particularly in the United States and Europe. Although this is cause for celebration, it also highlights that, in Palestine, because of the continuing state of discord between Fatah and Hamas and the erosion of the PLO, there is a decline in critical and creative thinking, which hinders the growth of these initiatives. Until recently, many Palestinians in Palestine were not aware of the One State movement, arising especially among the new generation of academics. However, we are seeing a growing number of Palestinians fleeing from these stagnant factions and coming into a movement that returns the conflict to its roots and reframes it as an anti-colonial struggle and not a border dispute between two states.

In light of this growth in the support of the One Democratic State discussion over the past few years, there was a clear need to frame this intellectual discussion in a way that builds on the achievements of past initiatives and avoids their shortcomings. So, the first two meetings we held early in 2018 attracted large numbers of Palestinian intellectuals and activists on both sides of the green line, as well as progressive Jewish activists and intellectuals. These two meetings, held in Haifa and in Britain, resulted in the drafting of a document of principles. This was followed by Zoom meetings with prominent activists and intellectuals in the Gaza Strip, the West Bank and the Diaspora. We called the initiative, the "One Democratic State Campaign."

Why a campaign and not a movement? We wanted to distinguish ourselves from previous initiatives that had defined themselves as "movements," some even naming themselves "popular movements." We believe that building a movement is an ambitious work that does not yet match our current limited resources. We are also seeking to be a campaign that can include all the movements and the individuals who have worked towards the one state solution in the past. Part of this has been achieved so far and, despite all the difficulties, we see an open horizon for further progress. The changing reality in Palestine demands a new emancipatory vision that can return our people's confidence in the struggle and reignite their hopes within a unified resistance.

## The Palestinian Intifada: The Restoration of Awareness

After Israel killed any chance of a two-state solution, entrenched its settlement projects, intensified its ethnic cleansing, fortified its apartheid wall, deepened Palestinian fragmentation and established a Palestinian Authority that acts as an agent of the occupation, it thought it had succeeded in resolving the conflict. But the "Hope and Dignity" Intifada in the month of May 2021, also referred to as the "Sword of Jerusalem," demolished Israel's illusion that the question of Palestine could be liquidated, and that Palestinian Resistance was dead.

The third Intifada, which was launched from the neighborhood of Sheikh Jarrah and Al-Aqsa Mosque in Jerusalem, which was amplified by the Palestinian people inside Israel, in the West Bank and in the Gaza strip and supported by all Palestinian factions, had a profound impact. While nothing appeared to have changed on the ground, its profound effect was that it generated an awareness of the oneness of the Palestinian people and their unextinguished determination. A younger and politically aware generation in Palestine was the spark. They were joined by an army of young Palestinian keyboard warriors, born and raised in exile, who played an important role in supporting and expanding popular resistance. They came up with innovative hashtags, the most prominent of which was #from_the_river_to_the_sea, demonstrating the tendency of the younger generation—born during the Oslo years into a pit of despair under the rule of a Palestinian leadership that is divided and unable to confront Israel's crimes—to call for the elimination of the Oslo paradigm and the myth of state-building under the yoke of colonialism.

The diversity of the current popular movements, and the accumulation of critical Palestinian intellectual discussions, is an expression of defiance toward both the deepening colonial reality and the subservient and incompetent Palestinian Authority. The past two decades reflect the growing undercurrents of new awareness, waiting for the moment to rise to the surface in every corner of Palestine, where our people are hungry for freedom and for an end to their oppression and humiliation. Even my small village joined the Unity uprising, and I was heartened to engage with and stand by hundreds of young people in their massive nightly demonstrations.

The Unity Intifada confirmed the legitimacy of the vision of the One Secular Democratic State Campaign. This is what we need. A Palestinian framework, armed with a liberating, democratic and humane vision that progressive Jews can participate in as allies in the struggle, a framework that mobilizes the Palestinian people and formulates a popular, civil resistance strategy in all of Palestine. The one secular democratic state is already the only option, the inevitable evolution of events that Israel itself is bringing into being through its official policies that seek to control all of historic Palestine through an apartheid system of oppression and discrimination. Israel, today, is even more polarized, more right-wing, more extreme, and is leaning toward outright undisguisable fascism. However, an aggressive colonial and apartheid regime cannot sustain or continue to live by the sword amidst millions of native inhabitants determined to go on struggling and in the middle of hundreds of millions in the Arab countries who view Palestine and Jerusalem as part of their geography, culture and history, and indeed view Israel as a threat to that as well, as so much of the Middle East lies in ruins due to that underlying Zionist agenda.

Our struggle for a single secular democratic state is long, and it requires long-term thinking, great wisdom and high skill in communication and organization, so we can find the right answers to all the challenges and all the big questions that present themselves. Yet, it is the only way that is in line with history and with the logic of justice and human dignity, and sustainable peace.

LAILA AL-MARAYATI *has been a long-time activist in the American Muslim community, writing and speaking extensively on issues of concern to Muslim women and Muslims in general, with particular focus on religious freedom, women's rights in Islam, reproductive health, sexuality and spirituality. She is the chair of KinderUSA (Kids in Need of Development, Education and Relief), a non-profit humanitarian organization that provides health, education and other forms of assistance to Palestinian children and their families living in the West Bank, Gaza and refugee camps in Lebanon. She has been providing obstetrics and gynecological services to women of all backgrounds, with a particular commitment to the underserved, and to educating the next generation of physicians specializing in women's health.*

# ON DIGNITY AND EMPOWERMENT
## The Role of Charity in Our Struggle

*Laila Al-Marayati*

WHEN I WAS growing up as the daughter of what I considered to be a strict immigrant Arab father, my sense of identity as an Arab-American in general, and Palestinian specifically, was conflicted. I struggled with the bifurcated worlds of my father's relatives who came over, one by one, from Gaza or Kuwait, and my mother's family who also migrated to California, but was from Missouri. I was not sure if we were Midwestern, Southern, Middle Eastern or just American. However, there was no mistaking my late father's resolve and dedication to all things Palestinian. It was not until years later, when I visited Gaza, that I was able to understand his attachment to Southern California, which was almost the spitting image of his homeland, down to the ubiquitous *sabr* plant, or prickly pear, whose fruit he adored, and which served as a sort of namesake as he was called Sabri.

The *sabr* plant felt like it should be the national plant of Palestine as it embodies the attributes of *sumud*, or steadfastness, which is the defining characteristic of the Palestinian people. Tough on the outside, protective of the tender, life-giving water on the inside; thorns for protection, but beautiful blossoms and fruit, to be shared generously. Growing in all conditions, with or without water, seemingly even without adequate soil, but ever present.

I knew little of the history of Palestine while I was growing up. I could not really find Jerusalem on a map and had a vague idea of the geography of the region in general. Everything changed when my father sent my sister and me to visit our family in Gaza in 1980. I thought it was a trip to help us identify with his homeland, to meet our relatives and to learn about Palestine. I figured out later (brilliant 19-year-old that I was) that the purpose was to introduce me to potential spouses from among my cousins, a common practice among our community. That did not happen but after traveling throughout Palestine with my aunts, uncles and cousins, my sense of Palestinian identity was forever solidified. Little could we have imagined that the ability to travel freely would not last and that this experience was never to be repeated.

My uncles met us at the airport in Tel Aviv, a mere 30-minute drive from our home in Khan Younis. On our way out of Gaza, young Israeli soldiers flirted with us and let us pass easily through what would become the nightmare of Erez. We drove to Haifa and Nazareth, where we enjoyed a picnic by a lake with an Iraqi Jewish family. On another day trip, we visited Bir Zeit in Ramallah where my lack of education was quickly addressed after a meeting with enthusiastic activist professors who loaded us up with brochures, books and other items describing the Palestinian struggle. We enjoyed the famous *knafeh* of Nablus and visited Bethlehem. A memorable visit to the Haram al Sharif in Jerusalem with a tour through the Old City and the souk reinforced everything else that we had taken in, while my Anglo-American identity quickly receded into the background.

That was in 1980.

In the years that followed, my relationship with my father was difficult as I navigated young adulthood as an American woman. I cared about what happened in Palestine and elsewhere, but it was not a priority for me at that time and I felt that the Palestinian cause was in good hands with my father whom I believed wanted to return at some point.

Indeed, he did. After leaving Gaza in the 1950s to pursue an education in the US, he met and married my mother in 1959. He returned to Gaza in 1964 with his wife and three of his children. He did not go back again until after Oslo, as he was one of the members of the diaspora who truly believed it would provide the opportunity for the creation of a Palestinian State. Although a physician by training, he threw himself, together with his brothers, into creating businesses to elevate Gaza: helping to construct the airport, investing in a flour mill, initiating projects to improve access to medical care and services. He wanted to enable Gazans to get the care they needed in Gaza and not have to travel elsewhere. Throughout those years, I was busy with college, then medical school, then residency, marriage and a new baby. I had dreamt of going back to Palestine with my father one day, now as a mature adult daughter, no longer a surly adolescent. Just one more year, and then we would go.

In the midst of my over-committed life, I agreed to serve on the US Commission on Religious Freedom (USCIRF) as an appointee of then-President Clinton. The year was 1998. My sons were four and six years old and I was working full-time. As an activist member of the Muslim American community, I felt that I had no other choice but to agree. I served with John Bolton, Elliott Abrams, Nina Shea, David Saperstein, the then Archbishop Theodore McCarrick, among others. Eventually, I knew that I had to ensure the Commission addressed religious freedom, and lack thereof in Israel as well. Their main focus, at the time, was on Sudan, Saudi Arabia, the former Soviet republics and East Asia, including China. Part of the fact-finding mission included trips to the region in question and, eventually, we decided a trip to the Middle East was in order. Of course, most of the Commission did not think that it should include Israel, but I insisted. I made up for lost time by further educating myself about Palestine, learning that day by day the Oslo agreement was breaking down, that infringements on freedom of movement throughout the West Bank and in Gaza due to Israeli settlements were creating an intolerable level of despair and frustration among the Palestinian people. My father encouraged me to continue, to have courage and to represent our community, even in the face of open hostility from other Commission members.

When I announced, a year later, that I was expecting our third child, a girl, my father suggested that we name her Jenin, after the town in northern Palestine. She was to be the youngest of 10 grandchildren. Three months after her birth, my father died suddenly at the age of 66, the day after returning from a trip to Egypt. As the patriarch, not only of our nuclear family, but of his extended Palestinian family—and, indeed, a huge segment of the Palestinian and Arab community—the loss left a gaping hole. My dream of traveling with him one day was gone. It became clear that he was the glue that kept his family together, as conflict quickly ensued regarding property and business matters in Gaza.

I eventually recovered from the immediate shock and had to get on with being a mother, working full-time, not losing control in front of my patients, and serving on the damn Commission. However, it became even more important for me to continue his work after he died, or some semblance of it, as an activist for Palestine. Several months later, I was on a trip to the Middle East, first to Egypt, then Saudi Arabia, and finally, to Tel Aviv. Of all of the Commission members, I was the only one harassed in Saudi Arabia, as a Muslim woman traveling without a *mahrem*, (or guardian) even though the group was worried about how a rabbi and priest would be treated. Misogyny can be relied upon to rear its ugly head under all circumstances.

Several Commission members chose not to travel to Israel since they objected to the notion that there were any religious freedom violations of any kind there. Meeting with non-Orthodox Jews, Christians as well as Muslims, told another story. I documented it, along with our knowledgeable staff member, Khalid el-Gindy, in a dissenting opinion.[29]

The day we visited the Al-Aqsa compound, I went to pray in the small mosque under the Dome of the Rock. I am not sure what happened, but I was overwhelmed with emotion, sobbing uncontrollably, thinking of my late father and everything he believed in. I knew, then, that I could not let his dream for Palestine die with him and that, as the next generation, I was obliged to continue. My first responsibility was to assert myself within a group of neocons

---

29 United States Commission on International Religious Freedom, Addendum to the Report of the United States Commission on International Religious Freedom, May 14, 2001, last accessed October 1, 2021, https://www.uscirf.gov/sites/default/files/resources/may%202001%20annual%20report%20addendum%20with%20dissent.pdf

and Zionists, to speak up for the rights of religious minorities in Israel. I had to show them what should have been self-evident—that preventing Palestinians in the West Bank and Gaza, both Muslim and Christian, from practicing their faith in their houses of worship was a matter of religious freedom no different from the violations faced by people of minority faiths throughout the world. Once again, on the way out of Tel Aviv, I was the only Commissioner who was interrogated, now by the Israelis, who only desisted when the US Embassy staff intervened. We issued our dissent to the official Commission report the day before my term on the Commission expired, as I knew that efforts would be made to prevent me from publishing it at all, using the timing as an excuse.

Not much happened as a result, but in Washington DC at the time, issuing such a statement from an official government body was unprecedented. Clearly, the battle continues in the American political sphere but shortly after that, I had to turn my attention elsewhere.

While the events of 9/11 occurred 20 years ago, it sometimes feels like they happened yesterday. Words cannot describe our shock, horror and even shame as Muslim Americans, when we watched in real-time the devastation in New York, Washington and Pennsylvania. The terrorist threat had come to the US with a vengeance, and we braced ourselves for what would be a horrible backlash. Countries that used terrorism as an excuse to engage in gross human rights violations would now get a free pass since the anti-terrorism fight was everyone's fight. This included Israel. Ariel Sharon, Prime Minister at the time, went on to wage war on Palestinians engaged in what had started out as a non-violent uprising against the oppression of the Oslo regime. Devastation and destruction reigned throughout the West Bank and Gaza; lives were lost, and the horror of reciprocal suicide bombings began, which resulted in global solidarity with Israel.

In the US, non-profit, charitable organizations which had been supporting Palestinians and other Muslims elsewhere were shuttered, as the Patriot Act enabled the government to freeze assets, make accusations about wrongdoing and harass donors and employees alike, with impunity. Now that Palestine was on fire and the people were suffering from Jenin to Rafah, our channels of support were cut off. Even though the perpetrators of 9/11 were from the Arabian Peninsula, all of the energy against US charities in the interest of fighting terrorism was focused on those who supported Palestine.

Barriers were created, seemingly overnight, to anyone around the world from Europe to the Gulf, who wanted to provide humanitarian support to Palestine. The bombs continued in a pattern that exists to this day on the part of Israel in response to Palestinian resistance: disproportionate, excessive force that results in collective punishment against a civilian population. Every. Single. Time.

So, as a former donor to the above organizations who was outraged that I could no longer support those in need, I joined with other like-minded individuals, friends and humanitarians, who had founded a new organization, KinderUSA (Kids in Need of Development, Education and Relief) in 2002. Little did we know that the US Treasury Department assumed that we would pick up where others had left off in supporting "terrorists." This resulted in the launching of a Grand Jury investigation that ultimately went nowhere, harassing and arresting our staff in Israel, interrogating my family and me upon return from a family vacation and more. Confident in our own practices and commitment to providing humanitarian assistance in a legal and transparent manner under all circumstances, we were certain that we could withstand the efforts to defame and undermine our work.

Shortly after I joined the organization, I was able to travel once again to beloved Palestine, this time with my youngest sister. We could not go through Tel Aviv anymore (Palestinians who do travel through Tel Aviv can tell you about their mistreatment there), so we had to traverse the Sinai desert by car, entering via Rafah. While there, we visited with our NGO partners on the ground who were implementing our projects. We also visited with people at the World Food Program and saw local Palestinians selling the dry goods that they had received. I was shocked to learn that the olive oil the WFP procured was not Palestinian and that their donations included canned meat and no fresh produce. In Gaza! One of the richest agricultural regions on the planet! Families were given handouts that they had no choice but to accept. Our executive director, always thinking outside of the box, came up with the idea of instead producing vouchers for families to use that could be redeemed by local merchants to purchase food, clothing, school supplies, etc. The use of vouchers is now commonplace among humanitarian groups in general; such a program was first implemented by KinderUSA in Palestine.

Similarly, insofar as we knew, then, that we needed to provide food assistance differently, in a way that supported the local community, while providing LOCALLY GROWN fresh and nutritious produce to the community, we launched our Farmer's Project. It provides seeds and other tools to local farmers who then grow the crops that we then purchased and provided to the neediest families. In addition, over the years, we have employed female heads of household to provide additional products such as cheese, dates, jam, etc. with the food baskets.

Early on, with our focus on childhood nutrition and well-being, we engaged with a female-run business to provide hot meals to children in the local schools in the poorest areas. This included schools run by UNRWA as well as the Ministry of Education. Eventually, UNRWA took over and began providing hot meals to their own students. So then we focused on the government schools, especially pre-schools, throughout Gaza. We continued to provide vouchers in both the West Bank and Gaza for school supplies and uniforms, the cost of which could often prevent families from sending their kids to school at all.

As has been widely reported, the availability of clean drinking water is limited throughout Gaza due to the high rates of salinization as well as to ongoing contamination due to constant disruptions to the processing of sewage. We have worked on projects that make clean water available in schools, just to bring them up to a level that would be expected for children anywhere.

I traveled again to Gaza in 2009 with another Board member, shortly after the attacks of that year had wiped out significant infrastructure, particularly in the northeast part of the Gaza Strip. On that trip, we focused on identifying partners to address the psychosocial needs of children who suffered from unprecedented cases of post-traumatic stress disorder. We learned, at that time, about the tremendous limitations of the healthcare system, in general, throughout Gaza and its shortcomings in terms of mental health, in particular. The siege of Gaza had begun a few years earlier and was beginning to take its toll since the ability to bring in skilled trainers from outside, to send Gazans abroad (even to the West Bank) for training, or to obtain needed equipment to repair hardware like CT scanners or ventilators, etc., was severely curtailed. Yet, our commitment continued, while our respect for the incredible resilience of the people of Gaza mounted. On that trip, I learned what they could do with recycled rebar, how they had to destroy the concrete remains of buildings by hand, how they turned small plots of land adjacent to their homes into thriving potato farms, how they created art and embroidery, and preserved Palestinian traditions through dance, music and storytelling. Their commitment to education and excellence meant that they would rebuild the destroyed schools and university buildings and get on with teaching, learning and growing, once again.

My last trip was in 2013, before Israel's onslaught of Operation Protective Edge in 2014. My sister and I traveled once again across the Sinai, this time with another aging uncle, who had business to attend to in Gaza. We were greeted warmly by the border officials in Rafah and stayed with relatives for 10 days, visiting our projects and partners in the refugee camps from Jabaliya in the north to Rafah in the south. We visited a school for the hearing impaired in Bani Suhaila, where the students were accomplishing amazing things in art, science, and language, while the staff was so enthusiastic in its efforts to support these children. They were also our partners in the hot breakfast program for local pre-schools that we visited, as well. Gaza City, as always, was a lively hub where we connected with other humanitarian groups and community members. Children everywhere loved to have their photos taken with us and to practice their English.

From 2002 to 2013, I was able to witness the growth of my own family in Khan Younis, meeting new cousins and their children every time. The El-Farra family has been in Gaza for centuries and is extensive, to say the least. On our first trip in 2002, right after we arrived in Egypt, a helicopter gunship had attacked an area near our town, Khan Younis, destroying a building and killing many of its inhabitants. Everyone was worried about our safety and tried to discourage us from continuing the journey. I called my aunt in Khan Younis, and she said, "Don't worry, that was in another neighborhood. Most welcome!" I thought, "Who am I to be afraid when she goes through this every day, when her daughter gets up each morning, gets her kids ready for school, and goes off to work as a teacher herself." That's when I really understood that just getting up and getting on with life is a form of resistance for Palestinians. Having a healthy meal, not going to bed hungry, wearing a uniform and shoes that fit contribute to a sense of dignity and well-being that is elusive, but essential, not just for survival, but for thriving. Similarly, on that trip, we attended a wedding celebration full of joy, and again I realized, life has to go on, in spite of the daily threats of death and destruction.

I remember watching families gather on the beach for the day, preparing elaborate meals, followed by hookah as they made the best of such a bad situation, not letting the reality of the ongoing captivity interfere with living.

In 2002, we were unable to go to the beach at all due to the presence of the Gush Katif settlement and over 20,000 Israeli soldiers. After they had left in 2005, Gazans were once again able to enjoy the shoreline, as they have few other outlets, living as they do in the most densely populated place in the world. Drinking Arabic coffee at a "resort" in southern Gaza in April, watching my uncle proudly ride a camel on the beach, made me feel like I was on vacation in the Mediterranean. We were so happy at that moment. Later, visiting the fields in eastern Gaza, smelling the jasmine and orange blossoms, reminded me of my father, who once had a farm of his own in Southern California. His whole life was an attempt to recreate the beauty of Gaza.

On that trip in 2013, my sister and I decided to approach Gaza from a different perspective, that is, as a destination of immense historical interest, both in ancient and modern times. With the help of local guides (relatives, once again) we sought out and found amazing places, like a Turkish bath from the Ottoman period that is still in use in Gaza City, an ancient Byzantine monastery (St. Hilarion), buildings from the time of the Crusades, one of the oldest mosques in the world (Omari), to name a few. Often, people think of Gaza only in terms of war, hardship and misery but, through the challenges, the people there find opportunities to laugh, love and give of themselves. Their rich history, abiding faith, and endurance enable them to see beyond the limitations of their present circumstances—though there should be no mistaking the degree of hardship faced both by the people of Gaza and their sisters and brothers under occupation in the rest of Palestine.

Watching horrific crimes perpetrated against our people while we live in comparative luxury, creates survivor's guilt, which many seek to assuage through charitable giving. We often struggle with the concern that we are just applying a band aid, when the real problem of the Occupation has to be addressed in order for the humanitarian catastrophe to end. We agree with that perspective but remain drawn to the reality that helping a child survive today means she will be able to thrive tomorrow and will be ready to do her part to end the Occupation. I once read an article featuring a business leader engaged in philanthropic work, who said something like "If you can't provide help on a large scale, why bother?" I have thought of that often, wondering if what we are doing on a small scale with a modest budget is truly making a difference in the larger struggle, overall. But I cannot underestimate the impact of the generosity of our donors that is expressed with love and support for the people of Palestine.

Each year brings different struggles and new obstacles in providing humanitarian support, but they are nothing in comparison to the hurdles Palestinians face on a daily basis. We have to do our part on multiple levels whether in raising awareness, speaking up, providing support, lobbying members of Congress and more. The struggle continues.

NORA LESTER MURAD *is an anti-Zionist Jew from the United States. Her books,* Rest in My Shade *(2018) and* I Found Myself in Palestine *(2020), were published by Interlink and her children's novel is forthcoming in 2022. Nora teaches international humanitarian studies at Fordham University, drawing on the 13 years she has worked as an aid accountability activist in Palestine. Nora organizes with Defund Newton Police and cares deeply about racism, debt, displacement, climate and other urgent threats to humanity and nature. She is the loving mother of three brilliant Palestinian-American daughters and lives with her husband on Pawtucket and Massachusett land.*

# AIDING LIBERATION

*Nora Lester Murad*

AFTER EVERY military escalation, I am bombarded with requests for suggestions about how people can send money to Palestine—and Palestinians do need money. The Gaza Strip, for example, is cut off geographically from the rest of historic Palestine and is denied access to most of Palestine's rich human and natural resources. Gazans have endured the collective punishment of an Israeli-Egyptian blockade since 2007, which has ravaged local agriculture and fishing and ruined export-import activities. In violation of Palestinian human rights, the blockade and occupation have severely restricted the mobility needed for healthcare, education, and industry. Palestinians in Gaza suffered major destructive Israeli aggressions in 2008, 2012, 2014 and 2021 that killed thousands, demolished housing and other infrastructure, and deeply damaged the population's mental health.

However, is sending money to US Friends of UNRWA, a US fundraising and advocacy group, the same as giving to UNRWA, the United Nations agency? Is giving to UNRWA the same as giving directly to a women's committee in a refugee camp? Is supporting healthcare through the UK-nonprofit Medical Aid to Palestinians the same as supporting healthcare through the Ramallah-based Palestinian Medical Relief Society?[30] Is it the same as supporting health by sending money to activists who directly help families whose homes have been demolished?

Clearly, throwing money at Palestine any which way is not the answer. The Occupied Palestinian Territory (OPT) is already among the largest per capita recipients of non-military international aid in the world. More than US $40 billion in aid since the signing of the Oslo Accords in 1993 has not protected Palestinians from harm. It has not led to statehood or achieved "development," or

30 Palestinian Medical Relief Society, http://www.pmrs.ps/

advanced independence, whether economic or political. And it has certainly not resulted in liberation. On the contrary, in the context of international aid, human rights, like the right to shelter, become subject to negotiation, programatization, and postponement. While it is true that taxpayer-funded bilateral and multilateral aid has kept Palestinians alive, Israel has been the largest beneficiary. International aid lets Israel off the hook for its obligations to Palestinians under international humanitarian law. In fact, it subsidizes the occupation,[31] and facilitates Israel's ongoing violations of Palestinian rights.[32] International aid has also fostered the development of the Palestinian Authority into a militarized security apparatus that works to ensure Israel's continued dominance.[33]

I partnered with Palestinian aid critics when I founded Aid Watch Palestine in 2014. Aid Watch Palestine was a community-driven aid accountability initiative in Gaza with the intention of transforming the relationship between Palestinian beneficiaries and donors of charity into one between rights-holders and duty-bearers. Aid Watch Palestine was informed by years of experience trying and failing to improve the international aid system. It has been 15 years since I started working with Palestinians to highlight the unintended consequences of the way international actors gave aid. When no one listened, we moved on to giving them examples of how they could do aid better. When no one responded, we called upon aid actors to comply with their own principles, declarations, and

---

31 Shir Hever, "How Much International Aid to Palestinians Ends Up in the Israeli Economy?" *Aid Watch,* September 2015, https://www.shirhever.com/wp-content/uploads/2018/01/InternationalAidToPalestiniansFeedsTheIsraeliEconomy.pdf

32 Nora Lester Murad, "Donor Complicity in Israel's Violations of Palestinian Rights," *Al-Shabaka: Palestinian Policy Network,* October 24, 2014, https://al-shabaka.org/briefs/donor-complicity-in-israels-violations-of-palestinian-rights/.

33 Yara Hawari (host), "Palestinian Securitization vs Liberation with Alaa Tartir," *Rethinking Palestine* podcast, https://podcasts.apple.com/us/podcast/palestinian-securitization-vs-liberation-alaa-tartir/id1537774938?i=1000529683048.

commitments. We evoked international law. We mobilized people to pressure aid actors. We linked our cause with others around the world who see international aid in its current state as an imperialist tool that maintains, rather than challenges, the dominance of the global north over the global south. However, nothing we did seemed to mitigate the aid-provision process or reverse the harm Palestinians experienced from international aid.[34] I ended up believing that the only way for Palestinians to claim power from international aid actors was for them to reject aid completely and only accept support from true allies.[35] Other than a noble but imperfect boycott of conditional aid in 2005 that was renewed in 2014,[36] Palestinians have not taken this tack.

In response to requests from friends for suggestions, I have tried to develop a set of guidelines to help "true allies" make their giving decisions. I suggested they prioritize grassroots groups over nonprofit organizations, Palestinian groups over international NGOs and I encouraged them to commit to giving regularly, and as a part of political action rather than as a substitute for it. I, myself, have integrated giving into my life with commitments to people in Gaza, Syria, and Lebanon, along with supporting formerly incarcerated people, housing insecure people and people without documents in the United States, where I live.

Unfortunately, giving to Palestinians has been intentionally made hard. The US-led "war on terror" targets Muslim communities

---

34 Nora Lester Murad, "Putting Aid on Trial: An emerging theory of change for how Palestinians can hold international aid actors accountable to human rights obligations," in Saul Takahashi (Ed.), *Human Rights, Human Security and State Security: The Intersection* (Santa Barbara: Praeger, 2014), 163–84.

35 Nora Lester Murad, "Should Palestinians Boycott International Aid?" *The Guardian,* October 18, 2012, https://www.theguardian.com/global-development/poverty-matters/2012/oct/18/should-palestinians-boycott-international-aid

36 See Palestinian NGO Network, "PNGO Network calls for the UN and INGOs to stand by their mandates, and hold Israel accountable for persistent IHL violations" (Position Paper), August 14, 2014, https://www.cordaid.org/media/medialibrary/2014/08/Position_Paper_14-08-14_1.pdf

and liberation movements with military, economic and political aggression. It creates disasters in places like Palestine and then obstructs people from helping the victims. Givers fear they might unwittingly give money to an identified "terrorist group" and get in trouble under US and other laws. The shocking and unjust incarceration of the "Holy Land Five"[37] is used over and over by international humanitarian and philanthropic organizations to justify denial or distortion of assistance to Palestinians. Moreover, increasing bureaucratization of these racist laws has resulted in deplatforming, delisting and other administrative tactics that probably do little to prevent funding for political violence but definitely make it hard for legitimate groups to raise money for humanitarian work, to say nothing of actual liberation movements. Want to send money to Gaza? Gazans who are lucky enough to have a PayPal account find them arbitrarily canceled without recourse. Western Union regularly rejects transfers without explanation. If a giver regularly sends money to areas considered risky, they are likely to find their sending privileges canceled. Palestinian groups cannot set up a GoFundMe campaign because they do not have bank accounts in the US. They cannot get onto Global Giving unless they are registered by Israel or the Palestinian Authority (both of which are subject to political approval), and also have a US fiscal sponsor willing to risk investigation by the IRS and FBI.

For these reasons, international organizations are very attractive to givers. They have legal and regulatory standing and may be certified by watchdog groups. They have websites with compelling photos. Their materials use good English grammar and demonstrate a history of "legitimate" partnerships, evoking credibility and trust. They also take credit cards and, in many cases, offer tax deductibility. Perhaps most importantly, they make givers feel like they are making a difference.

---

37 See "USA v. Holy Land Foundation for Relief and Development," *Charity and Security Network,* August 24, 2020, https://charityandsecurity.org/litigation/holy-land-foundation/

But institutionalized philanthropy is also problematic. Grassroots activists, like those featured in the classic anthology, *The Revolution Will Not Be Funded*[38] have exposed how institutionalized philanthropy uses legal, administrative, and normative control to undermine social movements, depoliticize community work, co-opt communities' achievements, distort narratives, disempower poor people, and perpetuate inequality, among other things. Alternative approaches are gaining some traction within the aid and philanthropic industries,[39] but options are severely constrained in capitalist economies where money is considered private property, not a shared good. People end up expending energy trying to convince rich and powerful people to be more generous, and the best outcome we can hope for is a behemoth like the William and Melinda Gates Foundation that does much good while consolidating power over the global health system in the hands of two people (literally) who are not even affected by the work they fund.

Recognizing the problems inherent in international aid and institutionalized philanthropy, I worked with a group of Palestinians to found Dalia Association, Palestine's community foundation, in 2007. Our idea was to replace international aid with Palestinian resources, both financial and non-financial. We believed that community-controlled grantmaking that was transparent, democratic, and accountable, could support a vibrant, independent, and accountable Palestinian civil society. Although the grant amounts were very small, unrestricted support enabled communities to pursue their own priorities rather than jump through hoops to access highly project-tied money that was pre-packaged to advance donors' interests from the get-go.

Dalia Association's experience showed that Palestinian control over their own resources is transformational, but in our view that

---

38 Incite! Women of Color Against Violence (eds.), *The Revolution Will Not Be Funded: Beyond the Non-Profit Industrial Complex* (Cambridge, MA: South End Press, 2007).

39 See *How Matters*, https://www.how-matters.org/ and Global Fund Community Foundations, https://globalfundcommunityfoundations.org/, last accessed October 1, 2021.

does not imply an obligation to provide unconditional support to all Palestinians and all Palestinian activities. This would imply that any kind of support to Palestinians is good and righteous, no matter who it is sent to and no matter what they do with it. We, who dream of liberation, must acknowledge that Palestinians are as diverse as any other group. There are Palestinians who build organic farms and those who invest in agribusiness pesticides. There are Palestinians, like my friend Fatima, who pride themselves on making every tank of water last and others who … "fight for the right to waste as much water as the Israelis."[40] If Palestinians end up with a state that is racist, sexist, extractive and militaristic, it will not mean they "self-determined" that outcome and that we should respect it unconditionally. It will mean that Palestinian capitalists succeeded in conspiring to trample the forces of liberation in their own community.

Do non-Palestinians only stand in solidarity with the struggle against Israeli settler colonialism? Or must we recognize that the struggle for actual liberation is bigger than statehood? Does our understanding of liberation include a critique of racial capitalism and neoliberal globalization and the ways they, too, perpetuate exploitation, inequality, and injustice? If so, how should liberation-minded activists interact with Palestinians whose interests diverge, like those who aspire to build a Palestine that is allied with US and European corporate interests or those who want to establish another Islamic state?

The question is not theoretical. In country after country around the globe, people have risen up against their oppressors, only to find religious and military dictatorships or corrupt, US-chosen "representatives" in their place. We need not look further than the Arab Spring to see that unity *against* oppression is not the same as unity *for* a shared vision of a better world. There is also the case of South Africa, which achieved political equality but found it incomplete without economic equality. Palestinian movements,

40 A quote by Clemens Messerschmidt, a Ramallah-based water activist. His articulation of how international aid undermines Palestinians' water rights is expressed in the German documentary, *Aid But No State,* among other sources.

coming after decades of anti-colonial independence movements around the world, have the benefit of learning from that history. It is not only the ends of movements that matter, but also the means. It is the principles and practices developed in the *process* of struggle (for example, leadership of young women) that will manifest in post-colonial institutions.

This is not to say that Palestinians are not ready for independence or that the resolution of internal struggles is a prerequisite for defeating Israeli colonization! It simply means that blindly throwing money at Palestinians is not a neutral stance. Like it or not, money we give supports certain interests and strengthens certain groups at the expense of others. However, here there is a BIG RED FLAG! Without understanding how "help" is embedded in systems of economic and political oppression, we risk replicating oppressive dynamics in our solidarity efforts. For example, when potential givers say, "I will support Palestinians only when they renounce violence," or "I will support Palestinians only when they denounce Hamas," or "I will support Palestinians only when they stand up against anti-Semitism," this is not actually giving. This is using money as a form of control. Like international aid and institutionalized philanthropy, neocolonial giving is not liberatory and should be resisted.

Those of us who stand in solidarity must listen to Palestinians' nuanced analyses of what kind of help is actually helpful. Just this year, three important events call us to upgrade our solidarity with Palestinians, including the role of financial support in that solidarity. In May 2021, the escalation of violence against the Gaza Strip pushed awareness of Israeli human rights violations into the mainstream in the United States, Europe and elsewhere. It made criticism of Israel more acceptable (though also triggering massive backlash). It brought the suffering of Gazans into the headlines, at least temporarily. At the same time, ongoing attempts at dispossession and expulsion of families in Sheikh Jarrah, Jerusalem strengthened unity of Palestinians across Israeli-imposed fragmented geographies and moved the frontlines into unlikely places like Nazareth, Lod, Akka and Haifa. The brave, compelling and charismatic leadership of Mohammad and Muna al-Kurd captured attention around the world, highlighting Palestine as a cause to be supported, not as a charity to be funded. In fact, the Kurds explicitly called on supporters not to send money but to come to Sheikh Jarrah to protect, bear witness and participate in resistance on the ground. Soon after, the danger of the aid-funded Palestinian Authority (PA) was brought into stark relief. Not only did the PA apparently murder critic, Nizar Banat, while in custody, the PA reacted to popular discontent with violent suppression, including the targeting of women. For many, this was a wake-up call.

So, while giving can build Palestinian self-determination and the sustainability of local civil society and, while small, unrestricted amounts of money can have tremendous impact when Palestinians themselves decide how to use it, money simply is not enough. What Palestinians and many other oppressed people really need is political solidarity. I remember speaking to my friend, Hamada, in Gaza during the bombing in 2012. Desperate to show support, I told him that Gazans were not forgotten for a second and that people were anxious to help. I mentioned that you could not pass a street corner in Ramallah without seeing a clothing drive for Gaza. Hamada surprised us both by erupting: "For goodness sake, don't send clothes! Get them to stop dropping bombs on us!"

If we listen to Palestinians, we will hear them say that folks in the global north, and especially in the United States and Europe, must demand that our elected officials stop unconditional support for Israeli actions and, instead, hold Israel politically accountable. We will hear them tell us to incorporate Boycott, Divestment and Sanctions into our daily lives so there is economic pressure on Israel to stop violations of Palestinian human rights. We will hear them implore us to speak out through the media, our faith groups, in schools and in every way possible to challenge problematic narratives that undermine Palestinian humanity.

When we do send money, it should be a long-term investment in movements and direct aid to people in struggle so they can remain steadfast. Palestinians need money for food, medicine, shelter, services, and to maintain institutions. As they say, "existence is resistance." Palestinians need and deserve consistent, reliable, and sufficient support prior to escalations, not one-off, non-strategic contributions motivated by guilt. I remember trying to raise money for Gaza on the occasion of my 50th birthday. I released a videotaped interview with a Gazan every day for 30 days in the run-up to my birthday in May, but only raised a couple of thousand dollars, most of which came from my mother, Kathie. The idea that money given before an escalation could go farther was not convincing. A few months later, during the 2014 Israeli attack on Gaza, everyone wanted to give. This kind of reactive giving is not liberatory.

Liberatory giving is committed, explicitly political, grounded in mutual relationships and part and parcel of political solidarity, not a replacement for it. Mutual aid is a great example of liberatory giving. US-based mutual aid influencer, Dean Spade, identified three key elements of mutual aid:

> Mutual aid projects work to meet survival needs and build shared understanding about why people do not have what they need.
> Mutual aid projects mobilize people, expand solidarity, and build movements.
> Mutual aid projects are participatory, solving problems through collective action rather than waiting for saviors.[41]

It is critical to highlight the concept of mutuality in "mutual aid." Breaking the hierarchy between givers and receivers requires us all to become givers and for us all to become receivers. I must not covet and possess that feeling of worth I get when I help others. To give is to be human and everyone has a right to give. For this to happen, I must develop my ability to receive. I credit my friend, Katsuko, for showing me how dehumanizing it is when I insist on always paying for lunch or rush to "pay off" a gift with a reciprocal gift because the feeling of being indebted to others is uncomfortable.

---

41 Dean Spade, *Mutual Aid: Building Solidarity During This Crisis (and the Next).* (London: Verso Books, 2020).

To be interdependent is to sink into our indebtedness, to give equal value to what others give to us.

Although the Covid-19 pandemic has brought renewed visibility to the ways we help one another through disasters, the traditions and practices of sharing are long and deep. Indigenous and other collectivist cultures resist efforts to obliterate their ways of living that are grounded in interdependence. Many of these values were incorporated into third world liberation movements in the 1950s and 1960s but, with the absence of a viable counterweight to capitalist hegemony, a lot of internationalist and anti-imperialist solidarity among oppressed societies has eroded or become distorted by institutionalization.

In the Palestinian context, mutual aid often looks like *Al-Ouna*, the Palestinian cultural tradition of volunteerism that recognizes well-being as a collective pursuit[42] and is often credited as the reason why Palestinians have survived decades of dispossession, colonization, and occupation. Palestinians cite the First Intifada as the heyday of community self-reliance, which enables political expression that is untainted by pragmatism. For this reason, colonial narratives seek to erase this Palestinian history and make people forget that they were not always dependent. Mutual aid and other non- or anti-capitalist movements and practices like degrowth, the commons, solidarity economies, sharing economies, etc.,[43] offer alternatives to both international aid and the nonprofit industrial complex. They encourage us to share resources with others because we understand need as a product of failed systems that threaten us all.

Reparations are a logical corollary. The movement for Black Lives, for example, calls on governments, corporations and other institutions to repair harm for past and ongoing harms with a range

---

42 Aisha Mansour, "Before Neoliberal Economics, We Had Al-Ouna: Concerns of a Citizen," Dalia Association, October 30, 2015, https://www.dalia.ps/content/neoliberal-economics-we-had-al-ouna

43 See Corinna Bukhart, Matthias Schmelzer, and Nina Treu (eds.), *Degrowth in Movement(s): Exploring Pathways for Transformation* (London: Zero Books, 2020).

of corrective measures that include the redistribution of wealth.[44] Activist groups, like Resource Generation, organize people with unearned wealth to relinquish money and power as a form of voluntary reparations.[45] What is common to these practices is an understanding that not only is the receiver of aid socially located within systems of oppression, but so is the giver. In other words, once I admit that others are needy because of unfair systems, I must admit that I have surplus because of those same unfair systems. Giving is not only a means to transform the conditions of the receiver, but also a means to liberate the giver.

Expressions of the Palestinian liberatory imagination abound and provide hope: Palestinian farming,[46] contemporary dance,[47] sustainable living[48] community building[49] and even parkour,[50] among many others. Despite this inspiration, my giving does not always flow smoothly; it still has to be conscious and intentional. I grew up in California in a culture that values individual advancement and the acquisition of stuff. There is an implicit belief that if you have money, you are smart and have achieved something good. On the other hand, if you do not have money, you have failed and somehow deserve your lot. Activists continue to push open space for discussions about our economic system, the historical context, and the notion that equality

---

44 See M4BL, "Reparations," last accessed October 1, 2021, https://m4bl.org/policy-platforms/reparations/

45 See "Sign the Redistribution Pledge," Resource Generation, last accessed October 1, 2021, https://resourcegeneration.org/redistribution-pledge/

46 "Liberating Farming, Agriculture for Liberation," webinar (Arabic), last accessed October 1, 2021 at https://www.palestine-studies.org/en/node/1651375,

47 See Stereo48 Dance Company, https://www.stereo48.com/, last accessed October 1, 2021.

48 See The Palestine Institute for Biodiversity and Sustainability (PIBS) and the Palestine Museum of Natural History (PMNH) at https://www.palestinenature.org/, last accessed October 1, 2021.

49 See Mariam Al-Asturlabi on *Instagram* @astrolabedemariem, last accessed October 1, 2021, https://www.instagram.com/astrolabedemariem/

50 See Aljazeera English, "Parkour offers freedom to Gaza youth," *YouTube*, January 23, 2019, https://www.youtube.com/watch?v=TLgPYKhdRD0.

is good for everyone, including those who currently profit from our existing system. Yet, I still get scared, sometimes, when I give away money. I fear that if I give away too much, I will become insecure, poor, unable to take care of myself and my family, that I will die alone. I understand how hard it is to trust that if we take care of someone else today, someone will step up to take care of us tomorrow.

Palestinians have helped me to become a braver and more politically strategic giver. I was a sophomore at the University of California at Los Angeles when I discovered that, as a Jew, I am implicated in the oppression of Palestinians. To learn more, I spent my junior year living with Palestinians at the American University in Cairo and my senior year with Palestinians at Hebrew University in Jerusalem. I learned about politics, and I also learned about giving. I vividly remember being back in my room at the housing cooperative in Los Angeles where I lived, after my two years living in the Arab world. There was a knock at the door and my mind bifurcated into my old self and my new self. My old self wanted to put away the cookies I was eating before I opened the door, because it would be rude to eat in front of a guest. My new self wanted to put the cookies on a plate and make tea so that I could show respect to the person who was visiting. This understanding of giving as an expression of humanity has developed into a way-of-living that is not about helping others but, rather, about creating the world I want to live in, by living it.

Liberatory aid is more complicated than just sending money, but it is also very simple. It includes the incorporation of radical love[51] into our solidarity. In the early 1980s, I was a volunteer proof-reader for a Palestinian, English-language newspaper in Jerusalem called "Al-Fajr." I remember going with a reporter to interview a young woman named Viola, who had been released from jail. It was before the First Intifada when Palestinian women regularly led resistance activities. In her living room, packed with neighbors and activists welcoming her home, Viola said that, when she was arrested

---

51 See bell hooks, "Love as the Practice of Freedom" (6 pages), last accessed October 1, 2021 at https://uucsj.org/wp-content/uploads/2016/05/bell-hooks-Love-as-the-Practice-of-Freedom.pdf.

by the Israelis, her greatest fear was not that she had been tortured but that her father would find out that she had been organizing with men. She inspired me. When the crowd left, I confided in Viola that I would be returning to the United States soon and worried that I would not be able to find a way to continue supporting the Palestinian cause. She dismissed my concerns. "Teach a person to read," she said. "Liberate your neighbor. Liberate yourself. That is the best way to help Palestinians." All these years later, I still ground myself in the belief that everyone's liberation is tied up with everyone else's. This means that the possibilities to advance Palestinian liberation are as infinite as they are compelling.[52]

---

52 I thank Jimmy Dunson from Mutual Aid Disaster Relief; Lama Amr from Build Palestine; and Muna Dajani, a Palestinian academic, for helping me to articulate my ideas. Anna Levy helped me analyze tax documents. I thank the many generous and courageous activists who have helped me over the years to become a better giver. I thank my daughters, Serene, Jassi and Maysanne for giving me reasons to keep up the good fight.

PROFESSOR ILAN PAPPÉ *was born in Haifa in 1954 and graduated from the Hebrew University in Jerusalem in 1979 and completed his PhD at the university of Oxford, Britain in 1984. Pappé was a lecturer in the department of political science at the University of Haifa from 1984 to 2006 and was forced to leave due to his support for the Palestinian cause. He was also at that time the director of the Emil Touma Institute for Palestinian Studies in Haifa (2000–2006).*

*Since 2007, Pappé is the director of the European Centre for Palestine Studies at the University of Exeter, Britain. He is the author of 20 books, among them* The Ethnic Cleansing of Palestine *and* On Palestine *with Noam Chomsky.*

# THE INTERNATIONAL STRUGGLE ON BEHALF OF PALESTINE

*Ilan Pappé*

*"International solidarity is not an act of charity: It is an act of unity between allies fighting on different terrains toward the same objective. The foremost of these objectives is to aid the development of humanity to the highest level possible."*

—SAMORA MACHEL

*"These men, women and children whose lives are massacred in the struggle for liberation are in Vietnam, in Laos, in Khmer, in Thailand; they are in Palestine, in the Sinai Peninsula and other Arab lands under Zionist occupation."*

—OLIVER TAMBO'S CALL ON MK'S TENTH ANNIVERSARY, 16 DECEMBER 1961

OVER THE YEARS, as an activist in the international solidarity movement for Palestine, I learned three major lessons. First, that a life of activism on behalf of the Palestinian cause is a journey on parallel routes. This is particularly true for an Israeli Jew, like me. One journey is out of Zionism and its comfort zone; the second is a journey of winning the trust of your Palestinian friends and assuring them that you are a genuine supporter and the last one is trying to take your own compatriots on these journeys that you, yourself, have undertaken.

Another feature of activism and, in particular, international activism on behalf of Palestine, is the tension between effort and tangible results. This could be quite frustrating, given the lack of any significant change on the ground in Palestine; if anything, the situation there has grown worse over the years. Most solidarity activists deal with this frustration by focusing less on how much they have achieved and focus more on asking themselves if they have done enough for the cause they believe in.

Finally, you learn something about the true meaning of solidarity. First, by learning its genealogy and history—and there is no better guide than the anti-apartheid solidarity movement in South Africa. International solidarity with the ANC was paramount in the struggle to topple apartheid, as was the support many African states in the newly decolonized continent gave the ANC in the 1970s, a time long forgotten, when these new African states also led the support for the Palestinian struggle at the UN, culminating in the UN General Assembly resolution equating Zionism with racism. This was revoked in 1991 due to American pressure.

Learning about the true nature of solidarity is something you cannot learn theoretically or study in a university: you need to experience it through your own activism. It involves understanding fully the difference between pity, empathy, solidarity and advocacy. What it boils down to is a full understanding that you have to listen to liberation movements and the colonized people and learn what they need from you and not preach to them what they should do. This does not mean there is no room for criticism and an honest dialogue; neither does this stance help much to overcome the lack of a present clear orientation of the liberation movement and its chronic disunity. However, in the need of the day, you grasp fully what solidarity means and you become useful and important to the overall struggle. Indeed, for me this was a personal journey of learning, and un-learning, which began in the late 1970s and continues to this day.

## The History of the Solidarity Movement

The world at large, governments and societies alike, was quite indifferent to the Palestinian plight in the early years after the *Nakba*. This crime against humanity was hardly acknowledged, recorded, or condemned. The early signs of solidarity could be detected in the Arab world and the colonized world of Asia and Africa. Solidarity with the Palestinians was first led by Gamal Abdel Nasser, the Egyptian President, and then by anti-colonialist liberation movements all over the Arab world, Africa, and Asia (and a decade later, also in Central and South America). In the Arab world, solidarity was sustained through a network of trade unions, students, and people from every walk of life, who identified with the Palestinian struggle and with the new body leading it in the 1960s, the PLO. After 1967, the traditional Left in the West began to sober up and understand that its enthusiasm about Israel as a socialist paragon was misplaced and it joined the solidarity movement (it is not surprising that, in the UK until 1967, the pro-Israeli lobby was led by the Left of the Labor party and the pro-Palestinian one by the right wing of that party, with allies in the Conservative and Liberal parties).

The international solidarity movement in the West, as we know it today, had its roots in the post-1967 period. Western public opinion seemed to be oblivious to the *Nakba*, the suffering of the refugees and the victimization of the Palestinians in Israel (who were under a cruel military rule until 1966). However, the occupation of the West Bank and the Gaza Strip and the emergence of the PLO as a classical anti-colonialist movement of liberation caused a dramatic shift in the attitude of many in European and American societies. For a while, it even seemed that some of the governments, in particular Britain, France, and the Scandinavian countries, were willing to pressure Israel to withdraw from the West Bank and the Gaza Strip; but this willingness soon petered out under American pressure (where AIPAC made itself felt as potent actor in American politics). Support for Palestine in the West now moved to the public and remains there to this day.

There was a difference between the solidarity of the Left and the support in some liberal circles in the West. The Left identified the Palestinian struggle with anti-colonialism and saw itself as part of a network between the Left in Europe and the anti-colonialist movements around the world. Thus, the Left accepted the legitimacy of the armed struggle alongside the political one, while among liberals, it was easier to voice support after Fatah adopted its plan to pursue liberation in stages (its willingness to accept at least as a first step—the two states solution)—in particular, after Arafat's famous 1975 speech at the UN when he held an olive branch next to a pistol as a symbol of the options, and his willingness to join the diplomatic effort. As a result of this support, the PLO in the early 1970s was able to open legations in many parts of the world and, unlike today, they were the principal address for the solidarity movement.

Thus, by 1975, for the first time since 1948, there was a visible section within global civil society that openly supported the PLO's demand to be recognized as the sole and legitimate representative of the Palestinian people (there was less talk about a solution per se, as the powers that be were not as yet discussing in full the two states solution—as readers will remember, until the fall of the Labor party in Israel in 1977, the "peace" talks centered on the "Jordanian option" (annexing part of the West Bank to Jordan), and after the rise of the Likud to power, the conversation was about Palestinian autonomy in the Occupied Territories, both avenues rejected by the PLO.

In many ways, in the 1970s, the counter coalition for Palestine was centered in the non-Western world, where liberated African countries did not miss its comparison with the struggle for a free South Africa. The result was the support these countries gave at the UN to the 1975 resolution equating Zionism with racism.

This enthusiastic network of solidarity was replaced by a short period of despair after 1982, such a year of disaster that, sometimes, its catastrophic impact on the liberation movement is forgotten or dwarfed. The PLO was exiled far away from Palestine, and an uneasy period of internal struggles ensued which did not help the solidarity movement to have a clear orientation.

## Joining the Solidarity Movement

This was the time I began my long journey out of Zionism to full activism on behalf of the Palestinian cause. I arrived in Britain in 1980 as a Ph.D. student at the University of Oxford; under the supervision of a pro-Palestinian supervisor, the famous Lebanese historian, Albert Hourani, I began exploring the archival material about the 1948 *Nakba* in various places. This was my first station out of Zionism, a process that did not occur in a day, but started more or less there, where what I found in the archives contradicted everything I knew about 1948, and the outbreak of the first Israeli assault on Lebanon in the summer of 1982. Only outside of Israel was I able to connect the dots and see the bigger picture that led from the 1948 massacres to the 1982 massacres of Palestinians in Lebanon. The same ideology was behind both sets of atrocities and crimes against humanity. Once you realize this nexus between ideology and praxis, there is no way back. With every passing day, my doubts about Zionism grew and I challenged openly its moral validity and that of its projects in historical Palestine.

What I encountered in the early 1980s in Britain, many others in the West experienced elsewhere, in particular in the USA. Identifying with the Palestinian cause was still irregular, equated with support for terrorism on the one hand but, on the other hand, at least in certain circles—among trade unions, academia, and ordinary people—the pendulum began to shift. The quantum leap, in this respect, was the global reaction to the sights and sounds of the First Intifada of 1987.

The images from the uprising and the relative ease by which activists from abroad could reach the Occupied West Bank and Gaza Strip (until 2000), provided more depth to the solidarity movement. The solidarity movement found it much more difficult to operate after the Second Intifada which erupted in 2000. Conversely, at that very time, the solidarity movement became more institutionalized, which was manifested by the founding, in August 2001, of the official International Solidarity Movement (ISM). It was a Palestinian-led movement consisting of groups of activists around the world who wished to do more than demonstrate or be active on the Internet. They became volunteers, arrived in Palestine with the aim of helping the Palestinians to defend their olive groves, protect their school runs and defend their homes and businesses from the Jewish settlers' violence and the army's brutality.

The ISM was a precursor of a much larger and informal network of solidarity that sprang to life in this century. One after another, various Palestine solidarity committees or campaigns (PSCs), sometimes under such a name, sometimes under a similar name, emerged in many parts of the world. This development coincided with a formative period in my own activism. On several fronts, while I was still a faculty member of an Israeli university, it became clear to me that genuine anti-Zionist solidarity with the Palestinian struggle would be nearly impossible from within the Israeli academia. You lose your job when you do that and, if you do not lose your job, it probably means you are doing it wrong. The developments elsewhere meant that, no matter how alone you were in some of the struggles from within, you were part of an ever-growing network of solidarity you fully identified with.

Processing the knowledge, on the one hand, that you would not be able to be part of the local academia and that you should work from the outside, on the other, takes a bit of time and only by 2006 had this process matured. I left Israel and began teaching in the UK at a time when a new dimension was added to the international solidarity movement with Palestine: the Boycott, Divestment and Sanctions movement (BDS).

## The Role of the BDS Movement

This movement was born in 2005 as a response to a call by Palestinian civil society, represented by more than 100 NGOs from all over historical Palestine and by Palestinian communities from around the world, demanding pressure on Israel through these three means—boycott, divestment and sanctions—until it respects the three basic rights of the Palestinians:

the right of the refugees to return,

the right of the people of the West Bank and the Gaza Strip to live free of military occupation and

the right of the Palestinians in Israel to live in equality.

At a time of disunity in the Palestinian polity and when it is clear that there is very little chance for change within Israel, the position of the world public opinion has become a crucial factor providing encouragement to the Palestinian cause as Palestinians face one of their most difficult moments in history. The BDS campaign gives this international community a focal point and a sense of purpose. It has snowballed into an impressive movement of protest, with famous artists refusing to perform in Israel, students' unions severing ties with institutions in Israel, and even big companies withdrawing their contracts from the Jewish settlements in the Occupied West Bank, while trade unions have withdrawn funds and investment form Israeli companies.

I moved to teach in the UK a year later and became deeply involved in the actions of the BDS and contributed, I hope, through my scholarly work to the making of a new vocabulary on Palestine that equated Zionism with settler colonialism, framed the *Nakba* as ethnic cleansing and substituted the call for peace with a demand for decolonization. In this new dictionary, Israel was no longer "the only democracy in the Middle East" but, rather, an apartheid state. All these new entries in the new vocabulary were presented, not just as political positions, but as findings of academic work and research.

In order to enhance the role, not only of academics but also of the academia itself in the struggle for justice and liberation in Palestine, I founded, in 2007, the European Centre for Palestine Studies—the first center of this kind within an academic institute in the West. There are now several such centers. Such centers seek to provide a safe space for writing on Palestine for postgraduate students and provide a hub for joint academic work on various aspects of Palestine past, present and future.

As could have been anticipated, the pro-Israeli lobby in Britain did all it could to foil the project, but my university was steadfast and did not cave into intimidation and pressure. Now, academic research and student activism in campuses are going hand in hand. In 2010, students all over the world organized the Israeli Apartheid Week, with the first recorded event at the University of Toronto, Canada. Thereafter, all over the world, once a year, a whole week is devoted to lectures, workshops and exhibitions on Palestine, stressing the fact that the *Nakba* is ongoing. The campuses have become hubs of pro-Palestinian activity, with a younger generation, willing to commit itself to the struggle emerging, including formerly pro-Israel Jewish students.

Again, as anticipated, Israel has reacted with vehemence. To this very day, Israel tries to encourage legislation in the West against the BDS. It has also established a special ministry, the Ministry for Strategic Affairs, to which it has accorded a huge budget to fight what Israel called the "delegitimization" of the Jewish state. This ministry employs networks of students and activists to challenge the pro-Palestinian activity on the ground and on the internet and tries, unsuccessfully, to commodify Israel as an oasis of human rights in the midst of a "barbaric" Middle East. The TV series, *The Lobby*, screened by Al-Jazeera, exposed only the tip of the iceberg when examining how the Israeli embassy was involved in smear campaigns against pro-Palestinian politicians and activists.[53]

The last few years, namely from around 2015 onwards, have seen the slow but steady influence the solidarity movement has had on politics from above. For the first time, leading candidates in the USA and Britain openly endorsed a pro-Palestinian stance, at least as far as the basic rights of the Palestinians for self-determination and statehood were concerned. The election of Jeremy Corbyn as leader of the Labor party and the high-profile candidacy of Bernie Sanders for the presidency, despite their failure eventually to win the desired positions of Prime Minister and President respectively, indicate that the pro-Palestine solidarity movement now includes members of the political elite. This also included the election to the House of Representatives of Alexandria Ocasio-Cortez, Ilhan Omar and Rashida Tlaib.

## Conclusion: The Struggle for International Legitimacy

Looking back at the solidarity movement in the last 50 years or so, one can have a good idea of its major contribution to the struggle for freedom and liberation of Palestine. To appreciate it fully, one should explain the difference between International Law and International Legitimacy. International Law is a set of clear international conventions and UN resolutions that may not have a

53 Al Jazeera Investigative Unit, "The Lobby Part 1: Young Friends of Israel," *Aljazeera,* January 10, 2017, last accessed October 11, 2021 https://www.aljazeera.com/program/investigations/2017/1/10/the-lobby-young-friends-of-israel-part-1

sanctioning power but are produced by legal bodies. For instance, the Palestinian Authority desperately tries to persuade these bodies to become the main tool that would help transform the reality on the ground, but to no avail.

It is much more difficult to define International Legitimacy. And, yet, we have an incisive definition offered by Martin Wright back in 1972, when he commented:

> International legitimacy is an elusive and nebulous notion, on the frontiers of morality and law. It may be briefly described as moral acceptability. Acceptability to whom?—To the remainder of international society. South Africa under apartheid provides a good example of a state whose legitimacy is doubtful. There is no question that the regime in South Africa is legal. The steps by which it has grown up have made no breach in constitutional law. But it is condemned by a consensus of international opinion, expressed in a number of resolutions by both the United Nations and the Organisation of African Unity, and leading to the withdrawal of South Africa from the Commonwealth … South Africa is a pariah state. It is not immediately to the point that she is a very prosperous pariah.

This distinction is important because of the historical context and the top-bottom approach that has turned International Law into a useless tool in challenging the ideology of Israel and, therefore, allows it to perpetuate its overall policies towards the Palestinians all over historical Palestine. This state of affairs caters well to the main defenders of the Zionist project and Israel worldwide: a group one can call diet-Zionists, or liberal-Zionists. The reluctance of International Law to engage with the ideological nature of regimes means that, whatever else might be challenged, Zionist theory and praxis would not be put on the agenda of an international jury; it would be, and is, scrutinized by the unique Palestinian concept of *al-Shariyya al-Duwaliyya,* International Legitimacy.

International Legitimacy does not have any formal bodies and does not subscribe to official conventions. In many ways, it is the distinction one should make between boycott, an act of civil society, and sanctions, an act of government, which is what the BDS is ultimately striving to achieve. In the case of South Africa, the world needed these definitions for the Apartheid regime in 1972, because the governments of the West refused to support international civil society's boycott of South Africa by applying sanctions against it (this only occurred years later). If we now substitute Israel for South Africa we can grasp the potential effectiveness of the position of international civil society in Israel's regard, making the full meaning of international legitimacy much less obscure. There are similarities with the struggle against Apartheid in South Africa, which included, at the time, public tribunals substituting for the formal International Legal one, insofar as the public felt they were not doing its required work. In the case of Palestine one such tribunal, namely the Russell Tribunal, enlisted famous human rights activists and lawyers and conducted a public trial discussing Israel's violation of civil and human rights.[54]

To judge by the Israeli reaction, it seems that struggle for legitimacy, at this point, worries them much more than the attempt to impose International Law ruling on Israel. As aforementioned, Israel has established special teams and, eventually, an entire ministry, the Ministry for Strategic Affairs, to fight against what it called "the de-legitimization of Israel" as, indeed, the state's very essence and the nature of the regime cannot be questioned by International Law but can come under such scrutiny by International Legitimacy.[55]

This is, indeed, the biggest success of the international solidarity movement to date. The insistence on justice, truth and the right of liberation should not depend on how unified the Palestinians are at this given moment, or how successful they are in the struggle

---

54 See Russell Tribunal on Palestine, http://www.russelltribunalonpalestine.com/en/

55 I have discussed this at length in my book, Ilan Pappé, *The Idea of Israel* (New York: Verso Press, 2010), 295–313.

on the ground against their mighty colonizer and the international coalition that helps it. Unity and success on the ground are the means to advance and, eventually, liberate the colonized people. The international demand for protection of their rights, their narrative and their history is a crucial dimension of the struggle against denial and in the name of human and international legitimacy.

My own modest part was, and still is, not to allow the 1948 crime against humanity that Israel perpetrated against the Palestinians to be erased from memory or distorted. This is a struggle that must still be carried on today, because despite huge steps forward, the denial is widespread and continues to play a crucial role in Israel's international immunity. This foundational crime is not acknowledged by presidents and prime ministers, governments, mainstream media or the political systems, in general. Their denial serves as the basis for Western perceptions on the Palestine issue; it is at the heart of the exceptionalism that provides Israel with impunity. International solidarity can play its role in an even more efficient way (alongside support for the BDS). My personal dream and hope, which begins to materialize as I write this piece, is to establish the first ever Center Against Nakba Denial. There are hundreds of centers against Holocaust denial, and this is good and fine, but the Palestinian struggle needs at least one against the *Nakba* denial.

Palestinians, themselves, will have to solve issues of unity and representation and chart for all of us their vision for the future and how they see the liberation project in our time. We, in the international solidarity movement, have to constantly work so that the international environment will be as conducive and supportive as it is today for Palestinian liberation on the ground, when the day for it comes—and it will come, sooner or later.

DR. RAMZY BAROUD *was born in the Nuseirat Refugee Camp in the Gaza Strip. He is a Palestinian American journalist, media consultant, author, internationally-syndicated columnist and editor of* The Palestine Chronicle. *Baroud taught mass communication at Australia's Curtin University of Technology, Malaysia Campus.*

*Baroud is the author of six books and a contributor to many others. His books include* My Father Was a Freedom Fighter: Gaza's Untold Story *and* The Last Earth: A Palestinian Story.

*Baroud has a Doctorate of Philosophy in Palestine Studies from the European Centre for Palestinian Studies at the University of Exeter and was a Non-Resident Scholar at Orfalea Center for Global and International Studies, University of California at Santa Barbara. Currently, he is a Non-Resident Senior Research Fellow at Istanbul Zaim University's Center for Islam and Global Affairs (CIGA).*

# POSTSCRIPT

THE CONTRIBUTORS to *Our Vision for Liberation* have offered herein their own vision of how to advance the Palestinian struggle, each in their own respective area of study and work. Their rich experiential insights have been further embellished by the proud legacies they have shared that, in some cases, span several generations. In light of the lessons we will have hopefully gleaned, a compelling question remains: where do we go from here?

This book is not, and was never intended to be, an alternative to a centralized Palestinian vision, one that originates from a cohesive Palestinian body politic, itself an outcome of a fair and representative democratic process. Instead, our goal has been to communicate several important messages, leading amongst them that Palestinians can and surely must speak for themselves, that their insights into the many levels of Palestinian struggle provide invaluable operational instruction to inform future efforts, and that united Palestinian political, cultural and historical discourses are achievable despite the factionalism of internal Palestinian politics and the deliberate marginalization of Palestinians regionally—whether through official Arab normalization with Israel or internationally through the disproportionate focus Israel has succeeded in bringing to bear on its "security" and its historical narrative, even as Palestinians are still denied their most basic human rights.

Our great hope is that future researchers and writers on Palestine can now appreciate the centrality of the Palestinian view in the so-called "Palestinian-Israeli conflict" or, more accurately, in the ongoing Israeli colonial project in Palestine. Telling the story of Palestine and the Palestinian people without Palestinian voices being at its core simply cannot be done. Period. Not only is denying the Palestinians a claim to their own narrative unethical, but impractical as well.

It must be emphasized that the 30 intellectuals who have contributed to this volume are but a microcosm of a much greater Palestinian intellectual phenomenon, one that can be witnessed in

Palestine, throughout the Arab world and, indeed, around the globe. When Palestinian poet, Rafeef Ziadah, wrote her seminal poem: "We Teach Life Sir," the meaning is applicable in both the realms of symbolism and tangible experience, as well. The fact that Palestinian teacher Hanan al-Hroub won the Global Teacher Prize in 2016 is but one of numerous examples of how Palestinians can extract hope from pain, and use that hope for the benefit of humanity. It is telling that al-Hroub's well-deserved award was in recognition for supporting Palestinian children traumatized by Israeli violence.

So, where do we go from here? We use this book as the beginning of a forward-thinking conversation on Palestine, led by engaged Palestinian intellectuals, whose allegiance is not to a political party or to a rigid ideology, but to the Palestinian people themselves. After all, as "Che" Guevara said many years ago, "liberators do not exist. It is the peoples who liberate themselves."

*—Ramzy Baroud*
*November 2021*

# CONTRIBUTORS

**ABDEL-FATTAH, Randa** is a Palestinian Egyptian Australian Muslim writer, academic, activist and former lawyer. She is a postdoctoral research fellow in the Department of Sociology at Macquarie University.

**ABDELFATTAH, Awad** is the Coordinator of the One Democratic State Campaign (ODSC). He is the former Secretary-General of Balad/Tajamoa party. Abdelfattah is a prominent political analyst and a speaker in various international forums.

**ABU NIMAH, Hasan Abdul-Rahim** was born in 1935, in Battir, Palestine. He is a former ambassador who has served as a Permanent Representative of Jordan to the United Nations.

**ABU SHARAR, Samaa** is an independent journalist and researcher. She heads the Majed Abu Sharar Media Foundation (MASMF), a non-governmental organization that works to empower youth in Palestinian refugee camps in Lebanon.

**AGEEL, Ghada** is a visiting Professor in the Department of Political Science at the University of Alberta, and the editor of both *Apartheid in Palestine: Hard Laws and Harder Experiences* and *Women's Voices from Gaza* series.

**AL-ARIAN, Sami A.** is the Director of the Center for Islam and Global Affairs (CIGA) and public affairs professor at Istanbul Sabahattin Zaim University. He received his Ph.D. in 1986 and was a tenured academic in the United States for many years, receiving several teaching awards and grants.

**AL-MARAYATI, Laila** is a Palestinian-American doctor, and long-time activist in the American Muslim community. She is the chair of KinderUSA, a non-profit humanitarian organization that provides health, education and other forms of assistance to Palestinian children and their families.

**ALFARRA, Jehan** is a writer, multimedia journalist and producer, covering Middle Eastern affairs and specializing in Palestinian political news and social issues.

**ALI, Qassem Izzat** is a media specialist, a founder and innovator in the television news industry.

**AOUDE, Ibrahim** is Professor of Ethnic Studies at the University of Hawai'i—Mānoa. He is the Editor of Arab Studies Quarterly and holds a Ph.D. in political science.

**BOULLATA, Terry** is a Jerusalemite who served on the boards of Jerusalem Cultural and Women's Centers in defense of cultural and women's rights.

**CHALMERS, Jan** is a nurse and embroiderer who worked for UNRWA in Gaza in 1969 and 1970. She founded the Palestinian History Tapestry Project in 2011.

**HALAWANI, Hanadi** is a prominent activist in the Old City of Jerusalem and a Quran teacher at Al-Aqsa Mosque.

**JABR, Samah** is a psychiatrist and psychotherapist living in East Jerusalem. She serves as the Head of the Mental Health Unit at the Ministry of Health in Ramallah and maintains an office practice for children and adults.

**JARRAR, Khalida** is a civil society leader, lawmaker, and human rights activist. She is a member of the Palestinian Legislative Council (PLC). She played a major role in Palestine's application to join the International Criminal Court (ICC).

**JUMAA, Jamal** was born in Jerusalem and attended Birzeit University, where he became politically active. Since the first Intifada, he has focused on grassroots activism. Jumaa is the coordinator of the Palestinian Grassroots Anti-Apartheid Wall Campaign.

**KARMI, Ghada** is a physician, academic and writer. She is a former research fellow at the Institute of Arab and Islamic Studies at the University of Exeter.

**MAJLUF ISSA, Anuar** is a Chilean lawyer of Palestinian origin who worked as executive director of the Palestinian Community of Chile until June 2021.

**MANSOUR, Johnny** is a historian from Haifa. He is a lecturer in history and political science. He has published several studies and research papers.

**MURAD, Nora Lester** is an anti-Zionist Jew from the United States. Murad is a writer, activist and educator. She teaches international humanitarian studies at Fordham University.

**MUSALLAM, Father Manuel** is a Catholic priest, political activist and writer. He is iconic in his native Palestine.

**NABULSI, Farah** is an Oscar Nominated and BAFTA Award Winning Palestinian British filmmaker and human rights advocate.

**QUMSIYEH, Mazin** is a scientist and author. He is founder and volunteer director of the Palestine Institute for Biodiversity and Sustainability (PIBS) at Bethlehem University.

**SABAWI, Samah** is a writer and scholar. She is a recipient of multiple awards including the prestigious 2020 Green Room Award for Best Writing. She received a Ph.D. from Victoria University

**SOURANI, Raji** has been an active lawyer since 1977 and has represented a wide range of victims of human rights abuses. He has received many honors during his career, the most recent of which is the "Right Livelihood Award" for 2013.

**TAHA, Hamdan** is an archeologist, an independent researcher and former Deputy Minister for Heritage in the Palestinian Ministry of Tourism and Antiquities.

**TALHAMI, Reem** is an artist, largely involved in the Palestinian cultural performing arts scene as a singer and actress.

**ZOABI, Haneen** is a political activist, a member of the National Democratic Assembly (NDA) of Tajamoa. She is the first Palestinian woman representing a Palestinian party in the Israeli Knesset (2009-2019).

# EDITORS

DR. RAMZY BAROUD was born in the Nuseirat Refugee Camp in the Gaza Strip. He is a Palestinian American journalist, media consultant, an author, internationally-syndicated columnist and editor of *The Palestine Chronicle.* Baroud taught mass communication at Australia's Curtin University of Technology, Malaysia Campus.

Baroud is the author of six books and a contributor to many others. His books include *My Father Was a Freedom Fighter: Gaza's Untold Story* and *The Last Earth: A Palestinian Story.*

Baroud has a Doctorate of Philosophy in Palestine Studies from The European Centre for Palestinian Studies at the University of Exeter and was a Non-Resident Scholar at Orfalea Center for Global and International Studies, University of California at Santa Barbara. Currently, he is a Non-Resident Senior Research Fellow at Istanbul Zaim University's Center for Islam and Global Affairs (CIGA).

PROFESSOR ILAN PAPPÉ was born in Haifa in 1954 and graduated from the Hebrew University in Jerusalem in 1979 and completed his PhD at the university of Oxford, Britain in 1984. Pappé was a lecturer in the department of political science at the University of Haifa from 1984 to 2006 and was forced to leave due to his support for the Palestinian cause. He was also at that time the director of the Emil Touma Institute for Palestinian Studies in Haifa (2000–2006).

Since 2007, Pappé is the director of The European Centre for Palestine Studies at the University of Exeter, Britain. He is the author of 20 books among them *The Ethnic Cleansing of Palestine* and *On Palestine* with Noam Chomsky.

# PRODUCTION TEAM

ROMANA RUBEO is an Italian writer and the managing editor of *The Palestine Chronicle.* Her articles appeared in many online newspapers and academic journals. She holds a Master's degree in Foreign Languages and Literature and specializes in audio-visual and journalism translation.

SYLVIA FERNANDES, of Goan origin, was born in Mombasa, Kenya. Originally a teacher in both primary and secondary education, Sylvia now works as a freelance proofreader and copy-editor—combining her passion for the English language and her deep interest in Middle East politics. She currently resides in Nairobi, Kenya.

SAMAH SABAWI is a writer and scholar. She is a recipient of multiple awards including the prestigious 2020 Green Room Award for Best Writing. Sabawi received a Ph.D. from Victoria University for her thesis, *Inheriting Exile: Transgenerational Trauma and the Palestinian Australian Identity.*

# INDEX

## C



## D

El Hassan, Hani, 61

## K



## L



## M

**R**



**S**